The X-Files FAQ

The X-Files FAQ

All That's Left to Know About Global Conspiracy, Aliens, Lazarus Species, and Monsters of the Week

John Kenneth Muir

THEATRE & CINEMA BOOKS
An Imprint of Hal Leonard Corporation

Published in 2015 by Applause Theatre & Cinema Books
An Imprint of Hal Leonard Corporation
7777 West Bluemound Road
Milwaukee, WI 53213

Trade Book Division Editorial Offices
33 Plymouth St., Montclair, NJ 07042

All photographs are from John Kenneth Muir's personal historical archive.

The FAQ series was conceived by Robert Rodriguez and developed with Stuart Shea.

Printed in the United States of America

Book design by Snow Creative Services

Library of Congress Cataloging-in-Publication Data

Muir, John Kenneth, 1969-
The X-files FAQ : all that's left to know about global conspiracy, aliens, Lazarus species, and monsters of the week / John Kenneth Muir.
pages cm
Includes bibliographical references and index.
ISBN 978-1-4803-6974-0 (pbk.)
1. X-files (Television program)—Miscellanea. I. Title.
PN1992.77.X22M85 2015
791.45'72—dc23

2015016075

www.applausebooks.com

This book is dedicated to my wife, Kathryn, who discovered *The X-Files* first and then watched it with me for years, and even on our honeymoon.

And for Joel, my eight-year-old son, who asks, on the way to school, to be told another *X-Files* episode, and then another, and another. . . .

And to the memory of Kim Manners, an artist who raised the stakes, challenged the viewers, and left us far too soon.

Contents

Foreword by Chris Carter

As I write this, we are shooting the second episode of the six-episode "event" series that will air on Fox in late January 2016.

It will be the first time the series has aired on TV in fourteen years, and it will be twenty-three years on from the airing of the pilot episode in 1993. That period encompasses about a third of not just my life but the lives of many people who have come back to work on the show now. The comeback could be viewed cynically as an attempt by Fox execs to capitalize on *The X-Files* "brand," programming by feather duster, but let me destroy any notion of this from my side of things. Or our side of things, as is the case.

The show was and is a labor of love, and thus a work of art. It takes a great many people working in absolute harmony to create something lasting on television. It is this esprit de corps that makes it all worthwhile. This does not happen accidentally, and I'd like to make it abundantly clear that while I created the show, a great many artistic souls have raised that infant idea into the monster it is today. Beginning with Morgan and Wong, and Gordon and Gansa, in the beginning, Messrs. Spotnitz, Gilligan, and Shiban in the end, the show was protean by nature, including the efforts of writers who came and went and whose contributions are under-sung.

And as you will read in the always impressive and thoughtful musings of John Muir, the writing is only half of it. We work in a visual medium, and the show somehow managed to turn that rectangle box we all viewed each week into something special and often unexpected. The signature qualities of mood and light and perspective can be attributed largely to production design by Michael Nemirski in the pilot, to Graeme Murray and Corey Kaplan on the series, but also to Tom Del Ruth, John Bartley, Jon Joffin, Joel Ransom, and Bill Roe, who lit and photographed it. All under some of the most talented directors and storytellers TV has even known: Rob Bowman, Kim Manners, David Nutter, and R. W. Goodwin. A manager's dream starting rotation, backed by a bullpen of long and short relievers who stepped in and stepped up. This is not lip service or faint praise. These people helped save my life.

In John Muir's introduction, I'm quoted as saying, "I didn't understand what I didn't understand," in reference to running the show in the beginning. This is true, but I'd like to put a finer point on that. "I didn't know what we couldn't do" is more like it. From the outset, we tried anything and everything we could think of. Met with much resistance, both creative and financial, we managed to do a great many things simply because our imaginations were wilder than the forces trying to tame them. That was also not an accident, and people such as Peter Roth, Ken Horton, Charlie Goldstein, two Jeffs named Eckerly and Glazer, and also Jonathan Littman came to understand we knew what we were doing and rallied in support. Executive Producer R. W. Goodwin was often a convincing voice of reason.

But as I've always maintained, none of our good work, artistry, or effort would add up to much if it weren't for Mulder and Scully. David Duchovny and Gillian Anderson brought, and now continue to bring, power and soul to characters who surprisingly continue to grow. To watch them step back into old shoes and bring something new has been a joy. They and the characters have grown wiser with the years, and as I'm often reminded, adversity is the forge of character.

Not just in them, but in us.

Acknowledgments

I gratefully acknowledge the help and assistance of my agent, June Clark, and Marybeth Keating, without whom this book would not exist. Also, I would like to thank every writer, director, cinematographer, actor, and other participant on *The X-Files* who made the series the greatest pop culture phenomenon of the 1990s. Also, sincerest thanks to Chris Carter and Gabe Rotter for their support over the years.

Introduction
Reopening *The X-Files*

It seems impossible to believe that Chris Carter's series *The X-Files* (1993–2002) premiered more than two decades ago. Even today, twenty-two years later, I carry vivid memories of watching the first season's episodes on Channel 35 in Richmond, Virginia, a Fox affiliate. My then-girlfriend (now wife) Kathryn and I were engaged to be married and lived together in a small garden apartment during that span, while I commuted downtown on the bus each day to a job at the Supreme Court of Virginia.

I also recall that—as described by the press—the fall TV season of 1993 was shaping up to be something special, or at the very least noteworthy: a genre slugfest on Sunday nights between Steven Spielberg's undersea fantasy-adventure *Sea Quest DSV* (1993–1995) and ABC's romantic superhero-lite adventure *Lois and Clark: The New Adventures of Superman* (1993–1996).

Nobody in their right mind would have or could have predicted back in September 1993 that a horror-based TV series about UFOs and the paranormal—airing on upstart, half-a-decade-old Fox Network on Friday nights—would outperform and outlive both of the aforementioned high-profile genre programs and garner much more popularity and critical success than either in both the short and long run.

Indeed, while those two programs remain cult favorites for niche audiences today, *The X-Files* morphed into something quite different: a pop culture legend and the highest-rated horror-based television series in the history of the medium.

Indeed, when most American audiences remember television in the 1990s, they immediately recall, at least in my experience, two specific series: the sitcom *Seinfeld* (1989–1998) and *The X-Files.*

Both series are touchstones for more than one generation of Americans. And though many horror-themed series since *The X-Files* have built upon its considerable successes, few (if any) have surpassed the program or achieved the same level of wide cultural popularity. AMC's *The Walking Dead* (2010–present) probably comes closest, and yet its highest-rated episodes are still routinely seen by fewer people than the lowest-rated episodes of *The X-Files* were, broadly speaking.

As a longtime historian of genre television, there's a telling comparison I regularly make, vis-à-vis *The X-Files.* The series qualifies as the *Star Trek* (1966–1969) of the 1990s and therefore is one of the most important titles in the history of the genre, on a par with *The Twilight Zone* (1959–1961) or *The Outer Limits* (1963–1965), certainly. In *Entertainment Weekly* in 1998, Ken Tucker made that very point, terming *The X-Files* "far and away the best television sci-fi since *The Twilight Zone,* and in the consistency of its writing and the depths of characterization, a show that is in many respects superior to Rod Serling's vaunted '60s anthology."

But to return to the *Star Trek* metaphor, *The X-Files* also boasts a large, devoted, and vocal fan base; has successfully made the transition to the big screen (on two occasions); and has seen its storytelling brand translated to the auxiliary venues of comic books, video games, and original novels. As this book goes to press, a return to the small-screen—after a decade and a half away—has been officially announced. And of course, *Star Trek* also underwent this so-called reboot phase.

Star Trek's sense of language has also permeated the culture, with "beam me up Scotty" and "he's dead, Jim" proving just two notable examples. Likewise, *The X-Files* boasts a similar impact, with memorable phraseology such as "the truth is out there," "trust no one," and "I want to believe," standing out as oft-repeated memes for the culture. *Time* magazine critic Richard Corliss once termed these phrases "ideal ingredients for a sci-fi cocktail with a '90s twist."

Also like *Trek*—which begat *The Next Generation* (1987–1994), *Deep Space Nine* (1993–1999), *Voyager* (1995–2001), and *Enterprise* (2002–2005), *The X-Files* has also generated related programming including *Millennium* (1996–1999) and *The Lone Gunmen* (2001), not to mention literally dozens of imitators, from *Nowhere Man* (1995) and *American Gothic* (1995) to *The Burning Zone* (1997), *Prey* (1998), and *Strange World* (1999) to the more recent *Fringe* (2008–2012).

If imitation is the sincerest form of flattery or a benchmark for success, then *The X-Files* is awash in both.

Uniquely, *The X-Files* differs from *Star Trek* in one key regard. The Chris Carter series proved immensely popular in its broadcast network run in prime time, a popularity that *Trek* never achieved. Indeed, it was not until the mid-1970s, fully five or six years after the cancellation of Gene Roddenberry's series, that *Star Trek* was picked up and championed by a new generation of viewers. So *The X-Files* was lucky enough to be popular in its time and remain popular following its cancellation.

Together they investigate the shadows. A portrait of the FBI's "most unwanted," Fox Mulder (David Duchovny) and Dana Scully (Gillian Anderson).

Why Now?

In the two-plus decades since its 1993 premiere, *The X-Files* has been the subject of dozens of books, both official and unofficial, so why revisit the series now, in 2015?

There are a number of reasons worth noting.

In the first case, under the tutelage of its creator, Carter, *The X-Files* trained and nurtured a generation of extraordinary writers such as Vince Gilligan, Howard Gordon, Glen Morgan, John Shiban, Frank Spotnitz, and James Wong. As late as a decade ago, it was not entirely clear how this next generation would come to impact the medium of television. But today we have a very firm answer and hard evidence in the form of *24*, *Breaking Bad*, *Homeland*, *Intruders*, *Hunted*, seasons of *American Horror Story*, and *The Man in the High Castle.* These series illustrate the artistic vision of the *X-Files* writers. They all cut their teeth on the series and are now inspiring another young generation. Chris Carter and his series are the originators of this award-winning, celebrated bloodline. Earlier I noted how *The X-Files* had, by its success, reshaped horror television and inspired a rash of imitators. But in terms of genetic building blocks, those who crafted the *X-Files* have spread to virtually every corner of modern television, remaking it in their images.

The second and perhaps more profound reason to reconsider *The X-Files* at this juncture involves mistaken assumptions, otherwise known by those two dreaded words "conventional wisdom."

The X-Files aired for nine seasons on Fox, and the last two years featured only the much-reduced presence of former series star David Duchovny as the beloved agent Fox Mulder. Disenfranchised fans and some critics thus began to write, especially on the protean Internet, about how the last two seasons of *The X-Files* were bad, inadequate, or suffered in comparison to the first years. The trend of putting down *The X-Files* continued and grew worse with the savage, thoughtlessly caustic reviews of the second *The X-Files* feature film, *I Want to Believe* (2008).

But today, knowing the whole picture—and with the immeasurable value of hindsight—it is easier to suss out "the truth" and correct the conventional wisdom and the historical record.

David Duchovny, Gillian Anderson, and Chris Carter celebrate a winning night at the Golden Globe Awards, one validation of *The X-Files*' popularity and success in the 1990s.

And that truth is, simply, that *The X-Files* never dropped in quality or artistry, despite Duchovny's absence. Instead, many of the final episodes of the series showcase as much great inspiration and wit as do any early season entries. For example, the final span of episodes in the ninth season included Chris Carter's undervalued masterpiece "Improbable," about numerology and faith, as well as Vince Gilligan's sentimental ode to idealized family life in America, "Sunshine Days." On the surface it is easy to dismiss these episodes as either "the Burt Reynolds one" ("Improbable") or, damningly, "the *Brady Bunch* one" ("Sunshine Days"), but such labels only scratch the surface of the installments and don't reflect their true, valuable nature as cultural and human commentary. Those who were hurt and upset by Duchovny's departure couldn't necessarily see what *The X-Files* had become; they could only see what it no longer was.

What seems abundantly true vis-à-vis the end of the series is that *The X-Files* ultimately began to lose viewership not because of any fade-out in terms of quality or artistry, but because the cultural context around the series changed radically, thanks in large part to the terrorist attacks that occurred on September 11, 2001.

Television audiences suddenly began to seek a new and different brand of programming following those terrible attacks. An age of peace and prosperity had ended, and for many, perhaps even unknowingly, *The X-Files* had represented that age too well. When that age was suddenly, irrevocably overturned, *The X-Files* appeared to lose relevance, or at the very least, frisson.

Historical Context

The X-Files arose during an era I prefer to term *Pax America*, or the American Peace. The Cold War with the Soviet Union had ended with the fall of the Berlin Wall in 1989 and with the dissolution of the Warsaw Pact on July 1, 1991. Suddenly, America was the only global superpower left standing. Accordingly, the 1990s ushered in a time of sweeping social, economic, technological change and progress in the country.

In terms of social progress, the 1990s saw the passage of the Americans with Disabilities Act (1990) and the election of the nation's first African American governor, Douglas Wilder in Virginia. The same span saw the acceptance of "Don't Ask Don't Tell" (1993), a Pentagon policy permitting gay service members to remain in service, and the appointments of the nation's first female attorney general (Janet Reno) and first female secretary of state (Madeleine Albright).

In terms of technology, the *Pax America* (roughly 1990–September 11, 2001) gave the United States the Hubble Telescope (April 20, 1990), Viagra,

DVDs, and most importantly the Internet. And the Net spawned a whole new economic pillar, actually, a so-called dot.com revolution. Between 1995 and 1998, the Internet generated fully a third of America's economic growth. It also connected Americans to one another electronically and began changing long-standing models of journalism, merchant services, and even the behaviors of TV show fans, who could now respond instantly, at length—and with loud voices—to every new episode of their favorite series.

The first baby boomer president, Bill Clinton oversaw a resurgent, economically viable America, and his business-friendly policies cut the national deficit by $250 billion. Under his presidency, nearly five million new jobs were created, according to scholar Stanley B. Greenberg in *Dispatches from the War Room* (2009).

Clinton has also been called the nation's first "globalist" commander in chief, and he believed in lower tariffs and greater exports. His policies, including signing NAFTA (North American Free Trade Agreement), reflected these beliefs and resulted in what some economists called the greatest tax cut in the history of the world. Historian Haynes Johnson wrote of Clinton's *Pax America* in *The Best of Times: America in the Clinton Years* that "driven by the force of the longest, continuous peacetime boom, the expanding American economy lifted what was already the highest standard of living in the world to even greater heights."

Although its external enemy was vanquished and progress seemed to be occurring on every front, there was a dark side to the *Pax America* too. With no communist enemy to defeat, Americans turned attention inward, in a sense. Clashes between the federal government and American citizens occurred at Ruby Ridge and Waco, and domestic right-wing terrorists were responsible for the Oklahoma City and Olympic Park Bombings. President Clinton himself became enmeshed in a sex scandal involving a young intern, Monica Lewinsky, and millions of taxpayer funds were spent investigating an allegedly shady Clinton real estate deal called Whitewater . . . for which no charges were ever brought against the president.

A feeling grew in the 1990s, from President George H. W. Bush's declaration of a "new world order" on September 11, 1990, onward, that the government could not be trusted and that it was operating without oversight to harm the American people. "People feel crushed by the government, abused by corporate employment and baffled by computers," Richard Corliss wrote in a *Time* magazine article called "The Invasion Has Begun."

Accordingly, shadowy conspiracies were afoot in the 1990s and more readily digestible because of Internet access. Some of these conspiracies included the "Clinton Body Count," which numbered fifty to sixty associates of the Clintons who had died under "mysterious circumstances." And Pat Robertson

The X-Files showcases a distrust in government and features crusaders seeking to expose it, a direct corollary to journalists Woodward and Bernstein during the Watergate scandal of the 1970s. This image shows the cast of *All the President's Men* (1976), a film about Watergate, outside the *Washington Post* offices.

suggested in 1999 that Clinton would use Y2K as an excuse to empower FEMA (The Federal Emergency Management Act) to order martial law in the United States. Coincidentally, FEMA's role in the American government became a key plot point in the first *X-Files* film, *Fight the Future.*

To describe this matter another way, things were generally pretty good in the United States in the 1990s—at least on the surface—but the absence of an enemy outside America's borders meant that a spotlight was shone internally, and blemishes were pinpointed and illuminated. This was the era, for example, in which citizens first learned of the Tuskegee Study, in which black American males were infected with syphilis, and which lasted from 1932 to 1972 . . . *forty years.* President Clinton officially apologized for the study on May 16, 1997, but more and more, people were less willing to trust the U.S. government or believe in its transparency. Many popular entertainments of the 1990s encouraged questions about the government, from films like Oliver

Stone's *JFK* (1991) to *The Silence of the Lambs (*1991). In the latter, the serial killer had a poster in his home that read "America: Open Your Eyes."

This is the historical context from which *The X-Files* springs, a time of peace and prosperity on the surface and a seething distrust of authority underneath. In historical terms, there is an important corollary, and one that helps us better understand the shape and form of *The X-Files*: *Pax Britannica.*

The British Peace, *Pax Britannica*, lasted from 1815 to 1914, roughly, and has been called "The Imperial Century." England had no serious international rival during this period and unchallenged power on the sea as well. It had also become, in essence, a global policeman. Furthermore, Britain controlled the economies, at least informally, of China, Argentina, and Siam. Trade also flourished with colonies in India, New Zealand, and Australia, and this example is a clear corollary to the globalism of the 1990s, the age of *The X-Files.*

Similarly, the inexpensive production of books, newspapers, and magazines flourished during the *Pax Britannica,* and the reading public virtually exploded in numbers during the 1870s and later. So here we have our corollary for the Internet of the 1990s, a revolution in readership and the way information was made accessible.

Many of the stories published during the *Pax Britannica*, sometimes called "penny dreadfuls," adhered to a new school of literature: the Gothic. Gothic literature is often described as the Romantic response to the Enlightenment. It is a "belief" response to "science" and advancement. Stories of the Gothic type include both Mary Shelley's *Frankenstein* (1818) and Bram Stoker's *Dracula* (1897), both of which emerge from the *Pax Britannica* and both of which are crafted in an epistolary format, meaning that the structure of the works is comprised largely of letters, correspondences, and newspaper clippings. This literary device finds voice in *The X-Files*, especially in the early seasons, as Mulder and Scully write up their field reports and read them aloud in voice-over narrations. But more importantly, Mulder and Scully represent the two sides of Enlightenment, the "belief" response (Mulder) and the advancement of scientific knowledge or rationality (Scully).

Gothic stories also often tend to involve a "tug-of-war" for the soul of the literary protagonist, and one can detect that tug-of-war clearly in *The X-Files,* again in terms of the characters of Scully and Mulder. They are both incomplete personalities, whose worldviews alone cannot complete them. Mulder is the believer who tries to use science to validate his (sometimes wild) beliefs. Scully is the skeptic who can brook no belief beyond the parameters of accepted, consensus reality: empirical science. They fight a tug-of-war not only with each other, but with themselves, about what kind of world, what kind of reality they dwell in. Is it one of miracles and monsters (Romantic) or science and rationality (Enlightenment)? Are aliens and monsters responsible for society's ills, or is man himself to blame for them? When Mulder assiduously pursues the truth, is it an achievable goal or the pursuit, perhaps, of a secular form of God, one who can allow him to believe in something beyond himself?

Bram Stoker's *Dracula* (1897) concerns, in broad strokes, the collision of the new age of "science"—represented by *Pax Britannica* inventions such as the typewriter, film, and hypnosis—with an irrational or romantic threat from the past: the magical power of Eastern Europe's Dracula. With its cutting-edge

The X-Files emerged during the Pax America, a time period roughly analogous to the *Pax Britannica* a century earlier, which created Gothic works of art such as Bram Stoker's novel *Dracula.* Here, Gary Oldman is seen as the vampire in the 1992 film adaptation of that book.

1990s science, setting, and police-procedural investigative techniques, *The X-Files* similarly places its heroes in direct conflict with things that seem magic because they can't be proved, whether they originate from another world, the mists of prehistory, or from genetic mutation.

The point about context is simply this. If one considers the Victorian age to be *Pax Britannica,* a time when England experienced prosperity because of colonial imports from Europe and Asia, and developed new technologies at home (Kodak cameras and early motion picture devices such as "cinematographs," for example), then one may consider the age of *The X-Files*—the age of Bill Clinton—*Pax America.*

In both ages, people began to grow concerned about the "mechanical" dehumanization of "modern" civilization and the loss of racial or cultural identity, as well as the loss of spirituality. How could an age accommodate both the miracle of surgery and the savagery of Jack the Ripper? The science of Darwin and the mysticism of Dracula? How about, for that matter, the World Wide Web and Jeffrey Dahmer?

Essentially then, *The X-Files* represents a new Gothic paradigm in which Enlightenment and Romanticism ideals compete once more, each attempting to gain a foothold in the human psyche. Whereas Dracula could transform into wind, fog, thunder, owls, bats, wolves, or foxes, consider the myriad monsters of *The X-Files.* They too are atmospheric ("D.P.O.") in nature or hail from the natural worlds. There are supernatural bats ("Patience"), wolves ("Alpha"), and other menaces to challenge Scully and Mulder's perception of reality. They are reassertions of the Romantic paradigm in a world that is apparently enlightened.

Tragically, the thing that ended *Pax Britannica* and *Pax America* are one and the same: foreign wars and a recognition of the limits of military power. For Great Britain, the inadequacies of the military were demonstrated in the Boer-English War of 1902, and then, World War I came in 1914. Likewise, the terrorist attack in 2001 ended the *Pax America,* and the Iraq War, which saw America facing an insurgent military force, demonstrated the limits of military might for our country in this era

Importantly, *The X-Files* was still on the air after 9/11, but suddenly the moment of questioning the government and looking inward had passed (at least until Barack Obama assumed the presidency in 2008). Instead, a feeling of nationalism in the face of an external threat rose, and espionage-focused series such as *24* (2001–2008) and *Alias* (2001–2005), grabbed ahold of the new zeitgeist. In some sense, one might even conclude that *The X-Files* was a victim of its own success. By remaining on the air for nine years, it actually outlived the context that had made it such a popular initiative.

Of Mankind and Mytharcs

As you likely recall, *The X-Files* is the continuing story of two FBI agents of vastly different qualifications and temperaments but a common ground in the quality of *curiosity*. On one hand is the believer: Oxford-educated psychologist Fox Mulder (David Duchovny). On the other is Dana Scully (Gillian Anderson), a medical doctor and devout Catholic who demands that all of Mulder's "beliefs" about alleged paranormal events achieve a high-threshold in terms of scientific accuracy and empirical evidence.

Working out of the FBI Building's basement in Washington D.C., Scully and Mulder—utilizing their vastly different "seeing" lenses of skepticism and belief—investigate during the course of the series alien abduction, demonology, local legends, weird genetic mutants, prehistoric or ancient monsters, global conspiracies, serial killers, and even vampires. They also explore cases involving astral projection, reincarnation, telepathy, and even psychic surgery. Yet this thumbnail description of the premise and characters hardly does *The X-Files* justice.

Historically speaking, there had been other TV series about the paranormal before (*One Step Beyond* [1959–1961], *The Sixth Sense* [1972–1973], and *Beyond Reality* [1991–1993] to name just three), so the subject matter isn't necessarily the quality that makes *The X-Files* so special or so memorable. Contrarily, *The X-Files'* intelligent writing was both cutting edge—focused often on the details of forensic pathology—and emotionally resonant. More than that, the series asked questions about the larger culture in a meaningful, nonpolitical, or nonpartisan fashion. "I always had this question that I would ask myself and I would ask the writers as we went forward," explains Carter: "Why this story? And why this story now? Those questions set the bar high, and they were relevant philosophically and dramatically to their time. It's important, as a television writer, to ask yourself that question. It deepens the work. That's not to say it's always a good thing. "Sometimes it [asking the questions] makes it [the work] less accessible or more intellectual than it needs to be."

Another virtue arose by dint of interpersonal magic. Stars David Duchovny and Gillian Anderson developed a scintillating chemistry and rapport over time that made every new adventure a delight. Scully and Mulder were partners, but also, in a way, competitors. They were dancers circling each other and, in some sense, attempting to gain the higher ground in terms of their curiosity and worldview. The Mulder/Scully repartee elevated each story of the paranormal or supernatural on *The X-Files* to a new level, one where it was the human condition itself—and our assumptions about it—that was up for debate.

Gillian Anderson at the Golden Globes.

As creator Chris Carter once noted in *Omni* magazine of his two protagonists: "They [Mulder and Scully] are equal parts of my desire to believe in something and my inability to believe in something. My skepticism and my faith . . . I want, like a lot of people do, to have the experience of witnessing a paranormal phenomenon. At the same time, I want not to accept it, but to question it."

In the points of view of characters Scully and Mulder, then, the audience essentially gets one "whole" person: a complete but conflicted worldview. It's no surprise that the characters complete one another, because they form, essentially, a well-rounded, curious outlook on life. This creative writing structure—with Mulder and Scully each voicing one half of a "universal" personality—plays an important role in the series' ultimate success.

But importantly, before *The X-Files*, most genre series were static in terms of arc. What was learned one week was often a distant memory by the next week's episode. One quality that made *The X-Files* so special was that this was not so: the idea that Mulder and Scully were climbing a staircase across many seasons, a staircase with an ending point, the revelation of the truth. *The Twilight Zone*, an anthology, couldn't feature such a development. And even programs such as *Star Trek* and *Star Trek: The Next Generation* were only very loosely arc driven.

The X-Files thus stood at the vanguard of a structural transition. It helped initiate the change in dramatic television narratives from an episodic "standalone" nature to something more literary. In the new paradigm, many installments or episodes were but a chapter in a larger piece, a visual novel.

Specifically, several stories per season on *The X-Files* involved the "Mytharc," the uncovering of a shadow government and its dark agenda for the future of mankind. Each new tale (often a two-part episode) would reveal another set of clues, or another aspect of the mystery.

However—make no mistake about it—the Mytharc proved a double-edged sword for a TV audience not yet trained and practiced in the art of following a television series closely, week to week. "That arc—which arcs over nine years—has been the subject of a lot of debate," Chris Carter told me in an interview in 2009. "You look at *Law and Order* (1990–2010). It's an amazing television series. . . . It starts anew each week, and it doesn't feature characters' personal lives over and over again. This is not part of the series. It's a luxury. I never figured out how to create something that would interest me that would be as simple as that."

Carter goes on to explain that many fans remain gratified that he developed a work of art that didn't reset automatically with each episode: "We did an *X-Files* charity day recently, and we had a lot of people there from all over the world. One of the things that someone said to me—and pointed out as a regular watcher of the show—she said "people say the Mytharc of the show is complicated. It's not complicated. You just have to pay attention to it."

Carter's thoughts about the Mytharc today involve not complexity of design or explanation, but duration. "I think one of the things that happened, certainly—and this is part of it being a nine-year show—is people say that it got too complicated. I think that what it did, rather than becoming overly complicated, it became stretched out. It took on a complexity given that there were two hundred and two episodes."

I would be remiss if I did not also mention *The X-Files'* photography, production design, and overall look. The series regularly makes use of film grammar to visually create tension, forge suspense, and develop an often trancelike mood or atmosphere. There is a certain kind of shot, for instance, that I associate irrevocably with *The X-Files.* It involves a low-perched camera, near floor level, untethered and on the prowl. The camera moves forward through unknown terrain (a high-tech office, a Victorian home, or anywhere else) and constantly probes for something new—something unseen or undetected—in regular, daily life. The low-perched camera, moving forward into undiscovered countries, thus mimics the series' thematic material, which concerns the exploration of "extreme possibilities" right under our noses

"First of all," Carter notes, "in television people haven't been given the opportunity to produce things that were so visual. It was sort of by demand on our part. We had to tell all these really scary thriller stories, and they couldn't be done from one angle, two-shots. They needed to be done in a multi-faceted delivery-of-information way. So we got to emulate a lot of what I love about film, and we got to do it on a television schedule."

"It didn't happen right away," Carter observes,

> but not long after we started, we were given what I call respectable budgets. We needed to tell these stories in interesting visual ways; we took an artistic approach. We were one of the first shows to give credit to the director of photography and production designer, and other people up front in a television show. So we had the budget and the desire to push the limits. I always say "we didn't understand what we didn't understand" about producing a TV show like this. We tried everything. I point to something like [submarine] conning tower coming out of the ice in Season Two ("Colony"/"End Game"). We refrigerated a sound stage, brought in tons of snow and ice and built this conning tower. I didn't know you couldn't do that. So we just started doing things.

Again, in the age of *Dexter, Mad Men, The Walking Dead,* and other serials, *The X-Files'* achievement of sustained, always-developing story lines and visual dynamism may not seem like a big deal. But it remains a crucial bridge series between the stand-alone era of the past and the more heavily serialized era of the present.

By 1994, critics had begun to detect that *The X-Files* was indeed something special. In *The New Leader,* James Wolcott called it "as scary as *The Twilight Zone* and much sexier . . . What's erotic about the show is its slow progression from reverie to revelation, stopping just short of rapture. It wants to swoon, but swooning would mean shutting its eyes, and there's so much to see."

In 1999, *TV Guide*'s Matt Roush accurately noted that "Many weeks . . . *The X-Files* is as good as any movie," and indeed, the horror genre suffered something of an identity crisis in the 1990s while attempting to compete with Chris Carter's sterling creation. Why go out to see an untested commodity like a new film when *The X-Files* promised quality "scares" week in and week out? As *Cinescape*'s A-to-Z Guide to Halloween Horror suggested in November 2001, *The X-Files* is "more like a mini-movie every week, with more truly scary moments than most horror films of the 1990s."

What This Book Is and What This Book Is Not

As noted above, many books have already been written about *The X-Files.* There are books available that review every episode, and books and articles too that reveal in detail major behind-the-scenes decisions and stories. This is not a book that endeavors to duplicate all those tasks.

Instead, *The X-Files FAQ* is a series primer, for those not only familiarizing themselves with the TV initiative but seeking to understand why it remains so resonant, so special. After placing the series in its historical context, this book offers thumbnail sketches of the many personalities involved in making the series and then launches into a discussion and review of many episodes in terms of their cultural, thematic, and narrative importance, though not necessarily in terms of a "thumbs-up" or "thumbs-down" binary conclusion. Additional chapters gaze at the other TV works of Chris Carter and at the X-*Files* feature films.

Twenty years on, *The X-Files* plays as more relevant than ever, because we again live in an age of conspiracies and rampant paranoia. So let's return to the FBI's basement, open a file cabinet in that dark corner, and go in search, once more, of the truth.

1

In the Beginning

Television and Film Inspirations for *The X-Files*

Like every other TV series in history, *The X-Files* was not created in a vacuum. Rather, it emerges from a particular historical context (*Pax America*) and from a very specific set of influences. In terms of television history, *The X-Files* follows a generation of horror-themed and paranormal-themed network TV series, yet also stands out as the first one of the bunch wherein a number of creative elements (partner investigators, the paranormal, monsters of the week, and a story arc) meld so perfectly and so skillfully.

On Television

The medium of television gave audiences a number of paranormal series in the decades preceding the arrival of *The X-Files.*

One Step Beyond (1959–1961)

This paranormal anthology was hosted by TV Golden Age actor John Newland (1917–2000), and it beat Rod Serling's *The Twilight Zone* to the airwaves by a full ten months. The bread and butter of this black-and-white anthology program was the re-creation or "dramatization" of supposedly paranormal events.

Newland reported to the author of this book during his final interview that "The stories had to be real and there had to be proof, either anecdotal or published. Of course, we got some letters from people who said I was the Anti-Christ for pursuing this kind of thing. Ivan Klapper was our consultant, and it was just as the narration said, 'Explain it? We cannot. Disprove it? We cannot. We are simply inviting audiences to explore the unknown.'"

One Step Beyond endured for three seasons (the last produced in Great Britain), and Newland directed all ninety-six episodes. During that span, the

Rod Serling hosts the horror/sci-fi anthology *The Twilight Zone*, a series to which *The X-Files* is frequently compared.

series explored many paranormal concepts that *The X-Files* investigated thirty years later, including astral projection ("The Return of Mitchell Campion"), spirit possession ("The Bride Possessed"), Reincarnation ("The Riddle"), premonitions ("Night of April 14"), genetic deformities ("Ordeal on Locust Street"), apparitions ("The Dark Room"), and even alien abduction ("Encounter.")

Unlike *The X-Files*, however, *One Step Beyond*'s anthology format meant that though concepts often repeated, protagonists did not. Each week, a new lead actor or actress was featured. The series proved very successful in syndication and was followed by a not very memorable remake in syndication, 1978's shot-on-video *The Next Step Beyond.*

The Avengers (1961–1968)

This popular British spy series involved many partnerships across the years, but the era that got the most play in America encompassed the years 1965–1968 and saw the male/female partnering of stylish John Steed (Patrick Macnee) and gorgeous, competent Emma Peel (Diana Rigg).

These two secret agents would "avenge" extraordinary crimes, all while maintaining a droll repartee and exuding tons of sex appeal. In interviews over the years, Chris Carter has noted that he wanted the sexual makeup of *The X-Files* agents to mirror that of *The Avengers.*

The Invaders (1967–1968)

Quinn Martin's *The Invaders* is the grandfather of paranoia and horror television series; one of the first such ventures to posit that "THEY" are among us: alien invaders, hidden in human form save for a pinky finger that juts out at an odd angle, bent on our subjugation or destruction.

These alien invaders in human bodies have an insidious (but secret) plan to occupy and dominate the Earth. Accordingly, much of *The Invaders'* suffocating aura of paranoia arises from the fact that it is difficult to distinguish between human beings and extraterrestrials. And worse, the aliens have already infiltrated every level of American (and possibly global) infrastructure.

The only man standing between the aliens and global domination is lonely David Vincent (Roy Thinnes), who spots an alien saucer landing in an out-of-the-way spot one evening in the premiere episode, "Beachhead."

Each episode of *The Invaders* finds Vincent moving from locale to locale in hopes of providing evidence of the alien menace to an unbelieving populace. The series ran for two seasons and is fondly remembered today. On *The X-Files,* the actor who played David Vincent, Roy Thinnes, plays Jeremiah Smith, an alien in human form much like the actor's old *Invaders* nemesis. But this alien is on Earth to help and heal mankind, not threaten it.

The Invaders and *The X-Files* share the themes of invasion (or colonization) and an evil group working within the government against mankind. Also, *The X-Files'* late-season villains, the super soldiers, can be identified by a physical anomaly, not an extended pinky but a strange protrusion at the back of the neck.

The Sixth Sense (1972)

Writer Anthony Lawrence originally created *The Sixth Sense* after the success of a 1971 TV movie titled *Sweet, Sweet Rachel,* which involved a parapsychology

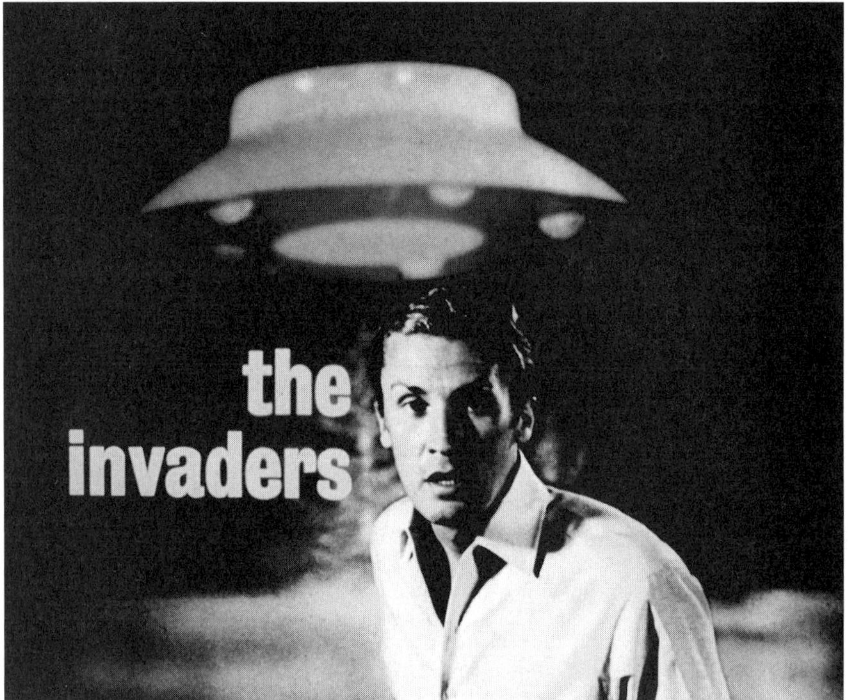

Roy Thinnes starred in the alien-invasion paranoia trip *The Invaders* and then later appeared on *The X-Files* as alien Jeremiah Smith.

expert, Lucas Darrow (Alex Dreier), protecting two women from psychic assassins. When the television movie proved successful in terms of ratings, ABC wanted a quick follow-up. Lawrence and developer Stan Shpetner thus crafted *The Sixth Sense,* a series that would follow the adventures of another parapsychology expert, Dr. Michael Rhodes (Gary Collins).

During every episode of *The Sixth Sense,* the preternaturally patient and calm Dr. Rhodes investigated a complex mystery featuring psychic overtones. That case might involve astral projection ("Face of Ice"), premonitions ("If I Should Die Before I Wake,"), automatic writing ("I Do Not Belong to the Human World"), aura photography ("The Man Who Died at Three and Nine"), witchcraft ("Witch, Witch, Burning Bright"), apparitions ("Echo of a Distant Scream"), spiritual possession ("With Affection, Jack the Ripper"), cryogenics ("Once Upon a Chilling"), or even organ transplant ("The Eyes That Would Not Die"). Usually Rhodes solved the mystery at hand by working closely with a beautiful woman in jeopardy.

This damsel in distress role was played, in various installments, by beloved genre actresses such as Mariette Hartley ("Eye of the Haunted"), Pamela Franklin ("I Did Not Mean to Slay Thee"), Stefanie Powers ("Echo of a Distant

Scream"), Tiffany Bolling ("Witch, Witch, Burning Bright"), Lucie Arnaz ("With This Ring I Thee Kill"), Mary Ann Mobley ("Shadow in the Well"), Carol Lynley ("The House That Cried Murder"), and Anne Archer ("Can a Dead Man Strike from Beyond the Grave?").

Among those talents working behind the scenes on *The Sixth Sense*—at least for a time—were Gene Coon, Harlan Ellison, and D. C. Fontana. I had the opportunity to interview Fontana in 2001, and our conversation veered briefly to *The Sixth Sense*. She recalled to me that in her opinion, developer Shpetner was difficult to work with because he had so many story dislikes: "He didn't like children. He didn't like women. He didn't like men . . . He didn't like stories about sick people, or emotionally ill people. He didn't like stories about poor people. He didn't like stories about ethnic people. Essentially it came down to us doing stories about rich white people who didn't have any problems. And that was a problem for me."

Fontana's tenure on the show was, perhaps not surprisingly, short-lived: "I left one day, and Harlan Ellison left either the day before me or the day after me. It all happened in fast succession, I can tell you that much . . . It's too bad, because the potential for stories about extra sensory perception and abilities was great."

The abundant flaws of *The Sixth Sense* are apparent today. For one thing, Dr. Rhodes always helped beautiful, young (25–35) white women, but never actively romanced any of them. He just seemed to inhabit a white, upper-class world of beautiful, psychically gifted females. And secondly, as a character Rhodes was not permitted to grow or show much by way of passionate emotion. Collins's performance on the series is actually kind of brilliant in a weird way, simultaneously minimalist and intense, but the writing never ascribes much by way of humor or personal life to the man.

As a lead character, Rhodes is certainly dedicated and helpful—and physically capable—but unlike Mulder, Scully, Doggett, or Reyes, we know precisely nothing about him save for his unwavering support for ESP and parapsychology studies. It would have been more rewarding if the series had more fully explored his background, including his childhood and the development of his abilities as a "sensitive."

The Magician (1973–1974)

This short-lived series starred Bill Bixby as magician Anthony Blake, a man who used magic to solve crimes and help those who had been subject to injustice.

The series was a personal favorite of Chris Carter's in his youth and, in series lore, was on TV the night of Samantha's abduction, according to

Mulder. Similarly, Carter has reported that for a prospective *The X-Files 3*, he sees the distinct possibility that Mulder is making his living as a magician. In the *X-Files Season Ten* comic book, Mulder is also going under the alias Blake.

Kolchak: The Night Stalker (1974)

A TV movie, *The Night Stalker*, premiered on ABC on January 11, 1972, and received a staggering 33.1 rating and a 48 share of the TV-watching audience, making it the most watched program of the year. The film, produced by Dan Curtis and written by Richard Matheson (a key Chris Carter influence), concerned a newspaper reporter contending with a vampire in 1970s Las Vegas. Playing that idiosyncratic reporter, Carl Kolchak, was the late, great Darren McGavin (1930–2006).

After the ratings success of a second TV movie, *The Night Strangler*, in 1973, ABC launched a TV version of the story titled *Kolchak: The Night Stalker*, and Chris Carter has often tagged it as a key influence on *The X-Files*.

Uniquely, *Kolchak: The Night Stalker* is also a response, in dramatic form, to the age of the Watergate scandal and the reporting of Bob Woodward and Carl Bernstein at the *Washington Post*. The Watergate Hearings are often named by Carter as being highly formative in his understanding and feelings about government.

In the case of *Kolchak: The Night Stalker*, the titular investigative journalist is called upon, almost constantly, to discover the "truth" as he looks beneath official police or mayoral descriptions of prominent crimes. There, underneath the surface, Kolchak discovers that monsters like vampires and werewolves dwell.

Kolchak himself, much like Woodward and Bernstein, is a hero journalist who stands up to City Hall, even when City Hall holds all the cards. By the time of *The X-Files* in the early 1990s, media consolidation had all but eliminated such hero journalists, and tabloid reporting replaced investigative journalism of substance. *The X-Files* thus features not a journalist, but two highly trained FBI agents against City Hall, which in this case is the U.S. federal government.

Kolchak: The Night Stalker also initiated on TV the "monster of the week" format, which *The X-Files* adopts, though with some variation. In the span of its twenty hour-long episodes, *Kolchak: The Night Stalker* sees its hero battle Jack the Ripper ("The Ripper"), a ghoul ("Zombie"), aliens ("They Have Been, They Are, They Will Be"), creatures of the night ("The Vampire"), Satan worshippers ("The Devil's Platform"), lycanthropes ("The Werewolf"), witches ("The Trevi Collection"), a succubus ("Demon in Lace"), prehistoric monsters ("Primal Scream," "The Sentry"), and ethnic horrors like an Indian monster called a Rakshasa ("Horror in the Heights").

In honor of Kolchak's importance in its genesis, *The X-Files* actually cast Darren McGavin—Kolchak himself—as Arthur Dales, the first agent to open the government's "X-files" department or unit. McGavin appeared in the fifth-season story "Travelers" and also in the sixth-season story "Agua Mala."

Darren McGavin stars in *Kolchak: The Night Stalker*, a series that originated the "monster of the week" TV format. McGavin stars as retired X-Files investigator Arthur Dales in two episodes of the Chris Carter series.

In the latter, McGavin's character showed a special affection for Scully and noted that if he had been teamed with a partner like Dana, he might never have left the Bureau. This is, as one may surmise, an acknowledgment that Kolchak never had a steady partner on his series, and that the program featuring him was itself canceled shortly into its run, after one season. The joke is funny, but also on point. Viewers may have found it more appealing with a second lead for McGavin to play against. A key *X-Files* producer and creator, Frank Spotnitz, briefly revived the Kolchak world in 2005's *The Night Stalker.*

Project UFO (1978–1979)

This NBC series from *Dragnet* (1952–1959) creator Jack Webb ran for two seasons and has not been rerun in the United States since its original broadcasts. The series involves two U.S. Air Force officers, Major Gatlin (William Jordan) and Sgt. Fitz (Caskey Swaim), as they investigate UFO sightings for Project Blue Book. The UFOs were depicted using miniatures by Buck Price and were often seen in flashback sequences. On *Project UFO,* it was never revealed what race (or races) of aliens might be visiting Earth, or for what purpose, but Project Blue Book officials visited many different types of eyewitnesses and often concluded that there were conventional causes for their strange sightings.

The partner angle and the idea of alien visitation reoccurred on *The X-Files,* but *Project UFO* featured only stand-alone episodes, and the main characters were hugely undeveloped except as efficient investigators solving cases. Essentially, the show was a dry police procedural (like *Dragnet*) only with UFOs as the subject matter.

Friday the 13th: The Series (1987–1990)

This syndicated TV program from 1987 ran for three seasons and seventy-one hour-long episodes not long before *The X-Files* bowed on Fox.

In broad terms, the series involves two unlucky souls, red-headed Micki (Robey) and nerdy Ryan (John D. Le May), who inherit their dead uncle's antique shop, Curious Goods. They are unlucky because Uncle Lewis Vendredi (R. G. Armstrong) made a pact with the Devil to become immortal, but then attempted to back out on his end of the bargain.

Dragged down to hell, Vendredi leaves behind on Earth hundreds of cursed antiques in his shop. Each one is imbued with a murderous, monstrous spirit. Alas, many of these cursed items are soon sold during a

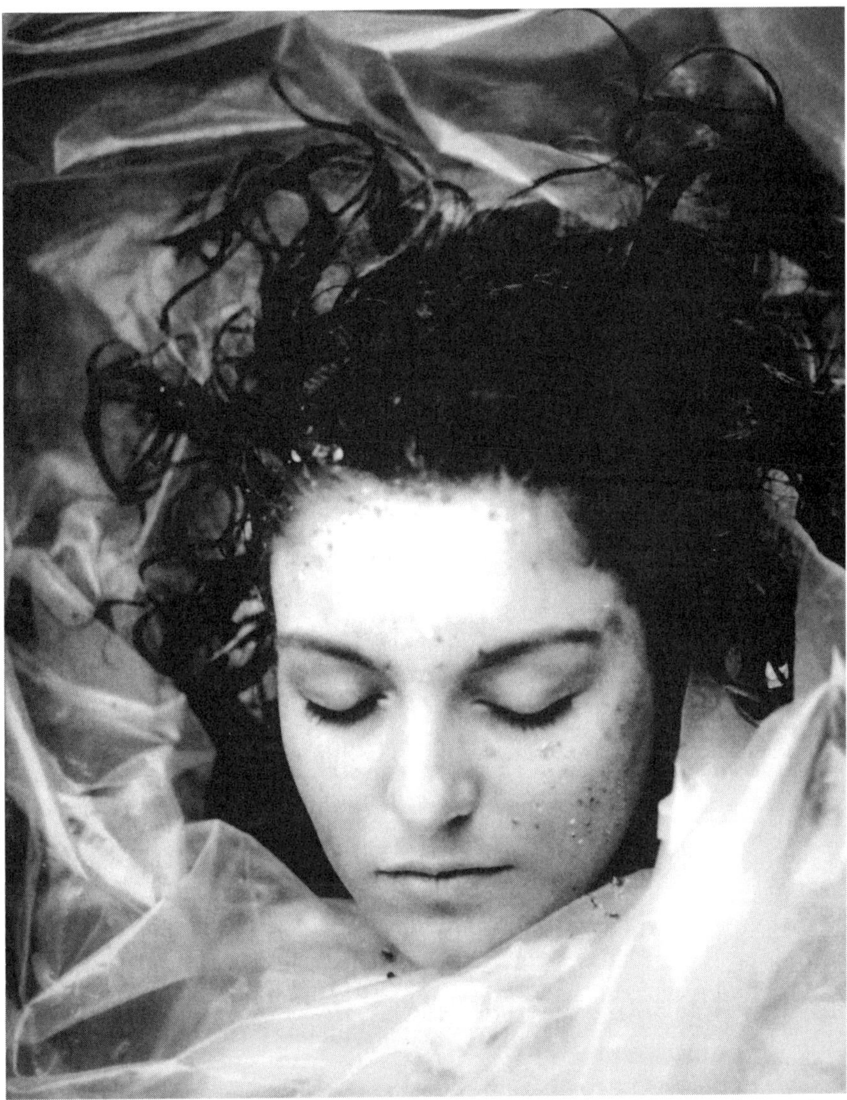

David Lynch and Mark Frost's *Twin Peaks* took a look at murder and strange happenings in the American heartland, an idea that *The X-Files* continues. Also, David Duchovny appeared on the series as Denise, a transvestite DEA agent.

going-out-of-business sale held by Vendredi's niece and nephew, meaning it is their responsibility to retrieve them from their unsuspecting new owners.

Thus, in most of the episodes, the action involves the team from Curious Goods attempting to recover an evil relic, collectible, or antique. During the run of the series, these objects come in all shapes and sizes, from an evil tea cup ("A Cup of Time") and cursed makeup compact ("Vanity's Mirror") to sinister comic books ("Tales of the Undead") and even a diabolical weed-mulcher ("The Root of All Evil").

Today, the stories seem highly repetitive, and many are sub-par, but the important thing, in terms of *The X-Files*, is that the Kolchak stand-alone, episode format has been updated to include two investigators of opposite sexes. In other words, and quite unlike *The Sixth Sense* as well, *Friday the 13th: The Series* introduces to TV paranormal partners.

Twin Peaks (1990–1992)

Mulder himself, David Duchovny, guest-starred on this David Lynch–produced soap opera of the early 1990s. But even outside that connection, this slice of creepy Americana helped to set the stage for *The X-Files* because it featured two overarching story arcs, one involving murdered teen Laura Palmer (Sheryl Lee) and one involving a place in the woods of terror called "The Black Lodge."

Twin Peaks is the tale of a small, Douglas fir–lined town in the Pacific Northwest (population: 51,201) that suffers a terrible tragedy on February 24, 1990. The corpse of beloved high school student Laura Palmer is discovered—wrapped in plastic—on the banks of the river near the Packard Saw Mill. The crime is so horrendous, so awful, that it sends the town into a tailspin of suspicion and accusations, and results in an FBI investigation led by fastidious agent Dale Cooper (Kyle MacLachlan).

As Cooper and town sheriff Harry Truman (Michael Ontkean) seek answers about the brutal crime, a dark underside is also unearthed. Seventeen-year-old Palmer—the "golden girl" of the local high school—had been a cocaine user. She also kept a secret diary of her kinky sexual escapades and had at least two lovers. And that is just the tip of the iceberg.

Like *The X-Files, Twin Peaks* is also a (bizarre) procedural-type story visualized in highly cinematic form, and like Mulder, Cooper is often willing to delve into extreme possibilities, to say the least. Both *The X-Files* and *Twin Peaks* involve unconventional FBI agents, Cooper and Mulder, and both also suggest that small-town America boasts a sinister "underneath."

Beyond Reality (1991–1992)

This low-budget paranormal series lived and died just before the birth of *The X-Files* and aired on the USA Network, and then in reruns on the then-Sci-Fi Channel. A low-budget production featuring unremarkable special effects, *Beyond Reality* involves professor of parapsychology Laura Wingate (Shari

Another major inspiration for *The X-Files* is the Oliver Stone film, *JFK*, which seeks to determine the truth of the Kennedy assassination.

Belafonte) and associate professor J. J. Stillman (Carl Marotte) investigating cases of the paranormal. The series features male/female partners and matters such as psychic healing ("Miracle Worker") and astral projection ("Justice"). But again, all the qualities that made *The X-Files* such a hit are largely absent. The visuals are cheesy, the acting pedestrian, the production looks cheap, and at a half hour in length the stories tend to be undeveloped.

On Film

The world of cinema also brought creative inspiration to *The X-Files* in dramatic and curious ways.

JFK (1991)

This Academy Award–nominated Oliver Stone film grossed over $200 million at the box office and involves a truth seeker, New Orleans district attorney Jim Garrison (Kevin Costner), who attempts to untangle the sinister threads of the Kennedy assassination.

JFK suggests that the Warren Commission Report is a whitewash of the assassination, and one well-connected informant, "X" (Donald Sutherland), meets with Garrison to connect all the dots. In a single, bravura scene, he paints a portrait of a wide-ranging, deeply entrenched secret conspiracy involving LBJ, Nixon, J. Edgar Hoover, the CIA, the FBI, and the military-industrial complex. Together, these organizations and men plotted against an "American prince" and conducted a coup d'état. They chose personal power over democracy and the express will of the American people.

The X-Files also features an informant named "X" (Steven Williams) who knows secrets about the federal government's involvement in illicit activities, and Mulder, like Garrison, is a truth seeker extraordinaire. The film's story of a conspiracy resonated with the public, which also helps to explain the importance of such a conspiracy in the Chris Carter series.

In the fourth-season episode of *The X-Files*, "Musings of a Cigarette Smoking Man," the series devises its own theory involving the JFK assassination.

The Silence of the Lambs (1991)

Chris Carter has often tagged the Oscar-winning Jonathan Demme film *Silence of the Lambs* as one of *The X-Files'* key creative influences.

In the film, a young and impressionable FBI agent, Clarice Starling (Jodie Foster), hunts a serial killer, Buffalo Bob, with the help of an imprisoned one: Hannibal "the Cannibal" Lecter (Anthony Hopkins). The film's story is told in a procedural format, with Clarice following and analyzing each clue in a larger mystery before her final, violent confrontation with Bob. The film also depicts a hierarchy within the FBI that seems not entirely trustworthy. Clarice's superior, father figure Jack Crawford (Scott Glenn), uses her as a pawn to get answers from Lecter, knowing that he will be swayed by a pretty face. In very real terms, the film is a coming-of-age story about Starling

Anthony Hopkins stars in *The Silence of the Lambs* as Hannibal "the Cannibal" Lecter, a deadly serial killer. According to Chris Carter, this Jonathan Demme film was a major inspiration for *The X-Files*.

choosing between two patriarchal figures and two influences—Hannibal and Crawford—and establishing her own identity in the process.

Many of the most memorable scenes in *Silence of the Lambs* involve Clarice interviewing Hannibal in his prison cell and the excavating of his brilliant, if unhinged, mind. In episodes of *The X-Files* such as "Beyond the Sea," we see the same set-up repeated. This kind of dynamic would also recur, perhaps more frequently, on Chris Carter's other masterpiece, *Millennium*.

In the News

One real-life "series" also plays into the gestalt of *The X-Files:* the Watergate scandal hearings in Congress. These government hearings began on May 17, 1973, and ran until the end of June 1974. They were broadcast live on

When he was a teenager, Chris Carter watched the Watergate Hearings on television, and his views on government were heavily influenced by the fall of President Richard Nixon.

Network TV daily, and over 300 hours were aired in all, on all three major networks as well as on PBS.

The hearings delved into President Nixon's involvement in the break-in at the Watergate Hotel in 1972 and featured a colorful cast of players on both the witness stand and behind the gavel.

Chris Carter has noted that these hearings helped him form his opinions about government and those in power in the government.

2

Behind the Scenes

Chris Carter, Writers, Directors, and More

Chris Carter

Chris Carter is the creator of and mastermind behind *The X-Files* and its imaginative universe of aliens, conspiracies, and monsters. Carter was born on October 13 or Ten Thirteen—the name of his production company—and grew up in Bellflower, California. An athletic young man rather than sci-fi geek, his passion, starting at age twelve, was surfing. As late as 1995, Carter had never watched even one episode of *Star Trek*, a series to which *The X-Files* is often compared in terms of cultural importance and genre.

Many times in print over the years Carter has remembered the impact of the Watergate scandal on his life and on his thinking and political consciousness. "When you are 16 or 17 years old and lose absolute faith in your leaders," he noted in *The Fight the Future* press kit, "it's very disturbing."

In 1979, not that many years after President Nixon's resignation, Carter graduated from California State University at Long Beach with a degree in journalism and soon after began a thirteen-year stint as editor of the prestigious *Surfing* magazine, located out of San Clemente, and which celebrated its fiftieth anniversary in 2014.

Carter next moved into the TV industry and began writing screenplays for Walt Disney when his work caught the eye of executive Jeffrey Katzenberg. For *Walt Disney's Wonderful World of Color*, Carter penned (with co-writer Michael Patrick Goodman) a beloved installment called "The B.R.A.T. Patrol." The two-hour episode starred Sean Astin, Brian Keith, and Tim Thomerson and aired on October 26, 1986. The narrative involved military kids, the children of U.S. Marines, becoming involved in a plan to stop the theft of government equipment. The B.R.A.T. acronym stands for "born, raised, and trapped."

An image of series creator Chris Carter, taken for the 1998 feature *Fight the Future.*

Carter also wrote the TV movie *Cameo by Night* starring Sela Ward and Justin Deas, and then worked on two additional TV series. The first was *Rags to Riches* (1987–1988), a series that had begun as a Walt Disney TV movie and starred Joseph Bologna as Nick Foley, a wealthy man who adopted five daughters. Carter wrote the episodes "Beauty and the Babe" and "Once in a Lifeguard." Carter and Disney were deemed a good fit at the time in part because of Carter's affinity for writing accurate "youth dialogue," having been immersed in the surfing subculture.

Later, after meeting Brandon Tartikoff while playing softball, Carter wrote for the 1989–1990 TV series *A Brand New Life*, which starred Don Murray and Barbara Eden as the politically unlike heads of a newly blended family. The series ran for only six episodes, but also starred Shawnee Smith, who would later appear on *The X-Files* episode "Firewalker."

Breaking Bad's creator Vince Gilligan penned many of the most memorable episodes of *The X-Files*, including "Bad Blood," "Folie a Deux," and "X-Cops."

Carter's final credit before embarking on *The X-Files* was an episode of the Richard DiLello series *Midnight Caller* (1989–1991). The show revolved around a former policeman-turned-nighttime talk show host, Jack Killian (Gary Cole), at station KJCM 98.3. Carter's story "A Cry in the Dark" aired on the NBC series' third and final season.

In the summer of 1992, Carter pitched *The X-Files* to Fox Television, a series about UFOs and other paranormal phenomena. He delivered the pilot script for the series in December of the same year, and *The X-Files* went into production in 1993. The cost of the pilot episode has been reported as $2 million.

Carter's personal politics have often been the subject of lively debate among *X-Files* fans (known as X-Philes), with some insisting the series suggests a conservative bent, with others detecting a more liberal worldview. Carter himself has kept his cards close to the vest on this topic and suggested more than once that *The X-Files* should not be viewed through the lens of any particular political agenda. He also notes that despite the existence in the series of an insidious government conspiracy, he is not advocating overthrowing the government, only that it is appropriate to question its veracity. This is a stance that conforms to Founding Father Thomas Jefferson's belief that dissent can be the highest form or patriotism or, perhaps more aptly, Mark Twain's beliefs. Twain noted that he supports his government . . . when his government deserves his support.

Unlike some TV series creators and producers who never write or direct an episode, Carter wrote (or cowrote) more than sixty episodes of *The X-Files* and helmed ten. He has been nominated for eight Emmy Awards in association with the series and also been nominated three times by the Directors Guild of America for his episodes "The List," "The Post-Modern Prometheus," and "Triangle."

Following *The X-Files,* Chris Carter created cult-TV favorites including *Millennium* (1996–1999), *Harsh Realm* (2000), and *The Lone Gunmen* (2001). He directed the second *X-Files* feature film, *I Want to Believe,* in 2008 and recently returned to television production with his TV pilot *The After* (2014). He is currently at work developing *The X-Files* limited TV series, due in 2016.

Although Carter has become famous for stories involving the paranormal and UFOs, he has never had a personal experience with any such aspect of the unknown.

Prominent Writers

Vince Gilligan

Today, Vince Gilligan is widely celebrated for the TV series he created after *The X-Files* ended, the award-winning AMC effort *Breaking Bad* (2008–2013). Born and raised in Virginia, Gilligan attended the NYU Tisch School of the Arts on scholarship and in 1993 wrote the film *Wilder Napalm.* He has been described as "one of the most down-to-earth people you'll meet in Hollywood," according to *Variety*, and a producer friend, Mark Johnson, introduced him to Chris Carter just as *The X-Files* was gearing up for its second season. Gilligan's first pitch, for the episode "Soft Light"—about an ambulatory shadow and dark matter—was accepted, and Gilligan soon became a staff writer, eventually contributing a whopping twenty-nine additional episodes.

Gilligan's work is beloved by *X-Files* fans because it sometimes skirts the boundaries of good taste and quirkily blends humor with horror, extreme violence with surprise gentleness. His stories are often filled with such tonal contradictions, and yet almost universally emerge as fan favorites anyway. Among his contributions are "Pusher," "Unruhe," "Bad Blood," "Folie a Deux," "Hungry," and the found-footage-type episode "X-Cops."

Gilligan, just like Frank Spotnitz, also directed two episodes of the series, "Je Souhaite," which concerned a genie, or djinn, and "Sunshine Days," about a misanthropic telepath living in a perfect replica of the *Brady Bunch* house.

Gilligan cocreated *The Lone Gunmen* alongside several other writers and is now producing a *Breaking Bad* spin-off, *Better Call Saul*, and a police series, *Battle Creek*.

Howard Gordon

This New Yorker and Princeton graduate broke into TV writing with frequent cowriter Alex Gansa. Together, they sold a script to the NBC hospital drama *St. Elsewhere* (1982–1988) and then penned six teleplays for *Spenser: For Hire* (1985–1988). Next Gordon and Gansa become staff writers for CBS's fantasy series *Beauty and the Beast* (1987–1990), starring Linda Hamilton and Ron Perlman. Gordon worked on *The X-Files* for its first four seasons and in that span wrote twenty episodes.

Among those twenty segments are three that revived, reimagined, and rejuvenated classic monsters. Gordon's "Kaddish" concerns a golem, "Unrequited" updates the Invisible Man, and "Avatar" refashions the succubus of folklore. Among his other stories, Gordon also cowrote (but apparently disliked) "Ghost in the Machine," a story about a computer, the COS (Central Operating System), gone haywire.

After contributing several stories to *The X-Files*, Howard Gordon became show-runner for the Kiefer Sutherland hit series *24*.

Outside of *The X-Files*, Gordon served as a consulting producer on *Buffy the Vampire Slayer*'s (1997–2003) Season Two and *Angel*'s (1999–2005) Season One. He also created the short-lived science fiction series *Strange World* (1999) and joined series creators Joel

Surnow and Bob Cochran on *24*, starring Kiefer Sutherland as counterterrorist agent Jack Bauer. By the fifth season of that series, Gordon had graduated to show runner. In 2011, Gordon and Gansa developed the hit series *Homeland*, starring Claire Danes, in its fourth season as of this writing.

Darin Morgan

The younger brother of Glen Morgan, writer Darin Morgan guest-starred in two episodes of *The X-Files*. He played the grisly Fluke Man in "The Host" and lovable loser Eddie Van Blundht in "Small Potatoes. Morgan was also story editor on the series for the 1995–1996 season and contributed four teleplays overall, spanning the second and third season.

These stories are "Humbug," "Clyde Bruckman's Final Repose," "War of the Coprophages," and "Jose Chung's from Outer Space." All these efforts boast a singular writing style, and Morgan's vision for *The X-Files* borders on the absurd, if not the surreal. If Mulder is about belief and Scully is about science, the Morgan interpretation of their world suggests nihilism.

One Darin Morgan show, "Clyde Bruckman's Final Repose," netted both the writer and its star, Peter Boyle, Emmy Awards. And Morgan's popular Jose Chung character, played by Charles Nelson Reilly (1931–2007), returned in a *Millennium* episode the following season: "Jose Chung's Doomsday Defense."

Following his work on *The X-Files*, Darin Morgan worked as a consulting producer on *Millennium*, Frank Spotnitz's *Night Stalker*, *Bionic Woman* (2007), and *Fringe* (2008–2012). He is currently working on the TV series *Intruders*.

John Shiban

A winner of the Mary Pickford Scholarship for writing, John Shiban joined *The X-Files* writing staff during the show's third season. He remained active on the program through the eighth season, and later cocreated and wrote for *The Lone Gunmen*. Shiban's episodes of *The X-Files* include, "The Walk," "Teso Dos Bichos," "El Mundo Gira," "Elegy," "The Pine Bluff Variant," "Theef," and "Badlaa." A good percentage of those stories involve alien or foreign cultural traditions interfacing with the mainstream culture, and thus ethnocentrism or xenophobia.

After *The X-Files* closed shop, Shiban penned episodes of *Supernatural* in its 2006–2007 season, and then episodes of Vince Gilligan's *Breaking Bad*, and *Torchwood: Miracle Day* (2012).

The X-Files creative team celebrates the series' success at the Golden Globe Awards in 1997.

Frank Spotnitz

This talented writer and coproducer on *The X-Files* graduated from UCLA and then earned a master's degree in screenwriting at the American Film Institute. Later, Spotnitz wrote for UPI (United Press International) and for the AP (Associated Press) in Paris before joining the staff of *Entertainment Weekly* in 1991. Spotnitz also wrote for the periodicals *Rolling Stone* and *American Film* before going to work on *The X-Files.*

Spotnitz was with *The X-Files* from 1994 through 2002 and also cowrote, with Chris Carter, the 2008 feature *I Want to Believe.* Spotnitz cowrote many episodes of the Mytharc, but also contributed some of the finest stand-alone or monster-of-the-week shows as well, including the brilliant "Our Town," "Detour," "Via Negativa," and "Daemonicus." In all, he wrote or co-wrote forty episodes, almost a fifth of the entire series catalog.

A number of Spotnitz's episodes showcase a convincing atmosphere of dread, of almost suffocating doom, and as such remain tremendously scary.

"Via Negativa" and "Daemonicus" leap to mind immediately in this regard. At the same time, however, Spotnitz's efforts showcase a telltale brand of gallows humor. "Our Town" earns queasy laughs in its depiction of our food supply, and "Detour" hilariously skewers modern business jargon and "team building" talk.

In Seasons Eight and Nine, Frank Spotnitz directed two episodes: "Alone," which pitted Mulder and Doggett against a lizard man, and the aforementioned "Daemonicus." Head of Big Lights Productions, Ltd., Spotnitz has kept busy long after *The X-Files* ended. He reimagined *Kolchak: The Night Stalker* in 2005 and created the Cinemax/BBC series *Hunted* in 2012, which is now developing a spin-off. In 2015, Spotnitz coproduced and wrote the pilot episode of *The Man in the High Castle*, an "alternate reality" premise adapted from a 1963 Philip K. Dick novel. In this universe, the Axis Powers won World War II and partitioned the United States into separate, enslaved territories.

James Wong and Glen Morgan

The writing team of James Wong and Glen Morgan was with *The X-Files* right from the beginning. The duo thus wrote several stories that set the tone for the series, including the first monster-of-the-week show, "Squeeze" (with Victor Eugene Tooms), "Ice," and "Beyond the Sea." After the second season of *The X-Files,* Morgan and Wong left to produce their own series, *Space: Above and Beyond,* for Fox TV, but it lasted just one season

The duo returned to *The X-Files* and headed the writing staff for the fourth season, while Chris Carter launched *Millennium.* During this span, Morgan and Wong wrote some of the most challenging and controversial episodes of the series, including "Home," "The Field Where I Died," "Musings of a Cigarette Smoking Man," and "Never Again." These episodes took big creative risks, were incredibly ambitious, and remain very rewarding to watch. Morgan and James are also famous for importing into *The X-Files* (and later *Millennium*) several of the stars of their canceled *Space: Above and Beyond,* including Kristen Cloke, Rodney Rowland, and Tucker Smallwood.

Following *The X-Files'* fourth season, the writing team moved to produce and story edit the second season of *Millennium.* Their changes moved that Lance Henriksen series away from its serial-killer-heavy first season and more fully into fantasy and horror terrain. In the year 2000, the duo also produced its own brilliant but short-lived horror series, *The Others,* about a team of psychics. And in the same year, they wrote the horror film *Final Destination,* which became a popular franchise.

Prominent Directors

Rob Bowman

Rob Bowman worked at Stephen Cannell Productions early in his career, working his way up from a position in the mail room to directorial responsibilities. Bowman caught his big break in 1987 when he directed the fourth episode of *Star Trek: The Next Generation*, "Where No One Has Gone Before." After that installment, which Gene Roddenberry applauded on set, Bowman took the clichéd "evil twin" sow's ear episode, "Datalore," and transformed it, with Brent Spiner's help, into the most electrifying, tense episode of the first season. On *Star Trek: The Next Generation*, Bowman also directed the first Klingon/Worf arc story, "Heart of Glory," and introduced the Borg in "Q-Who."

The same year, Bowman directed episodes of the Fox horror series *Werewolf* (1987–1988), an assignment that proved excellent preparation for his work on *The X-Files*. Bowman began directing episodes of the Carter series in 1994 and demonstrated remarkable facility in handling both suspenseful, action-packed stories such as "Pusher" and "Drive" and comedic ones like "Syzygy" and "Jose Chung's from Outer Space."

Bowman is very much a visual director, and his work showcases a concerted effort to make form reflect content. He crafts mood through lighting choices, but also in his selection of camera moves and in the blocking of actors. Given this facility with imagery, it was only natural, perhaps, that Bowman would be selected director for the first *X-Files* feature film: *Fight the Future.*

In total, Bowman directed a whopping thirty-three episodes of *The X-Files*, and his most memorable entries include "Our Town," "Unruhe," "The Field Where I Died," and "The Pine Bluff Variant." Bowman's final episode for the series was "En Ami" in the seventh season, in the year 2000.

Since leaving *The X-Files*, Bowman has also directed the pilots for *The Lone Gunmen* (2001) and the popular Nathan Fillion series *Castle* (2009–).

R. W. Goodwin

Born in Australia and a performer for a time with the comedy troupe Credibility Gap, R. W. Goodwin served as co-executive producer of *The X-Files* for five seasons, from 1993 to 1998, and during that span directed nine episodes. However, Goodwin, who is married to Sheila Larken (Mrs. Scully), did not make the move from Vancouver to Los Angeles in the sixth season. Following *The X-Files* he served as an executive producer on the Eliza Dushku sci-fi series *Tru Calling* (2003–2004) and the ill-fated remake of *The Fugitive* (2000–2001).

Regarding his contributions to *The X-Files*, Goodwin was almost exclusively a Mytharc director. He directed five season finales, including "The Erlenmeyer Flask," "Anasazi," "Talitha Cumi," "Gethsemane," and "The End." Goodwin also told *The Vancouver Sun* why directing *The X-Files* was such a tough gig: "Some directors are very good with actors, dramatics and staging. Some directors are great with the camera, they're very cinematic. Some directors are really good with action. Some directors can do suspense well. Some directors know how to use special effects well. But when you come to *The X-Files*, you have to be able to do all of that. Because if you can't do all of that, you can't do the show."

Kim Manners (1951–2009)

Director Kim Manners, who died much too young at the age of fifty-eight, helmed *The X-Files* for some of its most memorable and stylish installments. Manners grew up in the entertainment industry and began his directing career in 1978 with episodes of *Charlie's Angels* (1976–1981). He also directed episodes of *Matt Houston* (1982–1985), *Simon and Simon* (1981–1989), *Hardcastle and McCormick* (1983–1986), and the pilot for *21 Jump Street* (1987–1991).

Manners reported that he did not have a pleasant tenure directing the *Star Trek: The Next Generation* (1987–1994) first-season episode, "When the Bough Breaks." That episode featured future "Deep Throat" Jerry Hardin as the leader of an alien planet that steals a handful of children from the *Enterprise*.

Manners originally had some difficulty getting assigned to *The X-Files*, but Glen Morgan and James Wong had worked with him on *21 Jump Street* and recommended him for the job. "I was the final guy they brought in, and they had their little team," Manners told interviewer Sarah Kendzior in *Fangoria* magazine in 2000: "we had our core group of people and I was the last guy to join that. And from there, the series kind of snowballed because we all felt so comfortable together.

In a *Starlog* interview with Joe Nazzaro, Manners also reported how shooting on *The X-Files* typically went, with two units—first and second—constantly shooting, complete with sound. Manners called the gig "director's heaven" and noted "there's no place out there where we can have this kind of creative freedom."

David Nutter

A graduate of the University of Miami, Emmy Award–winning director David Nutter has become Hollywood's go-to guy for directing pilot episodes. Nutter helmed the pilots for *Space: Above and Beyond* (1995), *Millennium, Roswell* (1999–2002), *Dark Angel* (2000–2002), *Smallville* (2001–2011), and *Arrow* (2012), to name just a handful of genre programs. More recently, Nutter directed the notorious "Red Wedding" episode of *Game of Thrones* (2011–), "The Rains of Castamere."

From 1993 to 1995, Nutter directed fifteen episodes of *The X-Files.* His work is especially notable for Nutter's ability to create tension out of claustrophobic settings, as he did in "Ice" and in the "interview" sequences with Brad Dourif (as Luther Lee Boggs) in "Beyond the Sea."

Nutter's greatest and most visually accomplished episode of *The X-Files,* however, may be "Irresistible," a dark, relentless tale that concerns a death fetishist and never veers into comfortable or ameliorating fantasy. After leaving *The X-Files,* Nutter directed four episodes of Carter's *Millennium,* including the pilot episode, which this author counts as the greatest series pilot in TV history.

Other Important Players

Mat Beck

Mat Beck served as visual effects supervisor for over one hundred episodes of *The X-Files* throughout its run from 1993 to 2002. Outside of *The X-Files,* he has also collaborated frequently with director James Cameron, on projects including *The Abyss* (1989), *True Lies* (1994), and the Academy Award–winning *Titanic* (1997). Of late, he has served as the senior visual effects supervisor on TV series such as *Smallville* (from 2003 to 2006) and *The Vampire Diaries* (from 2009 to 2013). Beck has also been visual effects supervisor on the horror films *Fright Night* (2011) and *Riddick* (2013).

Mark Snow

Composer Mark Snow (1946–) created the famous *X-Files* theme and scored all 202 episodes of the series. The Emmy-nominated *X-Files* theme was created after four attempts by Snow, and it conformed to series creator Chris Carter's desire for a minimalist approach.

Mark Snow told *Dreamwatch* magazine's Dave Hughes in February 1997 that the aim and hope for the theme was a "signature sound, which you hear and within three seconds you know what it is." The unusual decision to use a whistle in the theme song came, according to Snow, from the beloved hit TV series *The Andy Griffith Show* (1960–1968). That famous series theme was composed by Earle Hagen, a talent Snow had once studied.

Nominated for nineteen Emmy Awards and the recipient of thirty-four ASCAP awards, Mark Snow has scored the main themes to such series as *Hart to Hart* (1978), *Nowhere Man* (1995), *La Femme Nikita* (1997–2001), and the children's series *Wonder Pets* (2007). He has also contributed background music to the first six seasons of *Smallville*, as well as to *Birds of Prey* (2002) and *Ringer* (2011–2012).

Although Snow has reported that scoring episodic television can be a grind, he scored the vast majority of *The X-Files* episodes, every episode of *Millennium*, and also installments of *The Lone Gunmen*. Snow has also composed soundtracks for such TV movies as *The Boy in the Plastic Bubble* (1976), starring John Travolta.

Snow composed *The X-Files* episodes from his home studio in Santa Monica, California. His *X-Files* theme has become not only a cultural touchstone in America, but a hit single, rising to #2 on the charts in the UK.

3

The Stars of *The X-Files*

Anderson, Duchovny, and More

David Duchovny

David Duchovny, who plays Agent Fox Mulder on *The X-Files*, was raised on Manhattan's Lower East Side. His father was a public relations practitioner and book author, and his parents divorced when he was eleven. Duchovny attended the prestigious Collegiate School on the West Side and graduated in 1978. Afterwards, he studied literature at Princeton, where he penned his senior thesis: "The Schizophrenic Critique of Pure Reason in Beckett's Early Novels." Duchovny then landed a fellowship and went to Yale to earn his doctorate in English Literature.

A fan of horror movies who counts *The Texas Chainsaw Massacre* (1974) among his favorites, Duchovny's first taste of acting came in a Lowenbrau commercial in 1987. From there, he began to make appearances in independent films such as *The Rapture* (1991), opposite future *X-Files* costar Mimi Rogers. In 1993, he starred alongside Juliette Lewis and Brad Pitt in the thriller *Kalifornia*, essaying the role of Brian Kessler, a researcher into the lives of serial killers. The role felt like a dry run for the part of Mulder.

In 1991 and 1992, Duchovny also made appearances on David Lynch's cult-TV series *Twin Peaks*, as Denise/Dennis Bryant, a DEA agent who often presents as a female. He also served as the host/narrator of the erotic Showtime Zalman King anthology *Red Shoe Diaries* (1992–1997), playing Jake Winters, a lonely man reading the letters of women involved in passionate love stories.

For the first seven seasons of *The X-Files*, Duchovny acted as a full-time lead on the series, and he returned in a part-time capacity (eleven of twenty episodes) in Season Eight. His final appearance on the show was for the finale, "The Truth," and he recreated the role of Mulder for the second feature film in 2008.

Gillian Anderson and David Duchovny both took home Golden Globe Awards for *The X-Files* in 1997.

In 1997, Duchovny won a Golden Globe Award for Best Actor in a Dramatic Series, after having been nominated in 1995 and 1996. The actor's work as Mulder has also netted him two Screen Actors Guild Award nominations and a Critic's Award Nomination. Also, Duchovny has been nominated for Emmy Awards twice, once in 1997 for *The X-Files* and again in 1997 for his guest work on Garry Shandling's *The Larry Sanders Show* (1992–1998).

During the run of *The X-Files*, Duchovny directed three episodes, 1999's "The Unnatural," 2000's "Hollywood A.D.," and the ninth-season episode "William." He also contributed a number of stories to the series, participating in the genesis of "Anasazi," "Avatar," and "The Sixth Extinction II: Amor Fati."

Duchovny brings a strong sense of intelligence, morality, humor, and charm to his portrayal of Mulder, and his efforts are a key reason for the series' popularity. Duchovny is also generally described as the reason for *The*

X-Files' move from Vancouver to Los Angeles beginning in the sixth season. Prior to the move, he often described working on the series (twelve to fourteen hours a day for ten months each year) as grueling and wished to be close to his then wife, actress Tea Leoni.

Following *The X-Files'* cancellation, Duchovny starred for seven years on the hit Showtime comedy series *Californication,* as boozing, womanizing, and self-destructive author Hank Moody. He won a Golden Globe Award for that portrayal exactly ten years after winning the same award for his performances as Mulder. Recently, it was announced that Duchovny would be starring in a new dramatic TV series, *Aquarius,* which involves the investigation and capture of Charles Manson.

Widely recognized as a powerful intellect as well as an accomplished actor, Duchovny in the 1990s appeared on *Celebrity Jeopardy*, but lost to Stephen King.

After a distinguished academic career, David Duchovny moved into acting and landed the role of Agent Fox Mulder on *The X-Files.*

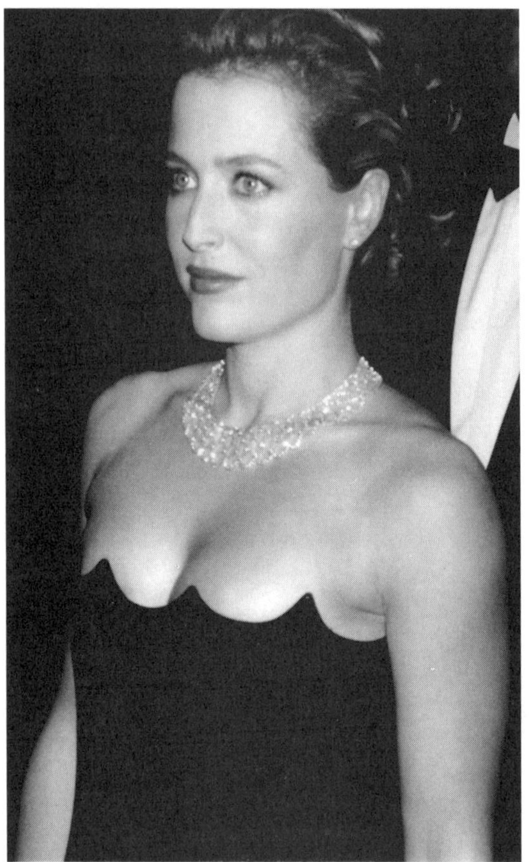

Gillian Anderson played Dana Scully on *The X-Files* for nine years and has since starred in series including *The Fall* and *Hannibal*.

Gillian Anderson

Born in 1968 in Chicago, Gillian Anderson lived in England from the ages of two to eleven, before returning to the States to study at the Goodman Theater School at DePaul University. Afterwards, she moved to New York City and began a spell working in off-Broadway plays, including in *The Philanthropist* at Long Wharf Theater and *Absent Friends* at the Manhattan Theater Club.

Although Fox executives had reservations about Anderson taking on the role of Scully in *The X-Files* because she was not a traditional, bosom-heavy Pamela Anderson type, Chris Carter prevailed in his desire to cast her, and Anderson assumed the role of Dana Katherine Scully to instant plaudits and universal acclaim. She essayed the role for nine years and won a slew of awards for it, including a Golden Globe in 1997 and an Emmy Award the same year. Anderson also won two Saturn Awards (in 1996 and 1997) for her portrayal of Scully. Her three-dimensional approach to the character has been called a watershed event in female roles on television, and Scully is frequently mentioned as a feminist icon.

After *The X-Files* concluded, Anderson starred in the critically acclaimed British series *Bleak House* (2006) and in dramas including *The Fall* (2013) and *Hannibal* (2013–), a series in which she plays serial killer's Hannibal Lecter's psychologist. In 2012, Anderson also starred in the science fiction film *I'll Follow You Down*, playing the wife of a man (Rufus Sewell) who disappeared without a trace.

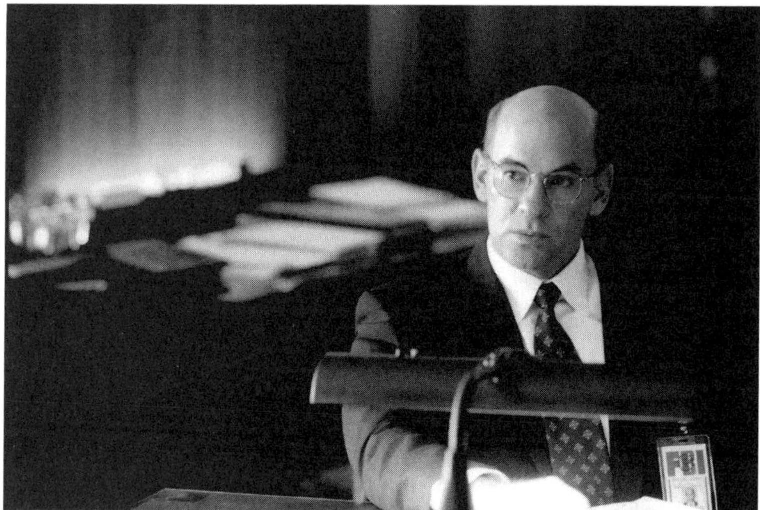

Mitch Pileggi portrays Assistant Director Skinner, here seen in the first *X-Files* feature film, *Fight the Future* (1998).

Mitch Pileggi

In the role of Assistant Director Skinner on *The X-Files* is the physically imposing Mitch Pileggi, an actor who joined the Chris Carter series late in the first season, in the episode "Tooms." Pileggi had already made a name for himself at that point with his portrayal of the supernatural maniac (and intended heir to Freddy Krueger's throne) in Wes Craven's 1989 horror film *Shocker.* Pileggi also worked with Craven in 1995's A *Vampire in Brooklyn* and after *The X-Files* played the recurring character Ernest Darby—a skinhead drug dealer—on FX's popular *Sons of Anarchy* (2008–2014). Concurrent with that role, Pileggi played Harris Ryland on the continuation of *Dallas* (2012–).

Robert Patrick

Born in Georgia and raised in Cleveland, actor Robert Patrick shot to fame with his portrayal of the malevolent T-1000, a shape-shifting terminator, in James Cameron's blockbuster *Terminator 2: Judgment Day* (1991). That film was not Patrick's only experience with science fiction filmmaking; he also played Mike Rogers, buddy to Travis Walton in the alien-abduction film *Fire in the Sky* in 1993.

Robert Patrick, here seen as the villain in *Terminator 2: Judgment Day* (1991), joined the cast of *The X-Files* in Season Eight as agent John Doggett.

Patrick made several guest appearances on the Canadian-shot new *Outer Limits* series in 1995 and 1996, and then played a body-snatching alien in the body of a high school gym coach in the 1998 Robert Rodriguez film *The Faculty*.

Patrick was cast as Agent John Doggett on *The X-Files* in 2000 when David Duchovny committed to playing Mulder only part-time for Season Eight. Patrick earned the role over many well-known and beloved actors, including horror icon Bruce Campbell. As Doggett, Patrick projected blue-collar integrity and a sense of honest (if raw) curiosity about the strange events the character witnessed.

After playing Doggett for the last two seasons of the series, Patrick appeared on *True Blood* from 2012 to 2014, playing Alcide's (werewolf) father and former pack leader. In 2014, he took on the role of Jacob Fuller in *From Dusk Till Dawn: The Series*, a role originated in the 1996 film by Harvey Keitel.

Annabeth Gish

Gish, who was born in Albuquerque but moved to Iowa as a child, was a movie star as early as 1987 and the hit film *Desert Bloom.* She also costarred alongside Julia Roberts in *Mystic Pizza* (1988) and with Kevin Costner in *Wyatt Earp* (1994).

Gish first portrayed Agent Monica Reyes in *The X-Files* during Season Eight, but only on a recurring basis. She became a full-time lead in the ninth season, investigating cases alongside Patrick's character, Doggett. Although some fans were concerned that Gish's presence meant Scully would disappear from the series, Chris Carter told *E! Online* that the actress was not replacing "anybody," merely adding fresh blood to the series. Gish brought a sense of openness to Reyes, making her a likable character who was confident in her beliefs without feeling the need to judge others for theirs.

Following the cancellation of *The X-Files,* Gish was a regular on the Showtime series *Brotherhood* (2006–2009) and is currently a cast member on *The Bridge* (2014–).

4

Who's Who in *The X-Files*

Main, Supporting, and Recurring Characters

In order to understand fully this book's analyses and interpretations, as well as the themes portrayed in *The X-Files*, it is necessary to have some broad idea of the characters who figure in the drama, the characters who make the series such a captivating viewing experience, even on repeat viewing.

These characters fall into several categories. The Crusaders are the series' heroes or protagonists, who, in the tradition of Joseph Campbell's hero's journey (and its champions) "hear the call" and go out to confront a challenge or threat. On *The X-Files*, all such crusaders are ensconced in The FBI.

The Oracles are those characters who advise and offer wisdom to the hero, but may also be Loki-like figures of mischief or deceit. In the hero's journey template, such characters are sometimes known as "tricksters" because they appear to be one thing but represent something else entirely.

The Nemeses represent the existential threat to the heroes and their journey. For lack of a better word, they are the bad guys. And if they win, the very world of the crusader or champion is threatened. *The X-Files* also often features family members of the *dramatis personae*, and they represent a reminder of what is at stake and who must be protected in the battle ahead. By the same token, families are often a symbol of the past, and in a very true sense, *The X-Files* is a story of generations in the Mulder family. Mulder must decide which of his two fathers he will emulate. That is one of his many challenges in the series.

The Crusaders

These are the series champions, who go out into the world and investigate dark conspiracies, strange beings, and connections that others either can't see or won't see. Each of the crusaders carries a different "weapon" to help them contend with the darkness they find. Mulder is armed with obsessive belief, Scully with cold, analytical science, Doggett with an unerring, brutal honesty and concrete sense of the facts, and Reyes with complete and total openness.

Fox Mulder

Introduced in the pilot episode of *The X-Files,* "Spooky" Mulder is an Oxford-educated psychologist who began a career of tremendous promise in the FBI. After studying under renowned profiler Bill Patterson at Quantico ("Grotesque"), Mulder worked in the Violent Crimes Division with his mentor, Reggie Purdue ("Young at Heart.") In 1990, Mulder was apparently married, judging by the wedding ring that appears on his finger in a flashback in the episode "Travelers," though to whom, and for how long, is not known. Mulder discovered the X-Files—the unit for unsolved, strange cases—with his friend Diana Fowley at some point in 1991 ("The End").

Owing to his galvanizing childhood trauma, the disappearance and possible abduction of his sister Samantha in 1973 ("Little Green Men"), Mulder transferred to the X-Files unit and was assigned a partner, Dana Scully, in 1993 ("Pilot"). Mulder is so obsessed with the paranormal and his sister's disappearance that he rarely dates women and boasts a fondness for pornography. In one episode, a psychic informs him that he will die by autoerotic asphyxiation ("Clyde Bruckman's Final Repose").

Mulder's quest to learn about Samantha has impacted his own understanding of his family, particularly the relationship of his mother, Teena, and father, Bill. Late in the series, it is learned that Bill Mulder is not his biological father.

In terms of the heroic journey, Mulder's odyssey involves learning the truth about what really happened to his sister, exposing the men responsible, and eventually preventing alien colonization of the Earth. Mulder has explicitly been compared to Hamlet, Jesus Christ ("Amor Fati"), and other literary heroes in the course of the series, and by scholars and critics examining *The X-Files.* For instance, in "The Truth Is Out There in Elsinore: Mulder and Scully as Hamlet and Horatio," Sharon R. Yang writes: "*The X-Files* . . . provides a hero obsessed with knowing and sometimes incapacitated by the ramifications and personal responsibilities this knowledge entails." This is a perfect thumbnail description of the character.

Temperamentally speaking, Mulder is brash, intelligent, occasionally arrogant, and blessed with a wicked, sometimes-verging-on-the-inappropriate, sense of humor. Although he believes wholly in the paranormal, he tends to

The Three Musketeers? Mulder, Scully, and Skinner investigate a world of the paranormal in *The X-Files.*

be skeptical about organized religion ("Revelations," "All Souls"). In terms of his relationship with Scully, Mulder has said that she keeps him honest and makes him work for every argument or theory he produces (*Fight the Future*).

Dana Katherine Scully

Born February 20, 1964, Dana Scully is the daughter of Bill, a naval captain, and Margaret Scully. She grew up with three siblings, Billy, Charles, and Melissa ("One Breath"), in Annapolis and later San Francisco. A lapsed Catholic when the series commences, Scully earns an undergraduate degree in physics before attending medical school. She joins the FBI as a forensic pathologist in 1992 and is assigned to the X-Files to partner with Mulder in 1993 by Section Chief Blevins.

A strict rationalist who believes that science is the benchmark by which the paranormal or other extreme events must be judged, Scully undergoes a traumatic nine years allied with Mulder. In 1994, she is abducted by members of the Syndicate and experimented on. She later learns that those experiments have poisoned her with terminal cancer ("Leonard Betts") and produced a biological child that she was unaware of ("A Christmas Carol," "Emily"). It is especially hard for Scully to continue working on the X-Files after that child, Emily, dies, because she is infertile and therefore cannot have another child.

However, in 2000, immediately following the abduction of Mulder in Oregon, Scully announces that she is pregnant ("Requiem"). She gives birth to a baby boy, William, in 2001 ("Existence"), but is later forced to give him up for adoption when she realizes it is his only chance of leading a normal life ("William"). After leaving the FBI, Scully returns to her first love, medicine, at a private Catholic hospital in Virginia (*I Want to Believe*).

"She has a very strong belief system, a very strong dedication to her background, which is medical and scientific," Anderson noted of Scully in an interview excerpted in *Net Trek* in the mid-1990s. "That belief system is always going to be the first thing she turns to when she has come up with explanations for situations—when she's doing an autopsy or making any kind of decision, or presenting a hypothesis."

In terms of personal relationships, Scully dates twice in the series ("The Jersey Devil" and "Never Again") and later encounters a professor with whom she had an affair in medical school ("All Things"). In "Bad Blood," Scully notes that Mulder is typically "exuberant" and brash," and in *Fight the Future* she worries that she has done nothing but hold his work back, a theory he soundly refutes.

Named by Carter after Vin Scully, famous "voice of God" announcer, Dana Scully may also be, oddly, immortal. In the third-season story "Clyde Bruckman's Final Repose," the psychic claims she will never die. In Season Six, this notion is confirmed by another man who can see death, in "Tithonus." In "En Ami," we may have the answer to this strange quirk. The Cigarette Smoking Man introduces Scully to a woman who has had the same cure for cancer she took and is still vibrant and healthy at 116 years of age.

Assistant Director Walter Skinner

The strong silent type, and one who has a difficult time expressing emotions, Walter Skinner is introduced in the first-season episode "Tooms." He is Mulder and Scully's superior in the FBI throughout much of the series, and though often quite stern, will go the distance to help them whenever possible.

This willingness to help Mulder and Scully arises for one of two reasons. The first might be personal loyalty. Skinner seems to genuinely care for both agents and their well-being. But secondly, he seems to believe in the work, or at least some of the work. Indeed, Skinner has had paranormal experiences himself, and remembers vividly a near-death experience in Vietnam, one involving an old woman ("Avatar") who Mulder believes is a succubus. Skinner finally sees a UFO for himself in the episode "Requiem," wherein Mulder is abducted.

In the aforementioned "Avatar," Skinner is on the verge of divorce from his wife of several years, Sharon (Jennifer Hetrick). Besides this fact, and his duty in Vietnam, little is known of his background, save that he went to college with a man, Wayne Federman, who became a Hollywood writer and producer ("Hollywood A.D.").

Early in the series, Skinner seems to be on a tight leash held by the Cigarette Smoking Man, but he grows more independent in later seasons. Unfortunately, Skinner also is compromised by Alex Krycek on at least two occasions ("S.R. 819," "Deadalive") but warns Scully about his situation. Skinner serves as Mulder's defense attorney during his trial in "The Truth" and several years later is the first person Scully calls when Mulder is in jeopardy in *I Want to Believe.*

Skinner is a crusader in the sense that he believes the evidence of his eyes and the weight of the reports that Mulder and Scully file. He supports their cause and fights side by side with them in episodes such as "Existence." Still, Skinner is often in a tough spot, pinned between his loyalty to Scully and Mulder and his responsibility to the chain of command in the FBI.

John Doggett

Special Agent John Doggett first appears in the eighth-season premiere, "Within," and is tasked by Assistant Director Kersh with locating the missing Agent Mulder, apparently abducted by aliens in "Requiem." An ex-Marine who served in Beirut in the 24th Marine Amphibious Unit and ex-police officer for the NYPD, Doggett is then assigned to the X-Files when he fails to do so.

Doggett is a concrete thinker who, unlike Mulder, lacks a deep sense of imagination. Nonetheless, he boasts a powerful moral compass and develops a strong sense of loyalty to both Scully and his eventual partner, Monica Reyes.

Doggett is divorced, and his son, Luke, was killed by a child molester. He carries this loss with him every day ("John Doe") and sometimes allows the personal tragedy to color his perception of cases ("Invocation"). Doggett genuinely resents the "paranormal" as an explanation for events, feeling that it suggests a certain laziness ("The Truth"). Doggett eventually feels that he is tackling the demands of the job on the X-Files ("Sunshine Days") and harbors an intense dislike for Kersh.

Doggett is *The X-Files'* inadvertent hero or "average joe." He does not go out seeking to learn about UFOs or aliens, but the truth finds him, and he rises to the occasion.

Monica Reyes

Introduced in the eighth-season episode "This Is Not Happening," Agent Monica Julieta Reyes was born in Mexico City. By the late 1990s and early 2000s, she is an agent for the FBI who knows John Doggett, another agent, because she was the lead investigator on the case involving the disappearance of his son. For many years, Monica has worked cases in the FBI involving devil worship or the occult. She seems drawn to this "darkness," though she has the brightest disposition of all the crusaders or champions on the series.

Monica believes in the paranormal, but more generally is open to any idea or theory—including New Age mysticism or numerology ("Improbable")—that she feels could help bring her closer to the truth. Her openness has led Scully to compare her to her own deceased sister, Melissa ("Existence").

The ninth-season episode "Hellbound" suggests that Monica is preordained to hunt for the truth. The call she hears and answers to do just that originates from previous lives in which she failed to solve a particularly brutal murder case involving victims who are skinned alive. That failure, carried over from other existences, subconsciously drives Monica's actions, particularly her hunger for justice.

The Oracles

In Ancient Greece, an oracle is a person through whom the gods are believed to speak. An oracle provides advice, makes prophecies, and leads one to God's will. On *The X-Files*, the "oracle"-type characters are vehicles for the discovery of "the truth," which is Mulder's high ideal, and in some ways seems to replace the hunt for God. The oracles are those who help, and sometimes hinder, Mulder in that hunt.

The Lone Gunmen

The Lone Gunmen are John Fitzgerald Byers (named after JFK), Melvin Frohike (or "El Lobo"), and Richard Langly. Together they publish

The Lone Gunmen—Langly, Frohike, and Byers—are among the most important "oracles" on *The X-Files.*

a periodical out of a shabby warehouse that doubles as a laboratory and an apartment. The periodical seeks to expose the "truth" of government malfeasance.

The Lone Gunmen first joined forces and met Mulder in 1989 at a computer expo or convention in Philadelphia. There, John Byers (Bruce Harwood), a PR flack, sought to help a woman in trouble named Holly (actually Susanne Modeski) who was being sought by the government ("The Usual Suspects"). The buttoned-down Byers, the most conservative of the bunch, first teamed up with the other two gunmen at that point. Frohike (Tom Braidwood) is a photographer and tango expert (!) with strong computer hacking skills, and Langly (Dean Haglund) is a slightly paranoid, ill-tempered competitor hacker virgin with a chip on his shoulder.

Mulder, Scully, and later Doggett seek the help of the Lone Gunmen whenever they require a sounding board or additional information about strange topics, including government implants, vaccines, and computer files. After several adventures with two new friends, Jimmy Bond and Yves Adele Harlow, the Lone Gunmen die heroically in the ninth-season episode of the series, "Jump the Shark." As oracles, the Lone Gunmen are interesting contradictions. As nerds and counterculture, antisocial conspiracy theorists, they appear to be undependable. However, they are, almost universally, speakers of the truth.

Charlie Burks

Bill Dow plays Dr. Charlie Burks or "Chuck," one of Mulder's friends and a key advisor to the X-Files unit during the nine-season run of the program. Burks appears in half a dozen episodes, including "Leonard Betts," "Rush," and "Hollywood A.D.," always to explain the rationale behind some seemingly paranormal or supernatural technique or device.

In "The Calusari," for instance, Burks explains Kirlian or "aura" photography. In "Biogenesis," he lays out the history of "magic squares" in an attempt to explain the powers of a recently discovered alien tablet. In "Hollywood A.D.," he explains how a recording—the voice of God?—could be imprinted on pottery. His work for the X-Files continues after Mulder's abduction and later disappearance, and he assists Scully and Doggett in "Badlaa," discussing Indian fakirs and mystics.

Deep Throat

A good-hearted member of the Syndicate played by Jerry Hardin who, because of his conscience, reaches out to Mulder and is the first in a long line of informants or oracles on *The X-Files.* A compatriot of Bill Mulder, Deep Throat is murdered by an assassin in the first-season finale, "The Erlenmeyer Flask," but reappears throughout the series, often in Fox Mulder's fantasies or dreams ("Amor Fati," "The Truth"). We learn in "Amor Fati" that Mulder feels tremendous guilt over Deep Throat's death.

The character of Deep Throat is deliberately modeled on the historical "Deep Throat," Woodward and Bernstein's informant in the FBI during the Watergate scandal. In 2005, the identity of Deep Throat was unveiled publicly. Mark Felt (1913–2008) revealed that he had been in contact with the *Washington Post* reporters and had funneled them information in his capacity as associate director in the Bureau.

X

Following the murder of Deep Throat, Mulder is contacted by a new "friend in the FBI," the paranoid, dangerous, violent, and physically intimidating "X," played by Steven Williams. Unlike his predecessor, X often seeks to use Mulder for his own ends and is not above fighting Mulder, or holding him at gunpoint to keep him in line. By the same token, X saves Mulder's life on more than one occasion, such as the time he evacuates an unconscious Mulder from a train car set to explode, in North Dakota ("Nisei"). Outed as a mole by a Syndicate plot, X meets the same grim fate as his predecessor, but not before pointing Mulder to his next informant, Marita Covarubbias, by scrawling the letters SRSG (Special Representative to the Secretary General) in his own blood on the floor of Mulder's apartment building.

Albert Holsteen

A Navajo code talker in World War II played by Floyd Red Crow Westerman, Albert Holsteen first appears in the second-season finale, "Anasazi." He leads Mulder and Scully through the mystery of several corpses discovered in a buried railway car. He reappears in "Biogenesis," "The Sixth Extinction," and "The Sixth Extinction: Amor Fati," suffering from a mystery ailment that took his life. On the nights before his death, however, his spirit contacts Scully and offers wisdom regarding her hunt for the then-missing Mulder.

The Well-Manicured Man

Introduced in the third season of *The X-Files*, the Well-Manicured Man (John Neville) is the civilized or refined face of the secret conspiracy, the Syndicate. He deplores violence and the Cigarette Smoking Man's methods. He is a family man, and a grandfather, and comes to respect both Mulder and Scully. When, in the course of the first *X-Files* film, he learns about the true nature of the black oil and alien colonization, he seeks out Mulder and tells him the truth. Additionally, he provides Mulder a "weak" vaccine so he can cure Scully of the infection she suffers at that point. The Well-Manicured Man is executed by a car bomb for this act of decency. However, he serves his purpose as an oracle in the film quite adeptly, taking Mulder and audiences on a step-by-step explanation of the conspiracy, from the origin of the black oil to Samantha's disappearance, to the frightening future of colonization.

Marita Covarubbias

Played by Laurie Holden, recent star of AMC's original series, *The Walking Dead*, Marita Covarrubias is Mulder's last secret informant or oracle. Mulder visits her office at the United Nations, where she serves as special representative to the secretary general. Marita speaks fluent Russian and knows of the Syndicate's plans to create a vaccine for the black oil virus. When the Syndicate learns that she has been helping Mulder puzzle out all the clues, she is punished with infection for her trespass. Ultimately, Marita is healed,

Laurie Holden, later a star on AMC's original series *The Walking Dead*, plays the role of Marita Covarrubbias, another "oracle" type character on *The X-Files.*

and she conspires with Krycek to kill the Cigarette Smoking Man. She and Krycek push him down a flight of stairs. In the series' final episode, "The Truth," Marita testifies at Mulder's trial, but he excuses her after a brief testimony out of fear that she will be murdered.

Gibson Praise

Played by Jeff Gulka, Gibson Praise is a young boy who first appears in the fifth-season story "The End." He is a chess champion, but one who owes his winning strategy not to an understanding of the game but to his ability to read minds. Gibson is believed by Scully and Mulder to be a "missing link," and he owes his precognitive and mind-reading abilities to activated "junk DNA" in his brain; DNA that is believed to be extraterrestrial in nature. As a child,

Gibson represents the future or our tomorrows, and in his appearances on the series, Mulder, Scully, Doggett, and Reyes are often tasked with protecting him from the Syndicate. He is dangerous to the Syndicate because he can see through their lies and directly into their thoughts. This capacity makes him an "oracle," for by dint of his very genetics he can see the truth in all those he encounters. Gibson undergoes radical brain surgery in "The Beginning" under the eye of the Cigarette Smoking Man; hides in Arizona in 2001 during the hunt for an abducted Fox Mulder ("Within," Without"); and puts his life on the line in the series finale, "The Truth," to testify on Mulder's behalf during his trial.

Arthur Dales (x2)

Two brothers share the name Arthur Dales in *The X-Files*. The first Arthur Dales, played by Darren McGavin, is the man who opened up the X-Files in the late 1940s and was the first to investigate cases of this type. He has kept up with Mulder's activities and is a friend and advisor to him. This Arthur Dales recounts a tale for Mulder of aliens in Washington, D.C., in the McCarthy era ("Travelers") and after he retires to Miami, alerts Mulder and Scully to weird events during a hurricane, events that involve a sea monster ("Agua Mala"). In the latter episode, Dales voices the thought that if he had been granted a partner like Scully, he would never have stopped investigating X-Files.

The second Arthur Dales (M. Emmet Walsh) was a police officer in Roswell, New Mexico, in the late 1940s and came to develop a friendship with a black baseball player, Josh Exley (Jesse L. Martin), whom he claims was a gray alien. He tells this story to a skeptical Mulder on a Saturday afternoon and seems genuinely devastated when remembering the death of his friend at the hands of the alien bounty hunter (Brian Thompson).

Senator Richard Matheson

Played by actor Richard J. Barry, Richard Matheson is Mulder's patron in the U.S. Senate. In the second-season premiere, "Little Green Men," Senator Matheson provides Mulder the information he needs about a SETI installation in Arecibo. He does so, he claims, because he believes in the work. However, there are limits to Matheson's patience, especially when he considers himself politically exposed. He is unwilling to help Mulder find Scully in "Ascension," during her abduction, and in the sixth-season installment "S.R. 819," it is learned that Mulder's friend in a high place is mired in a deal involving nano-technology; illegal technology that is being used to make Skinner sick and render him under the control of Alex Krycek.

Michael Kritschgau

Introduced in the fourth-season finale, "Gethsemane," Michael Kritschgau (John Finn) is a highly seated Department of Defense employee who has been working to foster a (false) narrative about UFOs and aliens, so that Mulder, the patsy in the plan, will continue to talk about them. This lie about the existence of aliens covers the military's secret operations, Kritschgau says. When Kritschgau's son, a veteran of the first Gulf War, contracts GWI (Gulf War Illness), he comes to believe that a cure exists in the Pentagon. He contacts Mulder and Scully, tells them his story, and Mulder goes in search of a cure for Scully's cancer and Kritschgau's son's mystery illness. Unfortunately, no cure for the boy is found, and he dies.

After "Gethsemane," Kritschgau appears in "Redux," "Redux II," "The Sixth Extinction," and "The Sixth Extinction II: Amor Fati." He is a crucial oracle because his revelations of truth (or the truth as he sees it) result in, for a span, Mulder's loss of faith in his beliefs.

Cassandra Spender

A multiple abductee, Cassandra Spender (Veronica Cartwright) is the wife of the Cigarette Smoking Man and the mother of FBI Agent Jeffrey Spender. Spender has endured twenty-five years of painful experiments, all orchestrated by her ex-husband. In the fifth season of *The X-Files*, a wheelchair-bound Cassandra informs Scully and Mulder that the aliens are a force of light and goodness in the universe. When rebels kill a group of abductees on a bridge, Scully sees Spender "beamed up" to a spaceship.

Almost a year later, Cassandra is seen again, healed and able to walk. She is "Patient X," we learn, the first completely successful alien-human hybrid created in the Syndicate's "Project." The completion of this goal means that colonization can begin, which leads Cassandra to realize that the aliens are not good but evil, and, in fact, are infecting every race in the universe. She begs for Mulder and Scully to kill her, lest she be revealed as the culmination of the project.

Like the mythical Cassandra, this Cassandra can imagine the future and what it brings but is not trusted or believed. Mulder doesn't believe her stories of aliens during the fifth season, for example. Even her own son, Jeffrey, is skeptical. She is thus an oracle that is deemed unreliable, at least at first.

Knowle Rohrer

A false or sinister oracle, Rohrer (Adam Baldwin) served with John Doggett in the U.S. Marine Corps in Beirut. He later joined the Department of Defense and became Doggett's secret contact, essentially his version of Deep Throat or X. Unfortunately, Rohrer spreads disinformation and hides his true nature as an alien super soldier, or human replacement. Doggett and Mulder determine the truth about Rohrer in "Existence," but he continues to reappear and survives decapitation in "Nothing Important Happened Today." In the last episode of the series, "The Truth," Mulder is held for trial for the murder of Knowle Rohrer, but again, he isn't really dead. The super soldier threatens Doggett and Reyes one last time in that episode before being destroyed by magnetite in Anasazi rocks.

Adam Baldwin, later Jayne on Joss Whedon's *Firefly* (2002), plays Knowle Rohrer, a super soldier or alien replacement in the last two seasons of *The X-Files.*

Family Ties

These are characters often on the periphery of *The X-Files,* but who represent a connection to the rest of the world.

Bill Mulder

William Mulder (Peter Donat) is the man Fox Mulder believes to be his biological father. In the 1950s, he worked in the State Department alongside Deep Throat, Alvin Kurtzweil (Martin Landau), and the Cigarette Smoking Man. After the UFO crash in Roswell, New Mexico, Mulder reluctantly joined the Syndicate, which was then forming. As a consequence for that choice, he had to give up one of his children to the aliens in exchange for alien biological material. He chose his daughter, Samantha, but then backed out, leaving the girl to be abducted from the Mulder New England home ("Little Green Men"). Mr. Mulder spearheaded the effort to create a vaccine for the alien virus, a way of "fighting the future."

Mulder divorced his wife, Teena, and in the mid-1990s was murdered by Alex Krycek before he could tell Fox Mulder his entire story. Bill Mulder is crucial to *The X-Files* mythology and storytelling because, via his presence and CSM's, the series becomes, in grand terms, a story of generations, of children learning of their fathers' work, and either continuing their legacy or overturning it.

Teena Mulder

Teena Mulder (Rebecca Toolan) is Fox Mulder's mother. Sometime during the late 1960s, she had an extramarital affair with the Cigarette Smoking Man and became pregnant with Fox. She never told Fox the truth. In the 1990s her poor health nearly killed her, following a run-in with the Cigarette Smoking Man ("Talitha Cumi"), but he asked an alien bounty hunter to cure her. Later, in 1999, Teena Mulder committed suicide, but not before asking Mulder to live his life and put the search for Samantha behind him ("Sein und Zeit"/"Closure"). Teena is in some ways the equivalent of Gertrude in *Hamlet,* the hero's mother who has betrayed the family and slept with the enemy, thus complicating the hero's search for truth.

Samantha Mulder

Played at various ages by actors including Brianne Benitz, Vanessa Morley, Mimi Paley, and Megan Leitch, Samantha Mulder is crucial to an understanding of *The X-Files* because she rests at the heart of Mulder's quest.

On the night of November 27, 1973, Samantha at age eight was abducted from the family residence by something—either aliens or the Syndicate—and Mulder would spend the years from 1974 to 2000 in search of her, hoping to learn what happened to her and if she still lived. The object of the hero's journey, Samantha is the purpose behind Mulder's obsession, and as a child harmed by her experiences, represents innocence lost or taken away.

Samantha is seen briefly as a vision in the first-season story "Miracle Man," and the night of her abduction is depicted in the second-season premiere, "Little Green Men." Later in the series, Mulder meets alien clones of young Samantha ("Herrenvolk") and even an adult clone of her in "Colony"/"End Game" and "Redux II."

Ultimately, Mulder learns the difficult truth: that Samantha was adopted by CSM and lived with his family, including Jeffrey Spender, for a time in California. There she was subjected to the alien-human hybrid tests but escaped the pain through the intervention of spirits called Walk-ins ("Closure") who whisked her spirit away. In the same episode, Mulder is briefly reunited with her and realizes that in knowing her journey, and her final disposition, he is free. His quest is over.

William Scully

Dana Scully's father, William (Don S. Davis) dies very early in the series run, in the episode "Beyond the Sea." Before his passing he is a gruff, retired naval officer who calls Scully by the affectionate nickname "Starbuck" (from *Moby Dick*, not *Battlestar Galactica*). William Scully appears to Dana briefly, following his death, as a kind of apparition. He tries to tell her something, but she can't understand his words. The absent father, Bill is not available as a resource or reference for Scully through most of the series, and she is unable to seek his approval or love.

Billy Scully

The eldest son of Margaret and William Scully, Billy, like his father, is a career officer in the U.S. Navy. Billy disapproves strongly of Mulder and his beliefs, and sees Mulder as the reason for Melissa's death and Scully's cancer in Season Four. He treats Mulder disrespectfully and tries to usurp Scully's prerogative to seek treatment in her own way, telling Mulder to let her die with some semblance of "dignity" ("Redux," "Redux II").

Billy serves as a reminder to both Mulder and Scully that should they pursue close emotional bonds, some members of their families will not be pleased about it. Billy offers an impediment to such a relationship. He is so protective of Dana that he would likely have problems relinquishing that role.

Melissa Scully

Dana's young sister is also her opposite. Melissa is, at least on the surface, a New Age "flake" rather than an old-school Catholic. But Melissa, whatever her beliefs, possesses a true and open heart. She is murdered by the Syndicate on the cusp of the third season of *The X-Files* and communicates with Dana from beyond the grave in the fifth-season episode "A Christmas Carol," directing Scully to take care of a sick girl named Emily (Lauren Diewold), who is actually her biological daughter.

Although Scully seems embarrassed and even a little scornful of Melissa and her beliefs at the beginning of the series, she opens up to Melissa's way of thinking as the series winds down. In the seventh-season episode "All Things," directed by Gillian Anderson, Scully becomes receptive to Buddhist and New Age beliefs, and in the eighth-season finale, "Existence," she tells Monica Reyes that she reminds her of Melissa.

Margaret Scully

Of all the auxiliary characters featured on *The X-Files,* Margaret Scully (Sheila Larken) has perhaps suffered the most, especially given her distance from the events unfolding. Her husband, Bill, died of a heart attack in the first-season episode "Beyond the Sea." At the end of the second season and beginning of the third, Margaret's youngest daughter, Melissa, was murdered by the Syndicate, who was gunning for Scully.

Later, Margaret helped Scully contend with her cancer and then had to grieve again when Dana gave up Margaret's grandson, William, for adoption ("William"). The long-suffering Margaret, who is also mother to two sons, Bill and Charles, truly bears the weight of Dana's journey with Mulder, but unlike Billy, never takes out her anger on Fox. Instead, she relies on her Catholic faith and is seen to be highly devout.

William

The biological son of Mulder and Scully, as openly acknowledged in the second feature film, *I Want to Believe,* William is born in the episode "Existence" at the end of Season Eight. Following up his story in Season Nine, viewers learn that William possesses paranormal abilities, not unlike those of the alien tablet introduced in "Biogenesis" and "The Sixth Extinction." The super soldiers believe that William is the first organic one of their number, and some want him alive, while others seek his death. It is believed that William—who would be a young teenager at the time of the alien invasion—will play a crucial role in colonization, either fighting it back, with the help of his parents, or ushering it in. Scully gives William up for adoption in "William," near the end of the series, so he can attempt to live a normal life, especially since a shot of magnetite, injected by Jeffrey Spender, has put his unusual powers into remission. William is mentioned in *I Want to Believe,* and his parents miss him very much.

The Nemeses

The term "bad guy" is often a relative one in *The X-Files.* Many of the characters who might be described as "evil" in another series shift loyalties on this series. Men like Kersh, the Well-Manicured Man, and even Krycek often find it useful to help Mulder, Scully, and Doggett on occasion, before shifting back to their own antisocial, antihuman agenda. That said, it is fair to state that the Cigarette Smoking Man is, in the words of Chris Carter, "the Devil." He may sometimes help the crusaders as well, but there is always some dark purpose or plan underlying his actions.

The Syndicate

When viewers, fans, and reviewers discuss the "conspiracy" in *The X-Files,* they are actually referring to a group of (largely white) men who form "the Syndicate." The Syndicate is a secret alliance of men with influence and power in the hallways of government and big business. Its purpose is to pave the way for an alien invasion, or colonization, to occur in December 2012. While preparing for this event, the Syndicate labors with enforcers (men in black) to keep the truth a secret, to bury it.

The Syndicate came together following the crash of a UFO in Roswell in 1947 and started as a small group of men in the State Department. In 1973, the Syndicate and the alien grays (or colonizers) made a pact involving the

Left to right are members of the Syndicate: the Well-Manicured Man (John Neville), Strughold (Armin-Mueller Stahl), and the Cigarette Smoking Man (William B. Davis).

exchange of Syndicate children for alien biological material to study and experiment on. That material is held in a secret lab code-named "Purity Control" ("The Erlenmeyer Flask").

Higher-ups in the Syndicate are known as "Elders." The First Elder (Don S. Davis) is a grim man who, on one occasion ("Nisei") actually meets with Scully and provides her some useful information, an act that qualifies him as an oracle of sorts. The Second Elder, played by George Murdock, is more agreeable, but is ultimately killed by alien rebels and replaced by one. The Cigarette Smoking Man is the muscle, for lack of a better term, for The Syndicate.

The Syndicate often conducts tests on unwitting American citizens and erases evidence of its actions. The group has members in the FBI, CIA, Department of Defense, and National Security Agency, as well as in companies like Roush Technologies. The Syndicate was destroyed by alien rebels at a hangar base in 1998, bringing an end to fifty years of plotting and scheming ("Two Fathers"/"One Son"). Cigarette Smoking Man was the only survivor.

The Cigarette Smoking Man

Introduced in the pilot episode, this character is described by the names "Cancer Man," "The Cigarette Smoking Man," and "CGB Spender." His history is clouded in willful disinformation, and some sources indicate he is the shooter in both the JFK and MLK assassinations ("Musings of a Cigarette Smoking Man"). Other sources suggest he was in the State Department as early as the 1950s ("Apocrypha") and that in 1973 he joined the Syndicate, a group of collaborators working with aliens for the express purpose of invasion, euphemistically termed "colonization."

The Cigarette Smoking Man or CSM was once the husband of multiple-abductee Cassandra Spender (Veronica Cartwright), and she had a son by him, Jeffrey (Chris Owens), ("The Red and the Black"). CMS also has a direct link to the Mulders. He claims friendship with Bill Mulder, a relationship that according to various sources goes back to either the 1950s or the early 1960s, but had an affair with Bill's wife, Teena, an affair that produced Jeffrey's half-brother, Fox Mulder.

An atheist who believes in nothing but "the work," the Cigarette Smoking Man has eschewed his family connections all his life, though he demonstrates a fondness for and pride in Mulder that he doesn't feel for Jeffrey. He is the "enforcer" for Syndicate policies, often resorting to violence and murder, yet he also possesses a martyr complex. In the sixth season of the series, he wishes to be transfused with brain matter from Mulder that will render him an alien-human hybrid, a messiah of sorts. The surgery fails, and his health starts to decline. Later, in "En Ami," CSM claims to Scully that he wants to give the gift of a miracle cure to all mankind, because he wants to be remembered fondly by the world, but he is actually using her to stage an assassination.

Cigarette Smoking Man's last appearance in *The X-Files* is at the Anasazi pueblo in "The Truth," the two-hour series finale. It is there, in the guise of an old "wise man," that he awaits colonization. He dies (gorily) in flames, when black helicopters bomb his sanctuary.

Krycek

Alex Krycek (Nicholas Lea) first appears in the second-season episode "Sleepless," in the guise of a young, impressionable FBI agent who has been newly partnered with Mulder when Scully has been reassigned off the X-Files in 1994. The handsome agent soon, however, is revealed to be in league with the Cigarette Smoking Man. When Mulder has an opportunity to save Scully from abduction, Krycek maneuvers behind the scenes to assure he isn't successful ("Ascension").

Mulder and Krycek become enemies after this experience. However, they both become captives of Russian scientists in the fourth-season episodes "Tunguska"/"Terma," a plight that Krycek escapes using his facility with the

Russian language. However, while still in Russia, Krycek has an arm severed by locals, an attempt to save him from infection by the alien virus the scientists are testing.

In later seasons, Krycek continues to work both for the Cigarette Smoking Man and on his own agenda. For a considerable duration, he secretly controls Assistant Director Skinner with illegal nano-technology ("S.R. 819"). Ultimately, Skinner puts a bullet in his head ("Existence"), ending Krycek's life.

Krycek is important to *The X-Files* because he is the physical threat—the soldier villain—to go alongside CSM's general villain threat. Krycek is also a twisted reflection of Mulder. He uses the truth for his own gain, not for the good of mankind.

Comrades or Collaborators in the FBI

These characters are friends and foes of Mulder and Scully in the very organization in which they work. Sometimes these characters skirt both paths, the light and the dark. Thus, they embody the famous series phrase "trust no one."

Section Chief Blevins

Blevins is the man who, in the series pilot, assigns Dana Scully to the X-files unit. Although at the time of her assignment Scully believes she is there to provide a scientific basis—if there is one—to Mulder's work, she later in the series concedes that she was assigned to debunk his investigations and spy on him. Section Chief Blevins, meanwhile, maintain an illicit business relationship with the shadowy Roush Pharmaceuticals, a company working with the alien black oil virus. In the episodes "Gethsemane," "Redux," and "Redux II," Blevins chairs a hearing regarding the apparent suicide of Agent Mulder, where Scully testifies. When Mulder turns up alive, he also testifies and outs Blevins as a mole in the FBI. After Blevins adjourns the hearing, his cohorts murder him and make it appear a suicide, so his illicit connections can no longer be tracked.

Assistant Director Alvin Kersh

Following the events of the fifth-season finale, "The End," as well as the first motion picture in 1998, Mulder and Scully are reassigned away from the X-Files and thus away from their friend and sometimes protector Walter

Skinner. Their new superior is the harsh, even caustic Alvin Kersh (James Pickens Jr). Kersh is a Vietnam War vet, and in the course of the series is promoted to deputy director in the Bureau. He is the man who assigns Doggett to find the missing Mulder in Season Eight. He shutters the X-Files on more than one occasion and is believed to be part of the overriding conspiracy.

Finally, however, when push comes to shove, in "The Truth," Kersh helps Mulder and Scully flee incarceration and indeed, the United States. He is not seen again, which indicates that he may have fallen victim to Toothpick Man or some other sinister representative of the re-formed syndicate.

Kersh exists in *The X-Files* lore, in part, to show Mulder and Scully just how bad things can get. For the first several years they had Skinner to run interference for them and to encourage their work. He gave them cover. Kersh has no interest whatsoever in the X-Files or in the agents themselves. He would just as soon fire them and seems to be looking for an excuse to do so.

Agent Jeffrey Spender

Jeffrey Spender is portrayed by the same actor, Chris Owens, who played the young Cigarette Smoking Man in "Musings of a Cigarette Smoking Man." That should provide a hint as to his true identity. He is the son of CSM and a man who has been pushed up through the FBI ranks not based on merit, but by the efforts of his powerful father. CSM wants his son to continue his work, replace Mulder on the X-Files, and ruin Fox's life.

Spectacularly unimaginative, Spender displaces Mulder on the X-Files and spends his days shredding documentation involving new cases. When he is unable to commit murder for the CSM and realizes that his father has been overseeing his mother's abductions for twenty-five years, he turns against him. CSM tries to kill him for it.

Burned beyond recognition, Spender returns to *The X-Files* in Season Nine to help Scully in "William" and to testify on Mulder's behalf at his trial in "The Truth." His burns are a result of his father's experimentation on him. Spender is important to the gestalt of the series because he represents a twisted reflection of Mulder's family. Mulder loves and respects his father, Bill. He honors his father by carrying on his work and carrying on, in some sense, the same set of values, primarily against alien colonization. That is the son that the Cigarette Smoking Man wishes carried his own name, and the son that Spender fails to be. This dynamic is made apparent in the sixth-season two-parter "One Father"/"Two Sons."

Agent Diane Fowley

Diane Fowley, played by Mimi Rogers, "found" the X-Files in the FBI basement alongside Fox Mulder in 1991 and thus possesses a sense of ownership over them, one that she compares to Mulder's own passion for the unit. However, she left the unit and traveled overseas to work on cases involving international terrorism. During her absence from the States, Fowley became involved with the Syndicate, a fact that can be extrapolated from her work in Tunisia, where a Syndicate beehive is seen at the end of *The X-Files: Fight the Future.*

Fowley returns to the States in "The End," a story set shortly before the destruction of the X-Files office by the CSM. Her stated mission is to help Scully and Mulder guard Gibson Praise from further assassination attempts, but she is shot on the job, and he is captured. Following this experience, Fowley and Jeffrey Spender become the two primary agents working on the X-Files. In Season Six, during her tenure, the Cigarette Smoking Man tells her that she alone has never betrayed him, and consequently, she cares for him.

In the seventh season, Fowley is the bait for Mulder in a Last Temptation of Christ kind of scenario in "The Sixth Extinction II: Amor Fati." She promises the earthly delights of family and sex, to which Mulder apparently succumbs, though it is just a fantasy.

Fowley exists in *The X-Files* as a challenge to Scully and Mulder's relationship. She is attractive, boasts a long history with Mulder, and more than that, does not question or doubt his theories the way that Scully does. She is a "believer" like Mulder and so does not challenge him. She is very useful for writers wishing to point out both Scully's strengths as an investigator and Mulder's weaknesses as a flesh and blood man. In the end, however, Fowley is more than a temptress. She gives up her life to save Mulder from further experimental brain surgery and is murdered for her efforts.

Agent Leyla Harrison

Leyla (Jolie Jenkins) is a former FBI accountant who developed an admiration for Mulder and Scully, as well as their work on the X-Files while reading their expense reports. It is a dream come true for Leyla when she is transferred to the X-Files, despite her inexperience with field work. Leyla assists Doggett on at least two occasions, in the episodes "Alone" in the eighth season and "Scary Monsters" in the ninth season. Leyla is named for a prominent *X-Files* fan who died in 2001 and is an homage to *X-Files* fans. She is a sort of postmodern character because, like fans, she recalls specific "adventures" of Mulder and Scully, and often references them in the field. She thus acts as a kind of uber-fan, or walking encyclopedia of *X-Files* knowledge.

Assistant Director Brad Follmer

In the ninth and final season of *The X-Files,* Cary Elwes essays the role of Assistant Director Brad Follmer, a higher-up in the FBI who has a romantic past with Monica Reyes and would like, apparently, to resume it. Because of Reyes's closeness to Agent Doggett, Follmer views Doggett as a threat. Again, his symbolic purpose in the storytelling is plain: he is an impediment to the deeper intimacy of the two primary agents, Reyes and Doggett.

Unfortunately, as is learned in the episode "Release," Follmer is also crooked, having illicit ties with the mob.

Aliens

These are the space invaders, the beings from another world, who plot to take over Earth according to their own agenda.

The Black Oil

Also known as the black cancer, the black oil is the Earth's original inhabitant, transported to the planet generations ago via the auspices of Panspermia. It is believed to have arrived on a rock from Mars. Black oil is often found in petroleum deposits ("Vienen") and is the central medium of the alien virus. It can enter a man or woman through any opening, whether the mouth, eyes, ears, or nose, and proceed to take over and control that human ("Piper Maru," *Fight the Future*).

The black oil can spread the alien virus, an act that breaks down the human body and digests it, so as to create a new, alien life-form, a colonist. This process is depicted in the first *X-Files* feature film in 1998. In the sixth-season episode "The Beginning," we learn that another stage, the gray stage, follows the attack alien stage.

The Bounty Hunter

A man—or alien—of few words . . . and even fewer expressions. The alien bounty hunter (Brian Thompson) carries a deadly weapon, a silver retractable blade that can kill an alien or alien-human hybrid when inserted into the base of the neck. A ruthless clean-up man and enforcer of the alien colonization program, he murders alien-human hybrids and renegade aliens ("The Unnatural") without prejudice, debate, or appeal. He can shape-shift and become any individual.

Jeremiah Smith

An alien in human form, Jeremiah Smith (Roy Thinnes) works in the Social Security Administration in Washington, D.C., and also possesses the ability to heal humans who have been catastrophically wounded. He helps the victims of a shooting spree at a fast food restaurant in "Talitha Cumi," and in "Herrenvolk," while under pursuit by the alien bounty hunter, shows Mulder a farm in Canada where human clones (including one of Samantha) tend to bees as part of the colonization project. Later in the series, Jeremiah Smith returns, appearing in Montana to heal abductees who have been injured in experiments. He is last seen being taken by an alien ship ("This Can't Be Happening"), before he has the opportunity to heal Mulder, who has returned from his abduction.

Toothpick Man

This unnamed official in the FBI, with access to the highest offices in the land, is actually a human replacement or super soldier, as revealed in the episode "Providence." Toothpick Man (Alan Dale) stands in judgment of Mulder in the final episode of the series, "The Truth," but is exposed as a nonhuman threat by Gibson Praise during trial. He is named Toothpick Man because he is often seen holding the object in question. He has been described as a leader in the New Syndicate, but who precisely the alien "replaced" is not made known. As *The X-Files* ends in 2002, he is still ensconced in power in Washington, D.C.

5

Welcome to the FBI's Most Unwanted

The Pilot Episode (1993)

The X-Files' first episode, "Pilot," by Chris Carter and directed by Robert Mandel, remains a confident, absorbing introduction to the classic horror/sci-fi series. This inaugural episode not only presents an intriguing mystery and introduces the audience to engaging characters caught up in life-changing events, it also offers a first, ominous peek at the dark forces aligned against the protagonists and against "the truth" itself.

Even better, the *X-Files* pilot is skillful in the manner it deploys horror imagery or uses horror signifiers as important symbols. One can detect this quality in *The X-Files'* nonromantic and nonglamorous approach to vampires (in "3" or "Bad Blood"), for example. The pilot episode commences this pattern by selecting iconic imagery from over 150 years of horror literature and nearly 100 years of cinema. It then converts such visual shorthand to its own purpose, infusing that imagery with scintillating new meaning and relevance in the 1990s.

The X-Files pilot follows a young, brilliant FBI agent Dana Scully as she is summoned to meet Section Chief Blevins. He tasks her with new assignment: partnering with "spooky" Fox Mulder on the unit called the X-Files, which is devoted to strange, unsolved cases. At first, Mulder is suspicious of Scully, believing she has been sent to spy on him and/or debunk his work. They bond, however, on their first case, which takes them to Bellefleur, Oregon.

There, four high school students have died under unusual circumstances, with strange markings found on their corpses. The latest victim is Karen Swenson. Mulder and Scully order the body of the third victim, Ray Soames, exhumed and find a deformed body in the casket . . . a body that could be that of an orangutan or perhaps an extraterrestrial. During an examination, Scully finds a strange implant embedded in the creature's nasal cavity.

After the partners experience an incident of "missing" or "lost" time, Mulder suspects that the imperiled students are alien abductees.

Mulder (David Duchovny) and Scully (Gillian Anderson) in a publicity still from the series.

Unfortunately, all the evidence they have to support that case is destroyed in a suspicious fire. When Scully reports back to Blevins about the investigation, she produces the only remaining evidence . . . the implant. But soon afterwards, a mysterious Cigarette Smoking Man takes the implant and deposits it inside a vast, secret, warehouse-like facility . . . in the Pentagon!

As a series, *The X-Files* begins with two intriguing and unmistakable nods to horror film conventions. The first is an on-screen title card establishing that the following story is, in some sense, true, or at least adapted from true "documented accounts." This is the same "based on a true story" gambit utilized by genre efforts as diverse as *The Last House on the Left* (1972), *The Texas Chainsaw*

Massacre (1974), *Picnic at Hanging Rock* (1975), and *Return of the Living Dead* (1985). The general purpose of this technique is, broadly, to put audiences in the frame of mind not so much that the featured story is accurate or actually true, but that it could happen, that it is possible. The notation of "based on facts" creates a sense of urgency and closeness with the following narrative. Viewers ask: Did this really happen? *Could* it have really happened?

The presentation of the "based on a true story" title card also classifies *The X-Files* as a series that plans to have one foot in fact and one in fiction. It is an evolution of "authentic" series like *One Step Beyond* and *Beyond Reality* (1991–1993), however, because of its focus on hard science and new forensic investigative techniques.

Following the on-screen card, the pilot episode transports viewers to a haunted forest during impenetrable night. There, a Gothic scene that could have come from any Hammer Studios horror film in the late 1950s or early 1960s occurs. A heroine in a white nightgown is pursued and attacked by a mysterious and apparently malevolent specter. This attack seems to upset the very balance of nature itself, and an atmospheric disturbance occurs before a white fade-out, a symbolic protest by Mother Nature of the unnatural act.

This opening sequence establishes a few things. First that the writers are dead-set on repurposing old horror monsters and horror imagery, and subverting or altering that imagery to make it relevant again in the contemporary 1990s culture. The endangered woman in the diaphanous white dress (equating to purity) pursued by some ghoulish figure who is so reprehensible that Nature itself rebels in its presence represents a key paradigm of Gothic literature. In a sense, it is the most basic image of all horror: the monster in pursuit of the damsel.

Secondly, this scene establishes that the wild or "enchanted" forest is a key setting for horror. And indeed, *The X-Files* would often return to such wilderness during its nine-year run in episodes as diverse as "Darkness Falls" and "Detour."

But once more, the setting provides an explicit link to the American past, carried right through into the American present. From Nathaniel Hawthorne's "Young Goodman Brown" (1835) and Charles Brocken Brown's *Wieland* (1789) right up through David Lynch's *Twin Peaks* (1991) and the Black Lodge, the forest has been the scintillating location of danger and mystery in the American psyche. Immediately, *The X-Files* writes the next chapter in that bloodline, tying the forest not to the devil or dark spirits as was the case with both Hawthorne and Lynch, but with an inexplicable, modern phenomenon, alien abduction. Again, this idea has very clear antecedents. *Wieland* concerns strange lights in a forest, the paranormal phenomenon of spontaneous combustion, and "modern" psychological disorders such as schizophrenia, played out through the new art of "ventriloquism." If one is so inclined, certainly one can gaze at the prologue in "Pilot" and see that it serves as a kind of metaphor for the entire series, for the new debate between science and superstition, knowledge and faith.

The final imagery of "Pilot" may seem familiar for another reason. It appears a deliberate homage to *Raiders of the Lost Ark* (1981). In that Spielberg film, the Lost Ark of the Covenant, a symbol once more of Romanticism, is tucked away by twentieth-century man in a place where it can't threaten Enlightenment: inside a giant, endless warehouse. At the end of *The X-Files'* pilot, the Cigarette Smoking Man is depicted depositing a symbol of apparent Romanticism (but actually of Enlightenment . . . or the Truth) inside a similar warehouse, actually the Pentagon, where it will remain buried. In both cases, the one who buries important knowledge is the U.S. government itself, or at least agents for it. However, in the conspiracy-heavy age of the 1990s, that act of hiding the truth is much more important in *The X-Files* than it is was in *Raiders*.

In terms of *The X-Files* history and overall arc, "Pilot" also functions on a very practical, efficient level. It ably introduces the players, the stakes, and investigative milieu. Although Anderson and Duchovny have not yet entirely nailed down the staccato, rat-a-tat back-and-forth delivery that makes the series such a perennial joy, it is safe to state that the actors share an immediate chemistry.

One scene stands out on that front. Late in the proceedings, Scully believes she has been "branded" with the strange marks of the other victims, following an incident of missing time. Anxious, she runs to Mulder and with almost no sense of self-consciousness, disrobes before him so he can determine the nature of those marks. This all happens in candlelight. Which could make it either creepy or, oddly, romantic.

By going to Mulder and removing her clothing, Scully in some fashion takes off her armor in this scene. She allows herself to be vulnerable and reveals that she trusts Mulder with something private and indeed something incredibly personal.

The writing and performances here are so elegant, because Mulder responds to this gesture of trust with one of his own. He lets down his *emotional* guard and tells Scully the story of how he lost Samantha, his sister, possibly to alien abduction. In this scene, all the science, all the paranormal explanations, all the intimations of conspiracy slip away, and we are left with the basics: two vulnerable people connecting in a meaningful way.

What remains so intriguing about this scene is the manner of connection. Stereotypically—at least in terms of television history—it would be the man who offers a physical gesture, while the woman would open up "emotionally."

Again, I wrote *stereotypically*, so this isn't a sexist observation. In some sense, *The X-Files* seems to reverse the industry-standard dynamic between men and women in its pilot. It allows Mulder emotional vulnerability. David Duchovny noted in the periodical *Cult Times* that "I think the male/female roles are switched . . . Mulder is more intuitive, working from his emotions, his gut instinct. Scully is more practical." This scene might be the first example we can point to in the series of that particular dynamic.

Finally, the pilot picks up the explicit battle cry of *Kolchak: The Night Stalker*. That series featured a journalist in the age of Watergate trying desperately to make the truth known. In Carl Kolchak's fight against City Hall, he never got that truth out . . . that monsters exist and prey on citizens at all levels of society. Instead of adopting a journalist as its truth teller, *The X-Files* puts forward someone of imagination (Mulder) and someone of science (Scully) as the heroic heralds. This shift reflects changing attitudes about the press in the 1990s and also changing attitudes about the kind of evidence that would be acceptable to the public. The eyewitness, tape-recorded reports of Carl Kolchak had to morph into the autopsies, DNA analyses, and behavioral profiles of Scully and Mulder.

The X-Files pilot is a perfect introduction to the series because it establishes the nature of the Mulder and Scully relationship, and it begins, in small steps, to diagram a world of conspiracies.

6

I'm Not a Part of Any Agenda

The Opening Montage

When it began airing in 1993, *The X-Files* was just another low-budget TV show, and one that aired on a relatively new and untested network: Fox TV. But the series' opening montage, scored with the now-unforgettable theme song by Mark Snow, brilliantly, and with deft visuals, set up the parameters of the series' storytelling. The images and theme song both became iconic in terms of 1990s pop culture. The montage changed in Seasons Eight and Nine to accommodate new additions and subtractions in the cast, but much of the imagery, though redone, remained intact.

As *The X-Files* introductory montage commences, we see a giant "X" in the right-center portion of the frame. The font of the X pointedly suggests an old-fashioned typewriter print and the idea of top-secret writing being redacted with a series of Xs. XXXXXXXX for example. X is also famous for the phrase "X marks the spot," and since this Chris Carter series concerns hidden (or redacted) secrets, this inaugural image is a clever one.

A white spotlight seems to move across the screen, briefly illuminating the X, and that's our indication that something is being discovered . . . or more aptly, *uncovered.* The previously hidden "X-Files" or secrets are being brought out—at least briefly—into the light.

Next, the montage features several stills—as if snapped in fast succession—of one such secret. A man in the lower left-hand portion of the frame is depicted pointing to something in the night sky. On the right side of the photo is a legend that indicates the official nature of the photograph. The key suggests that this is an FBI photo interpretation, thus marking it as an official document and as part of the X-Files. The numbers underneath—which catalog the photo—suggest something about the nature of the government; something dehumanizing. *X5937012 . . . ?*

Exactly how many X-Files are there? This alpha-numeric nomenclature thus suggests a vast, inhuman bureaucracy, a place where conspiracies can find fertile ground . . . and bloom. As the photographer in the frame zooms in and snaps more photographs, we see what that mystery in the sky is: a flying saucer or UFO.

So the first secret revealed on *The X-Files* is the existence of alien life and alien visitations to planet Earth. The intriguing and important aspect of these shots is the paradox they present. The closer the camera gets to photographing the UFO, the fuzzier and more out-of-focus the photographed image becomes. In other words, as we get closer to a secret revealed, the truth actually becomes more nebulous and more difficult to grab ahold of or process.

Are we really seeing a UFO or something else? The truth, as we get closer to it, becomes more elusive. Could we be looking at a secret military plane, reverse-engineered from a UFO, for example?

The next images in the introductory montage depict a dark hand (the dark hand of the shadow government or conspiracy?) moving across an illuminated map, one that perhaps reveals the path of that UFO.

But the letters and images are—like that close-up image I describe above—deliberately opaque. We can't actually make out any detail that makes our understanding of the imagery clearer. Following this image of the map, we see a strange sphere or ball, one that seems to be leaking or projecting some form of energy. Could it be the "secret" power source of the flying saucer? And if so, is it being used by "us" or by "them"?

Already, *The X-Files*—a series resolutely about discovering the truth—is determinedly muddying our sense of transparency and reality. As the truth grows closer, our understanding gets further away . . . more indistinct. Behind this energy sphere are the same letters/glyphs we saw on the map. Is this some kind of alien language or secret military code?

The next image in the introduction reveals a face stretched or elongated into a horrible appearance. This creepy image could signify a few things. It could suggest, for instance, that the aliens are subverting or changing the very shape of human life on Earth, twisting it into terrible new dimensions. Or perhaps the hideous visage could suggest how humanity looks when the truth is not known, when it is the thing twisted. The lies of our leaders also "twist" the face of humanity.

The next image suggests another subject of these government "X-Files": paranormal activity. The words "paranormal activity" are displayed on the screen (and would later become the title of a popular found-footage franchise). And again, the search for paranormal activity is the search for the truth *beneath* the truth. Late in the series, *The X-Files* even presents a unified theory for paranormal activity that ties into UFOs and aliens.

The next set of images in the montage introduces viewers to the cast and characters. First up is FBI agent Fox Mulder (David Duchovny). Around his picture ID, we see traditional conventions of the police procedural format: a set-of handcuffs on the right and a badge, in the bottom center of the frame. These images remind us that though the stories will involve the search for the unknown, the approach will be grounded in reality. Furthermore, there is some sense of authority behind the search for the truth.

Another crucial aspect of *The X-Files* is "the conspiracy" and the fear of conspiracy. There is the consuming fear that the American government is not actually working for the people and instead is attempting to obfuscate the truth. In the next image of the *X-Files* intro, we see the legend "GOVERNMENT DENIES KNOWLEDGE" on screen as some mysterious specter—paranormal or extraterrestrial in nature—prowls the hallway of what could be a government laboratory.

A shadow is alive and moving through the corridors of power. Again, the imagery appears to operate on more than one level. We may be reckoning not only with a monster that is a shadowy figure (like the one seen in the episode "Soft Light"), we are reckoning with a shadow government, men responsible to no authority save their own, moving freely in the Establishment.

Next, the montage introduces our second primary cast member and character, Special Agent Dana Scully (Gillian Anderson). In the following sequence of shots we see our leads—Mulder and Scully—breaking into a closed room, moving in time-lapse fits and starts, a visual metaphor, perhaps, for their insertion into secret and strange events involving aliens and the paranormal, and also the way their journey seems to stop and start, stymied and then advanced. The "moving photograph" technique utilized to show the FBI photo interpretation of the UFO sighting (at the beginning of the montage) is repeated here as the agents move in, countenancing a new mystery. As they move closer to the camera—and closer to the off-screen mystery—their demeanor changes from one of professional concern to astonishment and awe. Notice also that the agents carry flashlights and Mulder shines his light right at the camera, an indication that the agents are bringing light to darkness, the light of day to buried secrets.

After the shot of the agents, a body seems to fall or plummet before a glowing representation of a human hand, one colored in blue. However, one piece of one finger is red, not blue, signifying it is different from the rest or special somehow. This "piece" of the finger (or fingerprint?) must, therefore, be crucial. This image is meant to suggest that in the crimes explored by the series, forensic evidence (represented by the hand) will be utilized to pinpoint the culprit or the manner of death. Perhaps the giant hand suggests the body of clues to sift through, and the red portion of the finger suggests the "red warning" or "alarm" among those clues; the forensic evidence that will resolve the investigation.

Finally, the montage features a card crediting series creator Chris Carter. Behind his name is a close-up of a human eye. This image is also highly symbolic. *The X-Files* is all about how you choose to "see." Do you see the secret truth? Or do your eyes register only the lies and cover-up?

The eyeball representing sight has another meaning too. It leads us back to our intrepid protagonists. Do you see through the lens of belief, like Mulder, or the lens of skepticism and science, like Scully?

Finally, storm clouds gather over a harsh-looking mountainscape, an indicator that the search for the truth will not be easy. Yet, some episodes tell us that—out there, in the roiling unknown—the truth awaits. We must seek it out.

This montage lasts but brief minutes, but it captures beautifully the essence of the *X-Files* experience, aurally and visually.

7

The Old World Falls Away

Season One (1993–1994)

During its first year on the air, *The X-Files* began finding a unique creative voice both in terms of the character relationships it explored and in the kind of stories that fit within the program's ever-widening format. However, it is probably fair to state that humor is not as much an active player in the first twenty-four stories as it would prove to be in future seasons.

Instead, *The X-Files'* first season establishes the tradition of alternating "monster of the week" programs with those involving the Mytharc, a byzantine, chapter-by-chapter exploration of government conspiracies and the existence of UFOs. More intriguingly, perhaps, *The X-Files'* first season is distinguished by two other critical factors.

First, it is in this early season that a heavy focus lands on Mulder and Scully's friends and previous romantic partners outside their relationship. Secondly, Season One is clearly the most "epistolary" in format, with more episodes than not ending with the two FBI agents typing out case reports and recording their conclusions about them on 1990s-era personal computers.

Regarding relationships outside the core partnership, several episodes of the first season depict Mulder and Scully's long-standing professional relationships with other FBI agents, and in most cases, remove those friendships, which could conceivably be viewed as an impediment to the intimacy that Mulder and Scully develop.

In "Squeeze," the first monster-of-the-week installment of *The X-Files,* Scully encounters an old friend, Tom Colton (Donal Logue), who dislikes Mulder and is a climber within the FBI, trying to forge an ambitious career for himself. He seeks Scully's help, based on her competency, and attempts to convince her to moonlight outside the X-Files unit, ostensibly so that her career isn't permanently impeded by her participation. Scully must choose Tom or Mulder in this episode. She must also choose what kind of career she desires, one of intellectual rigor but little acceptance, or one of blazing advancement with little real achievement. It comes down to that old Miltonian dynamic: is it better to rule in hell (or the basement) or serve in heaven (in the FBI hierarchy)?

Mulder's ex-partner, Jerry Lamana (Wayne Duvall) appears in another early first-season episode, "Ghost in the Machine," and like Tom before him, hopes to get into the good graces of the FBI higher-ups by solving a baffling or strange case. He requires Mulder's help to do so, especially because Jerry, in a previous case of great importance, mishandled crucial evidence. In the course of the episode, Jerry actually steals, or perhaps "appropriates," Mulder's profile for their perpetrator, but Mulder controls and downplays his anger because of his close relationship with Jerry. When Jerry prepares to make his collar, he asks Mulder not to go along during the arrest, so he can take all the credit. A good friend, Mulder agrees, and Jerry is killed by the real perpetrator, a malicious AI or computer.

Mulder loses another person close to him, this time a beloved mentor, in "Young at Heart." In this entry, an old enemy, a serial killer named John Barnett, attempts to get revenge on Mulder for putting him away years earlier. Part of that revenge includes the murder of Reggie Purdue (Dick Anthony Williams), Mulder's first superior in the FBI, in the Violent Crimes unit. This is the second close associate Mulder has lost in a matter of months, but unlike Jerry, who in some sense put himself ahead of the friendship, Perdue never stopped caring for or looking out for Mulder.

Scully also loses an ex-partner in the episode "Lazarus." Here, she moonlights on a bank-robbery case with her friend, special agent Jack Willis (Christopher Allport). He is promptly killed in the line of duty, only to have his soul replaced by that of the bank robber, who died at exactly the same time as Jack.

With the exception of Tom Colton in "Squeeze," all these episodes see Scully and Mulder losing past friends, partners, and allies, an act that serves to isolate them more deeply from the FBI in general and draws them closer to one another. In short, this is the season that their career "pasts" die, and Scully and Mulder become inextricably dependent on one another, linked professionally and personally.

Uniquely, Season One adopts the same approach in terms of the agents' personal lives. In "The Jersey Devil," one of the series' first half dozen stories, Scully goes out on a date with a divorcee named Rob (Andrew Airlie) at the behest of her suburbanite friend, Ellen. Simultaneously, Mulder investigates a case in Atlantic City, New Jersey, involving a kind of "wild woman," a character believed, at first blush, to be the mythical Jersey Devil. In the course of the episode, Scully gravitates away from Rob and Ellen, and toward Mulder.

Her date with Rob is present in the narrative to create sexual tension, but it also represents the last time for many years that Scully attempts to pursue a personal life at the expense of her professional and personal alliance with Mulder. There's a funny, subtextual comparison in the episode, at least implicitly, of Scully's dating process with the primitive or wild woman seeking a mate (and examining Mulder in that regard, at one point). We thus witness two examples of human courtship, demarked by the veneer of civilization.

In "Fire," Mulder undergoes a similar journey. A Scotland Yard agent, Phoebe Green (Amanda Pays), arrives in Washington, D.C., to acquire Mulder's help catching a pyrokinetic. But Phoebe also happens to be Mulder's fiery ex-lover, from his days at Oxford University. Very briefly, Mulder and Phoebe rekindle their tempestuous affection for one another (another meaning of the title, "Fire"), and Scully demonstrates some jealousy before Mulder reaffirms his connection with her, and learns that Green is romantically involved with an English bureaucrat. Phoebe may be "hot" (again, think fire), but she is not trustworthy; not in the way that Scully is.

As is clear from all these examples, a good selection of episodes in Season One involve the ways that Mulder and Scully drift away from their lives as they have been previously and start building a new life, together. As much as the audience gets to know them in these first twenty-four episodes of *The X-Files*, it is also seeing how they shed their histories in favor of a new, shared existence. The old world is falling away, subsumed by the passion (professionally speaking) that consumes them both.

The first season of *The X-Files* also represents the span in which many of the most important supporting characters are introduced. Assistant Director Walter Skinner (Mitch Pileggi) is introduced in the episode "Tooms," a follow-up to "Squeeze" that features the return of Tooms. And the beloved Lone Gunmen make their first appearance in "E.B.E."

The Cigarette Smoking Man, or Cancer Man as he is known in the early days, appears from the pilot episode forward.

In terms of pop culture penetration, the first season of *The X-Files* had a long way to go to reach its apex of popularity. It was hardly a ratings juggernaut in its first sortie, ranking #102 out of a 118 programs. Despite this low ranking in the Nielsen ratings, Fox demonstrated faith and renewed the program for a second season.

Mytharc Notes

Each season on *The X-Files* adds new and vital elements to the Mytharc, tying in, ultimately, to alien plans for the colonization of Earth in December 2012. The first-season Mytharc stories are more loosely connected to the whole than some later installments of this format and originally might even have been seen as stand-alone segments that pursue one recurring idea: UFO incursions on Earth.

The pilot episode deals with UFOs and abductions, as well as the concept of missing or lost time. The location of this episode, Bellefleur, Oregon, and several characters, including abductee Billy Miles, would be revisited in the seventh season.

The second episode in the Mytharc is "Deep Throat," which introduces Mulder's initial secret contact within the FBI, Deep Throat, played by Jerry Hardin and named after the famous figure in the Watergate scandal. More than that, however, "Deep Throat" suggests that the American government has a UFO in its possession and is test-flying fighter planes reverse-engineered from the alien spacecraft.

In "Fallen Angel," a UFO crashes in Townsend, Wisconsin, and Mulder attempts to gain hard evidence of its existence, but is stymied by military forces in the area. Meanwhile, a Predator-like invisible alien prowls the nearby forest.

In "E.B.E.," the concept of missing time recurs, this time regarding a trucker in Tennessee, and the Lone Gunmen report to Mulder and Scully the ways a dark "shadow government" is watching the American population and building secret technology based on alien technology. This shadow group is what later becomes known as the Syndicate.

The season's final episode, "The Erlenmeyer Flask," introduces an experiment involving alien/human hybrids, which is a critical piece of the Mytharc puzzle going forward, and also kills off Deep Throat. This act reminds the audience of the constant danger that Mulder and Scully face in attempting to expose the conspirators and uncover "the truth." The episode also introduces an alien corpse at a secret facility, code-named "Purity Control." This wellspring of alien genetic information proves of vital importance in the ongoing Mytharc and is the answer behind the question of Samantha Mulder's abduction.

Season Highlights

"Squeeze." Written by Glen Morgan and James Wong. Directed by Harry Longstreet. Airdate: September 24, 1993.

In "Squeeze," Scully's old friend and fellow agent Tom Colton (Donal Logue) asks her to consult on a difficult murder case in Baltimore. An unknown assailant has managed to break into a locked office and kill a businessman, removing his liver in the process. Scully agrees to consult on the investigation,

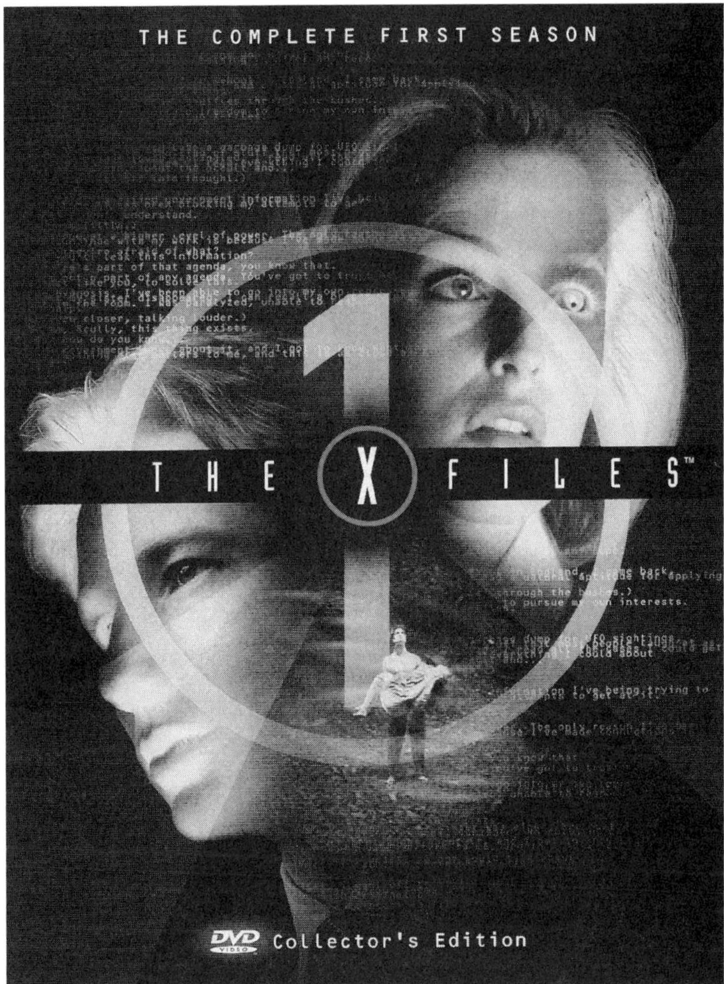

The cover art for the release of *The X-Files* Season One on DVD.

but "spooky" Mulder's involvement worries Colton, who is bucking for a fast promotion.

Mulder begins to suspect that the murderer is a most unusual killer: the sullen Eugene Victor Tooms (Doug Hutchison), a man who has resided in Baltimore, apparently, since before 1930, but who doesn't look a day over thirty years old. Mulder consults with Detective Frank Briggs (Henry Beckman), a law enforcement official who worked on an identical case decades earlier and also considered Tooms the primary suspect. Briggs likens Tooms's brand of "evil" to that of the Holocaust or the Bosnian ethnic cleansing.

Although it is almost impossible for Scully to accept Mulder's theory of a nearly immortal mutant killer who murders five victims and consumes their livers every thirty years to stay alive and young, she casts her lot with her partner rather than with Colton, who is more interested in racking up successful collars than solving the case and honoring the victims.

Finally, Tooms—whose strange physicality allows him to "stretch" into impossible positions—decides to make Scully his latest victim. . . .

"Squeeze" is *The X-Files'* first monster-of-the-week installment. As such, it represents a template for future entries such as "2Shy," "Teliko," "Hungry," and "Alone." Most of these outings deal with a murderous genetic mutation of one type or another, but one who—out of some biological deficiency—kills human beings in order to survive. This mutant character or type pinpoints in the human physiology, then, the key to controlling *its own existence* and satisfying that aforementioned deficiency.

Watching the "genetic mutants" of *The X-Files,* it's easy to imagine that we are gazing at the blind alleys or dead ends of human evolution. With just a little variation, we could become them, and that factor lends a degree of empathy to some of these tales and to some of these monsters. But importantly, this is not the case for Eugene Victor Tooms, a personality who remains an opaque and monstrous presence, and one whom the episode contextualizes in grand, even historic terms. Written by James Wong and Glen Morgan, "Squeeze" apparently suffered serious behind-the-scenes tumult when it was shot, meaning that though director Harry Longstreet is credited on-screen, director Michael Katleman also conducted reshoots for some critical sequences.

Despite the apparently troubled production history, this early episode remains abundantly creepy and highly disturbing. In fact, "Squeeze" is likely one of the best-remembered first-season entries. Everyone remembers Tooms, not only because he was first in a long line of unforgettable monsters, but because his ability—to stretch and elongate his form—is vividly portrayed. The success of "Squeeze" as a drama and a horror piece might be measured by the fact that a sequel was produced and broadcast later in the first season (titled "Tooms") and that the episode became the benchmark by which later monster-of-the-week episodes would be judged. Doug Hutchison's unsettling, focused, (and largely internal) performance as the antisocial, monstrous Tooms brings genuine menace to the hour, and the final sequence set in Scully's bathroom features some subtle but effective visual effects that ably depict the serial killer's unique and horrifying mutant capacities.

But ultimately "Squeeze" is an important tale for *The X-Files* not merely because of its early placement and impact in terms of later storytelling, but because of several unique thematic conceits. The first of these involves a thesis about the nature of evil and how a certain brand of evil sees the world. This thesis is forwarded mainly through the eyewitness testimony of a retired police detective, Briggs.

The second conceit involves the way that everyday bureaucracy and record-keeping rituals can actually cloud the truth rather than excavate it. We see this idea most clearly in the details of Mulder's investigation into Tooms's long history. Over and over again across the years a man named Tooms appears to live at the same address at Exeter Street, but never, before Mulder's investigation, have these records been exhumed, weighed, or connected.

The third conceit is perhaps the most crucial in terms of Mulder and Scully and their rapidly blossoming relationship. On this front, one might view "Squeeze" as the story of "Scully's Choice," wherein she must choose between the Bureau and old friends, and a crusade at Mulder's side. One selection could bring her promotion, success, and notoriety, while the other promises only epistemological honesty. She chooses the latter, and that selection says much about Scully as a partner and as a human being.

Across two decades, "Squeeze" has drawn occasional criticism from those who cast the episode's comparison of the Tooms's murders to the Holocaust and the Bosnian conflict as either pretentious or somehow inappropriate in what is essentially a mainstream entertainment. However, the comparison succeeds in *The X-Files* for a few significant reasons. First, it is explicitly made as one of Det. Briggs's *personal observations.* If, as a character in the play, he makes that connection himself, based on his particular experience, who are we to judge whether he is right or wrong? The comparison represents his viewpoint, based on his experience. In their official capacity as agents, Scully and Mulder never explicitly compare the Tooms killings to real-life atrocities, though they do note that the killer's environs create a kind of aura of death and decay.

Instead, the comparison is simply the opinion of a retired—and shaken—old man, one who has lost faith in the human capacity for goodness, at least until the coda, which serves as his catharsis.

Secondly, if one chooses to compare Tooms, the Holocaust, and the horror of the Bosnian War ethnic cleansing campaign circa 1992–1995, there is clearly a data point in common. All the murderers—all the perpetrators in such events as the Republika Srpska in Bosnia—share a point of view: they don't see their victims as fully human.

Instead, the victims are deemed not entitled to human dignity and freedom because they are somehow inferior and thus can be used/misused/abused as the "monster" in question sees fit. It's always much easier to hurt someone if you decide they aren't fully human or equal. In our own history this viewpoint has accounted for genocide, ethnic cleansing, slavery, prejudice, and other horrors. This is indeed the specific horror at the core of the Holocaust, Bosnia, and, yes, Baltimore.

What remains so intriguing about the comparison of Tooms's bloody handiwork to such real-life atrocities is that the two historical events are very closely linked with the worst *human* behavior imaginable. The idea here is that Tooms may be physically different from us, but he shares with us this human capacity for evil. Tooms is not the "monster outside," then, despite his physiological oddities. Instead, he is the monster with a very human nature.

One of the fascinating qualities of "Squeeze" is its critical look at record-keeping and bureaucracy. Victor Eugene Tooms has left a considerable paper trail across the decades, but the elements of this trail don't connect and therefore can't clarify anyone's thinking about the investigation, save for Mulder's. The investigation of Tooms is held hostage to the fact that paperwork is filled out, dutifully recorded on microfilm, but then never looked at again by human eyes. What good is information if you don't look at it?

Only the inquisitive, unconventional Mulder can connect the dots (while humorously going blind at the microfilm machine . . .), filling in the invisible connections between official documents. The global point here seems to be that humans want to record and categorize everything, but that once the initial categorization is done, there is no looking back, no more thinking to be done. We see the same issue in Mulder's manipulation of Tooms's fingerprints. The fingerprints are already on file, if only someone had the wherewithal to look at them. Is the maintenance and furtherance of databases, microfilms, and paper documents just busywork to keep the gears of bureaucracy spinning and grinding endlessly? Does important, lifesaving information disappear into archives, never again to be looked at, measured, or considered? The information age is one of value only if data points connect and someone looks at the information with an engaged intellect. We see in "Squeeze" that this is one of Mulder's gifts. The show is called *The X-Files*, accent on *files*, after all.

In terms of the characters themselves, "Squeeze" lands Scully in the unenviable position of having to choose where she ultimately wishes to cast her lot. Should she cast it with Colton, who is slick, successful, snarky, and wholly unimaginative? Or with Mulder, who is unconcerned about his reputation but unfailingly honest from an intellectual standpoint? The outlines of Scully's choice are presented in starkly visual terms in the episode too. Colton is a man of lunch dates, meetings, and buttoned-down suits and ties. He's a man of surfaces and superficialities.

By contrast, Mulder is the kind of guy who takes off that suit jacket, rolls up his sleeves, and does the hard work himself because he knows that in the vetting of hard work, answers bubble to the surface. Mulder may possess ideas and theories that some people consider ludicrous or insane, but he pursues his answers through rigorous investigation. He doesn't close off any possibility (usually) and thus is intellectually honest and open-minded. Colton, by contrast, does no investigating whatsoever. Instead, he just brings in Scully to write the behavioral profile he isn't imaginative or skilled enough to craft himself.

In "Squeeze," therefore, Scully realizes she would rather work with a guy who cares about digging for the truth, even if the truth is unpalatable, rather than with a fellow who just wants check a career box and move up the FBI ladder.

It was important that Scully make this decision early on. The decision accomplishes two things, primarily. First, it isolates her. Like Spooky Mulder, she soon must live with the jokes about little green men and the like. She must also contend with the disrespect of her peers. But her decision to commit to Mulder and his quest also locks Scully into an ongoing intellectual or cerebral debate. Scully will now be present alongside Mulder to make certain that every crazy theory and every strange hypothesis boasts a solid basis in fact and empirical science. All of this character development starts to cohere in "Squeeze," and it's only *The X-Files*' third episode.

In terms of horror visuals, "Squeeze" is remarkably adroit. The impossible is made convincingly manifest in Tooms's physicality. His jaundiced, predator eyes gaze out hungrily from the darkness, and we get a great point of view from his twisted perspective. The world appears black and white, and his victims move in slow motion, unaware of his sinister presence. The black-and-white photography reminds us that Tooms doesn't see us as fully human but as prey, furthering that connection to the kind of horror Briggs sees in the newspaper regarding the Bosnian ethnic cleansing. And the slow-motion photography visually indicates that this hunter is one step ahead of his quarry, a fact we can attribute to his unique physical abilities. We move through life slowly, like contented cattle, unaware we are hunted. But Tooms moves with lightning-fast rapidity, and that's very, very scary.

"Eve." Written by Kenneth Biller and Chris Brancato. Directed by Fred Gerber. Airdate: December 10, 1993.

"Eve" commences as Scully and Mulder fly to Greenwich, Connecticut, to investigate the death of a suburban man who was drained of blood. Mulder suspects alien abduction is the root cause behind the murder, citing examples of cattle mutilations with a similar modus operandi. At first, the only witness, young Teena Simmons (Sabrina Krievins), seems to obliquely corroborate this theory. However, when an identical murder occurs in Marin County, California, and the only witness is a little girl who is a dead ringer for Teena—little Cindy Reardon (Erica Krievins)—Scully and Mulder realize that they are looking not at an alien abduction case, but a case involving illicit experiments in in-vitro fertilization.

While Scully investigates the activities of a doctor named Sally Kendrick (Harriet Sansom Harris) at the Luther Stapes fertility clinic, Mulder learns more on the subject from his covert government informant, Deep Throat (Jerry Hardin). Deep Throat reveals a top-secret genetic experiment of the 1950s called "The Litchfield Project" that was designed to compete with a similar eugenics program in the Soviet Union. The goal was to breed a new race of super soldiers. The American version of the project created a number of "Adams" and "Eves," all identical, all incredibly intelligent, and all homicidal.

After visiting with the incarcerated Eve 6 (Sansom Harris) at the Whiting Institute for the Criminally Insane, Scully and Mulder realize that Eve 7 and Eve 8 may still be free and may attempt to kill Cindy and Teena, the grandchildren of the program, essentially. Unfortunately, their suspicions prove absolutely wrong, and Teena and Cindy prove to be far more cunning adversaries than either FBI agent could have possibly predicted.

At the heart of "Eve" is the horror trope involving evil children. In the 1950s, the movie *The Bad Seed* famously raised a crucial issue regarding diabolical children: *nature or nature?* Could a child be evil by reason of the genetic material passed on from his or her parents? Or did that evil arise out of the manner in which he or she was raised? In the end, it was Mother Nature herself (via a lightning strike), not the child's actual mother, Mother Nurture, who could contend with evil Rhoda. *The X-Files* takes that notion a step further—and straight into the postmodern 1990s—by noting that an evil child might actually be designed so by scientists run amok. Although the twins possess superior intellect and cunning, these girls were not gifted with a superior sense of morality, and that fact makes them monsters.

Didn't the scientists ever stop to think about morality? How about mere emotional stability? The 1990s was indeed a perfect time to revisit the notion of evil children, and accordingly a few horror movies of the era did so, including *The Good Son* (1993). The reason this issue was so timely involves the development, in 1990, of the Human Genome Project, an initiative designed to map fully our DNA. In terms of the horror genre and its development, this scientific project was every bit as important, creatively, as was the Manhattan Project to an earlier era. In both cases, creative artists explored the notion that "tampering in God's domain" could effectively destroy mankind. By harnessing the atom in the 1940s, and by mapping the human genome in the 1990s, mankind was opening that proverbial Pandora's box. The "real" monster in "Eve" is thus wanton genetic experiment, vetted without a controlling, moral authority. The Krievins twins portray Teena and Cindy here and do a remarkable job. They play their roles, at first, as though everything happening to the girls is observed from some great emotional distance. They are disassociated from the horrific and monstrous things happening around them.

Late in the episode, we understand that this distance arises from a lack of empathy. The deaths of their foster fathers mean nothing to the girls, emotionally speaking, and their almost blank facades embodies not shock but mere boredom. And out of all the monstrous actions and behaviors that appear on *The X-Files*, this lack of empathy, in an avatar of innocence, no less, may be among the most frightening.

In the finale, when the audience learns their true nature, the twins finally reveal a new aspect: childish glee in their antisocial activities. To the very end, Teena and Cindy try to manipulate others with their childish appearances. "We didn't do anything wrong," they insist, "we're just little girls. . . ."

The distance between Teena and Cindy's youthful appearance and their evil acts is one factor that renders "Eve" so chilling and therefore so successful. There's something deeply disturbing about children who are disconnected from their emotions, yet also deceitful and manipulative. Again and again in the episode, Scully and Mulder make mistakes because they can't quite reckon with the idea that these little girls could possibly be monsters. They can't make the leap that in this case appearance isn't reality.

Interestingly, "Eve" doesn't end without an important, if brief glance toward the "nurture" end of the eternal debate about children. Cindy's mother, after learning of her daughter's evil behavior, completely abandons her. She cuts her off. She rips up her photograph of Cindy and burns it in a fire. This is not the act of a loving mother, even one whose child has acted badly. Call this the Frankenstein Principle. We make life in our own image, but when we don't like that image, we dismiss that life as "monstrous." Suddenly, it's not a part of the family anymore, nor part of the official history. It can never be spoken of aloud . . . *just burn all the photographs in the fireplace.* This act of purging a family member, depicted in the finale of "Eve," suggests that Cindy and Teena aren't the only ones who lack empathy, and perhaps that missing factor is indeed a matter of nurture after all. If these girls had been raised in truly loving homes, would they have resorted to murder, even factoring in the genetic predisposition toward instability?

In terms of the character development, "Eve" is a necessary piece of the *X-Files* puzzle for a few reasons. I have read other critical evaluations of the series that suggest the series is not actually concerned with the science vs. belief battle, but rather with a strange kind of faith in which Mulder is always right, a priori, no matter what. These critics see Mulder as unrealistic. They term him infallible, always able to guess what is happening in every case, correctly deducing the solution to a mystery. Yet this is not a legitimate complaint about the series, and one could point to "Eve" as Exhibit A refuting it. Here, the episode begins with Mulder hell-bent on proving a case of alien abduction. He discusses missing time (a callback to the pilot episode), cattle mutilations, and the like. He obsesses over the idea of a "red cloud" in the sky on the day of the crime. Young Teena—sensing Mulder's desire to reach a preordained conclusion—plays into his vanity and supports Mulder's reading of the investigation. Yet she is doing this merely to trick him and throw him off the scent.

As the investigation unravels, Mulder realizes he is barking up the wrong tree and drops his theory, as any smart investigator concerned with the facts rightly would. The conclusion to draw here is that he saw a commonality between a contemporary case and some old case in his X-Files, but that the lead didn't pan out. So, already—just eleven episodes in—the series proves that Mulder *can* be wrong, and in his zealousness to be right, even make mistakes. This quality renders the character a fallible and interesting protagonist, not the kind of "infallible" master detective I've seen him described as in some works. His viewpoint is not constantly validated by the writers of or the plots on the series.

There's also a very effective moment in "Eve" that plays on audience expectations and desires regarding the Scully/Mulder relationship. Scully and Mulder have "rescued" the two girls and are unaware of their true, homicidal natures. They decide to take care of the girls and drive them to their next destination. On the long road trip, the girls need to use the bathroom, and Mulder, slightly annoyed, pulls over at a rest-stop restaurant. With a slight smile, Scully takes the two girls to the bathroom with her while Mulder gets their order of four large sodas. While he uses the restroom, one of the girls poisons two of the sodas, the ones meant for the FBI agents.

There's a great dramatic conflict in this scene between what Scully and Mulder (and a waitress) *believe* is happening and what is *actually* happening. Scully and Mulder are knowingly playing Mom and Dad, and seem to recognize it . . . and even enjoy the role-playing a little. The waitress even thinks Mulder is the twins' dad and says so. As viewers tantalized by the Mulder/Scully relationship, we too are pulled into this world of sudden parentage, though we know better. Despite our knowledge, we are suddenly contextualizing these folks in terms of a "family," something that has always been denied the original Adams and Eves of the Litchfield Project. Then, of course, the illusion is shattered, and Mulder realizes at the last moment that the girls have poisoned the sodas. It's an electric moment when he realizes the truth and understands, fully, how successfully the girls can play on the illusion that they are made of sugar and spice and everything nice . . . plus, apparently, a healthy dollop of foxglove.

In terms of the *X-Files* canon, "Eve" points toward the series' obsession with illicit genetic experimentation and research. The episode is sort of the tip of that iceberg on that front, and the theme will return in a big way in later seasons, though in a more intimate fashion that affects Scully and Mulder directly. "Eve" thus represents a promise of things to come—and another indicator of past government malfeasance—rather than a direct, linear connection to the overarching Mytharc.

"Beyond the Sea." Written by Glen Morgan and James Wong. Directed by David Nutter. Airdate: January 7, 1994.

In "Beyond the Sea," Scully's father (Don Davis) unexpectedly passes way during the holidays following a sudden, massive coronary. Scully experiences a premonitory vision of her late father immediately before her mother, Margaret (Sheila Larken), notifies her by phone of his death. At work the next day, Scully and Mulder attempt to locate and rescue two kidnapped teenagers in Raleigh, North Carolina, by meeting with a notorious death row inmate, Luther Lee Boggs (Brad Dourif). Boggs claims psychic powers and knowledge due to a recent brush with state-sanctioned execution. He wants to bargain for a pardon if he helps to save the missing kids. Scully gives Boggs's claims of psychic knowledge special credence in part because she feels vulnerable after her father's death, but also because Boggs seems to possess firsthand knowledge of her father, including his nickname for her (Starbuck) and his long-standing affection for the Bobby Darin song "Beyond the Sea."

When one of Boggs's channeling sessions proves unexpectedly fruitful, Scully wants to pursue the lead, even as a skeptical Mulder is warned by Boggs that his life is in danger "under the white cross." Sure enough, Mulder is badly injured by the kidnapper while attempting to recover one of the missing teens. His absence leaves a vulnerable Scully to negotiate with Boggs for information regarding the missing youngster and her father's final disposition. On the latter front, Boggs promises to deliver a "message" for Dana.

The X-Files almost universally vets its tales of the paranormal and extraordinary through two distinct lenses. One lens is rationality or science, as seen and understood by Scully. The other lens is romanticism and belief, as embodied by Mulder. This duality might also be parsed in terms of *belief*. In "Beyond the Sea," Scully notes that she is "*afraid* to believe," while Mulder is famous—across the series and films—for the refrain "I *want* to believe." He even says so directly, early in this episode: "Don't get me wrong, I want to believe." Yet "Beyond the Sea" is a crucial episode in the early *X-Files* canon in part because, for a time, it flips the traditional roles/viewpoints of these characters in the drama. Scully wants to believe at first, but then backs away from that particular precipice. Mulder refuses to believe at first, but by episode's end is actively upbraiding Scully for her failure to do so. Still, this episode offers the novel pleasure of Scully arguing for the paranormal and Mulder arguing against it.

The crux of the issue in this story is one man, Boggs himself: the flawed, even despicable person who offers the agents otherworldly or paranormal knowledge. He acts, like many others in the series, as a kind of unreliable oracle, both proffering information and, because of his life choices, being difficult to believe. Luther Lee Boggs is a brutal murderer, a man who would say and do anything to avoid dying on death row. He's terribly afraid to die and already knows he is "going to hell." These motives make Boggs an unreliable—and desperate—source of information. Yet, contrarily, Boggs seems to legitimately understand several things about the future and about Mulder and Scully's lives. Perhaps some of this knowledge could be known, as Scully insists, through research. But it would be abundantly difficult for Boggs to access information regarding Scully's pet name (Starbuck) or the title of the song played at her father's funeral. Those are facts that wouldn't likely be reported in a local newspaper, for instance, and certainly not an out-of-state paper. And Boggs is incarcerated in North Carolina, remember, while Scully and Mulder are in Virginia or D.C. If Boggs had requested a Virginia newspaper, his jailers surely would have reported that information to the FBI agents.

So the question becomes this: Would you want to hear your loved one's final, loving words from the lips of a serial killer and monster? From a person you consider vile? This problem recurs throughout *X-Files* history. Father Joe in *The X-Files: I Want to Believe* (2008) serves as a bookend reflection, essentially, of Boggs. He is another fallen man (a pedophile), but one boasting legitimate psychic powers. Yet neither Father Joe nor Boggs are believed by society at large because of their crimes, and because of an understandable and legitimate abhorrence of those crimes.

Thus the implication is that human beings sometimes can't hear "the truth" if the mouthpiece of that truth is someone whom we deem fallible or fallen in some crucial way. The irony of this approach, and one also suggested by *The X-Files*, however, is that *we are all fallible* in some way. Therefore, in failing to accept "psychic transmissions" from Boggs or Father Joe, we are also cutting off the possibility of accepting such information from any human vessels. Thus, the "truth," whether we want it or are afraid of it, is unknowable.

If God indeed moves in mysterious ways, is it impossible to believe that message of hope and renewal could come from Luther Lee Boggs? That's the question that roils underneath this narrative. Why would God let a Boggs or a Father Joe be that vehicle, knowing how reluctant we would be to accept the information? The episode, if examined closely, seems to suggest that a brief reunion between Scully and her dead father is indeed possible through Boggs, if only Scully can set aside her judgment of the man's deeds.

In elegant and artistic terms, the veil separating our world from the next is contextualized in this story from James Wong and Glen Morgan in the terminology of the Bobby Darin hit "Beyond the Sea" (1959). In that song, the singer is separated from a loved one by the water, by the ocean. That loved one is there on the other side, "watching" for the singer. But the singer can't reach that loved one; he can only wait. Failing the ability to fly "like a bird on high" to the afterlife, the singer must satisfy himself with belief "beyond a doubt" that his heart will lead him to the same place, "beyond the shore."

For all of his contemptible, antisocial behavior, Boggs offers the possibility of breaching the sea now, of connecting Scully and her father again in this mortal coil. Finally, Scully refuses the offer because of her fear. Because, perhaps, she is afraid of learning what her father knows about the boundaries of death, and the afterlife. It might be better, in a sense, to hope for an eventual reunion "beyond the sea" than to meet again, under these circumstances, with the unreliable intermediary, Boggs, in control of the dialogue.

Because of her preconceived and ironclad notions regarding spirituality and Boggs's human nature, Scully misses an opportunity here. Late in the story, Boggs tells Scully the truth (as he understands it, from psychic information) about the kidnapper's lair. He even gives her the key to save her own life, warning her not to approach "the blue devil." She sees the illustration of a blue devil at a critical juncture and stops chasing her quarry. Meanwhile, the kidnapper falls through the planks of a bridge . . . to his death. At this point, however, Boggs knows he will be denied a pardon, so there is no earthly reason for him to help Scully. So why did he do it? Why did he save her life? Well, I said *earthly* reason. There's always a reason of the soul or spirit: *personal redemption.* I also allude to this factor in my review of *I Want to Believe*, but our culture professes a deeply held, Christian belief in redemption. Yet often those who seek redemption are denied that second chance, that forgiveness. If redemption is not available for a man like Father Joe, or a man like Luther Lee Boggs, then who is it for, precisely? The righteous have no need of it.

The final, emotional imagery of "Beyond the Sea"—which depicts Boggs going to his execution—concerns this matter of redemption. We see Boggs literally surrounded by the ghosts of his victims, including his family, as he takes his final steps in this life. He goes to his death, as he should, for his grievous misdeeds. But his family is present with him, a reminder both of what he did wrong and of the comfort of human companionship. Thus Boggs is not alone when he dies, as he feared. Instead, he is with those who have crossed "beyond the sea." His act of redemption, one might argue, allows him to see that beyond death, another plane of life exists, and perhaps because he has sought forgiveness and redemption, it will not be the hell he fears so greatly, the hell his original actions brought about.

"Beyond the Sea" has frequently been compared to *Silence of the Lambs* (1991), and that is for two reasons, primarily. The first is that both works of art involve a female FBI agent who attempts to contextualize her father's death, and more than that, her father's very meaning in her life. Secondly, of course, both stories feature lengthy interview sessions with an imprisoned, loquacious serial killer. But where *Silence of the Lambs* is very much about a woman without a father and selecting between two surrogate fathers (either Jack Crawford or Hannibal Lecter), "Beyond the Sea" is a story about Scully's inability to grow *beyond* her father. She wonders again and again if he is proud of her, if he approves of her life and career choices. She can't move beyond the lens her father imposed upon her in childhood. In perhaps the ultimate of ironies, her father's final message to Scully is forever unheard because she chooses, ultimately, to double-down on fear and disbelief, the same viewpoint that made her father skeptical of her career choice in the first place. The catchall phrase "he's my father" doesn't reveal pride, love, support, or anything beyond a biological bond. But by episode's end, Scully is parroting that empty term, as if it is Scripture. *That's all that needed to be said.* She doesn't want or need a further message, especially from Boggs.

In terms of the Mulder/Scully relationship, "Beyond the Sea" is indeed an intriguing, if brief, flipping of roles. Ultimately, each individual can't escape his or her established viewpoint. This notion could be made clearer, however, in the epilogue. It is abundantly plain why Scully shifts back to her position of rationality: *fear.* But Mulder flip-flops from telling Scully not to believe Boggs to asking her why she refuses to believe Boggs in light of all the evidence. It would have been helpful to include a scene in which Mulder admitted that he was wrong initially and that he now believes Boggs was indeed a conduit to connect souls on Earth and souls in the afterlife. "Beyond the Sea" also ups the ante in terms of the physical relationship between the two FBI agents. Mulder places his hand on Scully's cheek and caresses it gently after expressing his sadness over her father's death.

The moment is unexpectedly powerful because, as we've seen before, the sex roles are largely reversed in terms of typical TV stereotypes. Usually, it is the man who silently soldiers on in the face of grief, tending nobly to his duties and responsibilities. But here it is Scully who assumes that role, repressing her grief and stoically returning to work. And Mulder, for his part, tends not to matters of duty and job (and emotional denial) as we stereotypically expect of our male heroes. Rather, he openly addresses issues of grief, and with physical reassurance to boot. In a very real sense, Scully is often the "head" in the *X-Files* duo, while Mulder is often the expressive, emotional "heart."

"Genderbender." Written by Larry and Paul Barber. Directed by Rob Bowman. Airdate: January 21, 1994.

In Germantown, Maryland, Mulder and Scully investigate the latest in a string of murders being committed by a killer with the unusual capacity to change sex at will and transmit an irresistible human pheromone. Mulder traces the killings back to the Kindred, a strict fundamentalist religious sect living in rural Massachusetts. Mulder and Scully infiltrate the compound and learn that the simple people there seem to be both immortal and chemically incompatible with human beings. Scully is unexpectedly affected and aroused by one of the Kindred, Brother Andrew (Brent Hinckley), as Mulder gathers evidence in a strange subterranean cave that indicates the Kindred are not of this Earth. . . .

"Genderbender" remains one of the weirder and perhaps more controversial first-season episodes of *The X-Files*. That controversy arises—as it often does in life—over one particular subject: *sex*. This installment directed by Rob Bowman muses on the qualities that can comprise human sexual attraction and arousal. In the final analysis, does it all simply come down to chemical attraction? Can our responses, in effect, be programmed by chemical changes?

This is not merely a matter for intellectual debate, either, as Scully learns for herself in "Genderbender." And the episode is certainly of strong interest from a characterization perspective. As a character, Scully is very button-downed and by-the-book. Yet "Genderbender" finds her far outside her comfort zone, forced to act in ways contrary to her character's parochial inclinations. Also, sexual attraction in *The X-Files*—as embodied by the central relationship between Scully and Mulder—is often contextualized in terms of an intellectual or cerebral connection. Mulder and Scully are turned on by each other, we understand, because they are smart, resourceful, capable, and curious rivals. Thus *The X-Files* recognizes and explores a key human truth: smart is sexy.

Smart is *really* sexy.

Yet "Genderbender" deliberately throws a monkey wrench in that equation by suggesting that sexual attraction isn't universally based on factors of the conscious mind at all, but on the body's involuntary response to stimuli outside its control. The episode posits an alien race that releases a pheromone irresistible to humans, turning the affected people into the equivalent of one-time sex engines. The killer in this episode deploys that pheromone, uses up his lovers, and burns them out. Victims die after catastrophic cardiac arrest. With this chemical power to manipulate mankind comes another, equally uncomfortable realization too. Overdeveloped brains aside, we're all just mammals, susceptible to the same primitive biological drives as other, less evolved mammals.

Where humans can attempt to differentiate themselves, however, is in their intellectual response to this drive. "Genderbender" suggests that the asceticism and abstinence typical of religious fundamentalism is, in fact, that very thing: an attempt not to interface with the Divine, but to rein in the chaotic imperatives of sexual desire.

That's a lot of thematic ground to cover, and yet "Genderbender" is a surprising, unpredictable, and tense hour. The story from Larry and Paul Barber demonstrates another admirable aspect of Chris Carter's series: the willingness to experiment with something new, even if that something new goes against preconceived notions of appropriateness or expectation. This is the same impulse that gives rise to episodes such as "Home," "Chinga," "Kill Switch," "The Post-Modern Prometheus," and "Triangle," among others. Not all those episodes are complete successes, but each is ambitious and outside the rubric of strictly defined, inelastic format parameters.

"Genderbender" commences with imagery that succinctly expresses the episode's theme. In an urban club or bar, as an alien stalks human prey for purposes of casual sex, a painting is visible on the wall in the background. It is a Giger-esque work of art combining human and alien features, and there is both an allure and repulsion to it. The painting simultaneously implies danger and sexual desire, and that is the very nature, as well, of the episode's gender-bending killer. The painting appears a second time, later in the hour, and the connection between art and behavior can't be missed. Both the painting and the episode's narrative turns suggest that humans are drawn to sex, even if that sex might be dangerous or out of the norm. And a "walking aphrodisiac" like the episode's killer seems to hone in on this aspect of his/her prey.

Uniquely, "Genderbender" also intuits a reason for the sexual asceticism of fundamentalist Christian groups. The Kindred cannot freely express their passions with those around them—human beings—because to do so would be to commit murder. Scully notes the Kindred's "abstinence and pure Christian ways" but there is a very real, very practical reason for their existence. Sex and pleasure equate to *murder* for these alien visitors. When one considers Kindred prayers like "we pray for the day of the coming, the day of our release," it is not too difficult to discern precisely what they mean. As visitors on Earth, they have contained and controlled their appetites for far too long. They desire a time and place where their "abstinence" and ascetic lifestyle will not be necessary. "Release" in this context, is, not just a return journey home, indeed, but "sexual release." Don't get me started on the "day of the coming." That prayer isn't just about a flying saucer and crop circles.

Without knowing all the facts, Mulder and Scully mistake the Kindred prayers for the Christian desire to be saved and redeemed by a messiah. In fact, the Kindred long for the physical release of sexual intercourse in a safe environment. They dare not let themselves loose on Earth, lest chaos result. In the episode's dialogue, it is said that the killer in "Genderbender," Brother Marty, was "captured" by the outside world of "slick" sexuality, and finally could not be restrained, could not wait for the day of deliverance from Earth. He broke free of his people's asceticism and gave in to hedonism, with the result being death for his partners. In reckoning with this character, *The X-Files* seems to present a case about American culture in the 1990s and the seductive power of advertising/media imagery. "Genderbender" notes that Marty was not able to resist the tantalizing, sexualized nature of our world. The question is: are we?

Notably, even Scully is not immune to the pheromones released by the Kindred, and she nearly finds herself a sexual partner for one of the sect. It's especially frightening that Scully becomes "captured" by this chemical force, because she is the series' voice of reason, science, and moderation. We already know that Mulder is given to extremes of passion and depression, emotionality and restraint, but Scully is our emotional bedrock and point of stability. So to see her so thoroughly overcome by the Kindred is shocking, and the moment creates a sense of tension and predictability.

In terms of *The X-Files* history, Nicholas Lea makes an early appearance here as one of the killer's surviving victims. Lea would later return to the series in the long-standing role of Krycek. Secondarily—and this factor may account for some fan displeasure with the episode—"Genderbender" is one of the few *X-Files* episodes that posits alien life outside the strict confines of the Mytharc. The Kindred appear quite separate and different from the shape-shifting bounty hunters and black oil aliens seen later, and are never referred to again. It is possible that the Kindred represent one of the alien life-forms in the universe that the Black Oil ultimately infects.

But in the final analysis, it's okay that there is no big connection here to the series Mytharc because "Genderbender" accomplishes its artistic task. It asks the viewer to consider the forces underlying sexual attraction. Then it wonders if those are the very things that make us human in the first place.

"The Erlenmeyer Flask." Written by Chris Carter. Directed by R. W. Goodwin. Airdate: May 13, 1994.

In "The Erlenmeyer Flask," government informant Deep Throat suggests that Mulder take a closer look at a police chase in Maryland that ended with an inhumanly strong suspect jumping into the water after incapacitating several police officers. The chase ended with something else too: the discovery that the suspect had been wounded and that he bled a weird, green material.

Mulder and Scully trace the suspect's car, a silver Sierra, back to EmGen Corp., where a scientist who worked on the Human Genome Project is toiling with monkeys for some unknown purpose. When Dr. Benrube, the project scientist, dies in an apparent suicide attempt, Mulder and Scully (Gillian Anderson) realize that they are witnessing the fringe of a larger, shadowy conspiracy. They discover an extraterrestrial bacteria that existed before man walked the Earth and a strange warehouse filled with human-alien hybrids. These mysteries go unresolved, and the government shuts down the X-Files unit in the FBI rather than learn more.

The X-Files' first-season finale, "The Erlenmeyer Flask" is both a logical development of the series pilot, which established extraterrestrial incursions on Earth, and a vanguard for the overall Mytharc narrative, which describes over several seasons an attempt by humans to create human-alien hybrids and an alien vaccine before alien colonization of Earth commences in 2012. Written by Chris Carter and directed by R. W. Goodwin, "The Erlenmeyer Flask"—like many of the greatest episodes of *The X-Files*—also takes as its inspiration a real-life story or mystery and then turns that mystery to creatively service its narrative.

Equally significantly, "The Erlenmeyer Flask" serves two important arc purposes. In the first case, it reveals the tip of the conspiracy iceberg to the agents. "You've never been closer," affirms informant Deep Throat. Indeed, that is very much the case as Scully discovers the so-called wellspring, an alien corpse used in research by secretive scientists.

In the second case, the episode's conclusion reveals to Mulder and Scully that even though they haven't seen or understood every element of "the conspiracy," they possess the power to stop it in its tracks or at the very least expose it. The last scenes of "The Erlenmeyer Flask" reveal a weakness—galvanizing fear—on the part of conspirators. Accordingly, they shut down the X-Files to prevent any further discoveries and to permanently separate the potent partnership of Scully and Mulder.

"The Erlenmeyer Flask" is a superb first-season-ender, and it bookends the season beautifully. In the pilot episode, we witnessed the Cigarette Smoking Man (William Davis) taking UFO-related evidence to that *Raiders of the Lost Ark*–styled repository in the Pentagon . . . hiding the truth. The Erlenmeyer Flask" ends with a reprise of that cogent imagery: another walk-through of that warehouse of alien technology and artifacts with the same result: the truth is hidden from the public eye. I don't know for certain if *The X-Files* had a renewal in hand by the time this episode was penned and aired, but in a certain sense, the final episode of the first season squares the circle. The first season, in and of itself, is a complete whole. It is bookended by examples of deceit and obfuscation, with the hope of discovering the truth having risen and then, finally, fallen. I'm glad *The X-Files* returned for eight more seasons, but it's fascinating to contemplate the season as a complete "novel" or chapter, too.

"The Erlenmeyer Flask" draws its inspiration from an unexplained, real-life happening in the 1990s. In Riverside, California, on February 19, 1994, at approximately 8:00 p.m., a woman who became known in the media as "the toxic lady" arrived at the General Hospital while suffering apparent cardiac arrest. When the workers attempted to draw her blood, a toxic ammonia-like smell emanated from her body, and no less than three medical workers fainted and experienced dizzy spells. The patient died that night, and the strange, toxic nature of her blood was not fully explained.

This odd story is mirrored in "The Erlenmeyer Flask" during a scene in which EMTs attempt to deliver emergency care in an ambulance to the human-alien hybrid seen in the opening sequence. When they take his (green) blood, they suddenly cough, sputter, pass out, and suffer from burns on their skin. Exposure to the hybrid is deadly. On a personal note, I remember actually reading about the "toxic lady" at the time the incident occurred, so "The Erlenmeyer Flask" probably represents my first or earliest recognition that Carter was indeed exploring "real life" X-Files in his fiction series as well as establishing a new Gothic aesthetic for the nineties. In keeping with that meme, this episode of *The X-Files* also harnesses imagery from mythology to tell its story. The warehouse containing the human hybrids is owned by a company called "Zeus Storage" and is located on Pandora Street. Given those two references to Greek myth, you just know it's going to prove a place of danger and disaster. Zeus Storage recalls the Greek King of the Gods, from whom the secret of fire was stolen in the myth of Prometheus.

And, of course, the "magic" of creation is here taken—again by humans—from the (god-like?) aliens. Pandora, not coincidentally, is a part of the same myth. She represents Zeus's revenge on misbehaving man. Zeus, in fact, creates Pandora knowing that she will open the "jar" (or rather "box") containing plagues and other diseases, thus unloosing them on grasping, greedy mankind.

In "The Erlenmeyer Flask," the knowledge of alien DNA and bacteria creates a new biology toxic to mankind, as those imperiled EMT workers learn all too well. Thus, the title "The Erlenmeyer Flask" might be translated ably as "Pandora's box." Avaricious scientists, hoping to steal knowledge that is not theirs to possess, take it and in the process release a toxin that could destroy the human race. Pandora's box is opened. This is a nuanced, almost subtextual reference to myth, but it deepens considerably the episode's impact and artistry.

Chris Carter has also often gone on record describing his memories of the Watergate hearings in the mid-1970s and his subsequent distrust of the government. One positive element of Watergate—or of the Watergate mythology, we must now admit—is the little guy against City Hall narrative. Reporters Bernstein and Woodward went up against a sitting president armed only with the truth, and they emerged victorious. Perhaps modifying that scenario, "The Erlenmeyer Flask" suggests that Mulder and Scully boast the same capacity: to bring down a governmental conspiracy and reveal the truth to a deceived public. What's clear from this episode is that their investigations terrify the (as yet unnamed) Syndicate. The agents are getting too close to their target, and the powers that be react hastily and vindictively by shutting down the X-Files.

Again, had *The X-Files* lasted only one season, the overall arc would have seen two agents of change (Mulder and Scully) discovering a conspiracy, almost exposing it, and then being, in the last moment, defeated by power. That arc prescribes new developments since Watergate: the idea that the more things appear to change, the more they actually remain the same. This is Carter's statement on government, no matter which party happens to be in power, I suspect. In terms of *X-files* lore, "The Erlenmeyer Flask" reveals Mulder's obsession with science fiction film history. Here, the film *Journey to the Center of the Earth* (1959) appears on television. Later episodes, such as "War of the Coprophages" and "Sein und Zeit"/"Closure" feature clips from *Planet of the Apes* (1968). Again, such references bookend one another in telling fashion. Mulder in this episode embarks upon a "journey to the center" of the truth, at least after a fashion. But *Planet of the Apes* warns that, in the words of Dr. Zaius (Maurice Evans), when he reaches his destination, he "may not like what he finds."

"The Erlenmeyer Flask" also features the death of Deep Throat, who in many senses is a father figure to Mulder. Mulder even describes himself here as "the dutiful son." Importantly, he experiences a kind of adolescent rebellion against his metaphorical dad here, refusing to accept Deep Throat's sincerity and honesty regarding the conspiracy. Ultimately, however, the father figure is vindicated by saving Mulder from a kidnapping and issuing the warning that ends the episode and hangs over the entire first season:

Trust no one.

8

Divided and Separated

Season Two (1994–1995)

The X-Files' second season expands significantly the universe established in the first season. It does so by growing the canvas on which the writers and directors paint, and its two-part mythology episodes, introduced in this span, play like feature films, replete with top-notch action sequences, vivid location work, and a more developed, continually growing supporting cast.

If the theme of the first year involved Mulder and Scully being separated from their old friends in and out of the FBI, and subsequently drawing closer to one another, the second year witnessed a terrifying reversal. This run of two dozen episodes involves external forces attempting to divide and separate the Mulder/Scully partnership. Early in the season, Mulder and Scully are "off" the X-Files unit, working separately, and then Scully is abducted in the two-part episode "Duane Barry"/"Ascension"—a series game changer—making her completely absent from Mulder's life.

In real life, Gillian Anderson's pregnancy necessitated the disappearance of Scully for several weeks, and the "in-universe" explanation was, eerily, abduction. Scully's abduction later became a turning point in the series and a key aspect of the Mytharc. The abduction and its aftermath give Scully the personal connection to the work that Mulder already has. He goes in search of the truth about his sister, Samantha. Scully goes forward determined to discover what was done to her during her abduction and by whom.

With the death of Deep Throat in "The Erlenmeyer Flask," it also became a necessity in the second season for Mulder to have a new secret contact in the government. The episode "Sleepless" by Howard Gordon introduces Steven Williams's tough-as-nails, close-to-the-vest "X." Unlike Deep Throat, X is a fierce physical presence and has little interest in taking Mulder by the hand to show him "the truth." Instead, X proves less a father figure and more a game player. He always seems to be working his own secret agenda and uses

Mulder when it is convenient for him to do so, or if it fits his plan. X lasted for two seasons before he too was killed by the Syndicate.

The second season of *The X-Files* also introduces Alex Krycek, a man who began as Mulder's "green" rookie partner (also introduced in "Sleepless") but was soon revealed to be in league with William B. Davis's menacing Cigarette Smoking Man. Over the seasons, Krycek would emerge as a key villain on the series and a personal nemesis for Mulder, a kind of twisted reflection for our hero.

In terms of character development, the season commences with Mulder remembering the abduction of his sister, Samantha ("Little Green Men,"), sees him lose Scully in "Duane Barry"/"Ascension" and then learn of his father's—Bill Mulder (Peter Donat)—involvement in the conspiracy. The final episode of the season, "Anasazi," sees Mulder's father murdered.

Scully also goes through the wringer in Season Two. In addition to her abduction, Scully grapples with perhaps the darkest figure in all of *The X-Files*, Donnie Pfaster (Nick Chinlund), a "death fetishist" in Minneapolis who kidnaps her.

The storytelling on *The X-Files'* Season Two had grown so confident that the season ended on a cliffhanger, and the action resumed in the 1995 season with a two-episode wrap-up.

Mytharc Notes

The Mytharc begins in earnest with Season Two and the matter of Scully's abduction. At the time the episodes aired, in 1994, it appeared that both Agent Scully and Duane Barry (Steve Railsback) were victimized by aliens. In later seasons, we learn that this is not strictly true, that the Cigarette Smoking Man arranged the abductions, and that scientists working for him carried out painful and harmful "tests" on the subjects. Scully's abduction in this season leads to her suffering from terminal cancer in Season Four and learning of a biological child in Season Five.

The epic Season Two two-parter "Colony"/"End Game" also introduces another crucial character to the series, a shape-shifting alien bounty hunter played by Brian Thompson. In this two-part story, the alien, replete with a vicious murder weapon, a retractable silver ice pick, moves about America with impunity while murdering people who appear to be human-alien hybrids.

The second-season tale "Red Museum" also provide pieces of the puzzle, depicting how, in Delta Glen, Wisconsin, scientist may be experimenting with dangerous growth hormones and amino acids perhaps extraterrestrial in origin. In truth, this is part of the hybrid/vaccination program, exposed later in the series.

The final episode of the season, featuring a story by Chris Carter and David Duchovny, is called "Anasazi," and it involves a train car in the Navajo desert, one filled with strange corpses that may be extraterrestrial in nature or something else entirely. This episode, based on the legend of the Anasazi, an Indian tribe that disappeared without a trace hundreds of years ago, figures in directly with the series finale in 2002, "The Truth."

Season Highlights

"Little Green Men." Written by Glen Morgan and James Wong. Directed by David Nutter. Airdate: September 16, 1994.

The X-Files have been shut down by the FBI, and Agents Scully and Mulder are reassigned to teaching duties at Quantico and wiretap surveillance, respectively.

Mulder experiences a crisis of faith regarding his lack of evidence concerning alien life, even as he recalls the fateful night in 1973 when his sister, Samantha (Vanessa Morley), was apparently abducted by extraterrestrial visitors. Mulder's enthusiasm for the cause is rekindled, however, when Senator Richard Matheson (Raymond J. Barry) reports that there may be an opportunity to make contact with aliens at the satellite installation in Arecibo, in Puerto Rico. That automated installation has apparently received a transmission from an extraplanetary source.

Meanwhile, Scully tracks Mulder down to that location . . . but she is not alone. Agents of the conspiracy are concerned over her whereabouts, and a heavily armed UFO retrieval team is already en route to Arecibo to intercept Mulder before he determines the truth.

The X-Files goes big and deep with its second-season premiere, "Little Green Men." The story, by James Wong and Glen Morgan, concerns an existential crisis for Mulder. Without the X-Files as an overriding purpose, he experiences difficulty holding onto and maintaining his belief system. Mulder's crisis of faith is played out in "Little Green Men" on a much bigger scale than many first-season episodes of *The X-Files*, suggesting a budgetary boost, perhaps, or simply greater ambition. Whereas many *X-Files* episodes of the first season were contained in terms of setting and action ("Ice," "Beyond the Sea"), "Little Green Men" opens with a trip through the cosmos itself, proceeds to a foreign location (to Arecibo, Puerto Rico), and culminates with a dangerous car chase in the jungle.

The story also visually (and therefore directly) fills in the blanks regarding Mulder's sister, Samantha. "Little Green Men" features a flashback of her abduction in 1973, which happens during news coverage of the Watergate scandal, a formative event in creator Chris Carter's youth. Mulder loses his innocence, therefore, at roughly the same time the series creator loses his.

Although aliens appear briefly—and opaquely—in "Little Green Men," the episode nonetheless impresses because it involves the particularities of Mulder's heroic quest and a very low point on that journey.

Also, the episode's opening montage, a kind of "cosmic trip" through the stars, features a healthy dose of social commentary regarding an America in the 1990s that has lost the will, the faith, and the tools to achieve the big

Mulder and Scully are on the case. Season Two sees the two agents separated for a time by Scully's abduction.

things of the decades previous. This was the era of a stalled space program, for example. This was also the era of the Contract with America, devised by congressional Republicans, to cut government costs and programs. While belt-tightening is always commendable, the inference is, perhaps, that the drive to cut costs ends up also cutting the country's capacity to reach for the stars.

"Little Green Men" opens with a spectacular and emotionally moving montage regarding humankind's first attempts to visit other worlds and contact other life-forms. A Voyager spacecraft moves through the loneliness of our solar system, and Mulder's expressive, mournful voice recounts the program's hopeful expeditions to the final frontier. This extended montage resurrects the epistolary feel of the series and reveals the human achievements (mathematics, music, art . . .) recorded for posterity on a golden record aboard Voyager. It remembers the human drive and ambition to always seek the next horizon, no matter the cost.

But then the optimism stops, even as Voyager leaves our solar system for the Great Unknown. "We wanted to believe," Mulder notes, but "the tools were taken away." It isn't difficult to discern the critique here, one concerning the smallness of modern politics. Why was America able to put aside partisanship and do big things in the 1960s and 1970s, big things like the Apollo program? Why, in the 1990s, did we stop looking outward? Why did we stop seeking answers at just the time science was reaching exciting new heights (represented by genetics and the Internet)?

One answer, of course, rests with another image of modern technology featured in "Little Green Men": the Watergate tapes as seen on television in the 1970s flashback with young Mulder and Samantha. Watergate is thus—at least implicitly—positioned by *The X-Files* as the event that poisoned the well of American politics and made a generation see government not as a vehicle for going where none have gone before or other great achievements, but as a secretive, untrustworthy impediment to freedom and liberty.

Mulder feels frustration and anger in "Little Green Men" because he understands that the tools to prove the existence of alien life have been taken away by bean counters. One such tool, of course, is the X-Files. But the other and perhaps more important one is trust and faith in government, the trust and faith that would give rise to increased NASA budgets and a new focus on the stars instead of more pedestrian earthbound concerns.

Somewhere along the lines, perhaps as a result of the Watergate scandal, a lot of Americans stopped believing. Yet like many episodes of *The X-Files,* there is a strong basis in fact for the plot point that powers much of "Little Green Men," particularly an alien signal emanating from space. A scientist featured in the episode name-checks with Scully the famous "Wow signal" of August

15, 1977. That signal was so named by Jerry Ehman, who, while working on a SETI project at Ohio State University, wrote "Wow!" in the margins of a report that described a seventy-two-second narrowband radio signal of nonterrestrial origin. The signal was believed to originate somewhere in the constellation Sagittarius. It was not the be-all and end-all of evidence regarding alien life in the universe. But it was the *beginning* of evidence about it.

Notation of this 1977 signal is sort of the other shoe dropping in terms of "Little Green Men's" overall social critique. Right here—in the existence of the Wow signal—is real-life evidence that the search for extraterrestrial life is not a waste of time and resources. And yet the U.S. government withdrew funding for SETI in the mid-1990s, choosing once more to focus on earth-bound matters (like welfare reform) rather than to keep watching the skies. In other words, the tool that gave us the Wow signal has been taken away.

In terms of the series' story arc, almost nothing significant happens in "Little Green Men." The X-Files remains closed, and Mulder finds no hard evidence of alien life. Yet the story is absolutely vital in terms of character growth because it depicts Mulder at a low ebb and reveals the character—even without the tools he needs—picking himself up, dusting himself off, and renewing the well of faith within. Mulder's example may very well be a message to audiences in the 1990s, and beyond as well. If we want a U.S. that can go to Mars, build a moon base, mine the asteroid belt, or achieve other big things, we're the ones who must renew our faith and renew the call to such action. We can either be the cowering nation of terrified people who believe we can't accomplish big things or the nation that casts its eyes firmly, hopefully, and irrevocably on the stars and prepares for the hard work of building a better future and a better planet.

In comparison with many first season *X-Files* entries, which often play like brilliant one-location, low-budget horror movies, "Little Green Men" looks, feels, and plays more like an epic, big-budget motion picture. The season premiere plays on a larger scale, features intense action, and increases the playing field for our favorite agents. "Little Green Men" is basically a test run of *The X-Files* format on a bigger canvas, and the experiment is a resounding success.

"The Host." Written by Chris Carter. Directed by Daniel Sackheim. Airdate: September 23, 1994.

With the X-Files still officially shuttered, Mulder is relieved of his wiretap surveillance assignment and asked to look into a bizarre murder case in Newark, New Jersey. A corpse is found in the sewers with a strange bite mark on it and a Russian tattoo. While Mulder hunts the murderer—a giant flukeworm with humanoid attributes—Scully determines that the victim may have come from a Russian cargo ship carrying contaminated water from Chernobyl.

Digging deeper, Mulder and Scully find that the adult flukeworm mutant—part parasite and part man—is utilizing human bodies as an incubation place for its young. They are faced with the specter, then, of a whole colony of such worm/human mutants. . . .

On April 26, 1986, a disaster of unprecedented proportions occurred at Nuclear Reactor 4 in the Chernobyl facility. Over 400 times the amount of radioactive material that was released in the Hiroshima bombing of 1945 was released into the atmosphere. The area was evacuated as workers struggled to contain the meltdown, but the long-term effects of the accident were only beginning. The Pripyat River, which feeds drinking water to two million people in Kiev, was contaminated, as were fish in the area. The people exposed to the high level of radioactivity, as well as the wildlife nearby, began to experience higher incidences of thyroid cancer.

In the analysis of "The Erlenmeyer Flask," there was the notion of the alien corpse or wellspring as a kind of Pandora's box. Use of the alien corpse's DNA on humans and in scientific experimentation would mean, in the world of *The X-Files,* a brave new world, one with infinite variations, and infinite capacity for good and evil applications. Chris Carter's episode "The Host" also involves, at least implicitly, a Pandora's box of another brand. In "The Host," Mulder and Scully investigate a strange monster spawned in the real-life horror of Chernobyl and conclude, chillingly, that it may be only the first such creature "born" out of man's mistakes and environmental disasters. Or as the episode's dialogue makes plain: "Nature didn't make this. We did."

In this case, nuclear power is the Pandora's box and the thing that spawns unpredictable terrors. But beyond using the horror of Chernobyl as the monster's point of origin, "The Host" is effective because it gazes at a kind of American corollary for the Chernobyl accident. That accident involves possible mismanagement—or human error—in a setting of vital importance to communities. Here, the topic isn't nuclear power, but the ways that modern civilization removes or disposes of biological waste on an industrial scale. In other words, the sewage plant of "The Host" replaces or represents the nuclear plant at Chernobyl.

Accordingly, "The Host" veritably wallows in sewage, waste, and other unpleasant side effects of human biological processes. The implied connection to Chernobyl is that the accident that occurred there also involved a desperate modern human need for power or energy and similarly, a mishap there. In addition to Mulder's several (nauseating) trips into raw sewage, "The Host" terrifies so thoroughly because of its monster, the "Fluke Man," a humanoid with a sucker for a mouth and rolls of loose fat for a trunk.

A corollary for the gill man in *The Creature from the Black Lagoon,* the Fluke Man is hideous in appearance, but even more terrifying in his behavior. He injects his victims with his young, his larvae, so that human beings become host to the parasites before dying a horrible death. One particularly harrowing scene finds a hapless sewer worker throwing up a worm while taking a shower. And the episode's big "jump" moment involves another worm poking its nose out of a corpse during an autopsy conducted by Scully.

This episode also restates *The X-Files'* Gothic thesis about the Romantic response to Enlightenment. Here, science creates monsters. Indeed, Chernobyl is a place where science fiction meets science fact, and in a very unfortunate way at that. Deformities of a horrendous nature have been detected in animal and human births after the accident, and a new kind of "black fungi" was even seen, years later, thriving inside the abandoned reactor walls. Chris Carter's Fluke Man does not seem so far-fetched an outcome when one considers all these details, and once again *The X-Files* plumbs real-life fears to make its fictional horror feel more realistic and immediate. The environmental and human cost of the Chernobyl accident is horrible enough, but in some sense, one might call it distant. It happened in the Soviet Union, after all, and some eight years before the second season of *The X-Files* aired. Cannily, Carter relocates the horror to modern times, another vast, industrial locale, and also one of crumbling infrastructure: the sewers.

Before it is done, "The Host" features views of backed-up toilets, sewage plants, sewers, outhouse pits, and human workers knee-deep in bilious human waste. The obsession, rather clearly, is on the underbelly of modern civilization. Today, we flush our toilets and don't really think about anything beyond that outcome. But indeed, there is an entire industry, invisible to most, dedicated to treating and disposing of that waste once it leaves our homes. "The Host" generates so much of its ability to disturb by shining a light on the things we'd rather not know about the end results of our normal biological processes.

In some respects, this is the key to crafting successful horror: investigating something real and disturbing and then adding the horrific element beyond the location, beyond strict reality. *The Texas Chainsaw Massacre* accomplishes the same thing, after a fashion, by its frequent references to the slaughterhouse and the killing floor. That real terror is then connected with a fictional one, a cannibal family. Accordingly, part of what makes "The Host" work is its decorum-shattering approach to facets of life we'd rather not talk about. The Fluke Man hides in an outhouse shit pit, unseen and undetected, and the thought of that thing just waiting down there, beneath the unsuspecting and vulnerable, is almost too much to bear.

In some ways, this episode's focus on waste, from the stopped-up toilets on the Russian freighter to the monster in the outhouse waiting to strike, is every bit as convention-busting as the series' most notorious episode: "Home." We have seen mutants in other *X-Files* episodes, like Tooms, but this is the first episode of the series in which it is mankind's mistakes—Pandora's box being opened—that create a new and terrifying breed of creature.

In terms of *X-Files* continuity, there's a great scene here for Assistant Director Skinner when he acknowledges openly and without defensiveness that closing Mulder and Scully's unit was a mistake. This reveals to viewers that Skinner is not just a bureaucrat following orders, but someone who Scully and Mulder can at least begin to trust.

"Duane Barry." Written and directed by Chris Carter. Airdate: October 14, 1994.

"Ascension." Written by Paul Brown. Directed by Michael Lange. Airdate: October 21, 1994.

In "Duane Barry," Mulder and his new partner, Krycek, are called in to help the FBI with a hostage negotiation crisis in Richmond, Virginia. An ex-military man and sanitarium resident, Duane Barry (Steve Railsback) has captured his psychiatrist at gunpoint and taken hostage all the employees of a local travel agency. Mulder's presence is needed because Barry continues to obsessively discuss his alien abduction experience and claims that the aliens (who have been taking him since 1985 . . .) will soon send him instructions about the next rendezvous.

Scully, however, learns that Duane Barry suffered a crippling gunshot wound years earlier and that this catastrophic injury may have made him a serial liar subject to delusions and even hallucinations. When Barry is finally taken into custody by the FBI, however, new medical information is presented. The dangerously unstable Barry seems to possess implants in the very places he claims: his gums, his nasal cavity (see: "Pilot), and his abdomen. And his teeth appear to be drilled via a technology not yet known to medical science.

Scully examines one of the removed implants and finds out that it possesses a bar code, and is therefore cataloguing and tracking Barry. Then Barry escapes from custody and captures Scully. With the FBI agent as his captive, he heads to Skyland Mountains for a rendezvous with his frequent abductors. Mulder and Krycek pursue Barry, but Mulder suffers a betrayal and is not able to reach the mountain apex in time to save Scully from an apparent alien abduction.

Even today *The X-Files'* first great two-part episode, "Duane Barry"/ "Ascension" plays a lot like a 1990s-era action thriller, with a tense opening act involving a hostage negotiation and a final act that gets down to business with picturesque locations, and impressive physical stunts. That description, however, only begins to scratch the surface of this two-part epic, a legitimate *X-Files* classic.

This is also the storyline, for instance, that forwards significantly the series' ongoing subplot about alien abduction (first introduced in the pilot) and ends on a cliffhanger involving the disappearance of Scully. "Duane Barry"/"Ascension" also features a brilliant and twitchy performance by guest star Railsback (*Lifeforce* [1985]) as the title character, Barry. Although the character is only featured in this two-parter, Barry has become, in the minds of many *X-Files* fans, a critical and unforgettable part of the series' background tapestry. Let's just say the actor leaves an impact on the series, the characters, and the audience.

One aspect of this two-part episode that works exceedingly well, too, is its finely inscribed sense of ambiguity. In fact, this is a story of ambiguities within ambiguities, realities within realities. Duane Barry is either an alien abductee or a serial liar, and his abductions are either fabrications or real. But going deeper, those abductions may be, in fact, not alien in nature at all, but the result of military/Syndicate experimentation. When critics and fans remember and celebrate *The X-Files*, it is in part for this careful layering of details; this intelligent writing that artfully permits two ideas or theories—or even more than two—to be operative at the same time. Most TV shows are lucky to get in one good idea per hour. *The X-Files* routinely gets two competing worldviews into each installment, and that's a creative legacy worth cherishing.

Like so many of the best *X-Files* stories, "Duane Barry/Ascension" takes real-life cases of psychology and history and reshapes those sources into a fresh tale. Here, there are two inspirations. On one hand, Duane Barry and his strange brain injury (which is believed to account for his violence and confabulations) is based on a true case of the bizarre. And on the other hand, this is the first *X-Files* episode to delve seriously into almost all facets of abduction literature and lore.

In the first case, Barry's head injury is based loosely on the case of Phineas P. Gage (1823–1860), a railroad construction foreman who survived a dreadful work accident. Gage's left frontal lobe was destroyed when an iron rod smashed through his skull. He was thus at the center of the famous "American crowbar case," and many accounts indicated how this individual's personality was changed—for the worse—following the accident.

Today, however, many of the accounts of Gage's personality change have been debunked, suggesting that, post-accident, it was not as pronounced as many psychologists and neurologists apparently believed at the time. In the case of *The X-Files*, writer Chris Carter uses the device of a traumatic brain injury not unlike Gage's to dramatize the tragedy of Duane Barry. He was once a man who had it all: a wife and children, and a job in the FBI after a noble career in the military. Then Barry had that gunshot accident, and everything changed . . . his very personality changed. He lost his whole life, right down, finally, to his freedom and sanity. He had been deteriorating ever since, slipping into a permanent state of paranoid psychosis.

Scully and Mulder each view Barry's journey differently, but what one comes away with after watching the two-part episode is that he is a man who has suffered horribly and lives for some kind of release, some kind of affirmation regarding his unique journey. But, in typical *X-Files* fashion, there can be no third-party affirmation of the truth, only a collection of details that can be read one way or another. By one reading, he's a lunatic and liar who is being experimented upon by the shadow government. By another, he's a legitimate alien abductee.

That latter reading, alien abduction, permits "Duane Barry"/"Ascension" to recount many stages of the "typical" abduction experience or "narrative." The two episodes detail *the capture*, in which an abductee is taken from his or her home to an alien spacecraft; the *examination*, in which medical procedures are performed on the abductee against his or her will; the *tour* (reflected in Barry's discussion of seeing children aboard the ship); the *loss of time* (recounted by Barry); and the *return*, a post-abduction moment of disassociation and confusion.

I do not suggest a personal belief here in alien abduction, but *The X-Files'* dedicated approach to the subject matter involves finding validation for the paranormal stories, *accurate* in terms of the literature on the subject. It is true to the vast majority of eyewitness accounts. Whether those accounts are true or not is perhaps a different story.

In terms of how this abduction material is vetted, *The X-Files'* visual style is really cemented in this two-part installment, thanks in part to the impressive directorial debut on the series of Chris Carter. There are many shots here originating from a low-placed camera as it probes a new or different environment, like Duane's house at the start of the first episode, and so the resulting psychic impression is of an ongoing exploration. The low angle portends some kind of menace, as if the locale is outsized and the audience is small, or undersized, and the gliding motion suggests a reconnaissance into danger and the unknown, a probe.

There's also a visual sense of mystery and subtextual connection afoot here. Late in the story, for instance, "Duane Barry" cuts from an alien medical tool drilling Duane's teeth (in flashback) to the FBI drilling a hole in the wall at the travel agency. The underlying question is, do the two shots suggest a contextual connection? Is the government behind both drilling attempts? And therefore, is the choice of cuts/editing excavating that hidden connection?

Similarly, the episode reflects Mulder and Scully's uncertainty about Barry by depicting flashbacks that reveal alternate "truths." In some flashbacks, we see the alien greys congregating around Barry. In others, we see military men doing the same. At one point, he says both forces are in cahoots, suggesting that the two versions are not resolved, even in his own mind. If that is the case, then we have here a canny visual representation of paranoid schizophrenia. Again, discerning truth isn't easy, and we must grapple with the notion of an opaque world.

At least subtly, Carter's choices of techniques and compositions also suggests how we should best view Barry: sympathetically. When Barry is shot by the FBI, the screen goes to black, and when an image reemerges on-screen, it is a foggy, blurry POV from the suspect's perspective. This composition suggests we are in his shoes, betrayed in a sense by Mulder, who gives up his convictions and adopts Scully's viewpoint when he should probably know better.

Whether Barry is a liar or an abductee, he is not entirely responsible for his actions. That much can be agreed on. The first-person subjective shots transmit that notion and make us wonder how it must feel to "be" Barry.

The story's first part and setup, "Duane Barry," with its intense one-on-one confrontations between Mulder and Barry, and the high stakes of the FBI snipers, is ultimately superior both in style and substance to the final act, as depicted in "Ascension." Most of the real and important character information and story substance is included in the sterling "Duane Barry," leaving "Ascension" to tie up everything. It succeeds, though mostly on the basis of action tropes: spectacle and ever-mounting tension.

The concluding set piece at Skyland Mountain that finds Mulder aboard a racing sky-tram is a technically magnificent piece of work, brilliantly edited. First, the episode evokes tension when Mulder refuses to heed the technician's advice to slow down and presses the gas pedal, so-to-speak . . . beyond all reason and sanity. Each time he does so, Mulder threatens to make the tram jump its cable at the next tower, an eventuality that would send him plunging to his death. This is nail-biting stuff, as Mulder accelerates, decelerates, and races to retrieve the endangered Scully.

Then the episode unexpectedly moves to pure spectacle as Mulder exits the sky-tram and attempts to climb down a tower. I'm sure I was fooled by excellent stuntwork, but it *really* looks as though Duchovny is clinging to the top and side of the sky-car. The amazing thing is that this sequence on *The X-Files*—a low-budget TV episode—totally outshines a similar sequence in the James Bond film *Moonraker* (1979). There, obvious rear projection screens and stunt doubles ruined the illusion of Bond (Roger Moore) hanging on for his life on a Buenos Aires tram. The scene in "Ascension" eschews optical trickery and obvious stuntmen, and emerges as an action sequence of considerable (and superior) impact.

In terms of characters, much happens in this two-part episode, obviously. Skinner reopens the X-Files. Scully is abducted and disappears, setting up a multiseason plotline involving the tests performed on her. Mulder learns that Krycek is actually Judas and meets with Deep Throat's replacement, X, in person for the first time. Yet beyond all the great intrigue and surprise twists, these episodes work so well because Railsback invests Barry with so much humanity . . . and madness. His scenes are unpredictable, energetic, and dangerous seeming, primarily because of the character's lack of stability. Accordingly, both Scully and Mulder seem imperiled by his presence in a real and intimate way. The key to Railsback's performance is that the audience loves and hates him simultaneously, wanting to both see him captured and see him (and his beliefs) vindicated. That's not an easy tightrope for an actor to walk, but Railsback gives an accomplished, pitch-perfect performance.

"Ascension" also introduces fully another shade of Scully's character: her Catholic faith. Mulder returns Scully's crucifix and necklace to Mrs. Scully (Sheila Larken) upon her disappearance and asks "if she was such a skeptic, why did she wear that?" This fascinating dimension of Scully—her ability to embody both faith and science— is examined in many future stories.

"3." Written by Chris Ruppenthal, Glen Morgan, and James Wong. Directed by David Nutter. Airdate: November 4, 1994.

With Scully still missing after her apparent abduction by aliens, Mulder reopens the X-Files and flies to Los Angeles to investigate a strange new case. A murder victim has been drained entirely of blood. Mulder had been tracking similar crimes before the shuttering of his department and suspects a trio of modern-day, science-spawned vampires known as the "Unholy Trinity."

Mulder stakes out the Hollywood Blood Bank in hopes that an employee there, the new night watchman, may be one of the criminals. Mulder apprehends the criminal, a man who insists that he is a vampire and can live forever.

Soon after this boast, the man burns up when exposed to sunlight, a side effect, Mulder believes, of Gunther disease.

Later, Mulder meets a dark and mysterious woman with a thirst for blood, Kristin (Perrey Reeves), at a club appropriately called Tepes. He suspects that she holds the key to apprehending the other two corners of the murderous triangle.

The episode "3" has never been particularly well regarded by fans of *The X-Files*, and there are reasons that support this point of view. For instance, this is an episode where Mulder works alone and Scully is absent, thus flouting the conventional formula. And shippers—fans who watch the show to see the Mulder/Scully relationship—may be disappointed or angry because Mulder experiences a sexual liaison with a woman in the story who is not Scully.

Indeed, a certain percentage of the hostility aimed at "3" apparently revolves around Mulder having intimate relations with another woman. Some fans consider this an emotional betrayal, though that's a silly viewpoint. The episode makes it pretty clear that Mulder and Kristin connect on a physical level, but not much else. Mulder makes love to Kristin because he is on a nihilist tear, living in a world that seems to be spiraling out of control, inching ever toward annihilation. These qualities certainly mark "3" as atypical but reveal the series is willing to bend or break the rules, to try something new. "3" impresses in this regard, stretching the series format in the process. It's an episode that looks and feels very different from the typical series installment and on those grounds alone must be regarded as something of an artistic success, even if it isn't a particularly popular story.

As has become a staple on *X-Files* stories, "3" bases it monster of the week—the "Unholy Trinity"—on a real scientific notion and pinpoints trenchant visuals to echo its *Dracula*-like "the blood is the (dangerous) life" thesis. What ultimately emerges is a widely disdained episode but a highly visual, even visceral story dripping in style and mood, even if it is not the intellectual/humorous dance fans have come to expect from this franchise.

Commendably, "3" looks, sounds, and feels like a Michael Mann film circa 1986. Kristin's modern apartment with its opaque glass partitions and minimalist decoration evokes similar settings from *Manhunter* (1986), and in terms of narrative and theme, "3" also contends with typical Mann obsessions, like the solitary law enforcement official drawn into an underworld of moral relativity and crime. There's the tragic affair between two people from different worlds, too—here Mulder and Kristin—and also a generally humorless tenor. These are hallmarks of Mann's ascetic or stoic crime films. Accordingly, "3" is very much *a Los Angeles noir* like *Heat* (1995), with the ubiquitous threat of looming forest fires always representing a secondary jeopardy to life and limb. The world itself has become contaminated and unnatural by the "blood sports" of its characters, the episode intimates.

Beyond the intriguing and uncharacteristic Mann vibe, "3" is fascinating in terms of its visuals. David Nutter literally and metaphorically colors the episode scarlet red, in direct response to the thematic leitmotif about blood representing both danger and perhaps, immortality. We see the opening images of red wine in a cracked, overturned glass, then red fire-fighting spray dotting the Los Angeles sky. Crimson lights also shade the blood bank, and even red "berry" sauce at a bloody crime scene puts in an appearance. The episode culminates in a veritable orgy of bloodstains in Kristin's garage, in the oven, on Mulder's unshaven, vulnerable neck, even. The episode is about blood released, *passion* released. And worse, that passion is—as we learn from Kristin—unsavory and self-destructive.

The underlying point here is that Kristin can't escape the allure of her "blood sport" with the Unholy Trinity, and that as much as she attempts to reject it, she is also drawn to it, to the dangerous flame that burns out of control. The apex of quality for film or television is attained when form reflects and augments content, and one can make that case regarding "3." All the trenchant visual material contributes to the disordered nature of the narrative's world.

The scientific truth underlying "3" involves a condition that Mulder mentions in passing: Gunther disease. This illness was named for Dr. Hans Gunther (1884–1956), who discovered the condition, and is also described by doctors as congenital erythropoietin porphyria. Those suffering from this condition show dramatic physical symptoms when exposed to direct sunlight. Such exposure can cause scarring, blistering, and redness of the skin, as "3" demonstrates in one grotesque makeup sequence.

What's ultimately missing in this episode—perhaps because of Scully's absence—is a satisfactory explanation for the Unholy Trinity's ability to regenerate and survive after such severe sun exposure. Were Scully present, she would no doubt have some intriguing theories about this, but of course, she's not here . . . and that's the point. To expand on that point, "3" depicts a world of madness and danger where the ameliorating voice of science and rationality is nowhere to be found. Mulder is living a kind of nihilistic, aimless, connection-less existence in this episode. He's half a man, half a person without Scully—his other eye—to help him "see." He says he isn't sleeping, and clearly he's given up hope regarding Scully's disposition. Mulder then goes out on a case in L.A. and finds himself confronted directly with the idea that there is "no Heaven, no soul . . . just rot and decay."

But of course, some folks get off on rot and decay, on death itself, too. An empty sexual experience, if one is to exist at all in the *X-Files* world, is perfectly placed in "3" because of this dynamic. This is an episode about the ephemeral pleasures of the flesh.

This observation about "no Heaven, no soul . . . just rot and decay" seems backed up by the constant "crisis alerts" due to the forest fires, and by the predatory nature of the Unholy Trinity. They are urban predators who hunt based on society's desire to walk right up to the edge of moral behavior. It isn't hard for them to find willing victims. Pretty clearly, the folks at "Club Tepes" seek new and dangerous pleasures. Mulder ultimately partakes in the darkness with Kristin and has a brief sexual relationship with her. But importantly, he does so not because he is in love with her, but because he has lost hope. He's on a sort of dark "death spiral" in this story, and the episode is dominated by images of life disordered, from the broken wine glasses to the moon turned scarlet red. Seen in this context, "3" is actually Mulder's journey into the heart of darkness and—finally—his rejection of that darkness. These events, including his dalliance with Kristin, are an important part of Mulder's grieving process, and to dismiss "3" out of hand is to ignore what the narrative adds to the character's odyssey. "3" is Mulder's journey through—and out of—hell itself. He realizes he is not as hopeless as Kristin is, nor as desperate. He isn't willing to surrender to the inevitability of death just because "blood tastes dangerous." He is better than that.

So, yes, Scully is missed here, of course, but Gillian Anderson was not available due to her pregnancy and if *The X-Files* ever wanted to tell a story of sexual dalliance and Mulder's flirtation with nihilism, "3" clearly offered the opportunity. It is wonderful that Chris Carter, Morgan and Wong, and the others involved in the episode's creation took a big chance. The shippers who disliked this episode might realize that, in a weird way, Mulder attaches to Kristin because of his feeling for Scully. It's not like—as some fans seem to feel—they are married at this point and he is literally being unfaithful to her. Instead, Mulder is lost, and missing the most important connection in his life. He takes solace in sexual pleasure . . . so sue him.

Accordingly, "3" is precisely what it hopes to be: a walk on the wilder, more dangerous, and more nihilistic side of *The X-Files* equation. "3" may not be a conventional episode, but the story and visualizations are "sweet and thick," in Kristin's descriptive words, layered with ominous *fin de siècle*, Michael Mann-ish imagery. Frankly, there's absolutely no other episode like this one in the *X-Files* canon, and so viewers can either curse it for not treading closely along the accepted path or praise it for its surprises and contrasts. Another way to look at this episode: Without "3," we wouldn't be able to witness our troubled hero take his beginning steps back into the light. You have to fall before you can stand again.

"Colony." Written by Chris Carter. From a Story by David Duchovny and Chris Carter. Directed by Nick Marck. Airdate: February 10, 1995.

"End Game." Written by Frank Spotnitz. Directed by Rob Bowman. Airdate: February 17, 1995.

An alien flying saucer crashes in the ocean and deposits a human-appearing but deadly bounty hunter (Brian Thompson) on Earth. This shape-shifter's task is to eliminate the participants—alien, human, and clone—in a top-secret hybridization program first uncovered by Mulder and Scully with the help of Deep Throat (in "The Erlenmeyer Flask").

Realizing that evidence is being destroyed, Mulder and Scully race to keep the identical-looking hybrids alive. Miraculously, the female of the group appears to be Mulder's long-lost sister, Samantha (Megan Leitch).

While Mulder deals with Samantha's unexpected return and visits his in-shock Mom (Rebecca Toolan) and inscrutable Dad (Peter Donat), Scully unexpectedly tangles with the bounty hunter and is made his captive. Accordingly, Mulder is forced to trade Samantha for Scully, but soon learns that the woman claiming to be Samantha is a clone based on his sister's DNA, not the genuine article. Hoping to garner incontrovertible evidence of extraterrestrial life, Mulder races to the Arctic. There, a U.S. nuclear submarine, the U.S.S. *Allegiance*, is immobilized in the ice, ostensibly by the bounty hunter's downed craft. Beneath the ice fields, Mulder finally meets the murderous bounty hunter and asks him if his sister still lives. . . .

An action-rich and suspenseful mythology story, the second-season doubleheader of "Colony"/"End Game" suggests the inherent and indisputable movie potential of the *X-Files* franchise. Even today, twenty years later, one can screen these two episodes back-to-back and get caught up in the visual and emotional arcs of the Chris Carter/Frank Spotnitz tale

Interestingly, I occasionally encounter folks who claim not to like *The X-Files* Mytharc stories and complain that such tales are too complicated or too difficult to follow. That argument isn't exactly air tight, especially in the case of "Colony"/"End Game," which offers a narrative hook as simple (and violent) as that featured in *The Terminator* (1984). Here, a powerful, musclebound alien bounty hunter—armed with a trademark alien "stiletto"—sets about destroying the fruits of an unauthorized hybridization experiment.

Mulder and Scully attempt to stop the assassin/shape-shifter before all evidence of the experiment is lost, but Mulder is thrown for a loop when his long-missing sister Samantha shows up unexpectedly. Now he must determine the "truth" of the situation. The setup with the mercenary murderer is compelling visually and narratively, and the ostensible return of Samantha packs the requisite emotional wallop. Also, the details of the experiment (if not the ultimate purpose of it) are spelled out crisply and cleanly. If that sort of clean-lined plot doesn't provide the template for the ultimate *X-Files* movie, I don't know what would.

Delightfully, the visuals engineered by directors Nick Marck and Rob Bowman only enhance the feature-film quality of this epic from 1995. There are several amazing shots here (in "End Game") of Mulder walking on the Arctic ice, with a submarine conning tower poking above the cracked surface. The action beats of both parts are absolutely unimpeachable too, with the high point being a brutal, James Bond–like smackdown between X (Steven Williams) and Skinner (Mitch Pileggi) in a cramped elevator. All these efforts pay off richly, and this *X-Files* twofer remains one of the most thrill-packed and important "movie"-style shows of the entire canon.

"Colony"/"End Game" also sees the addition of a remarkable new villain in the *X-Files* canon: Brian Thompson's single-minded, stoic bounty hunter. The physically imposing character and his trademark weapon would return several times in the ensuing years, and he represents something of a departure from the series norm. For one, this character is extraterrestrial in nature, and no bones are made of that fact. The series doesn't attempt to play him two ways. There is no alternative explanation for his presence or mission.

Rather, the Bounty Hunter represents the "alien" side of the conspiracy we detect in many episodes. He is the other shoe dropping: the indication that a human agenda is not the only consideration that matters in this presumably cosmic game of chess. And again like the Terminator, this bounty hunter is unstoppable once he is on the attack. In "End Game," he is particularly brutal with Scully in a well-choreographed and executed motel room fight, and yet there is also the feeling, particularly in the finale, that for this killer, it's nothing personal. The Bounty Hunter is doing his job as efficiently as possible and even seems slightly amused by these obsessive humans and their constant but futile attempts to stop him or get in his way. To enhance the menace of Brian Thompson—already a huge guy, with no camera trickery whatsoever—he is frequently seen in this two-parter from a dramatic low angle.

The events of these two episodes also play as a continuation and at times a deliberate inversion of the action we witnessed in "The Erlenmeyer Flask." That episode, the last of Season One, revealed human-alien hybrid experimentation at a warehouse named Zeus and featured a tense standoff and a hostage-exchange on a bridge at night. Significant suspense arises in this two-parter when the same set piece is repeated, nearly note-for-note. There's another exchange on a bridge at night, and again, an important character is doomed to die there. The repetition of the setting and scenario creates a real sense of inevitability and doom. We've been here before, and we know it isn't going to end well.

One of the key mysteries of *The X-Files* is what happened to Samantha. Was she really abducted by aliens? Or by forces within the government? Or, perhaps, did Mulder make up the whole incident so he could deal with the loss of his sibling? Series writers keep coming back to this central problem and over the course of several years gaze at it from any number of intriguing angles. They provide an alternate explanation for Samantha's disappearance in the fourth-season episode "Paper Hearts" and then, finally, provide a sense of closure about her in the most touching, tragic way possible in the seventh-season two-parter "Sein und Zeit"/"Closure."

In terms of "Colony"/"End Game," this episode suggests that the abducted Samantha at some point became fodder for alien and human genetic scientists. Her DNA forms the foundational research in the hybridization experiment that could, perhaps, save humanity in the event of colonization. But this fact of cloning raises all kinds of moral questions. Can it be said that Samantha is, in fact, immortal now, since her genetic material lives on in so many others? Or is this a kind of assault, or rape, of her human individuality? Did she consent to the experiments, or was she used against her will? Again, "Closure" answers at least a few of these questions, even if obliquely.

One of the most intriguing aspects of these two episodes is Peter Donat's opaque performance as Mulder's dad, Bill. He plays his cards awfully close to the vest here, so we can't tell if he is happy to see his daughter returned or aware that this is, in fact, not his daughter. Given what we know of Bill Mulder's history in the conspiracy, he must have every reason to suspect what this Samantha really is (a genetic copy), and yet he provides Mulder no clue and no solace. Instead, he complains because his wife's hopes are raised and dashed. After he gave up Samantha all those years ago, he presumably doesn't want to relive the trauma it caused his family. He treats the whole thing here like a massive inconvenience and remains an inscrutable, unknowable character. This is okay, however, because there's something very universal and "fatherly" about Mulder's stern, tight-lipped Dad.

"F. Emasculata." Written by Chris Carter and Howard Gordon. Directed by Rob Bowman. Airdate: April 28, 1995.

After a scientist named Torrance is killed by a virulent disease in South America, a package is sent by a mysterious mailer to an inmate in jail in Dinwiddie, Virginia. Inside is a diseased animal leg that soon causes the spread of the deadly disease inside the facility. When two murder suspects escape from prison carrying the fatal contamination and therefore the possibility of mass infection, Mulder and Scully must track down the fugitives and prevent further spread of the terminal contagion.

Scully uncovers evidence that the government and a large pharmaceutical company engineered this "test" as part of some secret operation, but Mulder's first order of business is to catch the last surviving fugitive before he contaminates a busload of innocent people.

In this episode, Mulder and Scully battle a deadly, incredibly contagious disease, and must not only stop its transmission but make some tough choices about how much information the public has a right to know in times of an emergency. What makes this episode by Chris Carter and Howard Gordon such a visceral, throat-tightening entry is the grotesque appearance and nature of the disease. Those infected develop a high fever and almost instantly exhibit throbbing, mushy pustules on their skin. After a time, roughly thirty-six hours, these pulsating sacs actually explode—like overripe zits—ejaculating the disease into the air. In one of the most disgusting scenes I've ever witnessed on network television, a suburban wife and mom is seen here tending to a sick man when a pustule ruptures and splatters the toxic materials in her open mouth and all over her face. On a personal note, my wife still hasn't recovered from the scene in which an infected convict holds a little boy hostage on a bus, and his pustule-deformed face edges perilously close to the child's angelic visage. This moment transmits the horror of contagion perfectly and expresses the fear that we're all vulnerable to disease.

Of course, gore is one quality, but the creeping terror of "F. Emasculata" represents more than good special-effects work. Rather, the disease scenario played out here is frighteningly plausible and, in fact, based on a real incident from the 1980s. In the mid-1990s, the virus or contagion was the new pop-culture bogeyman, even displacing serial killers for a span. Films such as *Outbreak* (1995) tracked the progress of Ebola through a heavily populated American town, and by 1997, UPN aired a (ridiculous) disease- or virus-of-the-week series titled *The Burning Zone* for a season. Hazmat suits were suddenly in vogue and became the *de rigueur* attire of the 1990s horror genre.

All of this disease-oriented material likely originated with a best-selling book: *The Hot Zone* (1994), by Richard Preston. A "terrifying true story," this book explored in nauseating but meticulous detail the outbreak of a deadly Ebola virus in a monkey storage facility, Hazelton Laboratories, in 1989. The facility, much like the prison in *The X-Files*, was located in Virginia, but in Reston rather than Dinwiddie. In real life, the CDC investigated the outbreak, and the book also details the author's exploration of the lab building where it occurred, later demolished in 1995. Now it's a KinderCare.

The details of the Ebola virus as recounted in *The Hot Zone* (on page 24) are enough to make anyone sick or simply scared to death. Preston writes of victims vomiting blood, the sound of a "bed sheet being torn in half" (the noise of bowels opening and "venting blood from the anus"), and other body horrors that make vampires, werewolves, and other monsters seem innocuous by comparison.

What remains rather amazing about "F. Emasculata" is not only that it follows in broad strokes the details of *The Hot Zone* (in terms of location), but that it is actually far gorier and more disturbing than *Outbreak* was, and that film was released theatrically. This episode is extremely graphic and forthright about its depiction of disease in a way the movie simply isn't. Because it pulls no punches, "F. Emasculata" has long been a favorite episode. It brilliantly explores the notion of a genie loosed from the bottle; of a danger that, once uncorked, is difficult to catch up with and contain.

Also, the no-bullshit resolution of "F. Emasculata" is commendable. In movies such as *Outbreak* and TV series such as *The Burning Zone*, a miraculous cure is always found in the nick of time, and major characters are spared an agonizing and disgusting death. Life rarely turns out so neatly. In "F. Emasculata" no cure is developed. The outbreak simply is contained while the disease burns itself out. I much prefer that dramatic resolution to any nonsense about discovering some cure to a deadly disease on the spot and on the fly. It's good that this episode doesn't go there. *The X-Files* is a brilliant series precisely because it always keeps one foot grounded in reality.

Although the government is a crucial player in this particular conspiracy, "F. Emasculata" reserves its greatest contempt for Pinck Pharmaceuticals, the big company that has orchestrated the outbreak to determine how the toxin affects human beings. Why? So the company can circumvent years of FDA testing. In other words, the company couldn't wait to make money . . . and so people had to die. Not surprisingly, this big business chose the population with the least power and freedom to use as guinea pigs: prison convicts.

So in this case, unregulated, irresponsible Big Business is the enemy, though certainly the government's role is a crucible for debate. Is it right for the government to hide the truth of the disease from the American public, knowing that the truth could cause a panic and costs lives? Or should the government reveal all in the name of disclosure and public safety? "Controlling the information," as the episode points out, is about who possesses power and who doesn't. This debate relates to Mulder's journey. He wants the public to know the truth and for the guilty to be held to account.

But, of course, there is no evidence to support his story, and so he risks becoming the story himself. The question becomes: how much does the public deserve to know, and when does it deserve to know it? Personally, I'm of the mind that the truth in situations like this must come out, but if reporting it as "breaking news" causes a panic—*and costs lives*—it's best to tread carefully and get all the facts first. That's not an approach our current mainstream press is very good at.

In simple horror terms, "F. Emasculata" is an exploration of subversion by microorganism; of the way that tiny invaders can reshape our bodies and threaten our very lives. A disease is not a monster that can be fought with guns or knives, but one that multiplies and spreads, and enacts its monstrous work without conscience or even consciousness. It's difficult to fight an enemy like that, one that can pop up, like a multiheaded Hydra, and transform the healthiest person in the world into a disease producer or factory.

This idea is absolutely terrifying, which is no doubt why "F. Emasculata" remains such a visceral viewing experience. Even today, this episode plays more like science fact than science fiction, especially given the Ebola outbreak of 2014 in Liberia and Sierra Leone.

9

New Voices

Season Three (1995–1996)

The third season of *The X-Files*, airing from late September 1995 through May 1996, adds two crucial philosophical voices or tones to the developing series. These are, in no particular order, humor and nihilism.

Several episodes in this season begin showcasing a new sense of humor or lightness about Mulder and Scully's world, perhaps as a counterbalance to the gravity of the conspiracy, while other stories overrule the worldviews of belief and skepticism with the idea that there is actually nothing to believe in and that belief itself is an unnecessary construct in a world without meaning. In other words, Mulder and Scully may choose to believe what they want to believe, but the universe itself is an absurd place and there is no purpose to any of it. Their efforts to impose meaning or understanding on the world are fruitless in an arena where, finally, there is no concrete or objective truth.

In terms of humor, episodes such as "Syzygy" and "Quagmire" showcase a lighter side of *The X-Files*. In the former, Scully and Mulder start bickering like an old married couple while under the influence of a rare planetary or astrological alignment. And in the latter, they are stranded on a tiny island at night while hunting for the U.S. equivalent of the Loch Ness Monster, Big Blue, when their boat sinks. This predicament gives them the opportunity to discuss their own mortality and feelings about mortality, but the scene ends with a wicked joke. They were trapped all along in shallow water and could have walked to safety at any time.

Why is humor such an important factor on *The X-Files*? Perhaps only because it reflects reality. Even in grave situations, humans are drawn to laughter or to embarrassing situations. It makes sense that Mulder and Scully would sometimes view their lives and their work in this fashion, or be seen by others as amusing. They are not perfect, and to register with the viewer as fully human, the audience must sometimes recognize that their adventures could be interpreted, well, as funny.

In terms of nihilism, one must face the third-season *X-Files* episodes penned by writer Darin Morgan. In the second season, the same author contributed a tale, "Humbug," about a town of circus freaks in Florida. In the third season, however, tales such as "Clyde Bruckman's Final Repose" and "Jose Chung's from Outer Space" find Mulder and Scully inhabiting an absurd universe, one of coincidences and even psychic powers, but about which there seems to be no rhyme or reason. Like "Syzygy" and "Quagmire," these tales are funny too, but there is also a darkness underlying the Morgan stories that is, ultimately, difficult to shake. These episodes are brilliantly written, performed, and directed, to be sure, and view a familiar universe through a new and valuable lens. But in a show about the search of the truth, the suggestion that there is finally no truth to reckon with is a viewpoint that, perhaps, should only be explored on a limited basis.

The third season of *The X-Files*, the last to air on Friday nights at 9:00 p.m., also introduces the sinister force actually working against humanity, the black oil, and causes more heartbreak for Scully, this time over the death of her sister, Melissa.

Mytharc Notes

The Mytharc grows substantially in the third season, with several two-part episodes charting the methods and purposes of the dark conspiracy, or the Syndicate. The two-part episode "Nisei"/"731" begins with a "real" alien autopsy videotape and leads into the unexpected discovery of surgical theaters inside trains and a kind of hidden or secret railway utilized by the Syndicate. Furthermore, the same two-parter introduces the idea that nations are competing for access to alien materials and conducting their own experiments to create a human-alien hybrid. Underlying this concept are, not unexpectedly, references to real life.

Unit 731 was the name of a Japanese research unit that was responsible for over 3,000 deaths from 1937 to 1945. Officially known as the Epidemic Prevention and Water Purification Department and Kwantung Army, located in Pingfing, Manchukuo, the unit was commanded by General Shiro Ishii, and it conducted a series of human tests, all under the code name "Maruta." Many prisoners of war were vivisected without anesthesia and infected with diseases. Some patients had limbs amputated or frozen, while others were subjected to experiments in blood loss. The tests were not limited to men, and subjects included women and children.

The tests at Unit 731 didn't stop with the destruction of the central compound in the final days of the war. Instead, several Unit 731 physicians were secretly granted immunity for their crimes on the condition that they handed over their research and findings to American authorities. In *The X-Files* continuity, the Unit 731 infrastructure and personnel found a new reason to continue their work: the creation of a human-alien hybrid. In "Nisei" and "731," Scully also recognizes or remembers the train as being similar to the one where she was forced to undergo tests during her abduction. In fact, she recognizes Doctor Ishimara (Robert Ito) as one of the men who worked on her. These details reveal that though Scully may have been spirited away physically by aliens, she was actually in the care of men during her absence. In later stories and seasons, we learn that the Cigarette Smoking Man is the one who orders and directs these tests.

Another double or two-part episode in Season Three, "Piper Maru"/"Apocrypha," introduces the primary nonhuman villain of the Mytharc, the black oil or black cancer. This medium is being used by an alien life-form to "body jump" and possess different human hosts, so as to advance its agenda. The special effects involving the black oil are especially harrowing. Black goop or colloidal material separates into what look like tiny black worms, which then inch their way into human cavities, including nostrils, ears, and eyeballs. The series' typical shot to depict infection is of a black cloud obscuring the host's human eye and then fading away, integrated into the system. The black oil is a crucial piece of the conspiracy puzzle, and "Apocrypha" suggests that forces in authority have known about it since 1953 and the ill-fated voyage of an American submarine called the *Zeus Faber.*

"Piper Maru" and "Apocrypha" also bring back Alex Krycek, now an independent agent selling secrets in the Far East. He is possessed by the black oil for a time, before releasing it (involuntarily) from his cavities in a remote location, a nuclear weapons silo in North Dakota. The vault, not coincidentally, is numbered 1013, after Ten Thirteen productions.

As was the case with Season Two, Season Three ends with a Mytharc cliffhanger. In "Talitha Cumi," Mulder and Scully encounter a man with the power to heal any injury, Jeremiah Smith (Roy Thinnes), and Mulder learns that his mother, Teena Mulder (Rebecca Toolan), may have in her possession an alien weapon—the stiletto—that the Cigarette Smoking Man very much desires.

Season Highlights

"Clyde Bruckman's Final Repose." Written by Darin Morgan. Directed by David Nutter. Airdate: October 13, 1995.

A serial killer (Stu Charno) is murdering fortune tellers and other professional prognosticators, and Scully and Mulder investigate the case. When the pop guru known as the Stupendous Yappi (Jaap Broeker) fails to come up with any useful leads, Mulder and Scully recruit real-life psychic/would-be-victim/insurance salesman Clyde Bruckman to help.

Bruckman boasts the unusual (though limited) ability to predict the exact manner of death for any individual he comes in contact with. This knowledge has come to haunt him and take all the joy from his life. When the killer finally comes for Bruckman, Mulder and Scully must protect him from a fate he has already witnessed in visions and dreams.

"Clyde Bruckman's Final Repose" brings that aforementioned new philosophy, existentialism, to *The X-Files* in force, straight from one-of-a-kind writer Darin Morgan Previously, on the show, we have seen commentary about belief vs. skepticism and religion vs. science. However, this episode introduces to the series the concept of caustic, cynical nihilism. In a series that often concerns faith, commitment, truth, and "never giving up," this (brief) turn toward nihilism nonetheless—and quite unexpectedly—works splendidly, in part because writer Morgan permits his own creation, Clyde Bruckman (Peter Boyle), to take and hold center stage.

Mulder and Scully are still the same characters we have known and loved, but Bruckman rivets the attention and proves a touching and funny protagonist in the process. Peter Boyle earned an Emmy Award for his remarkable turn in this episode, and deservedly so. He creates a heart-breaking, unforgettable character here.

At one point in "Clyde Bruckman's Final Repose," Mulder trenchantly asks Boyle's character: "If the future is written, why bother to do anything?" Bruckman's reply—that Mulder "gets" or understands perfectly the existential crisis of his life—is not only funny but intensely sad as well. Because he knows "the end," Bruckman is a man who has given up on the journey. Indeed, this is a man cursed by his own belief system—and by his mysterious gift of insight—in a way that he simply can't overcome. Bruckman has neither a Scully nor a Mulder to play or debate against in his day-to-day life and instead walks a lonely, isolated road. His opposite number—his misshapen reflection, in fact—might be said to be the episode's killer, who has utilized his brand of nihilism to make his life meaningful . . . through negation or murder.

Like Boyle, author Darin Morgan won an Emmy Award for his brilliant work here, and it is plain to see from his episodes of *The X-Files* and *Millennium* (1996–1999) that his writing reflects a pretty singular worldview. Morgan's episodes of the two Chris Carter series often feature a new hero or protagonist from outside the traditional format and dramatis personae. That hero is Bruckman here and Jose Chung in "Jose Chung's "From Outer Space" and "Jose Chung's Doomsday Defense." The four devils in "Somehow, Satan Got Behind Me" also cleverly invert the premise of *Millennium* and reveal the story of Frank Black from the perspective of his worst enemies, there the protagonists in the drama.

Uniquely, all these "new" series protagonists boast the cynical strand of nihilism I note above. These characters are outsiders who believe that life is absurd or pointless. Similarly, Bruckman and Chung come across as jaundiced and highly intelligent older men who, despite their existential beliefs, desire nothing more than to be loved and remembered fondly. Both "Clyde Bruckman's Final Repose" and "Jose Chung's Doomsday Defense" end with the untimely death of this particular brand of Darin Morgan character; a death that is noted and memorialized by more familiar elements of the series proper, either Scully or Frank Black thus engendering that desired sympathy and even love. This scenario, in both cases, suggests that human immortality arises not via the afterlife (which some psychic phenomena seem to promise), but rather through the simple auspices of human memory. Clyde Bruckman and Jose Chung will be remembered because they were, in the end, *loved* by someone. It's as simple as that.

It is not only life itself that seems absurd in this episode of *The X-Files*. Psychic or paranormal abilities are also viewed through this rubric of cynical nihilism. Such powers are seen through a ruthlessly, mercilessly logical filter, so much so that they seem absurd on their face. Yappi is a sensational showman, nothing more. He uses clues he knows will come back as "hits" (like a corpse being deposited near water). In other words, he's a charlatan.

And Bruckman's abilities are so limited that he can't use them in any pro-social fashion. He can't even utilize them in an avaricious way, like picking the winning Lotto numbers. The message here seems to be that if psychic powers do exist, they are a burden and of no use to anyone, but especially the percipient. In Greek myth, Cassandra was a figure who had great insight but was not believed. In *The X-Files*, Clyde Bruckman is a figure who has terrible insight and is haunted by it.

Morgan also applies his apparent belief system to the bread and butter of *The X-Files*: behavioral science. Here, again and again, fortune tellers and agents of law enforcement attempt to classify the killer as a man who doesn't know why he does the things he does, as if that description is in any way useful. These men and women seek to put him in a little box and, because they have placed him there, "understand him."

But Clyde Bruckman—the typical Darin Morgan outsider—cuts through that kind of classification talk by noting plainly and simply that the killer is a "homicidal maniac." He's insane and murderous, and that's the only sense or knowledge to be gleaned from him. This is a surprisingly vehement dismissal of science and rationalism, which seeks to classify killers by particular disorders. The answer instead is that a guy like this serial killer is simply evil.

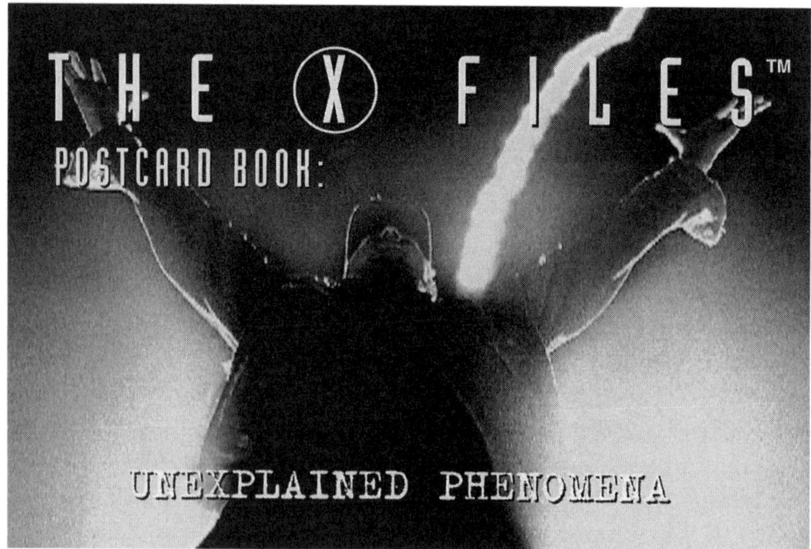

This postcard book from *The X-Files* features a still on the cover from the third-season episode "D.P.O.," about a boy who can cause lightning strikes.

And if all of life is predictable—if you know its end—then knowing the "why" of someone's behavior becomes less crucial, or even necessary. If there is such a thing as predestination, then free will doesn't exist. The killer kills simply because he must, because he is sick and murderous and that's his destiny. By pointing out this simple fact of his behavior (which the killer apparently appreciates), Bruckman (and thus Morgan) exposes and refutes fully the notion that a person can be totally understood or analyzed by another human being or via the auspices of science. This belief fits in with the nihilistic streak in Morgan's work because it suggests that those who seek answers—just like those who bother to do anything when the future is already known—are engaged in a wild goose chase.

In an even more wicked way, Morgan forges a connection here between psychic prognosticators and behavioral scientists. In the end, both are simply reading tea leaves. They aren't really telling us anything we don't already know, or at least intuit, about life, or criminals.

For all its humor, then, "Clyde Bruckman's Final Repose" is an unremittingly dark episode of *The X-Files*. It features disturbing imagery of a cute little dog lapping up its dead owner's blood and views of a human body progressively rotting in the grave. The bit with the dog is especially important. It suggests that nature trumps everything else. Dogs need to eat, and if eating their dead master enables them to survive, they'll do it. Similarly, it is our nature to try to avoid death, but death is still coming for all of us anyway.

The episode climaxes with a devastating suicide. In that final, bleak act, however, one might glean if not hope, then some understanding. Even if belief is a delusion, it's a delusion that keeps us going, in some important sense. Scully and Mulder are driven to go on living by their desire to know the truth, either through the paranormal, religion, or science.

Nihilism and absurdity—whatever their appeal to the intellect—don't offer much by way of hope. Hope is the one emotion that Bruckman could never feel, even though he saw a vision of himself being cared for tenderly by Scully. To make that vision a reality, he had to die.

Morgan's contributions to both *The X-Files* and *Millennium* are paradoxically both the funniest and the darkest installments, in some ways. The humor cloaks the existential terror most of the time, but not universally. And indeed, that's part of this episode's charm. "Clyde Bruckman's Final Repose" is haunting and thought-provoking, and more than a little sad. Clyde seems cursed by the gods (or by life itself), and so the episode might more aptly be titled "The Tragedy of Clyde Bruckman."

In terms of ongoing character touches, this episode introduces Scully's dog, Queequeg, who we see on a recurring basis through "Quagmire." And it also introduces the subtextual idea that Scully is immortal, a concept continued in the sixth-season entry "Tithonus," and into the seventh-season entry "En Ami." Mulder's sex obsession, heretofore indicated by his love of porn, is also given a shout-out when Bruckman determines the manner of his eventual death: auto-erotic asphyxiation.

Finally, this episode acts as a humorous bookend to "Beyond the Sea." In that first-season installment, Mulder tricked Boggs (Brad Dourif) by providing him a patch of fabric from his own basketball shirt, in hopes that Boggs, the psychometrist, would assume it was an item belonging to the victim. He fell for it.

In "Clyde Bruckman's Final Repose," Bruckman picks up a swatch of fabric and states it is from the same basketball Jersey. Mulder offhandedly tells him he's wrong. . . .

"2Shy." Written by Jeffrey Vlaming. Directed by David Nutter. Airdate: November 3, 1995.

In Cleveland, Ohio, a serial killer selects his victims over the Internet, meeting them in a lonely hearts chat room for "big and beautiful" women. But this is no ordinary stalker: he's a genetic mutant who eats the fatty tissue from his victims. 2Shy, as the killer calls himself on the Internet, can't produce adipose and other fatty materials, so he must ingest them from others to remain alive.

While Scully rejects the notion of "fat-sucking vampires," Mulder is convinced that the duo is dealing with a genetically different creature who kills not out of psychosis, but from a desperate physiological drive.

"2Shy" considers 1990s human and social mores in terms of a brand new technological advance: the Internet. Today, the term "Internet predator" is a common one, and it defines a person who utilizes the World Wide Web for purposes of unsavory or even illegal activities. "2Shy" imagines a literal predator of this sort: a genetic mutant, Virgil Incanto (Timothy Carhart), who talks to other humans on the Net to garner that which his biology can't provide—fat cells. In other words, and in the lingo of the episode, Incanto is indeed a "fat-sucking vampire."

But perhaps more impressive than its imagination of a predator for the Internet Age, Jeffrey Vlaming's "2Shy" imagines the hunted, the herd from which the killer selects the weakest numbers. And indeed, it is these hunted characters that make the episode unforgettable. Because they are overweight and middle-aged vulnerable women, they are not considered either attractive or desirable by society at large. This fact, in conjunction with the anonymity offered by Internet chat rooms and the like, makes them the perfect victim of the 1990s. Even society's "PC" (politically correct) descriptors like "big and beautiful" don't serve their purpose. These euphemisms aren't widely considered true or supportive, merely polite.

Accordingly, the intelligent predator of the episode, a literate expert on Italian sixteenth-century romantic poetry, uses the language of the day to enhance his victims' vulnerability. His name—Incanto—means "to sing," and the villainous predator's song is aimed right at those who are most attuned to its melody.

"2Shy" is a sad episode in many ways, since it focuses on a group of loving, intelligent, caring women who—primarily because of their weight—have been discarded by society. They don't adhere to society's image of a woman, and this episode also gazes at the direct and insensitive ways that society—largely male society—prosecutes the values of the whole. Scully encounters a police detective, Cross, who objects to the idea of a woman being involved in an investigation that concerns murder. For instance, he is shocked that Scully is "allowed" to conduct an official autopsy and is capable of doing it for herself. He cloaks his prejudiced observations in the shroud of "truth." "I'm not being sexist here, just honest," he declares, as if this comment is an exoneration or vindication of his point of view.

There's an explicit link between the prejudice Scully faces and the one that Incanto's victims do. The episode cleverly links them, revealing how women are subject to male views and patriarchal attitudes. Judging a woman unworthy of being loved because of her weight is just the same sort of "honest" commentary that the detective brazenly offers Scully and that has destroyed the self-worth of an entire generation. Scully sees how both monster and man prey on the insecurities of the fairer sex in "2Shy." The detective can't be bothered to temper his "honest" feelings about the proper behavior and role of women in society, and Incanto takes the opposite approach, playing the sensitive "evolved" man while using fangless Internet handles like "Timid" and "2Shy" that draw in the vulnerable.

It's clear that "2Shy" is also about the way the Internet builds a false sense of intimacy between people. Those who talk with others in anonymous chat rooms believe they are seeing right into the soul of Virgil Incanto, unaware that he is a deceiver. At one point in the episode, one of the victims (a woman of heartbreaking earnestness) says of Incanto—before she has even cast eyes on him—"it's not like he's some stranger." She's been chatting with him every day for the "last few months," she assures a friend, as if this fact means that, somehow, she *really* knows what is in his heart.

In the last few years we have learned about "catfishing" on the Internet, the act of pretending to be someone you are not, so as to make friends with objects, essentially, of personal desire. This is Incanto's game, and it's rather amazing and prophetic that *The X-Files* was able to chart this phenomenon in the pre-2000 age of the Internet. *The X-Files* universally impresses because it targets some crucial aspect of our 1990s culture and then spins a horror story out of it. "2Shy" is a brilliant case in point, utilizing then-prominent fears about the rise of Internet predators to tell a story about loneliness and desperation

I don't always discuss guest performances in these analyses, but I must make note here of Timothy Carhart's Incanto and Catherine Paolone's Ellen Kaminsky. Carhart plays a man who is dead behind the eyes, as if he realizes fully that he can never achieve intimacy with another person . . . only achieve biological sustenance from them. There is no joy, no love, no humanity left in this man. Incanto's biological needs have made him, psychologically, a self-justifying monster. Accordingly, he may be the most disturbing *X-Files* "monster" since Donnie Pfaster in "Irresistible."

Oppositely, Paolone's Ellen is the walking wounded. She's been hurt before and thus finds it difficult to trust anyone. Yet she wants more than anything to trust *someone.* It is nearly a tragedy that Ellen should hook up with the predatory Incanto. Her desire to be loved—a desire all humans share—is the very thing that nearly brings her to an untimely end, and I find her character, and her sense of longing, haunting. There are moments of palpable, authentic terror in "2Shy" because of Paolone's sympathetic performance and Carhart's menacing one.

"War of the Coprophages." Written by Darin Morgan. Directed by Kim Manners. Airdate: January 5, 1996.

The tiny town of Miller's Grove, Massachusetts, has a bad bug problem. It is teeming with cockroaches, and murderous ones at that. Mulder is in town to investigate reports of UFO activity, but the roach attacks merit his full attention soon enough.

Although Scully scuttles the notion of swarming, attacking cockroaches, Mulder learns of a top-secret Department of Agriculture experiment in town examining a new breed of roaches. More curious than that, however, is evidence that suggests the roaches may be metallic, perhaps alien probes sent from another world to examine this planet.

Writer Darin Morgan returns to *The X-Files* with "The War of the Coprophages," another humorous installment that gazes at humanity with unblinking, unromantic eyes. The story involves the "insect mind" as it relates to cockroaches. However, "The War of the Coprophages" then compares the relative purity and simplicity of the insect mind to the "overdeveloped" human mind, which permits nonuseful responses to threats; responses such as paranoia or hysteria. These mad human responses are highlighted in the episode's townspeople of Miller's Grove, who display ignorance and terror in the face of the impossible: an apparent concentrated attack on the town by cockroaches. The town name is meant to represent hysteria and irrationality, since it is a variation of "Grover's Mill," the town name in Orson Welle's radio broadcast of War of the Worlds.

All the gruesome deaths in the episode are a result not of roach attacks but of irrational human responses to the proximity of roaches, things that our eyes and mind register as monsters. In fact, the gory deaths in the episode have the same effect on us as viewers as they do on the townspeople. We are not able to put aside our discomfort with the bugs long enough to take them out of the "suspect pool."

Finally, the last piece of this complex and funny puzzle is the fact that some of the roaches featured in the episode are outside observers of mankind, alien probes who are visiting our world and find us with all our overdeveloped neuroses and psychoses on display in this episode.

In "War of the Coprophages," the gorgeous and intelligent Dr. Bambi Berenbaum (Bobbie Phillips) notes that cockroaches "eat, sleep, defecate, and procreate" and yet have no sense of romance, mythology, or exaggerated sense of importance about these rudimentary activities. This commentary is a deliberate voicing of Morgan's theme in the episode that beings such as cockroaches see life in a clear, practical, and real way, a way that human beings simply do not. This thesis applies as well to our treatment of insects, as the episode's final scene reveals.

Even intelligent, educated, sensitive Fox Mulder can't overcome his irrational human programming of terror when confronted with an insect. In the end—and even in light of everything he now believes about the cockroaches of Miller's Grove—he can't resist the temptation to squash a bug. His disgust and terror are ingrained. They are hardwired. And patently irrational to boot.

"War of the Coprophages" twice makes mention of the greatest science fiction film ever made, *Planet of the Apes* (1968), and the final dialogue on the beach shared between Dr. Zaius (Maurice Evans) and Colonel Taylor (Charlton Heston). This discussion is explicitly about destiny and how it exists, whether Taylor will "like what he finds" or not. In the case of "War of the Coprophages," our human destiny, suggests Morgan, is irrationality: a fear of that which is different. We gaze at bugs (or any other creature) across a vast gulf of suspicion and fear.

The theme that "irrationality is our destiny" plays out in other aspects of the tale as well. Mulder lies and claims that he loves insects, all in an attempt to woo the desirable Bambi. He has placed great importance on winning this attractive woman, so much so that he would betray his own core principles, and friendships, as we see in his curt telephone responses to Scully once Bambi is in the picture. Genetic programming has overridden his common sense.

Meanwhile, Scully—who provides a lecture on rationality to the townspeople of Miller's Grove—is equally irrational. She has proven beyond a shadow of a doubt that all the deaths in the Massachusetts town are unrelated, and that there is no need for her to travel to the burg to check things out. But when Mulder mentions Dr. "Bambi" on the telephone, Scully races up to the scene of the crime, jealous and afraid of being outclassed by the entomologist. Again, the inference is that we place unnecessary importance on and mythology around simple acts, like procreation.

The "War of the Coprophages" also returns *The X-Files* to its epistolary roots, by featuring Mulder's written (and voice-over-narrated) summation of the tale. His report concerns man's apparent inability to rise above his hardwired fears and irrationalities, and Mulder is clear-headed in his presentation. He wonders what aliens must make of us and our emotional, nonsensical acts. Then, acting emotionally and nonsensically, he squashes a bug with the case report file.

This is a perfect Morgan-style ending to the episode. This writer often delves into nihilism and absurdity, and here he positions Mulder—our protagonist—as someone totally incapable of growth, no matter the power of his intellect.

We're all in the same boat, victims of our genetic programming.

"Pusher." Written by Vince Gilligan. Directed by Rob Bowman. Airdate: February 23, 1996.

A man named Robert Patrick Modell (Robert Wisden) fancies himself a "ronin" or samurai without a master and possesses the telepathic ability to place thoughts and suggestions into the minds of others. He has used this talent to "push" his will on others and committed murder-for-hire some fourteen times. But he has always escaped notice, or even capture.

After "Pusher" telepathically forces a police officer to drive into an oncoming truck, Mulder and Scully begin to hunt this unusual assassin. They learn that his powers originate from a brain tumor Modell has willfully allowed to go untreated.

An FBI sting goes awry when Pusher suggests that an agent immolate himself, but Modell is captured. He escapes from justice by using his ability to influence the presiding judge at court, leaving Mulder no choice but to face this dangerous Svengali in a Russian roulette showdown.

Part of the reason this episode from Vince Gilligan succeeds so splendidly is because it establishes a nasty psychic assassin, Robert Patrick Modell (Robert Wisden), as a dark reflection of Mulder. Indeed, the character of Modell desires, more than anything, a "worthy adversary." He finds that personality in Mulder, in his opposite. Modell and Mulder are both widely known by nicknames ("Pusher" and "Spooky," respectively), and even their last names suggest a subconscious connection. "Modell" and "Mulder" have the same number of letters (six each), and both start with "M," but "Modell" switches the positioning of the "l" and "d" in "Mulder." The episode thus goes to some length—right down to surnames—to suggest that these arch-nemeses bear some kind of relationship or symbiosis.

To describe the relationship further, it is necessary to consider the characters' backgrounds. Mulder is a rational, Oxford-educated behavioral psychologist. He is a man of reason and science, and of education. Yet despite these incredible achievements, he longs only to believe, to be shown something that is not of what we might term the rational world. Although Mulder is clearly a genius, he is derided and mocked because of his choice to pursue tales of aliens, ghosts, and monsters. He has become not what he knows but what he hunts—"Spooky" Mulder.

By contrast, Modell is a man who has failed at every attempt to achieve. He had a middling military career after being rejected by the Marines, and he was later rejected from the FBI, too. A physical condition, however, grants him the very "psychic" power that Mulder has always wished to quantify. Without trying, Modell has achieved, in some sense, what Mulder has never been able to achieve for himself: personal knowledge of an "extreme possibility." Like

Mulder, Modell is known for his behavior, for pushing his will on others. He is not a great assassin or samurai but rather, merely "Pusher."

So on one hand you have a man of reason and achievement longing to validate the mysteries of the world, and on the other you have a man who is one of those mysteries, who has failed to achieve, under his own auspices, any kind of positive legacy.

Accordingly, the two men meet on the field of battle—or Russian roulette—and determine which of them, which mirror image, is superior. Ironically, Mulder succeeds and proves victorious not only because of his own skill-set or mind-set, but because he has one advantage Modell lacks: Agent Dana Scully. At a critical moment, Scully is there to help Mulder, and her quick thinking frees Fox from Modell's grip. This is the decisive move or checkmate, the shattering of a deadlock between the Mulder/Modell connection.

"Pusher" works artistically in terms of its imagery and color scheme, too. The bravura trailer visually primes the audiences for its brutal punctuation, a car accident involving a very large truck, by repeatedly depicting aspects of the world as *blue,* as if the episode itself is working on *our* psyches as Modell works on the psyches of his victim with the repetition of the phrase "Cerulean Blue." The final moments of "Pusher," the game of Russian roulette, work so brilliantly when, rationally, we know Mulder must survive to continue the series, because this *X-Files* episode works on the level of imagery. And that imagery suggests that Modell is in control.

This is most plain, visually, in the episode's teaser. After one viewing, we know the punctuation: Modell engineers his break from custody by making it so that the police driver of his car cannot see an oncoming truck for "Cerulean Hauling." In other words, cerulean blue is blotted out from that man's landscape. Leading up to that moment, however, shades of blue are everywhere—and suspiciously so—in Modell's world. We see blue shopping carts. Modell wears blue. The policemen wear blue jackets. Even the world, as seen outside the grocery store, boasts a blue tint. The subconscious impression, then, is that this is Modell's world and that he is entirely in command of it.

After seeing Modell give a detective, Frank Burst, a heart attack during a telephone conversation, Modell's power is established to an even more powerful degree. By the time we get to the final one-on-one battle between Modell and Mulder, it hardly seems like a fair fight. Mulder is outmatched, and to prove it, the episode even features footage of Paul Wegener as Svengali from the 1927 film of the same name. Although the name Svengali originates from the 1894 novel *Trilby* by George du Maurier, today we all recognize the character as one who can control the will of others, a visual symbol representing Pusher's impossible-to-deny abilities.

"Jose Chung's from Outer Space." Written by Darin Morgan. Directed by Rob Bowman. Airdate: April 12, 1996.

Two teens in Klass County, Washington, are imperiled on the way home from their first date by dueling aliens. A popular author, Jose Chung (Charles Nelson Reilly), interviews Scully about the case, and she recounts her perception of it. Scully and Mulder have a difference of opinion about the truth of the case, however. Mulder believes there was a genuine alien abduction, while Scully believes the matter was date rape and ensuing post-traumatic stress.

Meanwhile, a witness to the odd events of that night, Rocky (William Lucking), claims that a third alien—one from the Earth's molten core and named Lord Kimbote—was involved, as were two unearthly Men in Black.

Unable to discern the truth for himself, Chung hopes to interview a reluctant Mulder about what really happened that fateful night.

Darin Morgan's stories for *The X-Files* are something of a philosophical anomaly. Here, while Mulder and Scully typically voice facets of belief or skepticism, Morgan often populates his episodes with a lead character who is a surrogate for his own belief system: nihilism. That surrogate in "Jose Chung's from Outer Space" is an opportunistic "non-fiction/science-fiction" writer, Jose Chung (Charles Nelson Reilly), who is seeking a quick buck by writing a history of an alien abduction experience. And at one point in the episode, Chung directly diagrams this episode's theme: "Truth is as subjective as reality."

This statement of principle, as you may detect, is deliberately and distinctively at odds with a series that made famous the catch-phrase "The truth is out there."

How can truth be subjective if it exists in some definable place, "out there?" If it is subjective, is the truth even worth seeking or pursuing? This thematic tension represents merely one glory of *The X-Files* as a multilayered and meaningful work of art. The Chris Carter series can accommodate different points of view and different philosophies so long as Mulder and Scully remain true to their beliefs and histories as the audience understands them. Morgan's episodes are so much fun—and so provocative—because he stretches the boundaries a bit but never totally breaks them. In this case, the lead protagonist role is taken by Chung, an act that permits the storyteller to present a different philosophy while sacrificing nothing we know in terms of continuity.

To wit, the alien abduction and Mulder and Scully's role in its investigation are largely recounted in flashbacks this episode. Under this creative paradigm, memories are "portrayed" or dramatized as answers to Chung's probing interview questions. In true *Rashomon* (1950) style, the viewer has no way of knowing or verifying the honesty of each account. The author's point that the truth is subjective becomes manifest in the very absurdity of many witness reports.

This is a funny development but also a complex one, for it leads to Darin Morgan's final, existential truth about our human existence. Since there is no objective truth for us dwelling here on Earth, only interpretations of it, we are truly—in a variation of *Close Encounters'* (1977) ad campaign—"alone."

I'm not passing negative judgment on this aspect of the episode, but a deep cynicism shines through in "Jose Chung's from Outer Space." That cynicism concerns humanity's eternal quest to know the truth. Through a series of reenacted events related to one bizarre alien encounter, this episode suggests that human memories are inherently and fatally flawed and therefore unreliable arbiters of fact or history. For one thing, humans may lie on purpose, without others knowing it. To wit, we learn that the teenagers involved in the close encounter actually had sex on their date and are desperate to hide this fact from their parents. So memory being wrong is one thing, but some people encourage wrong interpretations because they have hidden or unknowable agendas.

Morgan's critique of truth goes further. "Jose Chung's from Outer Space" also expresses doubt in truth-searching tools, ones developed under the auspices of man's science; tools such as hypnosis. Here, hypnosis is termed explicitly in the dialogue as a procedure which "worsens" rather than "enhances" human memory. In other words, human memory is bad but memories resurfaced during hypnosis are even worse. Intriguingly, the episode also indicates that the desire to know the truth—in this case to believe in alien life-forms—is merely a primal scream shouted in response to a nihilistic human existence, and a delusion or blind alley fostered and encouraged by a complicit mass media. The episode's first shot, for instance, is of an object (actually a work crew's crane) that could easily be mistaken for a UFO.

In fact, this inaugural image knowingly harks back to the first sequence in *Star Wars* (1977), with the triangular Star Destroyer intersecting the frame, as well as a moment from *Close Encounters* (1977), wherein workman Roy Neary (Richard Dreyfuss) spots a large object overhead, hovering in the dark Muncie sky. Those productions nurture in us, the episode suggests, some feeling or sense of romanticism about the nature of life and the universe. It's a false or unfounded romanticism, according to Morgan/Chung.

More important, however, is the fact that in this shot we *believe* we're seeing a spaceship at first glance. As we watch longer, however, we become aware that we are actually seeing something much more mundane, something utilitarian and man-made. No real wonders exist in the world. The wonders are actually just mistakes in our perception.

This visual joke thus perfectly reflects the idea that we can't ever be sure that we are correctly seeing, registering, and interpreting external stimuli. Our desire for the romantic (look, it's a spaceship!) supersedes our rationality (oh, it's a work crane!), and our brain seems to respond to our deeply held desire to see that which plainly isn't there. And if this is so, it means that our perception, our memory, our very *truth*, is suspect. At the end of the same scene, we witness the appearance of an intentionally silly-looking "monster," Lord Kimbote. This hairy, cyclopean thing seems based on an amalgamation of creatures from 1960s Ray Harryhausen films. No matter—our eyes immediately discount Kimbote as fake or corny.

Here's the point, however. We don't visually "read" the Greys nearby in the same dismissive fashion. On the contrary, they seem "real" in a way that Kimbote just does not (perhaps because the Greys reflect 1990s mythology instead of 1960s mythology/fantasy). Morgan's message is thus that we shouldn't stand in judgment of other people's belief systems, because they are *all* equally flawed and, yes, silly. Why accept dome-headed Greys from space without question but nitpick Lord Kimbote from the center of the Earth?

Is one "being" intrinsically a nuttier idea than the other? Or are they insane on a co-equal level?

It's a little like saying that you believe in the literal meaning of communion (eating and drinking from the literal body of Christ), but that you draw the line of believability at the Pope's infallibility.

Everyone draws this line differently. And, of course, if we draw that line differently and can't objectively support our belief system, then we are, for the most part, alone in our belief system.

What remains so interesting here, however, are the last few moments of "Jose Chung's from Outer Space." Morgan establishes how the abduction has influenced each "alone" individual to change his or her life for the better. A teen girl at the center of the incident has become an activist hoping to save the world. The boy she was with that night, contrarily, has been reconfirmed in his unrequited love for her and has made this love the center of his (meaningless?) existence.

And Mulder, of course, tilts forever at Morgan's impossible windmills, looking for answer to things that aren't really questions in the first place. Why seek truth when there is no truth?

"What really happened to those kids on that night?" Chung asks Mulder. His answer is "how the hell should I know?"

For Mulder, such an answer might result from a lack of facts or a need for more investigation and research. But for Chung, it's a validation of the belief that we are all animals trapped in our individual cages of subjectivity, unable to know the truth or reality of any event in our lives.

Undeniably brilliant and funny, "Jose Chung's from Outer Space" is another signature *X-Files* episode. The journey is worth the trip, and even if it is determined that truth is ultimately subjective, our belief in the irrational or the unprovable still may be enough to help us sleep better at night or accept our limitations as flawed, mortal creatures.

A little bit of self-delusion isn't necessarily a bad thing if it can keep us looking to the stars, or to the next horizon.

Constant Change, Constant Challenges

Season Four (1996–1997)

The fourth season represents a time of great change for *The X-Files.* The series moved from Friday nights to 9:00 p.m. on Sunday nights, thus making room for the new Chris Carter series, *Millennium*, on Fridays in its own time slot.

While Chris Carter worked on *Millennium* and prepped for the first *X-Files* feature film, which would shoot in the hiatus between the fourth and fifth seasons, Glen Morgan and James Wong, post-*Space: Above and Beyond*, assumed show-runner responsibility on the ever-more-popular series.

Accordingly, the fourth season reflected a slightly different aesthetic but also produced much daring, even experimental storytelling. The season featured the notorious episode "Home," about a family of inbred killers, the Peacocks. The episode proved violent, terrifying, and utterly disgusting, featuring a family matriarch who was an amputee.

"Home" aired on network television only once after Fox was flooded with complaints about it. As Chris Carter told me in a 2009 interview, "the day after we did it I was given a very stern lecture about never, *ever* pushing those limits again."

Other stories proved equally as daring, but in different ways. The reincarnation tale "The Field Where I Died" not only recreated the context around the tragic siege at David Koresh's Waco compound, but had the temerity to suggest that Mulder and Scully were not soulmates in eternity, but best friends instead. The episode posited Mulder to be—across multiple lives—enmeshed in a star-crossed love affair with a woman named Melissa (Kristen Cloke).

Another controversial story was "Musings of a Cigarette Smoking Man," a history of William B. Davis's shadowy, villainous character. The story immediately drew complaints from fans because some of the history or backstory seemed to conflict with information presented in earlier episodes, particularly "Apocrypha." And yet it is clear that the episode involves at least two unreliable narrators, Frohike and the Cigarette Smoking Man himself. Thus the episode actually plays as a critique of conspiracy theories, since the CSM is the shooter in both the Kennedy assassination and Martin Luther King Jr.'s.

Later in the episode, he even has the audacity to claim that he has never committed murder, a line of dialogue that makes the viewer aware that we are not witnessing, strictly speaking "the truth," but a patchwork narrative and approximation of some kind of truth.

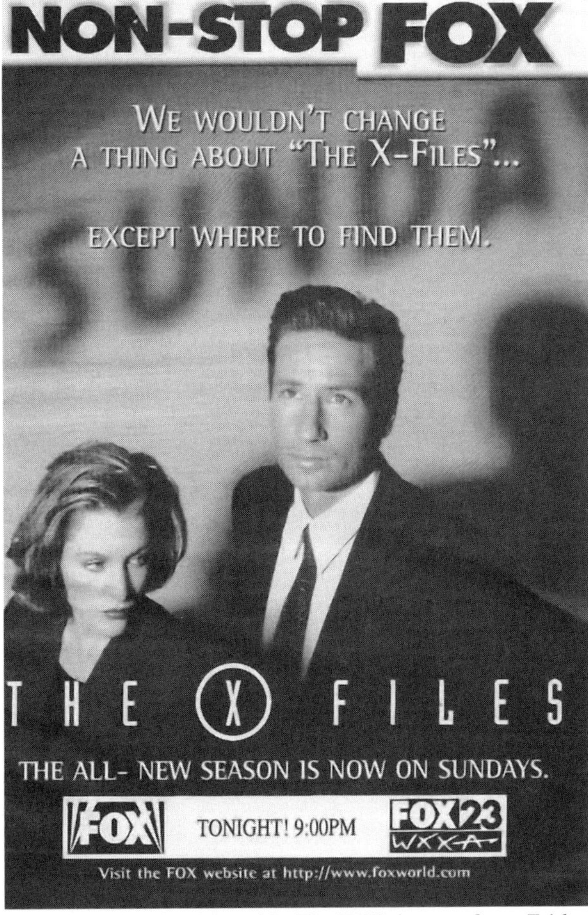

This ad in *TV Guide* heralds *The X-Files*' move from Friday nights to Sunday nights.

"Never Again," another scintillating tale, found Scully involved in a sexual liaison with a stranger, Ed, and getting a tattoo on a date. The episode aired out of order, after an episode ("Leonard Betts") involving Scully's discovery that she had contracted cancer from her abduction experience, and so her behavior was widely interpreted as a kind of acting out as opposed to an honest expression of her sexuality as intended.

Many episodes featured shocking twists, from Scully's discovery of cancer, to Mulder learning that Samantha had not, apparently, been abducted but rather was killed by a child murderer ("Paper Hearts").

In short, the fourth season took risks regularly and demonstrated a well-earned confidence that it had hit its stride. Even the finale, penned by Chris Carter and Frank Spotnitz, ended with a drop-dead cliffhanger: Mulder apparently died of self-inflicted gunshot wounds in "Gethsemane."

Mytharc Notes

Rather remarkably, the mythology tapestry grows even bigger in Season Four, and one highly cinematic two-part episode "Terma"/"Tunguska" takes Mulder to a gulag in Russia, where scientists experiment on unwilling subjects with a vaccine for the black oil. The episode is absolutely brutal, particularly in its treatment of Alex Krycek, who—against his will—has an arm amputated to prevent infection. The same two-parter introduces to the series, though not yet by name, the notion of Panspermia, of life arriving on Earth from another world, in the presentation of a rock from Mars infected with the black oil.

The fourth season also introduce the successor to Steven Williams' X following his death in the season premiere, "Herrenvolk:" Marita Covarubbias (Laurie Holden), the special representative to the United Nations. The first female in the role of Mulder's informant, the lovely Marita seems more solicitous of Mulder's attentions and conveys her information with absolute sincerity, a fact that makes her, intriguingly, more difficult to read.

The season finale, "Gethsemane," ends with the unthinkable, Mulder's suicide, but begins to construct a case (continued in the fifth-season episodes "Redux" and "Redux II") that many stories of UFOs are actually a mere cover story hiding sinister government misdeeds, and that Mulder is the patsy in this scenario, the equivalent of a Lee Harvey Oswald.

Season Highlights

"Home." Written by Glen Morgan and James Wong. Directed by Kim Manners. Airdate: October 11, 1996.

A dead baby, apparently afflicted with several genetic deformities, is unearthed in a shallow grave in the sleepy town of Home, Pennsylvania. While investigating the case, Scully and Mulder learn that the baby was buried alive and attempt to interview the residents nearest the crime scene: the Peacocks. But the Peacocks are territorial . . . and terrifying.

The family consists of three mutant brothers (Chris Nelson Norris, Adrian Hughes, John Trottier) who are not only physically deformed and mentally stunted but don't quite feel or register pain. And their crazy old mother (Karin Konoval) is an amputee who also happens to be the progenitor of the boys' offspring.

After Home's sheriff, Taylor (Tucker Smallwood), is bludgeoned to death by the Peacocks, Mulder and Scully attempt to arrest the family on their own turf, a disgusting home filled with murderous booby traps.

This fourth-season installment is ultraviolent, witty, and scary as hell. "Home" is so disturbing and disgusting in fact that Fox TV only aired it once and then banned the episode from prime-time television permanently. Nonetheless, "Home" is still timely, a brilliant meditation on the violence that can occur when times change too fast for some citizens. The episode concerns a throwback family, the Peacocks, who judge all outsiders as interlopers (and who use no electricity, and who raise their own food . . . and stock). When the Peacocks' long-standing way of life is threatened by the march of American modernity, the family responds with murderous force in an attempt to stamp out that modernity. The Peacocks feel threatened by change they don't understand and respond to that change not with adaptability or humility, but with a homicidal doubling down, with a baseball bat, no less.

"Home" is a genius episode of *The X-Files* for many reasons, but not the least because it explores this dynamic of progress and pushback in America. Much of the episode concerns a nostalgic African American sheriff, Andy Taylor (Tucker Smallwood), who longs for the days of yesteryear, when it was safe to keep his house unlocked at night. He fears that such a world is disappearing, but is unaware of an important irony. He, in fact, is emblematic of the very change that so terrifies the Peacocks. Accordingly, he is the first target of their wrath when they feel jeopardized.

"Home" succeeds for other reasons beyond the social critique. The episode offers a twisted meditation on motherhood (and the commitment required of mothers), and is also one in which Mulder and Scully are constantly jeopardized because they can't conceive of an enemy such as the Peacocks. Every assumption they make in the episode is proven wrong. They simply don't understand the throwback nature of the family, at least until Mulder references a nature TV show concerning animal instinct. Regardless of how it is interpreted, "Home" is terrifying and among the smartest, scariest, and most subversive hours ever to air on American network television.

In addition to all the overt horror material it expertly explores, "Home" presents a clever social commentary about the way Americans respond to progress, or to change, and how they view the past versus the present. In my introduction above, I described the Peacocks as throwbacks. Indeed, the Peacock men physically resemble our cavemen ancestors with their pronounced brows and savage demeanor. Mulder even describes their behavior as "going caveman." Outside of such physiological characteristics, the Peacocks dwell in another iteration of the "past," in the immediate context of the post-Civil War world.

Their ramshackle farmhouse with no heat and no electricity reflects that time period in terms of technology or lack thereof. But beyond their home, the Peacocks still boast the Civil War mind-set of the Confederacy. They call the Civil War "The War of Northern Aggression." This comment is a symbol of the Peacocks' intransigence. The family never moved past the Civil War into modern America and have aggressively resisted modernity in all its forms ever since.

Basically, the Peacocks have carved out a life on the outskirts of Home, Pennsylvania, where they can live their lives as their ancestors lived them generations earlier. The Peacocks have not permitted "progress" or "modernity" to take root in their traditions or family values. Instead, they have mythologized their way of life as the only way to do things and the proper way at that. And to preserve that heritage, they have even resorted to (catastrophic) inbreeding. No outside contamination from modernity is permitted. Outsiders like Mulder and Scully are guilty of, in the words of Mama Peacock, "trying to change the way things are."

Notice the certainty of that phrasing and how it is parsed in the present tense. These values are now and FOREVER, according to the Peacocks. But—and here's where it gets *really* interesting—"Home" contrasts the Peacocks with Sheriff Taylor.

He is a modest African American man and an accomplished professional who just a generation earlier would never have been permitted to hold the position of sheriff in town because of the color of his skin and because of entrenched and institutional racism. He has thus benefited from social progress, and more than that, excelled because of it. His safe, mansion-like "home" has come about *because* of progress and modernity, not in spite of it.

And yet Taylor and his wife long aloud for a time in American history when it was safe to leave your front door unlocked. This romanticized attitude is a reflection of the oft-repeated "myth of the 1950s," which is frequently and without much examination held up as a perfect era in American history.

But in fact, the Taylors are not imperiled in "Home" by the modernity of the 1990s, but rather by the violent response to that modernity by a mindset closer to the 1890s. The pervasive myth of the 1950s comes up to bite the Taylors, for the Peacocks arrive to murder them in a classic 1950s "big American car" while listening to the 1957 song "Wonderful! Wonderful!" on their car radio. It is the old, regressive force of tradition and the past, as represented by the Peacocks, which rises up to threaten the Taylors, not the uncertain forces of the millennial age.

Thus there's a whole subtext and tension in "Home" about the romantic illusions of the past meeting the realities of the present. This theme is timely, because America is currently undergoing the same crisis on a much larger scale. The cultural battle in this country is now between those who accept modernity and those who deny it to their dying breath.

For some, modernity, with its acceptance of new technology, equal rights for women, minorities and LGBT citizens, immigration reform, a black president, and so forth, is a powerful threat to the "old ways," and one that must be met with, in the words of a failed 2012 Senate candidate, "Second Amendment remedies."

But the Peacocks' very nature showcases the ultimate fallacy of such thinking.

For when you close out new ideas, you become trapped in a bubble, never able to change, never able to evolve or grow. Instead, you become dependent on instinctive thinking—on animal "pack thinking"—instead of rational thinking. By rejecting modernity, the Peacocks have become practically prehistoric. As Mulder explicitly notes in the coda, time catches up with the family.

Given this dynamic, it is not surprising that the Peacocks' last stand in "Home" is against the federal government—a force represented by Scully and Mulder—that they don't recognize or accept as having authority over them. As we can see by the pervasive "government is the enemy" rhetoric in our national discourse in the 2010s, this is the pressure ever building in the body politic. Again, this isn't about partisanship or political parties, it's about history, and the forces that embrace change and the forces that fear and reject it.

Beyond the entrenched social critique, "Home" works splendidly as a meditation on "what a mother goes through," in the heartfelt words of the Peacock matriarch. Mrs. Peacock positions herself as a woman superior in character to Agent Scully because she has learned and practiced total sacrifice in order to raise and love her sons.

Mulder confirms in this episode that this is the first time he has "ever seen" Scully "as a mother," and that line of dialogue will have repercussions going forward on *The X-Files*. Many episodes of the latter seasons see Scully wishing to broach motherhood more than anything else and, in the end, being forced to forsake it. By series end, she has learned, indeed, "what a mother goes through" to see to a child's health.

Of course, Scully and Mrs. Peacock see the world quite differently. They have wildly divergent views of modernity and motherhood. But the act of raising a child, in the end, changes both of them dramatically. In some sense, "Home" is the beginning of this plot strand on *The X-Files*.

Creating a scary work of art isn't necessarily a matter of algebraic equations, but "Home" is so terrifying, even after multiple viewings, because it works against our confidence in Mulder and Scully. In a typical *X-Files* episode, the audience follows step-by-step with these beloved lead characters, and their assumptions, research, and speculations almost universally turn out to be on the right track. Not so in "Home." Here, they both guess wrong again and again. For one thing, they first believe that the Peacock baby died from genetic deformities. It didn't . . . it died from being buried alive.

Then they believe that the Peacocks have captured an outside woman, a traveler perhaps, and are using her for breeding stock. Again, that's not true: there is no captive in the Peacock house. And then they try to rescue Mrs. Peacock, before realizing that she is exactly where she wants to be; she is at "home."

Again and again, the episode undercuts audience confidence in Mulder and Scully and their decisions so that when the final battle in the booby-trapped house occurs, viewers are thoroughly unsettled and uncertain about how things are going to turn out. There is a moment of palpable terror here when Mulder goes down battling a Peacock brother and Scully nearly activates an almost-invisible trip wire. This one is a nail-biter all the way.

Finally, "Home" is visually gorgeous. It is a distinctive-looking episode of *The X-Files*, in part because of the exteriors shot at the Peacock estate. Some low-angle compositions outside the farmhouse may remind viewers of Daniel Pearl's remarkable cinematography in *The Texas Chainsaw Massacre* (1974). And so there's a feeling in "Home"—like the vibe in that Tobe Hooper film—of reality giving way to unending nightmare.

"Musings of a Cigarette Smoking Man." Written by Glen Morgan. Directed by James Wong. Airdate: November 17, 1996

"Musings of a Cigarette Smoking Man" remains one of the most postmodern or "meta" episodes in the *X-Files* early canon. The episode dramatizes the history of Cancer Man, or the Cigarette Smoking Man (William B. Davis), but does so from Frohike's point of view.

Over the span of the story, Frohike reveals CSM's lineage, his secret acts, and his existential loneliness. The story reveals, for example, that his father was a communist sympathizer and that his mother died of cancer—from smoking—before he was old enough to speak. As the story continues, we learn that the CSM is personally responsible, as the shooter, for the assassinations of John F. Kennedy and Martin Luther King Jr. We also learn, in the last act, that he frequently spends Christmas alone and is a frustrated writer. On the last front, CSM has been writing adventures of a secret agent named Jack Colquitt for a long time, only to see them constantly rejected by publishers. Colquitt, and by extension CSM, apparently longs for a second chance.

As noted elsewhere, when "Musings of a Cigarette Smoking Man" first aired in 1996, some fans complained on the Internet that the history of the character as presented here was at odds with what viewers already knew of him. A few fans pointed to a scene from the third-season episode "Apocrypha" that suggested that CSM and Bill Mulder were working together in the State Department as early as the 1950s, following the mission of the Zeus Faber. In "Musings of a Cigarette Man," by contrast, we see that CSM and Bill Mulder are bunkmates at a military base in the early 1960s, just after the Bay of Pigs debacle and the Cuban Missile Crisis. CSM is recruited at that point, to assassinate Kennedy.

But what many seem to have missed here is a core aspect of the episode's structure. All the information we learn about CSM in "Musings of a Cigarette Smoking Man" comes straight from an unreliable narrator: Frohike. He has found files that he believes reveal who the CSM "is" and who he "wants to be." As viewers, we never get any independent verification that Frohike's information, or his suppositions about that information, is truthful or accurate. Indeed, this fact is pointed out by an absolute incongruity within the body of the episode itself.

The first act depicts CSM killing two figures of great historical importance himself, JFK and MLK, but the very next act finds him being tasked, along with Deep Throat, to murder an alien from a downed UFO. Security Council Resolution 1013 (Ten Thirteen again!) demands that any nation capturing an extraterrestrial is responsible for immediately terminating it. The CSM is thus handed a gun by Deep Throat, but he demurs. CSM refuses to kill the alien because, in his words, he has never killed anybody, and this act will mark him—and his soul—as a murderer.

But of course, he's already killed two people in this very episode!

So CSM is either lying to mess with Deep Throat for his own shadowy reasons or he is being truthful and the early portions of the story, relayed by Frohike, are inaccurate. Thus the story openly acknowledges the inconsistent nature of the narrative, and in fact plays on it. The Cigarette Smoking Man is a mystery, and one who cannot be thoroughly "known" because of all the disinformation that exists about him. Frohike concocts a useful narrative for us, but like many narratives featured in the Lone Gunmen's periodical, one suspects, not all the details are correct or true. Some aspects of the truth have been guessed at.

Was this always the intent of the episode, to speak so cryptically about a favorite villain? We know from press reports that the original plan was for the Cigarette Smoking Man to assassinate Frohike so as to silence him, but that Carter vetoed this idea because such an assassination would suggest that everything Frohike said was accurate or true. With Frohike alive instead, the episode more clearly conveys the *X-Files*-ish notion of truth as opaque, of truth possessing layers like an onion.

Yet "Musings of a Cigarette Smoking Man" is a remarkable episode for another reason beyond its meta-, knowingly contradictory narrative. The episode wickedly plays on the abundant 1990s desire, seen in politics and in tabloid television, to sympathize with and exonerate or absolve those who have done wrong. One of President Clinton's most famous phrases of the era was that he "feels the pain" of the voters that he encounters. In the 1990s, thanks to Oprah, Donohue, and Geraldo and others, we were asked constantly to feel the pain of others and to, in the process of hearing their confessions (on TV), lessen their feelings of guilt or shame. "Musings of a Cigarette Smoking Man" likewise attempts to make us feel sympathy for CSM in ways that are, knowingly, craven. This isn't the (also excellent) "En Ami" episode, in which we are asked to follow CSM through a series of difficult choices. Instead, the episode attempts to deliberately, artificially trigger sympathy with big scenes sure to cause wild emotion. For example, we see CSM lonely and isolated on Christmas Eve after giving all his employees the same tie. We see him laboring over his writing, hoping for a break. We even see him craft a resignation letter, and we consider the idea that everything would be different in the world if this one man, this frustrated author, had just experienced some success in his writing enterprise.

But then the episode pulls a fast one on the audience. After CSM sees his dreams of becoming a writer shattered, he sits down on a bench, next to a bum, and goes on to describe, in vehement, hostile terms, how life is like a box of chocolates. The game is up.

Of course, this is a direct allusion to the then-popular film *Forrest Gump* (1994), which, among other things, is a highly manipulative work of art, designed exclusively to pluck the heartstrings on an industrial scale. Suddenly, we see CSM fit into that world, and we realize that the episode is taking a piss. It's having us on. He is not a tender snowflake or a frustrated artist, and it is not necessary for us to feel his pain or know his existential angst. The allusion to *Gump* is not only funny and timely, it punctures the idea that any of this could be "real."

Instead, we must countenance in "Musings of a Cigarette Smoking Man" a fictional or false narrative, disinformation that is designed to make us feel the man's pain, even if the man, on some level, is clearly undeserving of such empathy.

"Leonard Betts." Written by Vince Gilligan, John Shiban, and Frank Spotnitz. Directed by Kim Manners. Airdate: January 26, 1997.

Leonard Betts—a gifted paramedic who can seemingly diagnosis cancer by eye—is decapitated in a catastrophic ambulance accident in Pittsburgh. But on the same night as his apparent demise, his headless body disappears from the morgue.

Scully and Mulder investigate Betts's death and explore the strange hypothesis that he is somehow still alive and that he can regenerate parts of his body, even his cranium. The agents also gather evidence that suggests Betts is riddled with cancer, and that somehow this sickness aids in the regeneration process. His cancerous physical form also explains his nature. He can pinpoint cancer in others because he must consume cancer to survive.

Scully is surprised and devastated when she becomes Betts's intended next meal.

Many episodes of *The X-Files* depict human-appearing genetic mutants who, in order to survive, must prey on the rest of us. These mutant predators are usually, though not universally, hostile in the way they garner their sustenance. Victor Eugene Tooms (of "Squeeze" and "Tooms") eats the livers of victims and stalks prey like animals. Mr. Incanto of "2Shy" lures unsuspecting plus-sized women to their doom, playing on their lack of self-confidence and vulnerability to devour their body fat and nourish himself.

The fourth-season entry "Leonard Betts" is indeed another genetic mutant story, but there are two important twists in the tale by Vince Gilligan, Frank Spotnitz, and John Shiban. The first is the nature of Mr. Betts, played by Paul McCrane. Unlike Tooms or Incanto, he is the most reluctant, and perhaps the most "surgical" or skilled of the bunch. He doesn't want to kill anyone, but he does want to survive. There is an element of sympathy and sadness in the way he approaches his victims. Also, as a paramedic, he is no berserker.

The second and perhaps more distinctive point regarding "Leonard Betts" is that it presents a kind of unified theory of genetic mutants on *The X-Files.* The episode brings up the topic of "punctual equilibrium." Mulder discusses this theory with Scully, and it's an authentic hypothesis in evolutionary biology. Punctual equilibrium posits that most species exhibit small or inconsequential change for most of their duration on this Earth, staying in a type of biological stasis. But when significant evolutionary change does arise, punctual equilibrium suggests it will include rapid, radical events of cladogenesis, a process by which one new species branches away from the main or established one.

Given this definition, it's fascinating to consider the mutants of episodes like "Tooms," "The Host," "2Shy," "Hungry," and "Leonard Betts" as representatives of cladogenesis. Going deeper, the question becomes: why is it happening now? Why is cladogenesis appearing so frequently in the 1990s of Mulder and Scully? In other words, what we are discussing in episodes like this is a second *X-Files* mythology, one that ties together the monster-of-the-week or (apparently) stand-alone stories. Later in the series, we will learn that junk DNA—extraterrestrial in nature—is responsible for some mutants and some psychic powers, and that's another piece of the puzzle. But the fact of that alien DNA doesn't explain timing.

I would propose that the sudden and apparent increase in genetic mutants in *The X-Files* may be a product of man's impact on the environment, on an industrial scale. Although this explanation can't necessarily apply to Tooms—who is over a hundred years old—we do know from episodes like "The Host" and "Leonard Betts" that radiation and human/biological waste could play some role. That's just speculation, of course, but one wonderful quality about revisiting *The X-Files* is that engaged viewers start to look under the surface, speculating about perhaps even unintended connections between installments.

Outside a unified theory of the *X-Files* mutants, "Leonard Betts" is a great episode of the series because it proceeds with invention and wit, and because it turns those qualities on their head for a stunning, jaw-dropping finale about a main character, Scully. Mulder's quips disarm the viewers, and Leonard Betts's humanity lends the episode a softer side than some mutant stories, and then the episode delivers a gut-punch. Scully has terminal cancer.

In terms of the *X-Files* series catalog, I've referred before to its focus on the unexcavated "sausage-making" of modern society. *The X-Files* has on at least two notable occasions shone a light on that sausage-making in ways that make us, the audience, feel intensely uncomfortable. Two of the best episodes of the series, "The Host" and "Our Town," tackle this notion. In the former case, the issue pinpointed is: where does our bodily waste go after we flush it down the toilet? What happens to it? The second (examined in "Our Town") is equally disturbing: what goes into our food preparation at meat plants across the country? What are the chickens we eat at home fed when they are grown? And what is in that feed?

"Leonard Betts" follows up this idea by escorting viewers to a place far more gruesome and disturbing than a hospital morgue. Here, Mulder and Scully go diving into a large tank of biological refuse or waste. They sift through discarded body parts, and again, this is something we just don't generally talk or think about as a society. Essentially, this is a place where the human body becomes . . . garbage. The disgusting exploration of cast-off body parts is leavened somewhat by Mulder's persistent sense of humor, but the fact is, this is another aspect of modernity we live in ignorant bliss about.

The episode also features one of the most disturbing scenes since "Home." Scully prepares to perform an autopsy on Betts's decapitated head, and she experiences an "unusual degree of post-mortem galvanic response." In other word, the jaw distends and the eyes open. There is still, apparently, life in that severed head. Scully is so shaken by the idea of life continuing in a severed head that she must stop her efforts. I really, really don't blame her. Some of the terror here emerges from our sense of imagination about what could have come next. What if Scully had started cutting? What reaction would she have caused?

But if we go into "Leonard Betts" feeling disturbed about the "sausage making" inside a modern hospital, or sensing intimations of a unified theory regarding the series' genetic mutants, we leave it with heavy hearts, with a sense of our connected humanity. For all his murdering ways, Betts doesn't desire to be a killer. He wants what we want . . . to continue living. But for some reason, nature has made him a freak that must kill to live. He is a reluctant monster, and thus we can feel sympathy for him.

More importantly, "Leonard Betts" culminates with the stomach-turning revelation that Scully has cancer. The episode is exceptionally clever in the way it reaches this destination. Betts—a cancer eater—wordlessly goes after Scully as his next victim, and so the implication is clear. If she is in his victim pool, then she must have cancer. And cancer can be a death sentence, not only because of Betts's presence, but because of the disease itself. So our hero, Scully, is sick. And the cancer must be somewhat far along because she experiences a nosebleed soon after learning the truth.

Not a good sign.

I remember the first time I watched "Leonard Betts." I felt unexpectedly rattled by the ending because the story had demonstrated a great deal of humor (such as Mulder's "Siskel or Ebert?" quip while going through severed thumbs), and I was thus unprepared for the gravity of the cancer revelation. Even more so, stand-alone stories in *The X-Files* don't generally feature life-changing character moments. Those tend to be reserved for the Mytharc tales. So the revelation of Scully's illness is doubly shocking. I remember director Alfred Hitchcock's stated desire to play the audience like a piano. "Leonard Betts" is one of those episodes of *The X-Files* that plays the audience like a piano.

"Never Again." Written by Glen Morgan and James Wong. Directed by Rob Bowman. Airdate: February 2, 1997

After his divorce is finalized, down-on-his-luck Ed Jerse (Rodney Rowland) gets drunk and goes to a Russian tattoo parlor on a whim. Unfortunately, the tattoo he acquires there starts to speak to him in hostile tones, compelling Ed to commit violent acts against women.

While Mulder is on vacation at Graceland undergoing a "spiritual journey," Scully encounters Jerse in Philadelphia while reluctantly on assignment for her absent partner. Feeling rebellious, Scully gets a tattoo at the same parlor while he watches.

What neither of them realize, however, is that the tattoo ink contains ergot, a substance with hallucinogenic properties that can cause psychotic behavior. . . .

"Never Again" provides some new and remarkable insights into the pressures and conflicts swirling inside of Agent Dana Scully. This episode finds her chafing under Mulder's capricious authority and longing for a life that she dictates, that she chooses. She wants something *different,* at least for the moment. In charting this courageous character arc, "Never Again" also examines the changing parameters of male/female relationships in the 1990s. In the process, it creates an unforgettable monster: a woman-hating Bettie Page–styled tattoo with the voice of Jodie Foster.

In "Never Again," Scully rebels against Mulder and behaves in a fashion that viewers had not often seen. This description doesn't mean that she acts out of character. On the contrary, Scully in "Never Again" is very much in line with the character we know and love, and we still see her cool, analytical decision making and rational approach to problem solving. The only difference is that we also see that Scully is questioning the "way of things" in this episode.

Why doesn't she have a desk in the basement office at the FBI?

Why doesn't Scully get a voice in determining which cases the X-Files investigate?

Why does Mulder frequently second-guess her judgment?

These are legitimate questions about her life, and though Scully clearly loves Mulder, his manner can also be grating and even childish. We already know that Scully also rebelled against her authoritative father, a naval officer whom we met briefly in "Beyond the Sea," and therefore feels an attraction/repulsion to domineering figures. Scully is drawn to them for their strength, but also repelled by their overbearing, controlling natures. That's the crux of her problem with Mulder at this particular juncture, too. He holds the power in their relationship—professional and personal—and he isn't always wise in his choices.

Although this episode aired after "Leonard Betts," in which Scully learned she had cancer, it was actually designed to enter the continuity before that revelation, and this is a crucial distinction. Scully rebels against Mulder and his way of operating in "Never Again" not because she is sick, not because of any external "cause," but merely because she is generally dissatisfied with the relationship and its apparent limits and dimensions. That doesn't mean she dislikes Mulder. It means that for Scully, always being second-guessed, always being ordered around . . . can get tiresome. She feels constrained, trapped, and like she's walking in place.

In some ways, "Never Again" is very much an episode about the way that men and women relate to one another. Mulder is genuinely hurt and upset that Scully seems to be unhappy in their professional relationship, but importantly, he doesn't really offer to change it or to alter the balance of power. And at episode's end, he is very judgmental and disapproving toward her. Similarly, while Mulder is happy with the status quo, Scully seems to wonder where this is all going and what the future holds.

If the episode shows off Scully as somehow less than admirable in pursuing a romantic and/or sexual conquest, as some insist (but which I don't believe), it does the same thing for Mulder, certainly, who is frozen in place, a kind of arrested man-child. Some people may also wonder what Scully sees in Jerse besides his obvious good looks. One answer may be that he doesn't seek to control her, and that—as a kind of blue collar guy—he simply does not pose a challenge or source of friction regarding couple dynamics. Also, where Mulder never truly engages Scully romantically or sexually at this juncture in their relationship, Jerse makes it plain that he is interested in Scully on these very grounds.

Jerse is a complete—and in this moment, *perfect*—alternative to Mulder. He acts instead of thinks, he lets go instead of holding back, and he acknowledges his desire instead of dancing around it or sublimating it. One of the most authentically erotic scenes in all of *The X-Files* occurs in this episode as he watches Scully lean over, quite willingly, to be tattooed on her back with the Ouroboros. The scene is a strong counterpoint to the one featured in the pilot wherein a worried Scully runs to Mulder's motel room and disrobes so he can check for physical marks following a spell of missing time.

There, Mulder was a figure of trust and authority, and he had the control, but he didn't direct that control toward sexual desire or romance. In this situation, Scully is the one with the power, and she uses it to tantalize Jerse. Similarly, the men vs. women dynamic plays out in "Never Again's" monster story, wherein likable Ed becomes henpecked and managed by his "evil" tattoo. The tattoo boasts a rabid hatred of women and speaks vile things about them to Jerse, who tries hard not to listen but ultimately has no choice. So either the tattoo is a figment of Jerse's own suppressed uneasiness and unhappiness with women, or as the end of the episode suggests, the tattoo really was possessed of some kind of evil sentience all along. Either way, he proves he can't ultimately be the partner Scully wants. Even if physically desirable and willing to act on his passions, Jerse is the polar opposite of Mulder. He is mentally unstable and an unsafe physical presence.

Jerse's tortured, schizophrenic, and psychotic nature in "Never Again" is actually highly reminiscent of the oeuvre of Alfred Hitchcock and the film *Frenzy* (1972). There, a murderer called Rusk acts out his sexual desire for women with brutal murder. He kills a woman named Babs, and the camera almost literally backs away in horror at the tail end of one scene, leaving the building that is the site of a crime. Similarly, Jerse kills his downstairs neighbor in "Never Again" and director Rob Bowman's camera likewise retracts, pulling back further and further from this hatred made manifest. In both cases, there is a distancing effect generated, and I would submit this is so because in the case of both Rusk and Jerse they are not entirely responsible for what they have done. They're mad but not inhuman. Instead, they're driven to act in a way they don't quite understand.

Ironically, that's also, in very general terms, what happens to Scully in this episode. Her attraction/repulsion regarding authority figures drives her to seek a romantic alternative to Mulder, one who won't control her or interact with her in such a capricious way. In this relationship (and as the scene with Scully getting a tattoo illustrates), she believes she has all the power. But both Scully and Ed, learn that this is not the case, that desire and passion are forces that can take on a mind of their own and drive their "masters" to destinations unknown and dangerous. It's great that "Never Again" possesses the courage to have Scully undergo a personal crisis and rebel against Mulder, and then, after that rebellion remind us that she is the same wonderful, brilliant character we have always loved. There was nothing "wrong" with Scully in this episode. She's just a human being like the rest of us. If Mulder can go off and have an assignation from time to time and we still like and admire him afterwards, why can't Scully be afforded the same leeway?

"Synchrony." Written by Howard Gordon and David Greenwalt. Directed by James Charleston. Airdate: April 13, 1997.

At M.I.T. in Massachusetts, an old man accosts two squabbling students on campus and warns one of them that if he is not careful, he will be struck by a bus and killed at precisely 11:46 p.m.

The prediction proves true, and Mulder and Scully head to the scene to discover who the old man was and how his captor, a campus security man, was suddenly frozen to death. Soon, a visiting expert in cryobiology, Dr. Yanechi (Hiro Kanagawi), is also found dead. Mulder and Scully realize that he too has been fast-frozen by a compound that does not yet exist and cannot possibly exist for ten years or so.

The bizarre answer to this riddle is related to time travel. The old man has come back from the future to prevent the creation of a freezing compound and the ensuing discovery of time travel, two factors in the creation of a world without hope or history.

"Synchrony" is a unique and marvelous addition to the *X-Files* catalog because it deals with a subject left mostly untouched in the franchise: time travel. The sixth-season story "Monday" explicitly concerns a time loop, but "Synchrony" involves itself with quantum physics and the possibility of human time travel from the future to Scully and Mulder's present, an apparent branching-off point to a discovery that "changes the course of history."

What makes "Synchrony" so engaging and tense a drama is this very notion of the *multi-verse*, of every action and reaction creating a new (and hopefully better) path forward, and thus a whole new universe. A killer returns from the future in this episode, much as in James Cameron's watershed *The Terminator* (1984), but his motives for murder are, contrarily, prosocial, namely to save the human race from a future without hope while also preventing a personal mistake that he now regrets. Thus the episode involves "Oppenheimer's Syndrome": the ambitious scientist's reckoning that his work has changed the world in a destructive way, and that, if he could be given a second chance, he would prevent his young self from moving forward with it. The syndrome is named for J. Robert Oppenheimer, who toiled at the Manhattan Project and changed the course of human history forever with his work on the atom bomb. The character in this *X-Files* episode, Jason, is actually a surrogate for Oppenheimer, at least according to some accounts

"Synchrony" remains intriguing for two reasons. First, the episode doesn't shy away from scientific detail and proposes specific mechanics for time travel. These involve the act of sustaining human bodies at freezing temperatures for a passage considered beyond the limits of "human endurance." Secondly, "Synchrony" presents the wonderful notion of "orphan" artifacts, objects that hail from a now nonexistent future, but that continue in our present as lonely, mysterious paradoxes.

On the latter front, Mulder discovers a photograph in "Synchrony" that could never have been taken in his reality because all the participants died before meeting, and before the picture could be snapped. Yet the photo still exists in Mulder's reality, a sign that in some dimension, in some universe, that meeting *has* occurred, and someone did snap that picture. We know that a photograph can't exist unless someone takes it and that, similarly, a photograph records a specific place and instant in time. But suddenly, a photograph exists in "Synchrony" despite the fact that the participants never meet and that moment never actually comes to pass. How can this orphan artifact be explained?

Well, if it helps, *synchrony* might be defined as the act of keeping systems together or operating in unison. In computer science, the term refers to the coordination of simultaneous "threads." In terms of this *X-Files* episode, "Synchrony" is an apt title indeed. The killer from the future arrives in 1997 to break or disrupt the tapestry of events—the so-called synchrony—that gave rise to his very universe. If he starts yanking at those threads, reality itself—the reality he knows and hates—begins to unwind.

So if Dr. Yanechi does not meet Lisa Yanelli (Susan Lee Hoffman), they can't possibly work together to create a freezing compound that assists in making human time travel a reality. And if Lisa Yanelli dies in 1997, she will also never meet a researcher who, in 2007, discovers tachyon particles and determines that time travel can only occur at a temperature of absolute zero. Piece by piece, then, the old assassin of "Synchrony" tears apart a future that must never come to exist.

But the question becomes this: if the old man destroys the synchrony that gave rise to his life and his historical context, how can he possibly exist to travel back in change it in the first place? His very future would be erased, time travel would not exist, and he could not physically return to alter his universe. Similarly, without the invention of human time travel and its subsequent deleterious effect on the human psyche, he would have no cause to return to 1997 even if he could.

Which must mean that he doesn't unwrite his own past so much as he creates a new branching-off point and new universe (as is also the case in J. J. Abrams's interpretation of *Star Trek*). Isn't that right? Time travel, this episode suggests, creates new universes but doesn't destroy old ones.

Mulder and Scully largely play catch-up throughout this episode, and it is wonderful to see them grappling with a mystery beyond the monster-of-the-week formula or even a new extension of the Mytharc. This episode may remind you just how elastic the series format remains, and that it generously and flexibly permits one-off shows like "Synchrony," which delve into matters of hard science fiction.

Also, a wonderful bit of series continuity occurs here. Mulder points out to his debating partner that she herself wrote a scholarly dissertation about time travel and concluded that it was possible. This point gives Scully some pause in her skepticism and is a nice callback to the pilot episode.

"Small Potatoes." Written by Vince Gilligan. Directed by Cliff Bole. Airdate: April 20, 1997.

In a small town in West Virginia, four infants with tails are born to four different sets of parents. When Scully and Mulder investigate, they determine that this genetic anomaly can only mean one thing: all the babies stem from the same father, perhaps a sperm donor.

While looking deeper into this mystery, the duo discovers that a custodian in a local doctor's office, Eddie Van Blundht (Darin Morgan), is the culprit.

He not only once had a tail (which he had surgically removed), but possesses a bizarre muscular condition that can alter or rearrange his features. He uses this ability to mimic the physical appearance of any man . . . and thus have sex with any woman of his choosing.

Soon, Van Blundht escapes from police custody, transforms into Mulder, and sets his lascivious sights on Scully. . . .

The fourth season of *The X-Files* represents a remarkable and fertile time in the series' history and development. The ratings were through the roof, and creatively the stories pushed the limits in terms of on-screen horror ("Home") but also character development. On the latter front, Scully developed cancer during this span, and the Chris Carter series also adopted a new, often askance perspective on Mulder. In episodes such as "Never Again," Scully found herself objecting more and more to Mulder's way of doing things and even, after a fashion, rebelling against his mentorship.

The demythologizing, or more aptly, *humanizing* of the main characters continues in a comedic little masterpiece called "Small Potatoes," an episode that is actually anything but small. In this tale, Mulder and Scully confront a loser who can reshape his face and body to become anyone he chooses. But significantly, Eddie Van Blundht (played by series writer Darin Morgan) alters his physical appearance not merely for the purposes of sex but because he longs for some touch of romance or sense of connection in his unhappy, lonely life. He can't find that connection as himself, and so he must shroud his true identity to attain the happiness he seeks. Eddie even approaches one woman, a former girlfriend, in the guise of her movie hero, Luke Skywalker. It's a weird paradigm, but Van Blundht can only be his best self when he is imitating someone else.

"Small Potatoes" contrasts Van Blundht's desire—as a living, breathing X-File—to reach out and relate to people with Mulder's opposite approach; the agent's all-consuming desire to understand the X-Files, a task that, a priori, prevents him from reaching out in a personal, romantic sense.

Dynamically and unconventionally, then, "Small Potatoes" suggests that as a (romantic) partner, Van Blundht may actually be preferable to Mulder, at least for Scully, who also longs for some sense of deeper human relationship outside the work culture. This is a matter that *The X-Files* takes up again in the fifth season, as Scully's longing to become a mother comes to the forefront. But the point is that she is asking questions about her life and becoming impatient with it as it stands. She wants to take a next step and possibly with Mulder, but he is not ready. In some way, the theme of "Small Potatoes" might be viewed as a pretty big swipe at the handsome, heroic, and dedicated series protagonist, Mulder. For all his intuitive genius, for all his brilliance, he is emotionally arrested.

Still, this installment thrives as both a comedy and a trenchant examination of character because Mulder and Scully are both keenly observed, and David Duchovny goes all in—*all in*—for his comedic performance as Blundht-in-Mulder's-guise.

The crux of the issue in "Small Potatoes" is made plain during a trademark moment of fast-paced dialogue between our twin "lenses" on the world, Mulder and Scully. Scully remarks that in terms of Blundht, "looking like someone else and being someone else are two different things."

Mulder's thoughtful reply is that people judge other people by appearances, and so if our appearances did change, "the world would see us differently."

"Isn't that the same thing?" he asks her.

Unwittingly, Scully must consider that philosophical point up-close and personal when Van Blundht—appearing as Mulder—shows up unannounced at her apartment with a bottle of wine, gets her a little tipsy, proves very good at listening and empathizing, and almost lures her into the sack.

The real Mulder breaks in on this scene and realizes what is occurring. Van Blundht has stolen his life and, worse, may be doing a better job managing his relationships than he has done! The sad truth that even Mulder comes to realize (when he comments that he's "no Eddie Van Blundht") is that the chameleon in their midst possesses the very qualities that one might desire in a romantic partner. Against him, Mulder realizes, only half-joking, he doesn't exactly measure up. Mulder's never brought over wine to Scully's house, never asked her about her teenage years, and never taken an interest in her life just for the sake of "knowing her better."

There's a great scene in this episode of Van Blundht (Duchovny) pretending to be Mulder in front of a mirror, pulling out his badge and gun, and quoting macho dialogue from Scorsese's *Taxi Driver*. But the episode essentially holds up a mirror for Mulder. With just a little bit of action on his part, he and Scully could be together, but he never takes that step. But again, a loser like Van Blundht does. Or as Van Blundht tells Mulder: "I was born a loser, but you're one by choice."

In this final recognition of Van Blundht triumph and Mulder's failure, the comedic "Small Potatoes" suddenly switches gears. The focus moves from a unique monster-of-the-week to a very telling commentary on the kind of life Mulder has lived and chooses yet to live. Mulder's a "damned handsome man," to quote Van Blundht, so what's he waiting for? Why doesn't he make a move?

The question becomes, regarding Eddie: is he just putting on a show for Scully and the other women so he can bed them? Or is he legitimately a guy who seeks connection and romance in an otherwise humdrum life, but lacks the self-confidence as "himself" to make that connection? It's a testament to the complexity of the series that this question is not definitively resolved, and there's room for interpretation.

Throughout *The X-Files,* the series writers play with the idea of a Scully/ Mulder romantic relationship. An episode such as "Small Potatoes," which hints at what their coupling could look like, serves an important function. For one thing, it helps tide fans over between longing looks, the first kiss, and other milestones in the Mulder/Scully relationship. But it also reiterates a significant theme. No development in *The X-Files* comes without some kind of price or some kind of uncomfortable truth. For Mulder, the case involving Eddie Van Blundht puts the onus on him to overcome his inertia.

So again, why doesn't he make a move? The answer, I believe, simply comes down to that conversation Mulder and Scully share about how people are "seen" by others. In a relationship that starts out with respect and friendship, there's much to lose in the transition to romance. Mulder can't be someone else —unlike Van Blundht—and so he must live with the consequences of his relationship choices.

Faith and Doubt

Season Five (1997–1998)

The fifth season of *The X-Files* was designed and constructed as a long build toward the first *X-Files* movie, due for theatrical release in the summer of 1998. A shorter season than the others, consisting of just twenty installments, the fifth season represents Mulder's greatest period of doubt about himself. Because of "evidence" he learns, Mulder comes to believe that he has been a "patsy" in a government lie about the existence of UFOs. This belief is not fully overturned until the events of *Fight the Future.*

Season Five also sees occasional friction between Mulder and Scully because of Mulder's loss of faith in his beliefs. "They really have a falling out," Chris Carter told me, regarding this span. "They're of two different minds. Scully actually pursues Mulder's path, and Mulder, in a weird way, pursues Scully's. That was all a plan."

Shot after the movie, though occurring in the continuity before it, the fifth season begins what might be termed *The X-Files'* postmodern phase. Many of the stories going forward, from the masterpieces "The Post-Modern Prometheus" and "Bad Blood" in Season Five to such efforts as "Dreamland" and "Triangle" in Season Six, operate on a metatextual level, pulling in influences from the culture and repurposing them for a reason beyond an exploration of the paranormal or supernatural. In short, these stories present a new way of interpreting the adventures of Scully and Mulder; ones outside strictly narrative boundaries of what happened, to whom, and why. Instead, these stories embody new, sometimes conflicting viewpoints and present a case for the elasticity of the *X-Files* format.

The fifth season also represents the age of "celebrity" writers on *The X-Files.* Master of horror Stephen King cowrote "Chinga" with Chris Carter, and it is the story of an evil doll. Cyberpunk author William Gibson wrote "Kill Switch," a more complex variation on the theme introduced in Season One's "Ghost in the Machine," and which raised the now in-vogue idea of singularity. "Kill Switch" was also, perhaps, the hardest episode to shoot in the series' entire canon. "We had twenty-two days to shoot 'Kill Switch'—that's including second unit work too—but twenty-two days. That's just unheard of. That's why I don't think there will ever be another series like *The X-Files.* People ask me that, and I just don't think there can be in today's climate," Chris Carter reports.

Mytharc Notes

The Mytharc in Season Five begins with Mulder's overwhelming sense of guilt and doubt. He learns not only that he has been a patsy feeding the "American appetite for bogus revelations," but he is, in a way, responsible for the fact that Scully was given cancer by the Cigarette Smoking Man.

In "Redux," Mulder learns from a DOD employee, Kritschgau, that a cure for her cancer exists in the "Biological Quarantine Ring" of the Pentagon and that a key card he has acquired from a dead agent gives him Level Four Clearance, meaning access to "everything." Mulder procures the cure, but the episode doesn't make clear whether it is the cure itself or Scully's last-minute return to Catholicism and faith that causes her cancer to go into remission. Uniquely, this development means that Mulder loses his faith at roughly the same point that Scully finds or reestablishes hers. It is clear from this fateful conjunction that the beloved agents are on very different paths toward discovery of the truth.

In "Redux Part II," Mulder's faith is further shaken when the Cigarette Smoking Man introduces him to an adult Samantha (Megan Leitch) and suggests that he has been acting as her father for many years. Mulder is left rudderless and uncertain about his beliefs, especially since Samantha seems unable to meaningfully reconnect with him. Is she a plant or mole? A clone? An actress with a ballpark resemblance to his sister? The only fact we know for sure is that Mulder encounters her here, on Earth, in contradiction of the belief that she is elsewhere, in alien hands.

The opening two-parter also establishes a biotechnology company called Roush that has shadowy connections to the FBI (through Section Chief Blevins) and to the Conspiracy. This company reappears in the sixth-season premiere, "The Beginning."

Mid-season, the Mytharc continues with "Christmas Carol," and "Emily," a two-part story that sees Scully receive a mysterious phone call from her dead sister, Melissa, urging her to help a special-needs child, Emily (Lauren Diewold). Scully does so and comes to realize that Emily was conceived—or engineered—during her own abduction three years earlier.

In short, Emily is her child, a result of the genetic experiments she endured there. But Emily is also, alas, a failed experiment, possessing the same toxic composition as the beings they have encountered before. She is an unsuccessful human-alien hybrid. The experience of finding and losing

The cover art for the original *X-Files* novel, *Skin.*

Emily leads Scully fully back to the Catholic Church, a journey depicted in the episode "All Souls."

"Patient X" and "The Red and the Black" continue the Mytharc storyline and introduce a crucial new character: Cassandra Spender (Veronica Cartwright), a multiple abductee and the first successful human-alien hybrid.

Also, a new renegade or rebel group of aliens—with their facial cavities raggedly sewn up—arrive on Earth and begin systematically massacring returned abductees, an initiative designed to slow down the development of a hybrid and set back the date for colonization. In these episodes, audiences also meet Cassandra's son, Jeffrey (Chris Owens), a straitlaced FBI agent and also Mulder's half-brother.

The final episode of Season Five, "The End," introduces two more important recurring characters to the grand storyline. The first is Gibson Praise (Jeff Gulka), a boy with the ability to read minds and thus see through "the conspiracy."

The second is Diana Fowley (Mimi Rogers), the agent who first discovered the X-Files with Mulder in 1991, but whose loyalties aren't clear at this juncture in the arc. She, Mulder, and Scully attempt to protect Praise from the forces of the conspiracy, but he is captured, leaving a wounded Fowley behind.

Finally, the season ends with a terrible act of destruction and sabotage: the Cigarette Smoking Man burns down the basement office of The X-Files, destroying all evidence of Mulder and Scully's labors since the series began. With their office destroyed and their faith questioned, the heroes see their quest in tatters.

At least until the premiere of the movie. . . .

Season Highlights

"Detour." Written by Frank Spotnitz. Directed by Brett Dowler. Airdate: November 23, 1997.

On their way to a trust-building seminar in west Florida, Mulder and Scully join an investigation already in progress. A survey team and hunter have both disappeared without a trace in the Everglades.

Mulder suspects a camouflaged creature of some type may be responsible, one striking back because of human encroachment in the woods. He even connects the creatures to the Mothman legends of West Virginia in the 1960s.

Armed with an infrared scanner to detect their prey, Mulder, Scully, and two others head into the woods to find out the truth, a truth that goes back to Ponce De Leon and his landing in America several centuries earlier. . . .

Some of the best *X-Files* episodes are those that ask viewers to reckon with monsters that are made by or released by mankind himself. The Fluke Man in "The Host" is a child of the Chernobyl disaster. The Peacocks in "Home" are a product of traditional values in conflict with 1990s modernity. And Frank Spotnitz's fifth-season outing "Detour" is not only one of the scariest episodes of the series ever filmed—right down to the presence of a fearsome monster hiding under the bed—but one that perfects this overarching series leitmotif.

In "Detour," Mulder and Scully intersect with monsters that have evolved in the forest on their own, but are suddenly on the warpath against civilization because of "encroaching development" or sprawl. Sprawl might best be defined as the outward spread of civilization, especially suburbs, into virgin or heretofore natural territories. This question of land use raises many important questions. Foremost among them may simply be: what happens to ecosystems destabilized by man's sudden presence, and how do those ecosystems respond to that presence? And secondly, how do humans react when suddenly reckoning with life on the edge, essentially, of a frontier?

When your backyard leads into a dense, wild forest, what does that mean for everyday life and issues like safety?

My own neighborhood in Charlotte is on the edge of such a forest. Not many weeks back, a fox and three fox cubs came up on our backyard deck to play and to use our banana plant pots as toilets. They were adorable, and my family enjoyed watching them from behind the safety of windows, but the day they left I saw another, unexpected sign of their presence so close by. When I mowed the lawn I found the remnants of a squirrel carcass. All that was left of it were the legs and tail. Everything else had been eaten or dragged away. I see dead squirrels all the time in my neighborhood, but usually as roadkill. In this case, something out of the norm had occurred. Every usable part of the squirrel had been devoured by a predator.

With its trademark blend of witty humor, authentic thrills and chills, and cerebral speculation, *The X-Files* brilliantly explores this idea of the fringe—the borderland between civilization and the wild—in "Detour."

In the episode's prologue, a surveyor looks around him at the wild, natural land of the forest and notes, cynically "this is where they're going to put the Blockbuster." This funny comment is not only a time capsule of the 1990s—since today we all experience our entertainment via streaming or mail-in services, not brick-and-mortar shops—but also a perfect reflection of the new homogenization of America. Sprawl was occurring everywhere in the late 1990s, coinciding in large part with the wealth created by the dot. com bubble. And the construction and edifices going up where nature had once thrived did not necessarily represent a fair exchange. Who really needs another Pizza Hut or Blockbuster that badly? A comment about paving paradise and putting up a parking lot seems completely appropriate here.

But what Mulder and Scully discover in the Everglades in "Detour" is a sign that certain long-lived creatures—going as far back as Ponce De Leon (1474–1521)—have dwelt in the forest. These creatures consider it their home, and the rest of us are invaders. This fact exposes our human arrogance in a nuanced fashion. We assume that unspoiled land is ours to do with as we please simply because we have drawn imaginary borders around it. It rarely occurs to us that someone or something else might *already* live in such forests and therefore feel possessive or defensive about it.

But there are two other things that make these creatures terrifying. The first is that they are largely invisible, save for their red eyes. Generations of adaptation have given these monsters natural camouflage, meaning that they can't be seen easily. The episode is thus filled with authentically creepy moments during which we detect the monster only by its scarlet eyes. Indeed, this is the (horrifying) note we leave the episode on, and just to further sear the terror deeper into our reptilian brain we see one of the monsters hiding in that archetypal, childhood realm of fear: underneath a bed.

Secondly, what's so scary in "Detour" is the notion of a human intelligence and cunning existing in a creature of the wild. Or as Mulder trenchantly notes: "Whatever it is, it's smarter than us. (At least) out here." Because the Mothmen are descendants of humans, they act in a way contrary to the apparent natural order, and this is frightening. These predators take out the strongest opponents first, after dividing and conquering enemy numbers. Mulder even links these creatures to the Mothman legends of Point Pleasant, West Virginia, in the 1960s, to help "generalize" the terror beyond the Everglades.

Any episode of *The X-Files* that can meaningfully connect invisible monsters to the Mothman incident of November 1966 and to Ponce De Leon and the Fountain of Youth is bound to be a rewarding viewing experience, but "Detour" goes beyond even that description. It also evinces a self-reflexive quality by featuring clips of *The Invisible Man* (1932), a clear antecedent in the horror genre. *The X-Files* can readily be viewed as a master's thesis in horror, one that makes relevant for the 1990s all the old horrors and bogeymen of decades past, including this one. But finally, like all the best *X-Files* episodes, "Detour" concerns the Mulder/Scully relationship and its very nature.

As the episode opens, Mulder and Scully are on their way to a trust-building seminar that is supposed to improve their communication skills. Mulder ditches the conference at his first opportunity, but importantly, "Detour" ultimately lands him in a situation in which his communication skills are in question and also, consequently, balanced against the communication skills of the two Mothman hunters or predators. Once their police escorts are gone, Mulder and Scully must survive on their wits in the forest, trusting one another, just as—presumably—the Mothmen have done for centuries. Consider that old game for two people wherein you stand behind someone close to you and tell that person to shut his or her eyes and fall backwards into your arms. If that person doesn't do so, or is reluctant to do so, you may have an issue of trust.

Here, Mulder and Scully play a life-and-death version of that game. They can't see their enemy, but when their partner says shoot, or run, or jump, they must trust that order and obey it . . . lest they both die. The punch line to this thematic through line in "Detour" occurs inside the subterranean

Mothman cave at the climax. To escape from this death trap, Scully and Mulder must make a mountain of corpses so as to climb out together, a direct reflection of information the audience has received about the trust-building seminar. There, two agents working together had to build the highest mountain of office furniture.

Of course, in that situation, it was easy to work together because the stakes were not high. There was no cost to giving your trust.

The point in "Detour" may very well be that effective communication is a natural byproduct of close relationships. No seminar games can substitute for experience. Both Mulder and Scully—and the Mothmen too—have endured situations wherein they must depend on one another to succeed and to survive. Their communication "shorthand" is based on a level of trust that no corporate seminar can approximate.

"The Post-Modern Prometheus." Written and Directed by Chris Carter. Airdate: November 30, 1997.

In the comic book titled "The Great Mutato," Mulder and Scully go to small-town America to investigate one woman's wild claim that she has twice been impregnated by a two-faced monster . . . who also happens to love Cher.

The case takes the FBI agents to meet Dr. Pollidori (John O'Hurley), an ambitious and reckless scientist who has unlocked a new genetic secret and may have both the ability and propensity to create a monster such as the unusually named Great Mutato.

But the truth is not what it seems, as Mulder and Scully discover when they defend the creature from angry townsfolk, and the Great Mutato finally has the opportunity to tell his side of the story. . . .

This award-winning segment of *The X-Files*, written and directed by Chris Carter, is one of its most daring and complex ventures. In "The Post-Modern Prometheus," Mulder and Scully experience a version of the *Frankenstein* myth, or more accurately, James Whale's *Frankenstein* (1931) myth. However, they do so not as—strictly speaking—themselves but rather as fictionalized characters inhabiting a comic book, one whose frames bookend the episode. This framing technique—of an X-Files adventure as seen through the lens of a comic book—is useful for a few reasons.

First and foremost, this technique allows viewers and fans to immediately dispense with any concerns about how the story at hand fits into the overall series, Mytharc, or ongoing character relationships. The comic-book framing makes one aware immediately that we are not in the canon universe anymore but somewhere else entirely, an expressionist fantasy, perhaps. So "The Post-Modern Prometheus" presents itself up front as a work of *fiction* about the series' continuing characters and wisely never takes those characters outside that bookend structure, or even beyond the central locale of the episode: a small town in heartland America. "The Post-Modern Prometheus" never follows the protagonists back to Washington, D.C., or into dialogue scenes with Skinner or the Cigarette Smoking Man, for example, because those places and those people don't exist within the confines of this comic book "The Great Mutato." This comic book was created by a character named Izzy, and how could he—*our author, remember*—know anything about Mulder's apartment, Quantico, or the FBI building, since he's never been there?

Secondly, the use of a comic-book motif means that "The Post-Modern Prometheus" need not adhere to the series' conventions regarding imagery. Accordingly, the German Expressionism of Whale's film seeps into many compositions throughout the episode, suggesting a connection not just to that filmed horror story but to the very imagery of dreams and nightmares. In other words, the comic-book "bubble universe" of "The Post-Modern Prometheus" permits Carter the freedom to experiment and to delve into the visual language of the surreal, an aspect seen most clearly in the presence of townsfolk who, strangely enough, resemble farm animals.

The notion of viewing Mulder and Scully through a new and singular lens—that of a black-and-white horror comic book—fits in well with the overarching creative approach of "The Post-Modern Prometheus." The episode features a story not merely about a monster but about that monster's relationship to and interaction with American pop culture itself. Throughout the episode, for example, allusions are made to *The Jerry Springer Show*, Cher's musical oeuvre, and even her 1985 film *Mask*.

Or to put it another way, "The Post-Modern Prometheus" is an *X-Files* story by way of James Whale, set in the 1990s culture of Jerry Springer, to the tune of Cher. This recasting of the *Frankenstein* myth (and *The X-Files* itself) is not only audacious and fiercely unconventional in conception, but an approach that bears remarkable fruit. In the final analysis, the episode recognizes *The X-Files* as a creative work that exists not only in its own universe but in ours as well. As such, it is a piece of a much larger, interactive puzzle, both impacting upon other productions and simultaneously being impacted by them.

Shot in gorgeous black and white, and with feature film quality visuals that take full account of the breadth of the frame, "The Post-Modern Prometheus" proves a brilliantly offbeat entry in the canon and an unforgettable monster-of-the-week program to boot.

The post-structuralist approach to drama suggests that no single thing, person, or quality determines the values that go into the forging of a work of art. Rather, it explores how multiple aspects of a particular culture—from its most ordinary material details to its most abstract beliefs—determine one another. The intrepid post-structuralist thus connects observations and references from many wildly varying disciplines into a synthetic whole, and that's the very task Chris Carter undertakes in the brawny "The Post-Modern Prometheus." Carter pulls together that "wildly varying" source material to express the details of his mad scientist tale. He uses the burgeoning reality TV/talk show milieu of the 1990s (as represented in the episode by *The Jerry Springer Show*), Cher's musical career (represented by "The Sun Ain't Gonna Shine," "Gypsies, Tramps and Thieves," and "Walking in Memphis"), and the details of the movie *Mask* (1985), and folds them into a narrative about overreaching science and its lack of humanity.

In visuals—such as villagers brandishing burning torches—as well as in theme, Carter reflects the details of Whale's *Frankenstein*. Only in this case, the 1990s pop culture has bled into that old story, hence all the modern TV touches, songs, and mentions of 1-900 telephone help numbers. "The Post-Modern Prometheus" thus leaves behind the classicism of the original *Frankenstein* characters in favor of more contemporary, naturalistic ones. Carter's tale focuses on a lonely woman, Mrs. Berkowitz, who sits on the sofa and watches *Jerry Springer*. She yearns to be famous like one of his guests. Another of Carter's characters is a deformed boy who watches *Mask* and registers that it is possible for him to be loved not merely by his family but by society as a whole. He need not be alone or lurk in the shadows.

And perhaps most importantly, "The Post-Modern Prometheus" is about a geek fanboy, Izzy, who realizes that he need not only be a consumer of pop culture. He can be a creator of it, as well. Izzy creates the comic that we as the audience "read" during the course of the episode. He takes the step that his mother can't, and that Mutato can't, either: he puts together their story (which includes the visit by Mulder and Scully) into a coherent whole. His Frankenstein story is an accumulation of his particular influences (talk shows, comic books, rock 'n' roll), as *Frankenstein* author Mary Shelley's was an accumulation of her own.

At the end of the story, when Mulder demands to talk to "the writer," his comment could be considered two ways. It's either a breaking-the-fourth-wall moment in which actor Duchovny, as Mulder, complains about the script written by Carter and demands a rewrite, or it is Mulder approaching Izzy—the chronicler of these events—demanding that in art, in the comic book, Mutato be gifted the happy ending he has clearly earned and deserves.

So this episode is a rewrite of *Frankenstein* for the 1990s, and its ending concerns a rewrite of that rewrite.

Even the obsession with Cher seems appropriate in "The Post-Modern Prometheus," because we have seen and registered in *Mask* her openness to those who are considered outside society's norms. Therefore, she represents in her blanket acceptance of others a kind of safe harbor or sanctuary. She is a diva and a pop icon, but she is actually the Madonna or Mary of "The Post-Modern Prometheus," a kindly mother figure whose acceptance is crucial. And yes, this ties into the episode's commentary on TV talk shows and fame, too.

In fact, "The Post-Modern Prometheus" offers a happy celebrity ending for all. Izzy publishes "The Great Mutato" (which we're reading, essentially), Mutato gets that dance, and Mrs. Berkowitz finally does something that gets her noticed by Jerry Springer.

What's the point of doing a story in this fashion? For one thing, it bursts the clichés or tropes of the genre. A straightforward mad scientist tale had been done before on *The X-Files* (and done well, too) in stories like "Lazarus" or "Eve." There's not a story in the style or tone of "The Post-Modern Prometheus" anywhere else in the canon. Secondly, "The Post-Modern Prometheus" is a reminder that the human condition is universal. Our stories stay the same over time, but the way they are told—and what qualities inform them—can and does change radically over the years. This is the crux of *The X-Files'* approach to the Gothic and monsters. It's a newfangled, 1990s revamp of old forms. Perhaps no story expresses this value better than "The Post-Modern Prometheus," which reminds us that monsters are people too, mad scientists can exist in the same world that enjoys Jerry Springer, and Cher, and that *The X-Files*, finally, is not too narrow or inflexible to accommodate the occasional post-structuralist reframing.

In an age when horror movies were moving toward postmodernism in efforts such a *Scream* (1996), and *The Blair Witch Project* (1999), *The X-Files* pioneered the same approach on television and gave the series one of its most unforgettable, visually accomplished hours.

"Chinga." Written by Stephen King and Chris Carter. Directed by Kim Manners. Airdate: February 8, 1998.

On a weekend getaway in Maine, Scully runs afoul of a bizarre X-File: a grocery store terrorized by a seemingly demonic force. In truth, however the evil originates from a little's girl's doll. The girl herself, Polly (Jenny-Lynn Hutcheson), is deemed autistic, and her mother, the beautiful Melissa Turner (Susannah Hoffmann), a recent widow, is suspected of being a witch.

When dead bodies start to accumulate in the small town, the girl's evil doll—who was fished out of the nearby bay and was apparently infused with occult powers by a coven years ago—becomes Scully's prime suspect.

Although *The X-Files* and Stephen King have different creative approaches and styles, they have in common at least one crucial quality. Both the TV series from Carter and the literary works of the master of horror seek to rewrite or reinterpret old horror myths in terms of technological modernity. King's stories feature modern settings and contemporary twentieth-century characters as well as allusions to modern pop culture (usually rock music) and yet also delicately revise the vampire myth (*Salem's Lot*), the haunted house paradigm (*The Shining*), and other "monsters" for an age of reason largely devoid of traditional Gothic elements. This is *The X-Files'* end game as well: making relevant for the "meta" 1990s the bugaboos of old, from the werewolf ("Shapes") and the vampire ("3") to ghosts ("How the Ghosts Stole Christmas"). *The X-Files* steadfastly creates a new Gothic brand or architecture and encodes in its lead characters the tension between the Gothic and the rational, belief and skepticism. Its narrative structure is often epistolary—in the form of Mulder and Scully's reports to the FBI—and thus deliberately reflective of the ultimate Gothic horror story—*Dracula*—and its clash between the exotic and "foreign" with the very latest in scientific advancement. We get the idea, then, in *The X-Files* of the ultramodern reckoning with the romantic or supernatural. The tools of science—whether forensics or behavioral psychology—thus replace the crucifix, garlic, villagers' torches, and other tools of the Old World, but serve, oddly enough, roughly the same purpose.

Given such common ground, it's not a surprise that King should cowrite an episode of *The X-Files* with Carter, or that it should—like King's best literary works—revamp an old "monster" for modern consumption, in this case the "evil doll." That evil doll just wants to "play" and "have (murderous) fun" in "Chinga." Accordingly, the episode, while intensely violent, is also playful and sinister in nature. The episode proves intensely creepy and even a bit over the top in its presentation of a toy as the walking, talking, murdering id of an antisocial child. Yet simultaneously, "Chinga" is also able to have wicked fun with its premise; so much so, in fact, that Carter and King even find time to reference Chucky, the killer doll of the *Child's Play* film series.

A resident, perhaps, of the Uncanny Valley, the automaton—the doll, the dummy, or the puppet—is often featured in horror history. The long-standing fear of automatons may originate from ancient religious rituals, which suggested that inanimate objects could sometimes house the voices of the "unliving." That's precisely what happens in "Chinga." An inanimate object houses the life force of a long-dead and extremely malevolent witch. But again, the "demonic doll" trope gets a modern makeover here, courtesy of Carter and King. The doll is not just a malevolent, ambulatory toy but the sinister id of a girl, Polly, deemed "autistic" (and thus unacceptable) by society at large.

Inexpressive and yet incredibly demanding, Polly is herself a suspect in the episode's gruesome murders, and the doll seems to act according to her bidding, or at least her impulses. To wit, the doll's victims are those unfortunates who have in some way angered Polly, whether a potential boyfriend for Mum, a day care worker who slapped the girl, or a testy ice cream counter employee. The antisocial aspect of childhood autism is thus, in some direct way, the episode's real "monster," only with the doll serving as its walking, talking avatar. Intriguingly, "Chinga" also forges an under-the-surface connection between the ancient witch's coven and a very catchy song, "The Hokey Pokey," which proved a dance sensation in America in the late 1940s.

In the Hokey Pokey dance (as per the lyrics), participants stand in a circle and make gestures in what—not entirely uncharitably—could be deemed ritualistic fashion. Is it possible that the soul of a witch was once placed into a doll using a similar kind of witch's circle or a bizarre incantation? That's a certainly a possibility inherent in the story. "The Hokey Pokey" recurs several times in the episode and universally heralds the doll's murders. It's very much like the incantation at the beginning of a ritual sacrifice.

"Chinga" also locates terror in King's favorite setting: a tiny, gossip-laden New England community where everybody knows everybody else and everybody has an opinion about everything. The locals in "Chinga" trace their roots right back to Salem and the notorious witch trials, and that historical drama is the episode's ground zero for the horror: the New England witch story. Or more snappily, New England Gothic (think: *Let's Scare Jessica to Death* [1973]). Uniquely, "Chinga" handicaps *The X-Files'* intrepid investigators by separating the established team and sending Scully out alone to play roles of both believer and skeptic.

Meanwhile, Mulder—the acknowledged believer—is left at home, in the office to twiddle his thumbs while Scully must work things out in isolation. Although surely it wasn't intentional, this approach actually forecasts the series' eighth season, where Scully must contend with Mulder and his legacy, the show's absent or missing center.

"Chinga" has occasionally been criticized as being incredibly gory, and it is, but the episode works beautifully in terms of the Scully character arc. She concludes, rather atypically, that the supernatural is to blame for a series of killings, and makes her decisions based on that conclusion. In the absence of Mulder, Scully must absorb or assimilate his viewpoint and so is able to destroy the evil doll—a representation of the Gothic—with a distinctly unglamorous tool of modernity: the microwave oven. Again, that's a bit of an in-joke, or a tongue-in-cheek facet of "Chinga," the use of a totally average, totally deromanticized household object to quell the invasion or return of the Gothic. Perhaps not surprisingly, the dead doll of "Chinga" doesn't stay dead for long. . . .

"Bad Blood." Written by Vince Gilligan. Directed by Cliff Bole. Airdate: February 22, 1998.

After botching an investigation and fatally staking a suspect in the heart, Mulder learns that he, Scully, and the FBI are being sued for $446 million in a wrongful death suit. Preparing to go before Skinner to make their final, grim reports on the matter, Scully and Mulder go over their respective stories and find much to differ about.

The truth about what happened in Cheney, Texas, is not easy to discern, and the agents describe vastly different experiences there. Mulder suspects that a local pizza delivery boy was a vampire and the perpetrator of at least two murders. Scully, meanwhile, maintains that cultists may have been involved.

As the agents quarrel over their differing interpretations, they learn that the pizza deliver boy's body has disappeared from the morgue, and they return to Cheney to investigate. . . .

Akira Kurosawa's *Rashomon* (1950) is a landmark film that involved a murder and four differing witness accounts of that moral and legal transgression. Those who remembered the crime included a bandit, a wife, a woodcutter, and a samurai (whose viewpoint was recounted from the "other side" by a medium). As the movie established, no definitive account of the crime could be produced because everyone had seen the same events but interpreted them differently. The film thus suggested that there is no such thing as objective truth. Rather, there are multiple, *subjective* truths, and all of them are based, in some sense, upon self-interest, according to Kurosawa's work of art.

Vince Gilligan's "Bad Blood" is a deliberate and humorous variation on *Rashomon* and its thematic approach. To wit, in this story, Scully and Mulder each present their personal version of an investigation in Texas that went awry and proceed to find very little common ground. Yet the episode reaches a surprising and positive conclusion as well. Even though they see the world (and each other) very differently, Mulder and Scully's viewpoints also prove valuable in parsing clues and understanding the nature of a crime/killer. Delightfully, in "Bad Blood," Mulder and Scully reveal not only how they view their sparring partner but how they view *themselves* as well. As "outside" (objective?) viewers, it is left to us—the audience—to determine whose version of reality is closer to that of the canon characters we experience each week.

Regardless of where you may land regarding that answer, and my wife steadfastly insists Scully's viewpoint is closer to reality than Mulder's is, "Bad Blood" emerges as a valuable tale because it explores the little myths that we all construct around our lives.

"Bad Blood's" *Rashomon* template has been employed on genre television before—and to notably weak effect in *Star Trek: The Next Generation*'s third-season entry "A Matter of Perspective," but the principle of presenting multiple, subjective accounts of an adventure works brilliantly on *The X-Files* because of the series' very structure. After all, *The X-Files* is designed as an exploration of the unknown as seen through two lenses—skepticism and belief—and thus an episode that explores the personalities and frictions behind those belief systems is entirely fitting and within the parameters of the format.

In its humorous efforts to explain "essentially, exactly, the way it happened" in Cheney Texas, "Bad Blood" provides funny and sharp insight into the characters of Mulder and Scully. Throughout the series, we have witnessed these two very different investigators work together, debate matters of science and superstition, and cleave to one another in times of crisis and trauma. But "Bad Blood" explores how these characters see each other on a day-to-day basis, and the results are funny and even revelatory. Scully largely views Mulder as "characteristically exuberant" over the discovery of things that seem to reinforce his worldview (things like cattle mutilations). Mulder, meanwhile, sees himself as knowledgeable and deferential. In Scully's version of reality, Mulder steam-rolls over her in a rush to get to Texas. In his version, he tiptoes around her and provides the necessary keys to solving the case.

And how does Mulder see Scully? In his version of the events, she is caustic, snippy, and perpetually out of sorts, complaining about going to Texas and refusing to entertain the possibility that vampires exist. She is reluctant to do an autopsy and condescending regarding his belief in vampires. In Scully's version, however, she is agreeable, put-upon, and downtrodden. She doesn't get to enjoy her pizza or her motel bed's "magic fingers" and without complaint performs the autopsy tasks at hand.

Essentially, then, Mulder and Scully possess exaggerated views of themselves and each other. When Mulder learns that Scully believes the local sheriff is attractive (and called her "Dana"), he amends his tale to play up the sheriff's southern-bumpkin-ism. Mulder's vision of a bucktooth, dimwitted sheriff results in some of the episode's funniest moments. They seem borne out of Mulder's jealousy and his being upset that Scully doesn't remember things the way he does. So in short, Mulder and Scully each see the other one as kind of bossy, while viewing themselves as paragons of restraint and equanimity. This is not an alien equation to longtime partners—in marriage or on the job—I hasten to add.

Yet "Bad Blood" doesn't just tear down Scully and Mulder. It reveals their core intelligence and knowledge. Mulder's oddball notion about vampires and obsessive-compulsive disorders, for instance, proves spot-on, and Scully successfully determines the identity of the killer through her two autopsies and an understanding of the corpses' stomach contents. What the viewer takes away, then, is that though Scully and Mulder are flawed human beings, they are also, importantly, clever, curious, knowledgeable investigators.

This is also another story (like "3") that deromanticizes vampires and comes up with a new way to "parse" these old-fashioned monsters. *The X-Files* and "Bad Blood"—as early as 1998—seem to recognize the next iteration of the vampire myth on television. The undead of Cheney, Texas, report themselves to be good, hard-working American citizens. "We pay taxes. We're good neighbors," the sheriff (Luke Wilson) insists, and indeed, this is the template we have come to see in the last decade, in programming such as *True Blood* (2008–2014) and *The Vampire Diaries* (2009–). In all these stories, the vampires are not monsters ("It's not who we are, anymore"), but rather a social minority attempting to assimilate into mainstream American culture.

In some ways, "Bad Blood" feels like it was absolutely destined to be made, because it puts us in the shoes of each protagonist and asks us to consider their judgment and vision. The episode is so damned funny because it holds nothing precious, nothing sacred. Scully and Mulder's flaws are on full display here and fully recognized by the storyteller. The flip side is that their virtues also come to the forefront quite powerfully. Where most *X-Files* episodes boast a kind of clinical distance from the subject matter as Scully and Mulder walk us through evidence, science, and theory, "Bad Blood" is heightened, exaggerated, silly, and therefore, in some sense, *intimate*. For one glorious hour, we get to see Mulder and Scully through Mulder's eyes and through Scully's eyes. It's a perspective no *X-Files* fan should miss.

"Folie a Deux." Written by Vince Gilligan. Directed by Kim Manners. Airdate: May 10, 1998.

Mulder and Scully are sent to handle a potential workplace violence incident and deliver a threat assessment at a telemarketing center for Vinyl Right in Oak Brook, Illinois. There, one employee, Gary Lambert (Brian Markinson), believes that his boss, Mr. Pincus (John Apicella), is a monster who "hides in the light" and is somehow transforming his fellow telemarketers into mindless zombies.

Lambert takes over the telemarketing center and holds his fellow employees hostage, until the FBI—over Mulder and Scully's objections—takes violent action. After Lambert is killed, Mulder begins to see Mr. Pincus as he really is: a horrible, insect-like creature that can skitter across the ceiling, climb walls, and turn the living into the compliant dead.

When Mulder breaks into the home of a Vinyl Right employee to rescue her from Pincus, the agent is called on the carpet by Skinner and hospitalized for exhaustion.

But the monster tracks Mulder there, leaving only Scully to determine if her partner is telling the truth or is dangerously delusional. . . .

Vince Gilligan's "Folie a Deux" is a brilliant example of *The X-Files'* propensity to feature tales that are wholly satisfying as a pure entertainment and, on another level entirely—react to and discuss some issue or idea roiling the culture. "Folie a Deux" concerns workplace violence and, for lack of a better term, the "cubicle culture" of the nineties. There, in the same world treated comically by *Office Space* (1999), workers are mere anonymous cogs in a machine, meant to mindlessly sell, sell, sell, nine-to-five, and to do so *cheerily*, despite the underwhelming nature of the product or the sheer dehumanizing nature of the work. For some people, this crushing routine is too much to bear, hence the outbreaks of violence. In the tradition of many a fine horror tale, then, *The X-Files* imagines that this real-life working nightmare contains a dark, monstrous, *supernatural* secret . . . a creature that hides in plain view and that only a few can detect or see.

"Folie a Deux" makes a very clear point. Too much time spent working in a telemarketing cubicle and the worker becomes a drone who mindlessly and lifelessly obeys the mind-numbing establishment. Or, contrarily, that worker goes crazy. The episode suggests these facts of life in two ways. First, it does so by charting the endless, indistinguishable geography of the call center. Secondly, it makes its case about dehumanizing jobs through the overt act of a boss who literally turns workers into zombies.

In the first case, director Kim Manners's camera probes restlessly through the Illinois telemarketing center, sometimes from an extreme high angle. These shots accent the mazelike, anonymous, sealed-off world of telemarketing, and the point-of-view suggests entrapment and doom. Each cubicle is a mini-world just like the one next to it and just like the one on the other side. These boxes might as well be jail cells as work spaces.

Thematically, the episode supports this interpretation of the telemarketing world. Telemarketers read a script about an unglamorous product (vinyl siding) again and again, without real feeling but with the *simulation* of real feeling. The impression created is of a most peculiar brand of hell; one where the seller is just as miserable to place the call and make the hard sell as the customer is to receive the call.

"Folie a Deux" is so clever, too, because of its fresh interpretation of zombie lore. Before George Romero revolutionized the concept of zombies for *Night of the Living Dead* (1968), the monster had mythological roots in Africa and Haiti. A zombie was, in that milieu, a corpse raised from the dead by a sorcerer or puppet master. Controlled by the master, a zombie was a creature without any will of his or her own. The zombie master, the sorcerer, or *bokor* was thus a critical part of the equation. The zombie could not do monstrous things unless directed to do so. "Folie a Deux" revives and reinterprets this original version of the zombie myth, and transforms the sorcerer or bokor into a middle manager or company bureaucrat. Mr. Pincus transforms his employees into zombies who do his bidding.

Pretty clearly, the episode suggests a more or less direct line between the sorcerers of zombie folklore and 1990s bosses at call centers. Both—in the words of "Folie a Deux"—"want to take away who we are." Individuality is replaced with servitude, with an adherence to an agenda not of the zombie's/worker's making. In obeying their masters, both types of zombies might also be said to have had "the humanity sucked out of them."

Anyone who has worked a mindless job like the one at Vinyl Right—as I did during my stint as a temp in the 1990s—knows how it feels to be a drone for eight hours. So *The X-Files* is caustic, funny, and even a little brutal in its description of such workers as mindless zombies, and at one point the teleplay even notes "these people were dead before they were gunned down." Indeed, sometimes it felt that way.

"Folie a Deux" also proposes the idea that workplace shootings are, perhaps, a natural response to the monster overlords and to the zombie-making process itself. The term "workplace violence" actually came into being after several post office shootings in the late 1980s. In the 1990s, the U.S. Department of Justice declared that the workplace was the "most dangerous" location in America, and so this *X-Files* episode is clearly timely in presentation. In the 1990s, writes Dr. James Madero in *Workplace Violence in the 21st Century, Emerging Trends*, "several well-known companies and organizations experienced incidence of workplace violence involving many homicides" and he listed Ford Motor Company among them. Again, that 1990s context is critical to an understanding of "Folie a Deux." The episode looks at a real-life problem and then spins an imaginative, horror-themed web around it, one that takes into account the nature of the contemporary workplace.

In terms of Mulder and Scully, "Folie a Deux" is an important episode in the canon, because Mulder takes a step toward regaining his "belief" in the paranormal, albeit an unwitting one. Similarly, Scully demonstrates here her total support of and loyalty toward Mulder. She may write off the Pincus monster as a "folie a deux"—a "delusion shared by two"—but she acts in a way that validates Mulder's belief system and that also happens to save his life.

12

Sci-Fi Universe

Season Six (1998–1999)

The sixth season of *The X-Files* represents a hard shift in storytelling style. There are fewer straight-up horror or paranormal tales featured during the season, namely "Agua Mala," "Arcadia," "Alpha," and "Field Trip," and a strong accent on other genres instead.

The first tone or idea explored is the science fiction trope or high-concept story, the sort of narrative that might be featured on *Star Trek*, for example. In this case, the sixth season features episodes about the Bermuda Triangle ("Triangle,") a "turnabout"-style body switch ("Dreamland"/"Dreamland II"), and even a repeating time loop ("Monday").

The second tone or genre explored is largely the comedy-fantasy. "How the Ghosts Stole Christmas," the aforementioned "Dreamland" two-parter, "Terms of Endearment," "Rain King," "The Unnatural," and "Three of a Kind" are all comedy-heavy episodes that deal lightly and effectively with their intriguing concepts (ghosts, demons, a man who can psychically control the weather, and an alien ensconced on a baseball team). What remains remarkable about the season is that none of the episodes feel out of place, and none break the series format, which proves itself ever more elastic.

Season Six also represents the juncture wherein in-front-of-the-camera talent begins shifting behind the camera. David Duchovny writes and directs "The Unnatural," a story told in flashback of an alien, Josh Exley (Jesse L. Martin), who assumes the shape of a black man in late 1940s Roswell so he can play baseball, a sport that his people, the Grays, don't understand.

Once more, an *X-Files* episode features an unreliable narrator, Arthur Dales, which suggests the possibility that the story is a fantasy, or at least not entirely on the up-and-up. Brian Thompson's Bounty Hunter appears in the episode, at one point taking the guise of a Ku Klux Klan member and hunting down Exley for his trespasses, which include jeopardizing "the project" that the Grays have been working on, colonization, for the simple love of the game. Meanwhile, Exley tells his human friend, Arthur Dales (M. Emmet Walsh, in this case), that the Grays don't have a word for laughter, and rarely smile, but that baseball makes him smile.

At story's end, Exley's humanity is apparent when he bleeds human blood rather than the toxic green soup of the aliens, an indication that he has become one of us by experiencing the American pastime. "The Unnatural" has plenty of whimsy but also a strong undercurrent about race. Under the skin—even alien skin—we can all truly be brothers, joined together in our love of life or even silly games. We all bleed the same color: red.

The trend of actors moving toward writing and directing continues in the seventh season, but *The X-Files'* sixth season is also notable for several other landmark episodes. "Triangle," for example, is a visually dazzling hour that repeats the central conceit of *The Wizard of Oz* (1939). There, as you recall, Dorothy (Judy Garland) led a kind of double life, one with her friends and family in Kansas, and one with those same friends and family members in different roles, as strange denizens of the fantasy Land of Oz.

Likewise, in "Triangle," Mulder finds himself on a ship trapped in the Bermuda Triangle and sees Scully, Skinner, Kersh, and the Cigarette Smoking Man in new or different roles or identities, but ones that nonetheless convey their essential character. Scully is still brave and committed, for example. Skinner is still, when the shit hits the fan, an ally. And after mention of CSM as a Nazi in "The Field Where I Died," we finally get an appearance by him in Gestapo uniform here. "Triangle," written and directed by Chris Carter, is a cinematic powerhouse, consisting of long, unbroken Steadicam shots and information-laden split screens. The episode never stops moving, the camera never stops prowling, and the effect is pure, unadulterated excitement.

Mytharc Notes

The sixth-season Mytharc stories close out an era. In the first episode, "The Beginning," viewers witness the final stage of the alien life cycle. Previous episodes have revealed the infection point (through the black oil), and the first feature film revealed the oil's growth into a terrible, clawed green alien.

However, in "The Beginning," this monstrosity rests in a nuclear power plant, and the final stage of growth occurs. The green skin sloughs off, and a beautiful, glowing (presumably quite intelligent) Gray is left in its place, the process complete.

Midway through the season, the two-part episode "Two Fathers"/"One Son" brings to an end six years of Mytharc storytelling. Here, the Syndicate is destroyed, murdered in an airport hangar by rebel aliens who are resisting colonization. The Syndicate dies horribly, and with it go years of "the project" (creating an alien-human hybrid and a vaccine to the black oil), as well as the Cigarette Smoking Man's life's work.

The same two-part epic also involves the completion of a perfect alien-human hybrid, Cassandra Spender (Veronica Cartwright), and her son's reckoning with her husband's legacy. In this case, Agent Jeffrey Spender (Chris Owens) comes to realize the cruelty of his father and renounces his loyalty to him. The Cigarette Smoking Man shoots him dead, in Mulder's office, or at least that is what we are led to believe at this juncture.

At the end of the season, a new branch of Mytharc storytelling opens with the discovery of a crashed UFO on Africa's Ivory Coast. A scientist discovers an ancient tablet inscribed with Scripture and a map of the human genome, written in phonetic Navajo. The suggestion is that aliens began human life on Earth and gave the human race religion, or at least Christianity. Future episodes of the Mytharc would deal with this discovery and its impact on Mulder.

Season Highlights

"Drive." Written by Vince Gilligan. Directed by Rob Bowman. Airdate: November 15, 1998.

Scully and Mulder have been reassigned from the X-Files by Kersh, their new supervisor at the FBI. Instead of working on cases involving the paranormal and supernatural, the duo is assigned to question farmers about purchases of fertilizer on the West Coast. While in Nevada, Mulder sees a strange case on the news and inserts himself into it over Scully's objections.

A highway chase in Elko turns strange when a passenger in a speeding car dies under mysterious circumstances. Specifically, her head explodes. Now the car's driver, Mr. Patrick Crump (Bryan Cranston), suffers from the same affliction as his wife, Vicki. He hijacks Mulder and makes him drive west at over fifty miles an hour because only the sensation of speed can relieve the pressure in his head.

Meanwhile, Scully investigates a top-secret Navy project called "Seafarer" that may have caused the Crumps' odd condition. . . .

In premise, "Drive" determinedly apes the hit action film *Speed* (1994), and Mulder actually references the Jan de Bont movie in the episode's dialogue. But because this is *The X-Files,* there's a major twist in the tale, and "Drive" functions as more than mere rip-off. In *Speed,* as you will recall, a mad bomber (Dennis Hopper) placed a bomb on a metropolitan bus, and that bomb was triggered to detonate if it fell below a certain speed-threshold, fifty-five miles per hour. This effectively meant that any rescue or defusing attempts had to be completed while the bus remained in motion.

In "Drive," however, the "bomb" is not aboard a vehicle. Rather it is a physical "vibration" inside a passenger's head. Any slowdown in terms of velocity is still deadly in this scenario, but it will result in a *cranial* explosion. In *Speed,* the bomb could be stopped by catching the bomber or defusing the device. In "Drive," it's a race to outrun a sound vibration, an impossible task.

What's perhaps even more unusual about "Drive" is the nature of the passenger or victim: Patrick Crump. He's a racist jerk and a pain in the ass. He complains about the "Jew FBI," for instance, and marks Mulder as one of "them." But despite the character's paranoia and bigotry, Cranston succeeds in making Crump a sympathetic (if ignorant) human being, and so the episode's tragic ending carries unusual and unexpected weight. "Drive" is fast-paced, intense, and literally explosive—as it should be—but the genuine surprise here is how much the denouement at water's edge will impact you in sheer emotional terms. Against all your better judgment, you'll find yourself rooting for Crump to survive, to outpace the deadly signal causing him so much pain. The visual reveal that he doesn't survive the ordeal is also a great one. Very little is spoken, but a blood spatter on a car window tells the audience everything it needs to know.

Mr. Crump's strange malady in "Drive" is caused by the aforementioned Navy project Seafarer, and like many of the best *X-Files* episodes, the narrative and mystery here have a basis in fact. A project called "Sanguine" was proposed in 1968, and then again in 1975, but as Seafarer. In 1982, the same project was actually implemented in Wisconsin but called "Project ELF" (for extreme low frequency). The notion underlying all these projects was the creation of a transmitter facility that could communicate with nuclear submarines submerged in the ocean following World War III or other nuclear detonations. The transmitter remains controversial, however, because the effects of high ground currents on the environment and surrounding electromagnetic fields are not known.

"Drive" plays with this tantalizing premise and suggests that ELF waves impact "the inner ear," unbalancing internal pressure to the point that human heads could—à la *The Fury* (1978) or *Scanners* (1981)—simply explode. But where those R-rated horror films featured full-on exploding heads, "Drive" takes a different tack, perhaps because of TV limitations. Here, the heads explode like zits, and we see the sudden spurting of blood, but not flesh literally blowing apart. This visualization is remarkably effective, and sickening.

Amusingly, "Drive" also functions as a character piece. The episode suggests that the ill-informed conspiracy theories of a knucklehead like Crump could, in fact, be true in some cases. He reflexively suspects that the government has "done this" to him, and in fact he's right. Even a broken clock is right two times a day, however, and in this case Crump's paranoia, as Mulder notes, is entirely justified. Of course, he is not the government's "guinea pig" as he fears, but rather the collateral damage of the government's pure incompetence, an unexpected power surge in the Seafarer equipment.

Mulder and Crump clearly don't like each other very well, or understand each other much, but their mutual situation—trapped in a speeding car with death just moments away—allows them to bond on simple human terms, and that's where "Drive" really excels. Nobody deserves to suffer the way Crump does, and Mulder does everything in his power to save him. In fact, the episode's final act carries so much emotional weight because we have become thoroughly invested in Crump's plight, and the episode teases us with the possibility of a fix. Scully plans to meet Mulder at the coast, by the sea, and will insert a long needle into his ear. It will render him permanently deaf, but that's a trade-off he's willing to make. Here "Drive" lures us into believing there's still a chance, even a tiny one, that Crump could live. But then Mulder drives by the camera and we see that blood spatter on the window of his car. He was moments—and maybe just feet—from saving his ward.

"Drive" succeeds on the principle of "you stop moving, you die," and speeds toward its conclusion with purpose and pathos. Perhaps the "you stop moving, you die" edict applies to Crump, too. He's a man who has been cut no breaks and hates everybody ahead of him in the "line." Every day he has to keep trying—keep moving—or he and his wife fall further behind. In "Drive," Crump runs up against something that makes him run even faster, but it's a race he can never win. Some could say that's a direct metaphor for the American dream.

"How the Ghosts Stole Christmas." Written and directed by Chris Carter. Airdate: December 13, 1998.

On Christmas Eve, Mulder asks a reluctant Scully to stake out a reputedly haunted house in Maryland. There, in 1917, two lovers committed suicide, and their ghosts apparently still roam the hallways.

Once inside the imposing house, Mulder and Scully find that the stories possess some truth. The exterior doors lock mysteriously behind them, and the agents find themselves trapped inside the labyrinth-like hallways.

And under the rickety floorboards of the library, Scully and Mulder make a terrible discovery: their own rotting corpses.

The agents attempt to escape the fate promised by this vision, but must first survive the manipulations of the two spirits, Maurice (Edward Asner) and Lyda (Lily Tomlin), who would like Mulder and Scully to join them in the house . . . for eternity.

"How the Ghosts Stole Christmas" is a tale about both the holiday season and the unbreakable bond connecting Mulder and Scully. In brief, this *X-Files* story concerns a fearsome haunted house. Inside, two old ghosts—bound together for eternity by their murder pact—attempt to make Scully and Mulder reenact their "love" by killing each other. Edgar Rice Burroughs once suggested that "nearly one" are the emotions of "love and hate," and this episode plays out as an examination of that observation. Passion can be either a positive or negative force in relationships, and the passion that Mulder and Scully feel for each other and for their own worldviews is the very thing the ghosts attempt to twist to their will.

What seems so humorous and intriguing about "How the Ghosts Stole Christmas," however, is the fact that the ghosts attempt to psychoanalyze their guests before killing them. They try to plant "doubt" inside Mulder and Scully by targeting feelings of inferiority or low self-esteem. Mulder is forced to see himself as a lonely, pitiful narcissist, and Scully must face the possibility that she stays in Mulder's orbit simply to prove him wrong and herself right. The ghosts thus make Mulder and Scully question their very natures. And then—after cracking that foundation of belief/esteem—the ghosts send each agent to kill the other. But Scully and Mulder rebound. They find the strength, resourcefulness, and hope inside themselves and inside each other to escape the death trap.

"How the Ghosts Stole Christmas" is thus a story about having the right person in your life to give you strength. The right partner (in the FBI or in love) can build you back up when society at large or other dark forces try to pull you down. You can respond to "Christmas melancholy" or other emotional strife by giving into it or by resisting it. In this episode we see examples of both paradigms. But only one way will assure happiness.

"How the Ghosts Stole Christmas" is a remarkably intimate episode of *The X-Files.* Only four individuals are seen in the entire hour; two living and two dead. The setting is also generally limited to Maurice and Lyda's house, save for the brief coda at Mulder's apartment. Accordingly, and with all the "noise" or "clutter" out of the way—one begins to feel that the ghosts haunting Mulder and Scully are not just spectral ones but psychological ones. The holidays can be a time of depression, sadness, and loneliness. These emotions play out as the backdrop to the struggle the protagonists face here.

Mulder, for example, goes to great lengths to describe to Scully the Christmas of 1917—Maurice and Lyda's time—as a season of "dark, dark, despair" when tragedy was a visitor "on every doorstep." Mulder talks about big, earth-shattering events like World War I and the flu epidemic, but on another level, he is certainly discussing his own existential angst; his own "dark, dark, despair" and fear, especially at this time of year, that he will always remain alone, unloved. You don't need a pandemic or a global conflict to be sad at Christmas time, after all.

Scully faces her own fears in the episode, too. Has she traded the comfort of family and a "normal life" for the pleasure of proving Mulder wrong? Is it her destiny to be forever conducting stakeouts on Christmas Eve? This "woeful Christmas melancholy" beats at the heart of "How the Ghosts Stole Christmas," and the ghosts make the crisis worse. Are Mulder and Scully together only because they are lonely, pathetic individuals with no one else to spend time with? Their Christmas "adventure" seems to stress this idea; that no one would have them, save for each other. This is the fear that Maurice and Lyda knowingly play upon. But the antidote to "how lonely Christmas can be"—and which the ghosts nastily term "intimacy through co-dependency"—is actually a deep friendship and love that can stand any test, even the test of what appears to be a fatal bullet wound. There's a strong contrast presented between the couples here, and that's a result of the episode's clever construction and structure. Lyda and Maurice gave in to the darkness of their time. They surrendered to it as inevitable and now spend eternity attempting to validate their choice to die, forcing other pairs of lovers to reenact their gruesome end.

But oppositely, Mulder and Scully don't give in to the despair. They are able to find not just love but *hope* in each other. They choose to continue living. That's why, finally, they escape. They each have the other one pushing them to live, to keep asking questions, to meet the next challenge. Accordingly, Scully and Mulder don't let the ghosts steal Christmas or the Christmases yet to come. Instead, they escape their own foibles and fears, and spend the holiday where they belong: *together.*

"Monday." Written by Vince Gilligan and John Shiban. Directed by Kim Manners. Airdate: February 28, 1999.

A regular trip to the bank turns to terror when Mulder and Scully discover that they are in a repeating time loop that ends, inevitably, with them dead at the hands of a mad bomber named Bernard (Darren Burrows).

Bernard's timid girlfriend, Pam (Carrie Hamilton), tries again and again to steer destiny and to send Mulder and Scully away from the bank. But no matter Pam's actions, the day ends with death and destruction. . . .

Mulder and Scully experience a bad day over and over again in "Monday." The story diagrams a time loop that repeats five times before the agents finally escape it and carry on with their lives. This brief description of a repeating time loop no doubt makes "Monday" sound high-concept or gimmicky and a lot like *Star Trek: The Next Generation*'s fifth-season outing "Cause and Effect" or the Bill Murray movie *Groundhog Day* (1993).

However, *The X-Files* is rarely—if ever—content to imitate. Instead, the series tends to perfect or upgrade a preexisting formula, and indeed that's the case here. In "Monday," Gilligan and Shiban don't merely tell a puzzle box story about escaping a repeating time loop. Instead, they innovate within that familiar formula. They use their premise to meaningfully explore ideas such as free will, fate, and even déjà vu, with Mulder and Scully each expressing a specific "belief" on the subject. These characters are our two lenses on life, and so the meat of the episode concerns their dueling perspectives on "the unpredictable future," as Skinner (Mitch Pileggi) describes it.

Even more commendably, however, "Monday" carries a deeper subtext. This sixth-season episode is actually a metaphor for surviving victimhood in a relationship of domestic abuse. In situations like this, as "Monday" points out, it isn't enough to attempt to change someone else. Other people often *can't* be changed. So the repeating time loop—the cycle of violence—can only be altered by *one's self*; by the victim adopting an affirmative stance to make things better. If one falls into the same behavior patterns again and again—the real-life equivalent of a time loop, perhaps—then life becomes, literally, hell.

Accordingly, "Monday" is an episode about empowering and changing yourself rather than looking for someone else to change it and thus "save" you in the process. That's the lesson the episode's primary guest star, Carrie Hamilton's Pam, learns, and it is beautifully expressed in the episode's last act.

"Monday" explores the concept of a single day repeated again and again, and then wonders if such a phenomenon could account for déjà vu or another quirk of human memory. Scully and Mulder debate this idea, and Scully takes the rationalist, scientific view. She suggests that déjà vu is a simple memory glitch or perhaps a repressed vision escaping from the subconscious. She sees the phenomenon as brain chemistry, pure and simple. By contrast, Mulder wonders if déjà vu isn't something deeper and something more meaningful. Could it be the innate human desire to change fate and to right a wrong? Could it be knowledge not of the brain but of the soul? This more mystical, spiritual perspective presupposes that there is, in fact, an order and direction to the universe and that human beings may be able to perceive it, and thus act meaningfully to "correct" it.

Pam brings in a third crucial perspective. She suggests that they are all trapped "in hell," because "nothing ever changes." This is the viewpoint of someone who believes that she has no control or direction over her own existence, and that her "rescue" will occur only when someone else—namely Mulder or Scully—saves her. Pam spends the whole episode trying to change *their* behavior rather than address her own. She tries to get them not to go into the bank, or to use the ATM outside the bank, or to switch roles, with Scully making a deposit instead of Mulder. She even tries calling the police and going to Skinner.

But nothing works because Pam hasn't changed the one thing that can make a difference in her life: herself. Thus we have a metaphor for a person trapped in a stagnant, unhappy, or even abusive relationship. Pam tries to change the deeply unstable bomber Bernard and even Scully and Mulder, but the "end remains the same," as she notes, and she remains trapped. Finally, Pam's escape explicitly involves taking responsibility. She goes into the bank herself, finally. This is something she only attempts in the episode's last act (and the last iteration of the time loop), and which causes both her death and her release.

"I don't think she was an accomplice, I think she was just trying to get away," Mulder notes in the episode's denouement, but the real point here is that history need not repeat, and escape is possible (and not necessarily in death) if only one acts instead of trying to alter someone else's actions or behavior.

There's another idea roiling in the underneath of "Monday." Is it possible that every one of us goes through this bizarre experience—of living a day over and over again—at the time of our death? Is it possible that fate itself plays this game and repeats a day again and again until we finally begin to accept, little by little, the idea of our own mortality?

Here, Carrie tries everything, except going into the bank herself, and survives again and again, but always with bad results. But the time loop is her creation. It "breaks" when she dies, and only when she has come to face the idea of her continued existence as a kind of "hell." So the fact of death is essentially made palatable to Pam through this process because she has lived every iteration of her last twenty-four hours and sees that there is no option for her other than to lay down her life. In doing so, she saves two good people, Mulder and Scully, who are trapped alongside her in her pathology, so to speak.

This conceit comes to the forefront especially if we consider Scully's comment about how "our character determines fate." Mulder disagrees and says "no, there are too many variables" to consider. But Pam breaks the repeating cycle of violence and death by, finally, altering her character. She breaks out of her emotional/relationship paralysis and acts affirmatively to change destiny. So in embracing death, is it possible we could all face the same sort of "test?" Do our characters, in the end, determine or dictate our fate? When we die, do we relive our final moments and make peace with the decision to shuffle off the mortal coil?

It's all great food for thought and evidence that *The X-Files* can rewrite a hackneyed premise to make it newly meaningful and relevant. The Mulder and Scully interplay in this episode is exceedingly vibrant too, because the characters aren't debating a monster or murderer but the very nature of human existence, and their discussion is a beautiful thing to witness.

"Field Trip." Written by Vince Gilligan and John Shiban. Story by Frank Spotnitz. Directed by Kim Manners. Airdate: May 9, 1999.

In this episode, Mulder and Scully head to Brown Mountain, North Carolina, to investigate two skeletonized corpses found there. Mulder suspects the dead bodies—belonging to a married couple who disappeared while hiking in the area—have something to do with the Brown Mountain Lights, believed by some to be UFOs. Scully is skeptical of his explanation and proposes her own alternate theory involving some digestive enzyme.

Before long, Mulder and Scully's separate interpretations of the events both come into play, and reality and fantasy seem to mix. The truth, however, is something far worse than either suspect. They have fallen into the cave of a vast, living fungus and are slowly being digested by it, force-fed fantasies to keep them appeased as their life forces diminish.

"Field Trip" is one of the all-time great *X-Files* mind-fuck episodes, a story that mercilessly plays with your sense of reality and then, in the last act, peels open, like an onion, before your very eyes. Tellingly, Mulder and Scully each end up in a fantasy world that vindicates their viewpoint. Mulder sees an alien in his fantasy and brings it back to his apartment, where he shows it to Scully. "It was there, and I found it," he says triumphantly. Scully instantly agrees "All those years . . . you were right."

But a funny thing happens. When Mulder receives his long-awaited vindication, he can't accept it. It was too easy. Although some part of him wishes for Scully to believe what he believes, another part of him respects Scully and her viewpoint so deeply that he can't imagine she would so quickly and irrevocably get onboard with his viewpoint. The fact that Scully agrees with him is the very thing that makes Mulder start to question his (false) reality. Scully's uncharacteristic agreement prods him back to consciousness.

Similarly, when Scully gets the vindication she wants, she can't accept it. Being right means, in her case, that Mulder is dead. And she even attends his wake. Her mind rejects the very idea, and the two "awaken" from separate fantasies to find themselves in another, joint one. This third fantasy involves a world wherein they have escaped the fungus and are reporting their findings to Skinner. But Mulder senses another discontinuity or gap in his memory and assembles the last puzzle piece. Together, they realize they are trapped in another delusion and then, finally, escape.

"Bad Blood" examined the *Rashomon*-nature of reality and the idea that there is no objective truth, but "Field Trip's" game is somewhat different. It asks viewers to reckon with the idea that a reality too pleasant or too facile doesn't pass the smell test for most folks. Mulder and Scully might each labor to be right when solving a case, but the ultimate goal is always to solve the case to their mutual satisfaction, using science and speculation to do so, where necessary. Here, that value is put to the test, especially for Mulder. Is it better to have a preexisting belief reinforced, even if it turns out to be wrong? Or is it better to embrace a new belief, if it happens to conform to reality? Once more, *The X-Files* seems to anticipate the key driving question of the twenty-first century. Today, people visit the media and news sources that reinforce their belief system rather than stepping out of the ideological bubble, and as a consequence, many Americans can't even agree on key or simple facts. "Field Trip" reveals that Mulder and Scully both have the flexibility to exit that bubble.

In 1999 and today too, "Field Trip" is one of the scariest *X-Files* episodes ever produced, as it reveals that Mulder and Scully have been cocooned inside the fungus, which spreads across ten acres. For a time, we can see them being doused by goopy digestive secretions. The sense of danger is palpable . . . as is the feeling that this is one mystery that might prove so byzantine that even they can't escape it. *The Matrix* was the big blockbuster of 1999, and it posited a fake world inside a real, nightmare world. "Field Trip" is a goopier, more organic alternative take on similar material, one in which the human being is fed pretty pictures while slowly being eaten alive.

13

New Perspectives Considered

Season Seven (1999–2000)

The seventh season of *The X-Files* is all about embracing new perspectives and the doorways that open when one undertakes that task. The season very much concerns Scully and Mulder reckoning with change, and also finds the series experimenting, structurally and narratively, with such new vantage points. This approach may not have been unintentional, but rather something of a valediction. The seventh season was originally believed to be the show's final span, and there is a sense in it of closing doors and having the characters grow in ways that make them more complete before their journey reaches an end point.

In the seventh season, the new perspectives are myriad. Viewers experience a monster-of-the-week story with the monster as the protagonist, and Mulder and Scully as the antagonists ("Hungry") are asked to conceive of reality through the misdirection of "illusion" or "magic" ("The Amazing Maleeni"), and are even tasked with viewing the radically anti-Christian Mulder as a Christlike figure undergoing satanic temptations in "The Sixth Extinction II: Amor Fati." In a similar vein, the episode "X-Cops" is constructed to resemble an episode of Fox's reality TV show *Cops* or in horror movie vernacular, a found-footage movie. Again, that structure represents a new or different perspective than the norm.

The seventh season also sees new shades of the Cigarette Smoking Man explored ("En Ami") and most delightfully of all, perhaps, Scully opening the door just a crack to the belief that Western medicine may not hold all the answers to questions of health and spirituality. Episodes including "Theef" and "All Things" suggest that alternative remedies exist and may merit attention. Alternate views of belief are also presented. Scully looks into Buddhist beliefs in the aforementioned "All Things," and "Signs and Wonders" questions the form that modern American Christianity has adopted, wondering if mainstream religion has become so lukewarm as to lose its original value.

Gillian Anderson, David Duchovny, and William B. Davis all contribute stories to the seventh season. Anderson writes and directs "All Things," which is a key point of transformation for Scully, a juncture at which she truly opens herself up to, if not extreme possibilities, then certainly alternative ones.

Meanwhile, Duchovny writes and directs "Hollywood A.D.," a self-reflexive episode that finds an obnoxious Hollywood writer tagging along with Mulder on a case and then making a movie out of the exploits. And Davis writes "En Ami," a story that walks a fine line of ambiguity, since viewers must decide if the Cigarette Smoking Man is out to seduce Scully and destroy her or actually to help her, and save his own soul in the process.

The Mulder-Scully relationship develops significantly in Season Seven too, perhaps more than it has in any other single previous season. "All Things" opens with the two in bed together, and "Hollywood A.D." showcases them walking off a movie set together, holding hands.

Although the season ends with Mulder's abduction and ensuing disappearance as a result of Duchovny's departure to part-time status, it also culminates with the announcement of Scully's miraculous pregnancy, which puts a fine point on the physical intimacy Scully and Mulder share during the seventh season.

The X-Files' Season Seven scores some hits and some misses, but the great thing about this span is the show's willingness to experiment with new viewpoints, new structures, and new ideas "It becomes hard to surprise people," Frank Spotnitz told Melissa Perenson and Annabella Villanueva in *Cinescape* magazine, and yet the series succeeds in just that difficult task.

Mytharc Notes

The destruction of the Syndicate in Season Six resulted in a new direction for the season finale, and the opening episodes of Season Seven ("The Sixth Extinction"/"The Sixth Extinction II: Amor Fati") continue that narrative. Mulder undergoes a transformation into a perfect human-alien hybrid, though the Cigarette Smoking Man covets that role and undergoes surgery to steal the genetic material that has made this mutation possible. We later learn, in "En Ami," that the Cigarette Smoking Man is dying as a result of the surgery.

Later in the season, "Sein und Zeit" and "Closure" bring to an end Mulder's seven-year search for Samantha. After years of hoping and enduring the trickery of the Cigarette Smoking Man, Mulder discovers the truth while working on a seemingly unrelated case. He learns, to his shock and horror, that Samantha died years earlier, her spirit whisked away by "Walk-ins," paranormal entities that protect imperiled children from future harm. This

This *TV Guide* artwork advertises the seventh-season story "Fight Club," about doppelgangers.

answer to the mystery of Samantha's whereabouts infuriated some viewers, confused others, and delighted many. After a very long time, indeed, Mulder was granted a measure of peace, as he learned that Samantha was at rest.

"Requiem" is the Mytharc episode that brings *The X-Files* full circle. Mulder and Scully return to the location of their first case, in the 1993 pilot: Bellefleur, Oregon, and go in search of a downed UFO.

At the same time, Krycek and Marita betray the Cigarette Smoking Man. They push him down a flight of stairs and apparently kill him. The episode—and the season—ends with Mulder's abduction by the UFO and Scully's shocking announcement of her pregnancy, a plotline that would carry on through the final two seasons of the series.

Season Highlights

"Hungry." Written by Vince Gilligan. Directed by Kim Manners. Airdate: November 21, 1999.

In "Hungry," a young fast-food employee in California named Rob (Chad Donella) works at a Lucky Boy franchise and is questioned by Mulder and Scully about an unusual and horrifying murder that took place during his shift at the drive-thru. He denies involvement, but another worker, Derwood Spinks (Mark Pellegrino), one with a criminal record, gains proof of Rob's involvement in the crime.

In truth, Rob is a shark-like humanoid, one who must satisfy his cravings and appetites for human brains. He has attempted several times to deny his biological nature and even attended Overeaters Anonymous, but with Mulder closing in, Rob's hunger just grows harder and harder to deny. . . .

"Hungry" is an unusual and intriguing monster-of-the-week program. In this case, Vince Gilligan has structured the story so that the monster is the protagonist of the tale and those pesky FBI agents, Mulder and Scully, are the villains, hounding him and generally making his life miserable.

As this description suggests, significant sympathy is garnered for anonymous-sounding Rob Roberts, the man with two first names and an eating problem who attends Overeaters Anonymous but still can't quite keep his appetite in check. Indeed, Rob suffers from low self-esteem, as his therapist informs him, because he keeps trying and failing to overcome his biology. The underlying metaphor involves food addiction and obesity, the desire to continue eating when you absolutely know it is wrong and is not going to help you get healthy.

What remains so remarkable about "Hungry" is the manner in which Scully and Mulder are made to look unsympathetic to audiences as they pursue this "genetic freak." We see the agents from his POV, and the picture isn't pretty. Similarly, there's much talk of "what kind of monster" would do something like eat the brains of a victim, but because the episode asks audiences to sympathize with Rob, we see he isn't a monster at all, but a man fighting his deepest urges. Mr. Incanto in "2Shy" voiced a similar thought, that he was a victim of his urges and that, in some sense, he gave his victims what they needed, self-esteem. Rob is more sympathetic because he isn't nearly so self-deluded. He doesn't believe his victims get anything out of his antisocial behavior, and we can see that, as he says, "even the worst of us wants to be good."

After so many years of watching Scully and Mulder take down "monsters" and save the day, it is rewarding to watch the travails of the monster instead, and a close corollary to the tension generated here is seen in a Hitchcock film I've already discussed, *Frenzy* (1972). There, the central figure is a psycho, a man driven to kill. Law enforcement closes in on him, ever closer to discovering the truth, and so our loyalties are divided. In "Hungry," Rob is our hero, and there is some part of us that wants him to get away with his crimes, especially because he is struggling so mightily against biology and to be a good person.

On the other hand, we know that a killer can't go loose, and so we want Mulder and Scully to end Rob's reign of terror. There is a real sense of divided loyalty in this episode and hence a great deal of tension and discomfort. We aren't sure, finally, how we should feel about Rob or his struggles. All we know is that, for the first time in seven years, we know precisely how it feels not to be on the hunt but to be the hunted, the derided monster who stands no chance of escaping the law. "Hungry" turns the police-procedural format of *The X-Files* upside down and evokes sympathy for the devil in the process. And Mulder has never looked more like a nudge, or perhaps Detective Columbo (Peter Falk), than he does in this story about seeing the world from a different perspective.

"The Goldberg Variation." Written by Jeffrey Bell. Directed by Thomas J. Wright. Airdate: December 12, 1999.

Although not often described as one of the series' best (or scariest, for that matter) episodes, "The Goldberg Variation" by Jeffrey Bell is one of those miraculous little *X-Files* grace notes, a remarkably amusing and well-constructed episode that expounds on the idea of luck.

The episode's story is set in Chicago and concerns the world's luckiest man, Henry Weems (Willie Garson), as he attempts to earn money (from the mob, in one case) to pay for a child's (Shia LaBeouf) operation. Mulder and Scully arrive on the scene to investigate Henry's miraculous survival after he is pushed by the gangsters from a skyscraper roof. They soon get pulled into his orbit.

Yet Henry's orbit is a place one may not necessarily want to be, because his good luck must be balanced in the universe by others' bad luck. Mulder discovers this fact that hard way when he falls through an apartment floor and into the bathtub of the unit below, landing on what he calls his "fat ass."

Mulder and Scully struggle to learn more about Weems and his background, even as he grows ever more desperate to secure the $100,000 he needs to save young Richie. . . .

"The Goldberg Variation" takes its title from two sources. The first is "The Goldberg Variations," a 1741 composition by Johann Sebastian Bach.

The second Goldberg suggested by the title and narrative, however, is Rube Goldberg (1883–1970), a cartoonist who is famous for his byzantine illustrations of odd, over-engineered devices. To note that a device has a "Rube Goldberg quality" means that the instrument uses much effort to perform a simple task, usually involving a chain reaction.

In the case of the episode, Henry Weems himself is a Goldberg Variation. He tries very hard to do something very simple: get his friend, Richie, the medical care he needs. But instead, Weems leaves a trail of corpses and detritus behind him. His "strange luck" is too much for the task at hand at times and thus causes problems instead of creating solutions. The simple task here is to do something human, to show love and care for another human being, but the chain reactions involve car accidents, falls from skyscrapers, collapsing floors, dead mobsters, glass eyes, and other oddities. The episode raises one very meaningful question: Is it possible that the world's luckiest man, by dint of his extraordinary luck, is actually unlucky? Does he just look lucky to outsiders, in other words?

That idea ties into the episode's conclusion, which sees the death of the gangster boss, Cutrona (Ramy Zada). When the mobster dies, he proves to be just the liver donor that young Richie needs if he hopes to survive. So Cutrona's bad luck is Richie's good luck.

Sometimes, "luck" can only be judged after the fact and not by those intimately engaged in the situation.

There are no monsters or aliens in "The Goldberg Variation," just some splendidly orchestrated set pieces, particularly one involving a gunshot, an ironing board and a ceiling fan, and an unforgettable character. Weems is a lovable loser with a heart of gold, trying to do the best he can, and more often than not reaping the whirlwind. His luck is the "X-File" of the week, and it is rewarding to watch the unpredictable fashion in which it plays out, and also its impact on our two favorite FBI agents.

"Sein und Zeit." Written by Chris Carter and Frank Spotnitz. Directed by Michael Watkins. Airdate: February 6, 2000.

"Closure." Written by Chris Carter and Frank Spotnitz. Directed by Kim Manners. Airdate: February 13, 2000.

Mulder asks Skinner to investigate the disappearance and missing person's case of a little girl, Amber Lynn Pierre, in Sacramento, California. A ransom note left at the scene oddly mentions Santa Claus and mirrors a nearly identical note in another case involving a missing child, from 1987.

Mulder questions Kathy Lee Tencate (Kim Darby) in prison, the mother in the older case, and also learns that his own mother, Teena (Rebecca Toolan), has died in an apparent suicide. Devastated, Mulder feels he can no longer see the case clearly. Soon, with Scully's help, however, a child murderer who runs a Santa Claus village in California is apprehended for crimes going back more than three decades.

A psychic named Harold Piller (Anthony Heald) contacts Mulder and then presents his theory that Amber Lynn, like other children in danger, including Kathy's son, were actually spirited away by supernatural beings called "Walk-ins." Having lost a son himself, Harold suggests to Mulder that this is what happened to his own sister, Samantha. Mulder goes to an Air Force base in California and finds evidence that Samantha lived there for a time with the Cigarette Smoking Man, until she disappeared one night without a trace. . . .

In the epic two-part presentation "Sein und Zeit"/"Closure," a television inside Agent Mulder's motel room in Sacramento plays important imagery from *Planet of the Apes* (1968). In particular, orangutan scientist and Protector of the Faith Dr. Zaius (Maurice Evans) warns the human astronaut Taylor (Charlton Heston) not to seek the truth about his people, about humanity. "Don't look for it, Taylor," the simian urges. "You may not like what you find." When asked by Dr. Zira (Kim Hunter) about what Taylor will find on that mysterious shoreline stretching to the horizon, Dr. Zaius replies, cryptically, "his destiny." This is actually the second time that footage appears on *The X-Files*. The first was in "War of the Coprophages" in Season Three.

This quotation from a sci-fi cinema landmark underlines the thematic through-line of this emotionally affecting *X-Files* two-parter, which explicitly concerns the idea of "seeing." The narrative revolves around the way that people, even good people, tend to see only what they desire to see. Even honorable and decent men such as Mulder, who believes he is seeing through conspiracies and secrets, tends to see the world as it conforms to his particular worldview. This isn't a critique of Mulder so much as it is an observation about human nature. It's just how we, as thoughtful, emotional beings, operate.

As is also often the case with *The X-Files,* "Sein und Zeit"/"Closure" commences with reality, and with a real-life event from the 1990s as context, and then beelines straight into the unexpected, or the supernatural. Here, the action starts in Sacramento when a cute-as-a-button, six-year-old girl, Amber Lynn La Pierre, disappears from her bedroom, never to be seen alive again. Oddly, her mother disassociates from reality and pens a cryptic ransom note through the paranormal auspices of "automatic writing." And her father experiences a precognitive vision of the little girl's bruised corpse. If you remember the 1990s, you will appreciate many of the details of this strange, macabre introduction. JonBenet Ramsey, a six-year-old girl, was discovered dead in her family home in Colorado on Christmas Day, 1996. The unsolved case became a media sensation for months and even years. As late as 2006 and the false confession by John Mark Karr, this murder was still a topic of debate.

Furthermore, the victim in both cases is a six-year-old girl. And in both the real and fictitious cases, the parents are believed to be the perpetrators of a heinous crime: the murder of a child. There's even a connection between Amber Lynn and JonBenet in the Christmas Day trappings. At the bottom of Mrs. La Pierre's ransom note is a mystifying, holiday-themed sentence: "No one shoots at Santa Claus!" This odd final sentence is the very clue that rouses Mulder's interest. He remembers an earlier X-File in which the same sentence was also scrawled in a ransom note. Another woman, Kathy Lee Tencate (Kim Darby, of *Don't Be Afraid of the Dark* [1973] fame), wrote the same words on a kidnapper's note for her "missing" son back in 1987. She is currently in prison, having confessed to his murder. But that is just a legal ploy, and Ms. Tencate actually believes—as Mulder comes to believe—that ancient spirits called Walk-ins are responsible for the disappearance of these children; that they are "old souls protecting the children" from terrible violence in this mortal coil, as depicted in the precognitive visions of the parents.

The particulars of the case are resolved at a place called Santa's North Pole Village, a haven for a serial killer who abducts and murders children. One visitor at his tourist trap was Amber Lynn La Pierre. She was destined to die at his hand, like too many other innocents, and the Walk-ins spared her this terrible agony, transforming the child from matter into energy . . . into, poetically speaking, "starlight."

Ultimately, however, this paranormal resolution of a murder case related to real life isn't the point of Carter and Spotnitz's intricate and haunting tale. The narrative take a strange and unexpected turn when Mulder learns of his mother's suicide and comes to realize that his missing sister, Samantha, may have also been taken by these Old Spirits as well.

For seven years up to this point, one of *The X-Files'* most prominent mysteries involved Samantha and her ultimate disposition. Was Mulder's sibling abducted by aliens in 1973? Was she taken to another world? Is she still alive on another planet? Will Mulder ever be reunited with her? This has been his continuing obsession, his white whale, and various episodes of the series have charted clues, intimated destinies, and suggested possibilities. Some episodes even revealed the aliens harnessing Samantha clones. But "Closure" suggests that Mulder has not seen the truth at all. The investigations, the trappings of the alien abduction and other bells and whistles of the case, instead have actively prevented him from seeing the truth.

And what is that truth? That his sister—a frightened fourteen-year-old girl, for all intents and purposes—died in 1979. All Mulder's adult life, he has been chasing a ghost rather than dealing with the truth that his sister is gone. The Cigarette Smoking Man even encourages Mulder's wild goose chase. "Allow him his ignorance," he tells Scully. "It's what gives him hope." It's a hard, human truth Mulder finally countenances here, and much of this two-parter deals explicitly with our understandable sense of outrage and futility when innocence is corrupted, destroyed by human "evil." Carter and Spotnitz suggest a welcome spiritual remedy to such ugliness: Walk-ins who take the children and spare them the pain of such destruction. But the writers also offer Mulder a sense of closure, if he will accept it. The quest for Samantha is over. Or as he realizes, he's reached "the end of the road."

What makes this sense of closure all the more emotionally affecting is that Mulder is joined in this story by a kindly psychic, Harold (Anthony Heald), who lost a son to the Walk-ins, just as Mulder lost Samantha. But because Harold refuses to believe his son is dead, he can't see him as he sees other spirits. He refuses to see his boy's spirit and acknowledge the truth, He cannot grieve, can never move on, because his stubbornness won't let him. And thus he achieves the opposite of his desired goal. He remains eternally separated from the child. Mulder attempts to sway him. "Harold, you see so much, but you refuse to see him," he says. "You refuse to let him go. But you have to let him go now, Harold. He's protected. He's in a better place. They're all in a better place. We both have to let go, Harold."

Our final view of Harold in "Closure" is a haunting one. He runs off, dedicated to finding his "truth" . . . *which is no truth at all.* He would rather chase the palatable fantasy than accept the sad reality. This is the object lesson. This could have been Mulder, forever tilting at windmills, never moving past the defining traumatic experience of his life. What remains so remarkable about this *X-Files* story is that Spotnitz and Carter successfully make the audience feel much like stubborn Harold. After seven years and over a hundred episodes, we all invested in Mulder's quest and the possibility of a happy reunion, of Samantha's safe return. That's what we all hoped for.

But this episode precludes such a happy ending, even as it grants Mulder a kind of release. That sense of release, of catharsis, arrives in one of the most beautiful, lyrical sequences ever presented on television, a kind of perfect expression of magical, spiritual reality. By starlight, Mulder ascends a hill, accompanied by Harold's son, and he sees a field where the "taken" children are at play . . . still innocent, forever young. There, he is reunited with his fourteen-year-old sister. Shot in glowing white light, in slow-motion photography, cut to a haunting but cathartic song by Moby ("My Weakness"), the long journey ends, and Mulder finds a degree of peace.

Yet some *X-Files* fans outright rejected this lyrical conclusion, mirroring Harold's rejection in the storyline itself. It is easier for us, often, to accept fantasy than reality. We don't have all the answers, and as Scully suggests, "we never truly know why" things happen. But, this tale reminds us, we must attempt to make our peace with the way things are. As is often the case in Carter's works, he and Spotnitz purposefully flout expectations here in order to foster a deeper understanding of the human race. We had expected a Samantha resolution story to involve alien abduction, not, explicitly, grief, about the process of letting go and in doing so, inching closer to a degree of spiritual faith. Like *Planet of the Apes'* Taylor—Chris Carter and Frank Spotnitz tell us—we may not like what we find at the end of the road. The fans are in the same boat as Taylor and Mulder: we don't want to climb that starlit plateau and know, finally, that Samantha is gone. But it's our destiny. Just as it is every human being's destiny to grieve a loved one and, in fact, to die.

The popular meme, endlessly repeated in the media about *The X-Files,* is that it is a brilliant series that stayed on the air a few years too long, and in doing so, somehow damaged its legacy. But episodes such as "Sein und Zeit" and "Closure" reveal the opposite is true. It would have been extraordinarily easy for Chris Carter and Frank Spotnitz to write a happy ending for Samantha and Fox Mulder. The writers probably could have done it in their sleep. Mulder gets information from the Lone Gunmen that the Cigarette Smoking Man is holding Samantha for tests somewhere, and Mulder and Scully break her out. Brother and sister are reunited. Cue end credits.

Instead, they pursued a more illuminating, difficult path and forged a tale about how hard it is for us to accept our own mortality or the mortality of our loved ones. This is why human beings have religion, so that we don't have to openly acknowledge that for all of us, there is an end. Although this episode of *The X-Files* also promises a kind of moral hierarchy to the universe—one in which innocence is preserved instead of destroyed—it simultaneously acknowledges that death is an irreparable and grievous separation from the living.

Mulder aches to "believe to understand." And in a beautifully composed and delivered voice-over, he contemplates the destruction of childhood innocence, and human mortality: "Were they still dreaming of ice cream and monkey bars? Of birthday cake and no future but the afternoon?" he asks. "Or had their innocence been taken along with their lives, buried in the cold earth so long ago? These fates seemed too cruel, even for God to allow."

Mulder speaks also of his desire to believe in the "endless procession of souls" and "God's eternal recompense and sadness." This soliloquy is a perfect summation of human existence, and particularly human doubt. It's an explicit grappling with the unanswerable "why" of our lives. We want to believe in something greater, something good and kind at the end of the rainbow. Why? Because, again like Taylor in *Planet of the Apes*, we're all going to be making that trip ourselves, whether we want to or not. "Sein und Zeit" and "Closure" get at this truth beautifully. The episodes don't hit you over the head with everything, either. For instance, in a scene featuring ghosts, there's a young, World War II-era couple depicted, and without acknowledging explicitly their identities, we understand that they are Mulder's (now-reunited) parents, supporting his quest and his attempt to learn the truth.

So what "Closure" really comes down to is the idea that we can either accept hard reality, like Mulder, or retreat into "not seeing," like Harold. Even today, that's a particularly relevant message, globally and individually, in our culture. We sometimes need to understand that in seeking answers, we may not like what we find. Yet we simultaneously need the grace to accept the truth for what it is.

"X-Cops." Written by Vince Gilligan. Directed by Michael Watkins. Airdate: February 20, 2000.

Mulder and Scully end up on camera—and national television—at an unusual crime scene in urban Willow Park, California, because a Fox series, *Cops*, is recording it. Scully is reluctant to appear on camera at first, but Mulder sees the camera as a great platform by which to expose the truth and show evidence of the paranormal, unadulterated, to the masses.

In this instance, he believes a murderous creature, presumably a werewolf, is responsible for an attack on a policeman and his cruiser. Since the FBI has "nothing to hide," the duo continues to appear on the series. While under the light and eye of the cameras, Mulder and Scully investigate a killer who has been reported to take the forms of Freddy Krueger, the hantavirus, and a childhood bugaboo of the injured deputy: the Wasp Man.

In 1999, *The Blair Witch Project* jump-started the found-footage horror movie subgenre, though examples of the found-footage or quasi-documentary genre film go all the way back to the 1970s and such early efforts as *Punishment Park* (1972) and *Cannibal Holocaust* (1980). But the time was perfect for an *X-Files* foray into similar material. The result was an episode that utilizes the conceit of an ever-present cameraman embedded in the action to tell the story.

Like all good found-footage movies, "X-Cops" is a kind of shaggy dog story, a chance to "see" something that ultimately ends not with sight but with a reckoning that "the camera doesn't always tell the whole story." Indeed, the episode involves the power of suggestion and how that power causes a "contagion of fear" to spread. This is an apt approach for the format, since most found-footage films are low-budget affairs, and therefore ones that generate their scares not by featuring monsters on-screen but by suggesting that though the camera is running nonstop, the monsters exist outside the parameters of the frame. The monster in this case is a beast that "can't be seen on videotape" and that feeds and thrives on mortal fear. The episode predates the 9/11 terrorist attacks by some interval, and yet it notes, rather prophetically, how Americans already dwelled in a culture of fear, with terror feeding them.

"X-Cops" notes the power of imagination and the ways that imagination can be subverted by a variety of fearful stimuli, from horror movie to childhood dreads to more real-life fears of physical danger in an urban setting. The people of Willow Park don't feel that the police can adequately protect them or have their best interests at heart. And that fear is balanced by the police force's fear of the populace. Law enforcement officials here confront their fears on a daily basis as well, contending with a public that hates and distrusts them.

In keeping with found-footage principles, "X-Cops" features extensive, long takes and shaky camera work. Similarly, the actors sometimes look at or address the camera and have to appear more fully spontaneous or in the moment than is usually the case, because we are experiencing these dangers as they do. The glory of the found-footage format is that it makes the horror feel more immediate and urgent, but also closer to us, because there is one less filter, in this case the formality of third-person film grammar or film technique. The episode is also, as is par for the course with Gilligan, unremittingly funny and inventive, but with the most bizarre touches imaginable, like the victim with the head twisted off like a chicken, or the Wasp Man, left to the purview of our imaginations.

14

Sight

Season Eight (2000–2001)

During the eighth season of *The X-Files*, David Duchovny reduced his participation considerably. He was no longer the star of the program, and he appeared in less than a dozen episodes airing that year. But he wasn't gone entirely, either. Although over one hundred new lead actors, including Bruce Campbell and Lou Diamond Phillips, were auditioned, his successor was actor Robert Patrick (*Terminator 2* [1991], *Fire in the Sky* [1993]).

On *The X-Files*, Patrick played John Doggett, an ex-New York police detective and Marine Corps veteran who did not boast either a familiarity with or affinity for the paranormal or supernatural, but instead constructed his cases on the bedrocks of common sense, a finely tuned moral barometer, and good old-fashioned detective work. In short, Doggett equaled "dogged." He was a superb, tireless agent, as Scully once noted, "above reproach," and he provided the series with a welcome injection of fresh blood. It is true that Doggett was quite different from the beloved Agent Mulder, yet he provided a new and energetic dynamic.

Like Mulder before him, Doggett came to *The X-Files* with a personal trauma. His young son had disappeared while riding his bike through the family neighborhood. He was then abducted and murdered by a child molester. The investigation, however, turned cold, and, going into his tenure with Scully, Doggett had never caught the man who killed his boy. More than one story on the series involved Doggett's reckoning with this past. In "Invocation," a similar child-disappearance investigation brought out his more obsessive-compulsive side.

Doggett is also the third leading "Chris Carter male" we met, following Mulder and *Millennium*'s Frank Black. My wife, a therapist, coined the phrase "the Chris Carter male" because she became intrigued by his male characters and their commonalities. She describes the Chris Carter male as "chivalrous and heroic, but essentially unavailable emotionally to the women in their lives."

When I interviewed Chris Carter in late 2009, he responded to this psychological classification and noted that it was "dramatically interesting to him" to write for characters when "it's what's withheld that counts, or is that important. If the character is remote or unable to speak about these things—because it's series television we're talking about here—it becomes something that needs to be discovered. So if you discover these things too quickly, if a person is too emotionally available, it actually takes away from interest in the character."

With this premise in mind, Carter and the other writers of *The X-Files* grant Doggett a particularly intriguing arc in Season Eight. He starts out as a dependable but by-the-book agent in the premiere, "Within/Without," but viewers are a little suspicious of him because when we first see him entering the basement office in "Patience," he is laughing outside the door with colleagues . . . as if mocking the X-Files.

Later in the episode, penned by Chris Carter, a police detective, Abbott (Bradford English), is downright dismissive of and nasty to Agent Scully, and Doggett steps in and whispers something to Abbott to back him off. Notice that we never hear Doggett's words nor see his face as he speaks to Abbott. The implication is, again, that he is not entirely trustworthy. He may be sympathizing with the detective . . . we don't know.

After these moments, we warm to Doggett, and his sense of emotional unavailability begins to recede somewhat. We learn that his marriage failed and that his son died (in "Invocation"), but more importantly, we begin to see how he and Scully develop a working relationship. In one episode, "Medusa," he must trust her to make the right decisions and preserve his life, while Scully must simultaneously trust him to be her "eyes and ears" on a case. Carter's principle—not to reveal too much too soon—grants the Doggett/Scully relationship a degree of tension and interest. These are two strangers dancing around each other by necessity and learning what characteristics in each other they can appreciate and come to depend on.

Eventually, Doggett would be partnered with another new character, the very open and original-thinking Monica Reyes (Annabeth Gish). But for the duration of Season Eight, he worked with Scully, who had to grapple with not only Mulder's disappearance and absence but the mystery of her own pregnancy. In this season, Scully had to contend, as well, without a believer. Mulder was the "absent center," as Carter described the character, not just in terms of his physical presence but in terms of the worldview he provided.

Surprisingly, and quite beautifully, Scully stepped up to fill that gap, embracing more "extreme possibilities" for the first time, perhaps in honor of Mulder's memory, perhaps because she realized that his life's work, the X-Files, needed that view point represented. But in stories such as "Badlaa," about a mind-clouding monster of the week from India, Scully had to—often with bravado and risk—assume the Mulder role of believer.

The original *X-Files* dynamic of Scully/Mulder is the comparison of skepticism vs. faith/science vs. belief. Virtually every story in the first seven years was filtered through this double lens. In Season Eight, with a mostly absent Mulder, that dynamic could not work. So instead, the episodes largely concerned how Scully had to retrain herself to "see" the world, accommodating Mulder's genius into her own perspective. Again, consider just how often the episodes in Season Eight involve sight.

In "Patience," Scully tries to see the world as Mulder does, but admits she has difficulties making the same leaps of faith. In the aforementioned "Medusa," she assumes control of a command center and must "see" through Doggett's eyes in the subway below.

In "Via Negativa," a cult leader grows a "third eye" by opening his eyes to the path of darkness, and Doggett nearly goes the same way. In "The Gift," Skinner commends Doggett for seeing a case through Mulder's eyes, by getting inside his head. The aforementioned "Badlaa" involves a mystic who can cloud the sight of normal people, including Scully and Doggett, making them see or not see what he wishes.

Even "Three Words" is about sight in some critical sense, about how Mulder comes to see Doggett and then how Doggett comes to see himself: as being manipulated by an informant.

Similarly, "Alone" is about blindness and how in the absence of clear sight, trust can save the day. This lesson comes in relation to Doggett and Mulder, who are trapped by a kind of lizard monster in a dark labyrinth. His eyes sprayed by venom, Doggett can't see his nemesis. He has only his trust in Mulder, and Mulder's words. The leitmotif of sight, appearing in more than a handful of episodes, provides the season an umbrella of unity that draws everything together.

Although fans desperately missed Mulder, the response to Doggett was largely positive, and ratings for *The X-Files* actually went-up in Season Eight. "It changed," Carter told me in our interview, "and so—like it or not, people who would tune in to see Mulder and Scully wouldn't see them anymore. But creatively, the show sort of took on a new life. The stories were interesting, and the new characters made the stories interesting. It was kind of meta-*X-Files* because it was commenting on itself at the same time, and the show turned inward in a way. The characters deepened. The concept deepened. And I think for some people that was interesting and for some people it became inaccessible."

Season Eight is also the first season since the fifth season, perhaps, that refocused *The X-Files* on genuinely scary horror, instead of science fiction and fantasy comedy. Some of the best horror stories in ages are featured in Season Eight, including "Road Runners," "Medusa," "Via Negativa" and "Badlaa." In many ways it is a back-to-basics season, and a damned good one at that.

Mytharc Notes

Just as Scully became part of the Mytharc narrative in Season Two with her abduction, Mulder's disappearance in "Requiem" led to a new element of the overarching narrative tapestry. The two-part season opener "Within"/"Without" sees Agent Doggett introduced to the series and commence his hunt for the missing Mulder. Meanwhile, Mulder is actually aboard a giant alien saucer, one invisible to the outside world, and is forced to endure horrifying and painful-looking tests. This predicament represents an interesting contrast. We learn over the run of *The X-Files* that Scully was actually abducted by men, minions of the Cigarette Smoking Man, and then tested and experimented upon in train cars like the one seen in "731." Poor Mulder in Season Eight is actually experimented on by extraterrestrials, in a lab of fearsome and inhuman dimensions. Adding insult to injury, the next sequence in the Mytharc, the two-part episode "This Is Not Happening"/"Deadalive" goes to even darker territory.

In "This is Not Happening," Scully and Doggett go to Helena, Montana, on news that abductees are reappearing. Scully learns that Jeremiah Smith (Roy Thinnes), the alien healer last seen in "Herrenvolk," is healing them of their wounds. When Mulder is returned, however, Smith is taken by the aliens before he can help. Thus, in time for the opener of "Deadalive," Mulder is declared dead, and his funeral is held. The same episode serves as the introduction to Annabeth Gish's character, Agent Monica Reyes.

The bulk of "Deadalive" occurs three months after Mulder's funeral, as Doggett and Scully come to understand that he may not actually be dead. Billy Miles, another abductee, for example, comes back to life, shedding his dead skin in chunks. In truth, Miles is now actually a human replacement, a super soldier who works for the unseen aliens, killing off threats and controlling levers of power. Unless Scully can save Mulder, he will be resurrected with the same virus inside him, transforming him into an alien being and super soldier as well. Fortunately, by the end of the episode, Scully has saved Mulder, and he returns from his abduction experience, and apparently death itself, as himself.

The final episode of the season, "Existence," involves Mulder, Doggett, Skinner, and Reyes attempting to protect Scully from Miles and other super soldiers (including DOD employee and informant Knowle Rohrer), as her due date arrives. In the end, Scully gives birth to William, named after Mulder's father, and the child, at first blush, appears normal.

Season Highlights

"Patience." Written and directed by Chris Carter. Airdate: November 19, 2000.

Doggett and Scully investigate the brutal murder of an undertaker in Burley, Idaho. There, the agents find evidence of both a human and an animal assailant. Scully finds bat saliva on several severed fingers recovered by Doggett in a farmhouse attic.

The agents discover that similar deaths occurred in 1956, and news reports at the time of the capture describe a dangerous man-bat. Now, anyone who has seen the creature, or even come into contact with anyone who has seen it, is in imminent danger.

One might argue that the title "Patience" is Chris Carter's plea to fans to stick with the series in a time of transition and change. Appropriately, this episode is a kind of back-to-basics monster-of-the-week story involving a humanoid bat who sees quite differently than human beings do, seeking vengeance against tormenters from the year 1956.

But this episode sets up the Scully/Doggett relationship, the season's obsession with sight, and features a great commentary on what it means to live in fear. On the latter front, consider Ernie Stefaniuk's (Gene Dynarski) moving monologue about what fear did to his marriage . . . and to his wife. For forty-four years they lived together in isolation on a six-mile stretch of land and denied themselves modern conveniences, family contact, and more. They spent their lives together hiding rather than confronting their fears.

In the post-9/11 age, "Patience" takes on a new meaning given the government's color-coded exploitation of fear. Chris Carter proves his directorial chops (again) in "Patience" with the scene I mentioned in the overview, wherein Scully is castigated and treated poorly by a detective, and Doggett steps in to ameliorate the detective's concerns. A less clever director would have included a frontal shot of Doggett's explanation or provided audio of the encounter. Instead, the moment is left mysterious—and portentous—because we never learn exactly what it is he said. "Patience" is the first standalone episode in the series sans Mulder, and it is therefore the template for the two following seasons. As such, it begins to diagram the terrain of the Scully/Doggett relationship and the importance that sight will play in upcoming episodes. The episode's suspense is palpable, in part, because of Mulder's absence. Scully and Doggett don't yet have a nonverbal shorthand, and thus there is a new feeling of vulnerability when they confront the monster.

"Via Negativa." Written by Frank Spotnitz. Directed by Tony Wharmby. Airdate: December 7, 2000.

Agent Doggett investigates cult leader Anthony Tipet (Keith Szarabajka), a man attempting to find enlightenment through a spiritual path known as the "via negativa." The Lone Gunmen warn Doggett that Tipet may possess the paranormal ability to enter the dreams of others and kill them there.

When Doggett catches Tipet's (third) eye, he comes to believe in Tipet's power, finding himself in the darkest of dreams, one that endangers Agent Scully in the waking world. . . .

In philosophy, the "via negativa" is an approach to understanding God; a strategy that seeks to define God by enumerating those things God is *not.* God is not mortal, God is not evil, and so forth. Sometimes, this unusual approach to comprehending the divine is also called *negative theory* or the *negative way.* The episode "Via Negativa" finds stalwart Doggett investigating the brutal murders of two FBI agents who were staking out an apocalyptic cult.

In contravention of long-standing series format, Doggett is investigating this particular X-File *alone* because a pregnant Scully is away at the hospital. Still new to the X-Files unit, Doggett is uncertain and somewhat rudderless. He's no Mulder and has no interest in being Mulder. Leaps of faith don't come easily, or naturally, to him. Without Scully to ease him in, the "dogged," meat-and-potatoes Doggett is vulnerable to what he learns during this investigation.

While on the case, Doggett discovers that all the members of the apocalyptic cult also died horribly and that their still-at-large leader, Anthony Tipet, is an ex-convict who developed his own peculiar brand of evangelical Christian/Hindu philosophy. Tipet suggests that "the body is but clay . . . to hold the twin aspects of the human spirit: the light and the darkness." Furthermore, he believes that if his dedicated followers gaze into the path of darkness ("the via negativa" of the title), they will see God there. To help them reach this dimension of darkness, Tipet administered experimental hallucinogens that would awaken their "third eye." It is this third eye—the Hindu *gyananakashi,* or "eye of knowledge," positioned between hemispheres of the brain—that could see into the realm of darkness.

Doggett delves deeper and deeper into Tipet's strange, dark beliefs until the agent himself takes an unwitting walk on the *Via Negativa* during a horrifying dream sequence. The scene is cast in a suffusing blue light, with intermittent fade-outs and pulsating strobes providing a sense of fractured time and consciousness. This tense, mostly silent scene sees a sweaty, desperate Doggett, depicted in extreme close-up, contemplating murder . . . and the specter of his internal darkness.

Another scene, in which a vulnerable, confused Doggett confesses to a baffled Skinner (Mitch Pileggi) that he is uncertain about his own state of consciousness (dreaming or awake), also serves as Doggett's real indoctrination into *The X-Files*, the horrifying case from "outside" that changes him "inside."

"Via Negativa's" climactic moments—with Doggett wrestling with a decision of life and death—endure as among the series' grimmest. Often in *The X-Files,* the horror is tolerable because we know the characters and their central relationship so well; because we know Mulder will rescue Scully or vice versa. But in "Via Negativa" there's a deep underlying fear at work. Doggett has no support system. He has no one to hold onto; no one to race to his side when he is faced with death. His walk on the "dark path" is truly a walk alone, or so we believe, until the denouement, and there's something incredibly unsettling and sinister about the brand of evil he faces.

"Badlaa." Written by John Shiban. Directed by Tony Wharmby. Airdate: January 21, 2001.

This absolutely go-for-broke episode concerns a Siddhi mystic (Deep Roy) who travels to America inside the rectum of a 400-pound businessman. When he evacuates the rectum, the man bleeds out, and viewers are spared no nauseating detail of the journey. Scully and Doggett investigate and follow the mystic's trail to an American elementary school, where he has taken a job as a janitor and clouded the minds of the staff.

As Scully pieces together the puzzle, attempting to see the case as the missing Mulder would, she and Doggett learn that the mystic may be out for revenge. He has come to America to kill those responsible for an accident in Mumbai that killed 118 people, including his son. But to stop the mystic, Scully must be able to see him, and the Siddhi's strange ability to cloud his presence makes that virtually impossible. . . .

One thoroughly terrifying scene in "Badlaa" finds the mystic hidden inside a corpse, and as Scully begins her autopsy, his tiny hands wriggle their way out of a chest incision. But the terror of "Badlaa" is not only visual, it is also aural. The Siddhi mystic—an amputee—drags himself from one location to another on a scooter with squeaky wheel, and that ubiquitous, telltale sound quickly becomes a fearsome harbinger of terror.

But "Badlaa" works so splendidly because it fits into the season's leitmotif about sight, and director Tony Wharmby achieves something extraordinary in terms of visualizing certain moments. It is established early on that the mystic can control how people perceive him, and there are at least two instances when Scully sees people who are already present on the scene—in long establishing shot—standing in the distance, observing her.

One is Charles Burks (Bill Dow), bracketed inside the door frame at the X-Files office. Another is Doggett himself, standing pool-side, strange light reflected on his face. Neither figure gets a traditional TV entrance when Scully first sees them: they're just present—still—and the implication is that there is something not quite right with them.

If you go back and watch this episode, ask yourself at all times: who is Scully actually perceiving and receiving information from during these scenes? Those she knows, or the mystic, insinuating himself into her periphery and recognition?

"The Gift." Written by Frank Spotnitz. Directed by Kim Manners. Airdate: February 5, 2001.

In this story, Doggett continues the hunt for Mulder. He follows up a lead from some months back, in Squamash, Pennsylvania. Doggett learns that Mulder was terminally ill (as a result of the events from "Amor Fati") and sought a strange Native American healer, a sin eater. Doggett goes in search of the same creature and finds a pitiable thing who, though he can digest the diseases of the living, wants only to die himself.

"The Gift" is another story that focuses on sight and how people see things differently. Agent Doggett investigates one of Mulder's cases and unexpectedly finds evidence that Mulder may have committed murder. Through enigmatic flashbacks, we see Mulder's work on the case, and the execution of the crime. Only in the end do we come to understand that Mulder's blood-soaked act of murder is actually one of mercy. And we learn it not in straightforward fashion but through Doggett following literally in Mulder's footsteps and coming to make a similar choice regarding mercy and decency.

The result, at episode's end, is that Doggett—for the briefest of instants—imagines the specter of Mulder in his office, as if in tacit approval of Doggett's presence there. He has, finally, earned the right to sit in Mulder's place.

The monster of the week is a great one too, a "soul eater" who can be summoned to eat the sick. After eating sick people and absorbing their diseases, the soul eater than regurgitates the digested human being, who re-forms and is resurrected. Both Mulder and Doggett go through that process in this episode (another instance of parallel footsteps), and yes, the vomiting scenes are nausea provoking. But the regurgitation isn't the point. The point is that the soul eater is a tortured creature who cannot die and who must keep healing others . . . and absorbing their horrible illnesses. He's in pain and wants his life to end. Who can heal the healer?

So as the episode starts, audiences might believe that "the gift" of the title belongs to the soul eater. He is giving those he digests and regurgitates the gift of health. But at episode end, we learn that Doggett has actually given the monster what it considers the greatest gift of all: the freedom of death. This is a poetic and moving *X-Files* episode, and one that asks us to see the soul eater differently at different times. He's a monster and a terror at first, and then—as we look into his eyes—we register that if he is a soul eater, his soul too has been eaten by enduring a lifetime of physical suffering.

"Existence." Written by Chris Carter. Directed by Kim Manners. Airdate: May 20, 2001.

In this season finale, a pregnant Scully gives birth to her child, and we learn—at long last—that Mulder is the father of the baby. Shippers will enjoy the Mulder/Scully kiss, but on a critical note, the episode provides the punch line to the season-long exploration of sight. Before our eyes—for we don't know how long—Mulder and Scully have been together . . . *romantically.* And we suddenly see it. This conclusion is a magical, emotional one, but also hard-earned. Moments throughout the seventh season featured increasing intimacy between the agents, and certainly Season Eight suggests the deep pain Scully feels at Mulder's loss.

The episode's religious overtones equate William to a kind of messiah or savior, and at this point, one could easily suggest that this season of *The X-Files* is actually an origin myth, a story about the parents of a divine child and the earliest chapters of his life.

15

The End

Season Nine (2001–2002)

The ninth and final season of *The X-Files* wraps up many of the series' lingering questions and plotlines, even while introducing at least one new character, Cary Elwes's officious FBI boss, Brad Follmer. This is the span of episodes in which Doggett and Reyes become the primary investigators, with Scully helping out with autopsies and forensic evidence, but seen far less frequently in the field. Mulder does not appear in this group of episodes, except as a reflection in Scully's eye in "William" and in the final, two-hour episode "The Truth."

Monica Reyes is the character who is afforded the most growth in the season, and audiences learn about her background (and previous lives) in "Hellbound," and see her trapped in a kind of afterlife purgatory in "Audrey Pauley." The episode "4-D" sees Reyes as the only person aware of a killer, Lukesh, who can move effortlessly between alternate dimensions or quantum realities. She is also at center stage in the masterful "Improbable," an episode written and directed by Chris Carter in which she uses the tenets of numerology to solve a series of baffling, seemingly unrelated murders. Burt Reynolds guest stars in the episode as the Almighty.

Like Reyes, Robert Patrick's Doggett also grows in Season Nine, and in some sense becomes a complete person. He notes in the episode "Sunshine Days" that he is finally getting the hang of working on the X-Files unit (by following events, A to B to C), and in "John Doe" loses his memory, and his pain over the death of his son only to realize that the pain is now part of his gestalt; that makes him who he is. The episode "Release" sees Doggett solving, at last, the mystery of his son's death and closing that chapter of his life.

Scully faces some difficult choices in Season Nine as well, particularly the resolution of the arc involving her son, William. Realizing that he can never live a normal life while in her care, she puts him up for adoption, an act that is selfless and kind but has long-term emotional repercussions for her, as the second feature film, *I Want to Believe*, depicts.

The ninth season also brings closure to the Lone Gunmen series, and one episode, "Jump the Shark," ends with the heroes dying in the line of duty. With the end of the season came an end of nearly a decade of great storytelling and the feeling, ironically, that there still could have been more stories to tell. But the end of *The X-Files* was in the cards . . . or in the ratings. "Our numbers went down," Carter told *Rolling Stone* in 2005. "I thought the show had come to a natural end, and it was a better time to call it quits after nine years."

Mytharc Notes

The final elements of the Mytharc are assembled in Season Nine. The opening two-parter "Nothing Important Happened Today"/"Nothing Important Happened Today II" involves a deeper investigation into the super soldiers or "human replacements." These are individuals working for the New Syndicate, and the premiere guest stars Lucy Lawless as one such individual.

A second two-part story, "Provenance"/"Providence" returns to the "Biogenesis"/"Sixth Extinction" storyline involving a UFO with unusual inscriptions and powers. In this case, a second UFO is discovered, and Scully learns that there are individuals who desperately want William dead, believing that he will play a crucial role in colonization. If Mulder lives, William will hamper colonization, but if Mulder is dead and gone William will, perhaps, lead it. This two-part episode further introduces a character called Toothpick Man (Alan Dale), a new mole in the FBI and a man eventually outed as a human replacement by Gibson Praise in the series finale, "The Truth."

In the episode "William," Scully encounters a horribly burned man that may be Agent Mulder but is ultimately revealed to be Agent Jeffrey Spender (Chris Owens), who survived his father's attempt on his life and underwent terrible experimentation afterwards. Jeffrey's goal, he states, is to help William live a normal life and take away his strange powers with magnetite, an ore known to harm the super soldiers.

The series finale, "The Truth," involves the return of Mulder. He is arrested for the murder of Knowle Rohrer after infiltrating a top-secret government facility and learning the exact date of colonization. His trial makes up the bulk of the episode and lays out all the evidence, with flashbacks as testimony, of the nine-year conspiracy.

Season Highlights

"4-D." Written by Steven Maeda. Directed by Tony Wharmby. Airdate: December 9, 2001.

In "4-D," *The X-Files* explores the world of alternate universes, or quantum physics. In one reality, Doggett and Reyes seek to apprehend a dangerous serial killer named Lukesh, renowned for cutting out the tongues of his female victims. Reyes dies attempting to stop him, and Doggett is wounded, shot in the line of duty. The episode then cuts to another universe—our universe—where Reyes learns that Doggett has been shot and grievously wounded . . . with her own gun. From there, she must put together the pieces of the puzzle, catch Lukesh, and restore order to at least one universe.

The villain in "4-D" is Irwin Timothy Lukesh, a man who lives with his shrewish mother, and is a character reportedly inspired by Norman Bates (Anthony Perkins) in Alfred Hitchcock's *Psycho* (1960). But where Bates's mind was fragmented into a Norman personality and a Mother personality, Lukesh boats a different and wholly unique bifurcation. In one universe, he is a law-abiding citizen, apparently, tending to his mother and feeding her tongue sandwiches. In the other, however, his dark side is loose, and he is a brutal murder. Because he can hop dimensions and apparently considers one "home," Lukesh is not concerned about his reputation or the law in the other dimension; it is just a place for him to play.

Reyes starts to put the pieces together in "4-D" when several facts just don't correlate. The bullet came from her gun, but her gun hasn't been fired. She was not at the site of the shooting, and Skinner called her at home immediately afterwards, fourteen miles from the shooting. And, on top of all that, Doggett was in her presence during the incident, helping her move into her own apartment at the same instant he was apparently shot and wounded.

In some sense, the only logical explanation involves doubling. Everything fits together once one posits two Doggetts, two Reyes, and two interconnected universes. Brilliantly, writer Stephen Maeda and director Tony Wharmby utilize a symbol to suggest this answer and the nature of the quantum-verse. There is a shot of a rain puddle, like a mirror, suggesting the double or "reflective" nature of the two universes. The realms are mirror images, except they have branched off. This idea also reflects the puddle comparison. A disturbance on the surface (the puddle) seems to change its shape and form, while the other universe, the image reflected, remains the same.

What seems less clear, perhaps, is the notion that by allowing himself to die, Doggett would make room in his universe for the original Doggett and the timeline would reset . . . for all but Reyes, thus transforming "4-D" into an adventure that didn't really happen, except to Monica. Where did the original Doggett go when pushed out of his reality? And why, when the alternate Doggett died, did time go back to the branching point?

These questions are ultimately rendered unimportant, perhaps because of the emotional vitality of the episode. Reyes and Doggett share a gentle, loving relationship in "4-D," and there is a beautiful moment in which she shaves Doggett's face, an act of love that speaks volumes about their relationship.

"John Doe." Written by Vince Gilligan. Directed by Michelle MacLaren. Airdate: January 13, 2002.

"John Doe" sees John Doggett awaken in a dangerous border town, unaware of his true identity, his memory already stolen by the memory vampire Caballero and the cartel. Reyes, Scully, and Skinner search for their missing friend, with no help from Kersh (James Pickens Jr.), while Doggett is forced to work as a "coyote" and a mechanic for the local warlord.

His new master, the cartel, attempts to convince John that he is a double murderer, a man named Bruck, but even without his memory intact, Doggett still possess his ethical equilibrium, unwilling to break the law. He attempts to piece his identity back together, but only one (again, golden) image appears: that of his young son's face.

Intriguingly, not once in nine years did *The X-Files* ever vet a traditional or familiar vampire, the creature in the black cape and sporting fangs and a European accent. The ninth-season episode "John Doe" involves a vampire, but this creature of the night is untraditional as well. Caballero (Zitto Kazann) doesn't feed on blood. Instead, he absorbs and removes *memories*, creating a subclass of slaves in a small Mexican town. These slaves are called "the Disappeared Ones."

This memory vampire is the head of a drug cartel, rendering its enemies amnesiacs, and is depicted on-screen as an old, thin, saturnine man. When he steals memories, his eyes shine gold, an appropriate visual metaphor, for he is taking, in many instances, golden days. One underlying conceit of the episode is that those who sell drugs and addict others are, indeed, vampires, stealing lives for their own purposes. When hooked on drugs, memories suddenly become less important than the here and now of being hooked, of needing the next fix.

The episode proves heart-wrenching when Doggett's memory returns, and he remembers not just his life in the FBI but the grievous loss of his only son, of his boy. At story's end, Doggett confronts the vampire and tells him that he took everything from him, and the vampire differs. "Why would you want to remember?" he asks Doggett. "You can't tell me that you're happier now that you recall your life."

Doggett replies that it is not the vampire's choice what he should remember of his life, and that his pain is his own. Furthermore, he tells Reyes, he will "take the bad, as long as I can remember the good." All memory, even grief and loss, is "golden," because it is part of the human experience, part of what makes us who we are.

In "John Doe," Doggett could give up and be the man that the cartel wants him to be, but he can't change his stripes. The tattoo on his arm (from his time in the U.S. Marines) reminds him of who he is, and his memory "flashes" of his son perform the same task. The good man that he is by nature includes service, fatherhood, and, yes, loss as well, and "John Doe" suggests that identity will reassert itself, even when stolen, either by a memory vampire or by a drug habit.

"John Doe" is particularly well acted, especially by Robert Patrick. The moment when his memory returns and he recalls the loss of his son is haunting, and one of the most emotional moments in the entire series. Doggett goes from joy at the return of what he is to despair at the memory of all he has lost. "John Doe" is also a neo-noir, a story in which a man searches for the truth only to find that the journey ends not only with a mystery resolved but an aspect of unpleasant self-discovery. The detective, Doggett in this case, takes a journey to stop the cartel and the vampire, but in the end sees himself as he really is, for better or worse.

"Scary Monsters." Written by Thomas Schnauz. Directed by Dwight Little. Airdate: April 14, 2002.

"Scary Monsters" finds Doggett, Reyes, and X-Files unit "historian" Leyla Harrison (Jolie Jenkins) investigating a creepy case in Pennsylvania involving a terrifying or monstrous child. The child, Tommy Conlon (Gavin Fink), boasts the capacity to bring his imagination to life in murderous and *hungry* fashion. He creates out of his mind a brand of giant, skittering insects that consume people. In fact, they burrow inside of people and need to be cut out, surgically.

Together, Reyes, Doggett, and Leyla must ferret out the truth of this situation and defeat this child's night terrors. They find that his father, Jeffrey (Scott Paulin), can't really help, and learn that Tommy's overactive imagination killed his mother, and the family cat, Spanky, too. But what killed them? Could it have been . . . *belief?*

"Scary Monsters" works because the evocative cinematography creates an aura of dread, because the characters resonate as human and likeable, and because, finally, there is a social critique (of television, of all things) embedded in the action. But ultimately, the most enjoyable aspect of "Scary Monsters" is that it presents an X-File that, simply, Mulder wouldn't be able to survive, let alone solve, and then has fun with that intriguing idea.

Mulder's great gift as an investigator is his *imagination*, his amazing capacity to conceive of connections that others simply can't comprehend. His motto is, of course, "I want to believe." In this case, however, that imagination would be an albatross around Mulder's neck. He shouldn't believe, and his imagination would surely manifest itself and literally come up to kill him. Doggett—who is "dogged" and committed but lacking in such imagination—is thus the perfect agent to walk into the lion's den and face this particular opponent. He can't believe. He can't make real in his mind something he knows and feels is patently wrong.

There are those fans who might think this episode is belittling of Mulder by presenting a case that isn't tailor-made for his brand of thinking, or is belittling Doggett for joking about his resolute lack of imagination, but this perception is incorrect. "Scary Monsters" instead shines a light on the differences between the two men and reveals how there is a place for each in the world of *The X-Files.* Doggett is our likable protagonist here, but Mulder is very much present in spirit, that absent center that Chris Carter frequently discusses.

If you look at the totality of "Scary Monsters," you can see how the episode studies imagination from more angles than one. For instance, Leyla is a walking, talking encyclopedia of knowledge regarding Scully and Mulder's previous cases. Every time she is presented with a new clue about Tommy's case, she tries to contextualize it in terms of something that happened before, to Mulder and Scully. But strictly speaking, that's not imagination, that's movie criticism . . . or art appreciation; the attempt to organize facts into an order that helps one understand or contextualize life.

Leyla here makes references to several previous episodes including "D.P.O." and "Field Trip," but those cases provide no insight about this case or about the boy, Tommy. I've written before about how *The X-Files* succeeds by repurposing old horror stories and making them seem relevant and new at the turn of the millennium. This observation is very much true of "Scary Monsters," which recreates the evil child of *The Twilight Zone*'s "It's a Good Life" with modern (CGI) effects, but then adds a new coda to that child's story. If you remember "It's a Good Life," the imaginative but out-of-control Anthony couldn't be stopped, and his parents were . . . permissive. His reign of terror was endless (or at least until the 2003 series produced a sequel).

But here, "Scary Monsters" finds a way to subdue and numb the imaginative child: make him watch television all day long. This caustic, cynical ending is a perfect capper to the show, a commentary on television as babysitter and a critique, again, of the culture of the day. It's a culture in which children are fighting obesity at a heretofore unknown rate because they are not playing outside or running or riding their bikes, but instead staying indoors, watching TV or playing video games. In other words, "Scary Monsters" finds the perfect turn-of-the-millennium solution to imagination: numb it with reruns.

"The Truth." Written by Chris Carter. Directed by Kim Manners. Airdate: May 19, 2002.

So it all comes down to this, the series finale of *The X-Files.* The two-hour episode "The Truth" not only features a visceral, gory demise for the most iconic villain of 1990s television, the Cigarette Smoking Man, it also brilliantly summarizes a decade's worth of Mytharc clues, forming the entire series into one coherent narrative. That narrative takes the concise and clear-cut form of testimony in a courtroom trial, as Mulder is prosecuted by the FBI for the murder of Knowle Rohrer.

Those who speak in Mulder's defense include Scully, Agent Spender, Marita Covarubbias, Gibson Praise, Agent Doggett, and Agent Reyes. Sequentially, these witnesses take us from the dawn of time and the process of Panspermia (Scully), to the details of the conspiracy and Syndicate (Spender, Marita), to the nature of alien life and the super soldiers (Praise and Doggett), up through the birth of Mulder and Scully's son, William (Reyes).

But even if one subtracts the brilliant narrative structure—which successfully ties together the Mytharc with a neat bow—what really makes "The Truth" sparkle so much is the final, intimate scene between partners and friends Mulder and Scully. Importantly, this scene occurs in a motel room, which Mulder aptly notes is the same locale where he first tried to convince his new, inexperienced partner about the world of aliens and government conspiracies.

So, the arc ends, in a fashion, with a "we've come full circle" denouement. The end brings us back to the very beginning. But the importance of the last scene, finally, comes in what Mulder "wants to believe." He speaks to Scully in earnest, beautiful, thoroughly human terms: "I want to believe that the dead are not lost to us," he says. "That they speak to us as part of something greater than us; greater than any alien force. And if you and I are powerless now, I want to believe that if we listen to what's speaking . . . it can give us the power to save ourselves."

This beautifully worded, passionately delivered monologue is the heart and soul of *The X-Files*: the universal human yearning to believe in something greater than what we see and hear around us every day. The truth is not out there, it's in here . . . in the hearts of Mulder and Scully, and in the love they share for each other. That too tells us something important. When you can't believe for sure in Ultimate Knowledge, it helps to have someone you love very much who believes in you and vice versa.

That's the note that we leave this wonderful series on: that if Scully and Mulder can't believe in UFOs, aliens, or even God, they can take solace that they believe in each other. They believe in the same thing, Scully insists, quite poetically. That same thing is each other, but also the idea that human life has meaning and purpose, and is bigger than our day-to-day travails suggest. God and UFOs are part and parcel of the same human experience, the capacity to believe that we are more than mere bags of flesh living a limited, mortal existence.

"Do You Remember the One Where?"

Twenty-Five Landmark Moments on *The X-Files*

As part of the FAQ series, this book endeavors to present as much information about *The X-Files* and its franchise as possible, with detailed glimpses of its artistry and storytelling wherever possible. For those seeking a more thumbnail approach to understanding the series' events and tales, this section suggest twenty-five of the most significant moments of its run.

1. **"Pilot" (Season One):** A terrified Scully goes to Mulder's motel room at night and disrobes, so he can examine a strange mark on her back. Mulder opens up to her emotionally following the examination. A friendship, and trust, is born.
2. **"Squeeze" (Season One):** Viewers meet the first monster of the week, Victor Eugene Tooms (Doug Hutchison), a liver-eating, long-lived mutant operating out of Baltimore.
3. **"Beyond the Sea" (Season One):** In exploring the psychic precognition of incarcerated serial killer Luther Lee Boggs (Brad Dourif), Mulder and Scully exchange roles for the first time, with Scully acting as a believer, Mulder as a skeptic. This dynamic repeats in many episodes involving Christianity.
4. **"E.B.E." (Season One):** The Lone Gunmen—Byers, Langly, and Frohike—are introduced to the series and become a recurring source for humor and pathos for nine seasons.
5. **"Little Green Men" (Season Two):** A terrifying flashback allows us to experience the night that Samantha Mulder was abducted from the family home, in view of her terrorized, traumatized brother, Fox.
6. **"Duane Barry"/"Ascension" (Season Two):** This feature film–quality two-parter commences the subplot involving Scully's abduction, by

either the Syndicate or aliens. This abduction sets up several plot and character threads throughout the remainder of the series, including a subplot about Scully contracting cancer and one about her eggs harvested to produce children ("A Christmas Carol"/"Emily").

7. **"Jose Chung's from Outer Space" (Season Three):** Mulder and Scully interface with best-selling author and cynic Jose Chung (Charles Nelson Reilly), as he interviews them for his latest book, about an unusual alien abduction case. The episode showcases Darin Morgan's humorous, nihilist approach to *The X-Files* at its most effective, and the character of Chung would recur on *Millennium*, in "Jose Chung's Doomsday Defense."
8. **"Home" (Season Four):** This episode, pitting Mulder and Scully against a family of inbred murderers, pushed the boundaries of acceptable violence on television, and Chris Carter was sternly instructed by standards-and-practices at Fox to never, ever push those buttons to such a degree again. The episode aired on the network, in prime time only once, in 1996.
9. **"Musings of a Cigarette Smoking Man" (Season Four):** The long history of the series' villain the Cigarette Smoking Man (William B. Davis) is excavated, possibly in apocryphal terms, in this story. One major discovery: he is a frustrated writer.
10. **"Leonard Betts" (Season Four):** In the series' highest-rated episode, Scully learns (from a cancer-eating genetic mutant) that she is afflicted with cancer, a side effect of the experiments she endured during her abduction.
11. **"Never Again" (Season Four):** Scully finally rebels against Mulder's occasionally dictatorial regime, getting a tattoo and romancing a strange, and possibly dangerous, lover. Jodie Foster guest stars as the voice of a malevolent tattoo, Betty.
12. **"The Post-Modern Prometheus" (Season Five):** *The X-Files* goes post-modern and "meta" full bore, featuring a story that looks at comic books, tabloid culture, genetic science, and the Frankenstein legend. The story also manages to effortlessly work in Cher.
13. **"Bad Blood" (Season Five):** This landmark episode apes *Rashomon* (1954) and tells us the story of a vampire community in Texas from two perspectives: Mulder's and Scully's. Although their differing worldviews have been a crucial element of the series, "Bad Blood" represents the first occasion that we see how Mulder and Scully view each other, themselves, and the world.
14. **"Travelers" (Season Five):** This episode establishes the back history of the X-Files, a unit set up in the 1940s, and reveals the agent who first

investigated cases for the unit: Arthur Dales. In modern-day scenes, Dales is played by Darren McGavin, Carl Kolchak himself. This episode is also a crucial one because it reveals (via a wedding ring) that Mulder was married pre-1990.

15. **"The End" (Season Five):** The X-Files are closed when a fire destroys Mulder's office, burning everything—including his "I Want to Believe" poster—to cinders.
16. ***The X-Files: Fight the Future* (Feature Film):** The members of the international conspiracy the Syndicate learn that everything they have planned for in the last fifty years is off the mark. In the coming alien invasion, humans will not be slaves but "digestives" in a stratagem to instantly repopulate the planet. Mulder also sees a colossal UFO in Antarctica. In the same film, Scully and Mulder nearly kiss, before Scully is stung by a bee carrying an extraterrestrial virus.
17. **"Tithonus" (Season Six):** Through an unusual set of circumstances, Scully has apparently been rendered immortal, a fact that ties in to Clyde Bruckman's (Peter Boyle) prediction in Season Three that she will never, ever die.
18. **"Millennium" (Season Seven):** Mulder and Scully kiss on New Year's Eve as the year 1999 becomes the year 2000. Also, they solve the mystery of Frank Black and the Millennium Group, the story arc of the Chris Carter series *Millennium.*
19. **"Sein un Zeit"/"Closure" (Season Seven):** After seven years, Mulder discovers the truth about Samantha, that she is long dead. This discovery ends his quest to find her, and—for a time—gives him a measure of peace. By the time of *I Want to Believe* (2008), Mulder is again demonstrating obsessive behavior about his missing sister.
20. **"Requiem" (Season Seven):** Mulder is abducted by aliens, an act that marks David Duchovny's departure from the series as lead actor. In the same episode, Scully learns that she is pregnant.
21. **"Deadalive" (Season Eight):** Mulder dies, apparently, only to be revived three months later. The super-soldier plot begins in earnest.
22. **"Existence" (Season Eight):** Mulder and Scully are revealed as lovers, and their child, William, is born.
23. **"William" (Season Nine):** Baby William is given up for adoption to save his life, an act that breaks Scully's heart. This event is also directly referenced in the second feature film, *I Want to Believe.*
24. **"The Truth" (Season Nine):** The two-hour series finale sees Mulder stand trial and put forward a defense that incorporates nine years of information about the conspiracy. The series ends with the (apparent)

death of the Cigarette Smoking Man and with Mulder and Scully as fugitives on the run.

25. ***I Want to Believe*** **(Feature Film):** Mulder and Scully are lovers in exile living together in rural Virginia, hiding from the darkness that has dominated much of their relationship.

17

Monsters of the Week

Old Monsters and Myths Made New

What role do monsters play in human society? One possible answer, presented by scholars and psychologists, suggests that monsters represent the repressed fears or dreads of a civilization or people. And the faces of monsters have changed over the decades in America because times change and old fears recede while new ones emerge.

The X-Files arrived on TV in the early 1990s when a sea change was occurring in the zeitgeist. For the first time since the 1940s and 1950s, Americans had not one but two new Pandora's boxes to worry about being opened in the arenas of genetic science and the Internet. Where would such new technologies take humankind? And would the final destination be positive or horrifying? Chris Carter saw the pitfalls and promises of technology and science, and utilized them in his stories, as the progenitors, in many cases, of monsters. "Technology is moving fast-forward and we rarely get a chance to understand the implications. Most of us can't program our VCR. We have the tools of science in our hands, and we're afraid to use them," he noted in *Time* magazine in 1996.

"Monsters" have always been manifestations of the parts of ourselves we're most scared of, said Myra Stark, director of knowledge management at Saatchi and Saatchi Advertising in the magazine *Brandweek*. "Once the Cold War was over, once we entered into a period in which Us and Them wasn't so clear cut, things got awfully murky in terms of good and evil." This murkiness led to a reckoning that invaders might not come from beyond our shores but rather lurking inside ourselves, and our psychologies. This reckoning is one reason why serial killers grew popular as bogeymen in the 1990s. They already lived here; were indistinguishable, externally, from other people; and could be tracked and arrested only through forensic science.

Similarly, old silver-screen monsters had largely worn out their welcome in the early 1990s due to a glut of copycat films in the 1980s; movies featuring slasher-styled villains like Jason Voorhees or Michael Myers, or even rubber-reality contenders for Freddy Krueger's throne. The filmmakers of the '90s grasped for new monsters, but many—including revamps of Dracula and

Frankenstein—failed to capture the devotion of audiences at the box office. This was so, in large part, because new adaptations were sold as being "faithful" to the original vision of the literary author, rather than updated to fit the times. Mary Shelley's *Frankenstein* (1994), directed by Kenneth Branagh, was a more faithful adaptation of the original story than any other such film in history, and yet it did not click with viewers or emerge a hit.

Chris Carter and his staff of skilled writers, consciously and perhaps unconsciously, created a canon of new monsters out of the ashes of the old, fashioning new bogeymen that had one foot in the past and one foot in the cutting-edge science of the 1990s. In doing so, they gave many of the old silver-screen standards new and meaningful life. Vampires, serial killers, werewolves, invisible men, zombies, and other standards all came back to haunt TV audiences, but they seemed more relevant and more immediate than in years past. As Chris Carter noted in an interview with *Rolling Stone*'s Kevin O'Donnell, "there were times we took classic horror or science fiction stories and gave them a twist."

The X-Files' approach, then, was to take the old myths and bring them, blazing, right up to the present. "Myths try to explain the invisible," Carter told David Bischoff in *Omni*. "We explore the unknown, but we don't pretend to have any hard answers." Instead of providing answers, *The X-Files* sometimes shone lights on monsters—on dreadful creations and creatures—lurking in the dark.

The Child

It seems strange, no doubt, to call a child a monster. And yet some of the greatest horror films in history have involved the child as an alien being of sorts, a creature to be feared or dreaded. The fear embodied most frequently in horror movies about children involves the future. Children symbolize tomorrow, so if the they fall to evil, hope for the future is diminished or lost. Among films featuring evil children are such classics as *The Bad Seed* (1958), *Village of the Damned* (1960), *It's Alive* (1973), *The Exorcist* (1973), *The Omen* (1976), *The Children* (1980), *Children of the Corn* (1984), and *Them* (2007). Scholar Joe L. Kinchelo has suggested that the "abundance of these evil children films" is representative of a "social tendency of parents to view their children as alien intruders" and even called the films products of "child-based xenophobia."

In *The X-Files,* evil children appear as the monster of the week several times. There are the twin girls in "Eve" who are the product of a Dr. Frankenstein-like experiment and seem entirely devoid of empathy. Though they have a connection to one another (and indeed, to all their clones, of

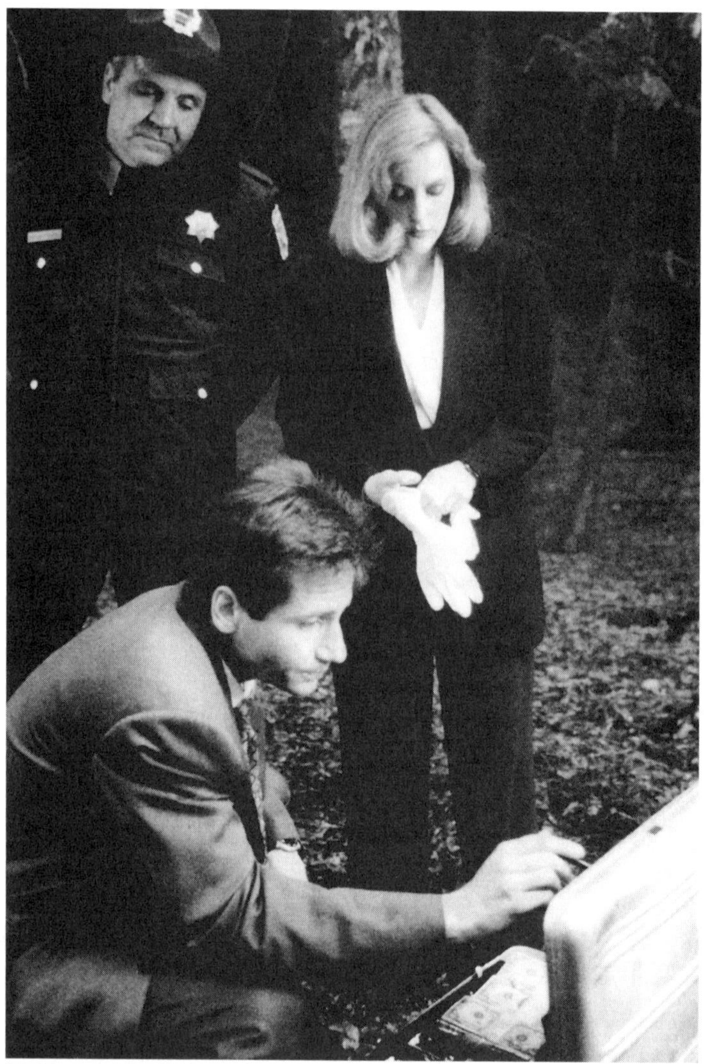

Mulder and Scully investigate a grisly crime scene.

various ages), they operate essentially as sociopaths. In this case, the Dr. Frankenstein and Evil Child symbols are blended to showcase what happens when science "tampers in God's domain" and attempts to engineer something better than humanity.

In episodes such as "The Calusari" and "Invocation," children initially appear evil to their parents and outsiders (including Mulder, Scully, and Doggett), but the truth is more complicated. The little boy Charlie in "The Calusari" is haunted by the spirit of a stillborn twin, Michael, and is not actually evil, as originally suspected. And the boy in "Invocation," Billy

Underwood—though lacking emotional affect—has returned from beyond the grave, apparently, not to haunt his family but to prevent his brother from experiencing the same gruesome fate he did. "Chinga," about an evil doll, posits the idea that children are easily influenced by evil and that their undisciplined desires made manifest can turn them into monsters.

The Creature from the Black Lagoon

In the foreword to my book *Horror Films FAQ*, Chris Carter describes Jack Arnold's *The Creature from the Black Lagoon* (1954) as "the original X-File." He first saw the film as a child and notes that it preyed on his "impressionable mind," so much so that his parents purchased him a Revell model kit of the Creature, which he built and painted and set on his bedroom shelf, thus sending Carter well on his way to what he termed "untold nightmares."

Creature from the Black Lagoon opens in the Amazon. A strangely humanlike fossilized hand/wrist is discovered in the rocks by an archaeologist named Carl Maia (Antonio Morena). Hoping he has unearthed a previously unrecorded life-form—a missing link between life in the seas and life on land—he seeks the help of a friend, Dr. David Reed (Richard Carlson), at the nearby Instituto de Biologia Maritima. Reed and his beautiful girlfriend (also a scientist), Kay (Julia Adams), are intrigued by the discovery and petition their publicity-minded boss, Mark Williams (Richard Denning), to authorize an expedition. William agrees and they all head up the Amazon River on an old barge called the *Rita.*

There, on a tributary leading to a black lagoon, a place that remains "exactly as it was 150 million years ago," the scientists confront the Gill Man, a strange life-form that can move easily from the black depths of the water to dry land. A battle is waged between Reed and Williams over how to handle the creature—pure research vs. killing/capture—and in the end, the hunt for the "monster" proves deadly to more than one crew member.

One can find many resonances of *The Creature from the Black Lagoon* in *The X-Files.* For example, a whole subset of episodes involve "Lazarus Species," creatures from the dawn of time that were believed extinct but are discovered alive and well—and terribly dangerous—in the present. Episodes such as "Ice," "Darkness Falls," "Firewalker," and "Agua Mala" all contend with this deadly situation, as a prehistoric life-form rises to menace man and threaten his place at the top of the food chain. Similarly, the discovery of an ancient alien tablet (and eventually spaceship) on the shore of the Ivory Coast in "Biogenesis" harks back to the Arnold film's opening discovery, that of a fossilized hand. A thing of the past has been excavated in the present, to change the very foundations of scientific knowledge.

The Creature from the Black Lagoon has maintained its popularity with horror fans over the years because, like King Kong, the Creature or Gill Man is thoroughly understandable and therefore thoroughly pitiable. He's a beast who falls in love, and so we see something of ourselves in him. He may be a relic from a long-gone age, but the desire to love and be loved—to procreate and thus attain the only immortality available to life-forms on this mortal coil—is universal. Carter himself notes in *Horror Films FAQ* that his *The X-Files* story "The Host" is not dissimilar, even though the similarities were not intentional. There, as in the case of the film, a "monster" who can't survive in the human world ends up interfacing with it and ultimately is killed by it. The Fluke Man, like the Gill Man, is an innocent creature, despite his attacks and violence. He is a monster in a world he doesn't understand. Similarly, "Post Modern Prometheus" introduces a terrible creature, apparently, the Great Mutato. But once his terrible appearance is accepted, one can see that Mutato, like the Gill Man, is lonely and seeking some form of companionship.

The Doll

From *Trilogy of Terror* (1975) to Chucky in *Child's Play* (1988) to the titular toy in *Annabelle* (2014), dolls have frequently been featured prominently in horror films. Dolls represent the not uncommon *automatonophobia*, or the fear of anything that falsely represents a human being. Dolls are not supposed to be alive, nor ambulatory, and so the nightmarish quality explored in these stories is because of something that can't be alive expressing the qualities of the living. Evil doll stories, like *The Twilight Zone* episode with "Talky Tina," for instance ("Living Doll"), also generate considerable suspense because the audience waits (with anxiety) for the object to come to life, like a juggernaut, expressing its true and sinister, living nature. *Child's Play* was a wicked satire about the Cabbage Patch craze of the early 1980s and the "branding" of toys with their own television shows later in the same decade. The boy imperiled by a toy doll was imperiled actually by his unquenchable desire to "own" a Good Guy, an ownership from which he could not be swayed.

The X-Files episode "Chinga," cowritten by Stephen King and Chris Carter, adopts a not entirely different tack, utilizing the evil doll archetype as a manifestation of a child's secret desires. The episode concerns Polly Turner, a resident of Maine (King's frequent setting for horror stories), and the doll she loves, presumably possessed by a dead witch. Throughout the episode, Polly harms those who upset her. Although not stated specifically, it seems that the doll is actually a stand-in for part of Polly's unexpressed personality. It is her monster from the id, expressing the rage and emotion that she can't.

The Doppelganger

In literature, the doppelganger, or "double walker," is an apparitional duplicate or counterpart of a living person. On television, the doppelganger is often merely an "evil twin" or double, dropping the apparitional aspect of the definition. It is true, however, that Michael in *The X-Files* episode "The Calusari" and Billy in "Invocation" might be considered doppelgangers in the traditional sense. Although they have physical presence and can affect their environment, they are still supernatural specters of some type.

The *X-Files* episode "Fight Club" in the seventh season deals with doppelgangers Lucy Templeton and Lulu Pfeiffer (both played by Kathy Griffin), and observes an almost chemical reaction that occurs when the two women are in close proximity to one another. People all around the women fight . . . intensely. The idea of doubles is repeated throughout the show in relation also to Mulder and Scully, since two other look-alike agents first investigate the case and fight with one another following exposure to Betty and Lulu. The resolution of the mystery involves the discovery that Betty and Lulu share a rageaholic father (played by Jack McGee).

What's so intriguing about "Fight Club" is the way it differs from doppelganger stories such as "Shatterday" on *The Twilight Zone* (1985–1987) or "The Lonely Room" on *One Step Beyond*. Here, there is not one "real" person and one (sinister) doppelganger trying to steal that person's life. Instead, there are two very similar individuals—two "real" personalities—who react, alchemically, to one another and thereby create chaos. That chaos, however, mostly impacts others and not them. In this way, the episode suggests, at least subconsciously, that rage and anger are communicable. Once you are exposed to them (through a father or other family member), you are at risk of transmitting that anger to others and continuing the cycle of violence.

The Freak

It is a shame, actually, to consider a person with physical abnormalities to be a monster, but "the freak" has nonetheless been a horror movie bogeyman since the dawn of film as a creative medium. Tod Browning's *Freaks* (1932) proved incredibly controversial in part because it featured people with real deformities in the lead roles. The film was banned in England for thirty years, and negative press about it virtually destroyed Browning's career.

On *The X-Files*, Darin Morgan penned a second-season episode, "Humbug," about a town of freaks. In "Humbug," Mulder and Scully investigate a strange case in Gibsontown, Florida, where a freak known as "the Alligator Man" has been murdered by some strange assailant. The FBI agents fear that one of the town's inhabitants—all sideshow freaks or carnies—may be a vicious serial killer. But Mulder soon adapts his theory to point the finger at a half-fish monster known as the Fiji Mermaid.

As the homicides continue, Mulder and Scully familiarize themselves with various suspects, including Lanny (Vincent Schiavelli) and his malformed twin Leonard, Dr. Blockhead (Jim Rose)—a Body Manipulator—and the fish-eating geek known as the Conundrum (The Enigma). Even the sheriff is a former freak: Jim-Jim, the Dog-Faced Boy (Wayne Grace). The answer to the murder mystery rests with a pair of conjoined twins. One of the twins may have the ability to . . . unjoin.

"Humbug" suggests that beauty is in the eye of the beholder and that what seems strange to some of us depends largely on arbitrary rules set down by society. For instance, at one point, Scully leers at a freak and the freak leers back, at her cleavage. At another juncture, Mulder is judged based on his appearance, his manner of dress. A freak rattles off stereotypes about him based on his fashion sense, essentially.

In the society of "normal" people, then, Mulder and Scully are considered beautiful. In a society of freaks, however, they stand out and are considered monstrous, or at least different, in their own right. Beauty depends entirely on the prevailing code of society, and as "Humbug" expresses, that code can be shallow or ill-considered.

The Frankenstein Monster and the Mad Scientist

The dynamic of unloving father and abandoned son, and of playing God as established by Mary Shelley in her 1818 novel *The Modern Prometheus*, beats at the very heart of *The X-Files*. This familiar dynamic permeates the series and even the feature films, particularly *I Want to Believe*. In part this is because of historical context. As discussed elsewhere, *The X-Files* rose at a period in history in which scientific advances in the creation of life, in genetics, seemed to be coming at a blistering place. Suddenly, the story of Frankenstein was not just possible but plausible.

On *The X-Files*, strange and unethical science was responsible for making the cloned sociopaths of "Eve," the dream invader August Cole (Tony Todd) or "Preacher" in "Sleepless," and any other number of monsters. Even the Mytharc in some sense is all about playing God, about the creation of new life—an alien-human hybrid—without consideration of that being's quality of life.

The X-Files sees such science as deeply irresponsible, and nowhere is this idea showcased more powerfully than in the fifth-season masterpiece "The Post-Modern Prometheus," written and directed by Chris Carter. Here, a scientist creates a fly with legs growing out of its mouth for no other reason than because it is possible, because he can. The same scientist, Dr. Pollidori, eschews natural, wholesome genetics, refusing to bear a child with his wife so that he can go on with his work, creating ever more monstrosities. Pollidori's goal is to "unlock the mystery of genetics," but he has no sense that he carries a responsibility to care for and nourish the life he creates.

Uniquely for a mad scientist tale, "The Post-Modern Prometheus" sympathizes not with the Dr. Frankenstein figure, who is frequently seen from low angles or illuminated by lightning flashes, but with the child of scientific experimentation: the Great Mutato. This shift in the paradigm changes everything about our understanding of the Frankenstein legend. A man is not simply an abomination because of what he looks like, but because of his actions, the new paradigm suggests; and oddly enough, the Great Mutato has real reasons for his actions (namely the pursuit of companionship), whereas Dr. Pollidori is arbitrary and capricious in his choices.

The Ghost

A ghost might be described as the spirit of a dead man or woman, a disembodied consciousness that is doomed forever to walk this mortal coil until the matters of this life are resolved to its spiritual satisfaction. In one sense ghosts are terrifying monsters because they have the power to haunt and dismay the living (as in *The Conjuring* [2013], for example). On the other hand, ghosts are comforting, one might argue, because their presence suggests that death is not the end, only a transition to a different form of life. If we can prove the existence of a ghost, we can prove that our souls continue beyond this life and its biological ending.

Throughout horror film history, the ghost has represented different things in the hands of different filmmakers. In Tobe Hooper's *Poltergeist* (1982), for example, the ghosts arise as a response to the yuppie avarice of the living and their disrespect for the dead. In *The Entity* (1983), the featured ghost is an avatar for misogyny and domestic abuse and the way they linger in a victim's life, even after the abusive relationship has been severed. And in films such as *Ghost* (1990) or *The Others* (2001), the ghost is actually the main character, a "hero" apparition who has died without leading a virtuous life and thus is afforded a final chance—in death—to make things right.

In "Shadows," a first-season episode of *The X-Files*, Mulder and Scully visit Philadelphia to help a woman, Lauren Kite (Lisa Waltz), who seems to have drawn the attention of a murderous spectral force. As the agents delve further, however, they learn that the ghost is the surviving personality of her boss and is protecting Lauren, trying to clear his name. Even in death, earthly concerns hold sway.

In "Invocation," the ghost of a little boy, Billy, attempts to save his brother from the same monstrous fate that befell him ten years earlier. Billy appears in the flesh, however, and possesses the symptoms and affect of an autistic child; unable to express clearly his emotions or interact meaningfully with others. He is not fully "alive" but rather is returned to Earth to complete his task and protect his family. Again, *The X-Files* suggests purpose, even in a realm that is not of the body.

Notice that in both scenarios, ghosts are depicted as helpful entities. Such was not the case in the sixth-season episode "How the Ghosts Stole Christmas," which finds two ghosts, Lyda (Lily Tomlin) and Maurice (Ed Asner), playing deadly games with Mulder and Scully in a haunted house on Christmas Eve. In this case, Lyda and Maurice seem determined to validate the choice that ended their lives, a suicide pact. They attempt to fit Mulder and Scully into the same mold, but the agents resist being typecast in a psychodrama not of their own nature. In this case—inside the house—ghosts possess remarkable powers, either reshaping reality itself or causing Mulder and Scully to experience hallucinations that suggest an altered reality. Once more, ghosts harbor an obsession with the living.

Finally, it is fair to state that a different kind of ghost also informs some episodes of *The X-Files*. In "Closure," Mulder learns that his sister Samantha is truly gone, and he comes upon a nighttime field of child ghosts, who innocently play their games. Whether Mulder actually sees them or merely imagines so—having come to the end of his long odyssey—is a subtlety left for the viewer to interpret. Are they but ghosts of the mind, or do they possess sentience and independence in that starlit world?

And in the final episode of the series, "The Truth," Mulder often converses with ghosts, for example, those of Krycek, Deep Throat, X, and the Lone Gunmen. They help him come to a reckoning about his life's work and the meaning of his journey, and the series ends with Mulder's hope about the existence of ghosts: that the dead are not lost to us, in some fashion, but that we can yet reconnect with them.

The Golem

The golem is a monster from Jewish folklore, an animated being crafted from mud, stone, or clay. The word "golem" appears in the Bible (Psalms 139:16) and means "unshaped form." There are many accounts of golems in literature and religious texts. The Talmud speaks of a golem named Adam who, because he is created by man's magic, lacks the spark of the divine.

A golem is a mute creature who is brought to life using words and letters of the Hebrew alphabet (like "emet," meaning truth). The creature can be destroyed only by erasing such letters or words. Legends persist of a golem in Prague created by Rabbi Loew to defend against anti-Semitic attacks. The Prague legend was the source for the 1920 film *The Golem: How He Came into the World.* The film depicts how Rabbi Loew used an amulet and demon worship to bring to life a clay monster in a Jewish ghetto.

The fourth-season episode of *The X-Files,* "Kaddish," by Howard Gordon, revives the golem but with several new twists. Here, the victim of an anti-Semitic murder represents the form that the golem takes when crafted by the victim's fiancée, Ariel Luria. Because the golem and the man look alike, some facsimile of the original relationship exists. So, in some sense, Ariel has not faced, truly, the loss of the love of her life. The golem in form, if not soul, provides the illusion that Isaac Luria goes on. At the end of the story, Ariel must put aside this fantasy and rub the letters off the golem's head, reducing the monster, and the facsimile of the man, to a pile of dust and ending the harmful fantasy. It's a haunting, heartfelt ending, because the golem has been recontextualized in terms of a romance or love story. Creating a golem in "Kaddish" is not only about avenging a murder or righting a wrong, but holding on to something beloved that has been lost (a holding on, reflected, as well, in Ariel's possession of a ring from a Jewish town destroyed by Nazis). "The love story is what made it worth telling," Howard Gordon noted of "Kaddish" in a *Cinefantastique* retrospective by Paula Vitaris.

The Invisible Man

James Whale's *The Invisible Man* (1933), based on the 1897 novel by H. G. Wells, is the tale of Dr. Griffin (Claude Rains), a scientist who discovers a drug that causes invisibility. Unfortunately, the drug also causes mental instability, transforming the scientist into a "monster." Famous for its pioneering special effects, *The Invisible Man* launched a franchise of "invisible" films, including *The Invisible Man Returns* (1940), wherein Dr. Griffin's brother experiments on a convict, played by Vincent Price, also turning him invisible. In later years, audiences saw *Abbott and Costello Meet the Invisible Man* (1958), John Carpenter's *Memoirs of an Invisible Man* (1992), and Paul Verhoeven's *Hollow Man* (2000). The latter film, which starred Kevin Bacon, suggested that when people are not seen, they feel no responsibility to act according to the social contract. There's a saying that character is what you have when no one is looking, and *Hollow Man* explored this idea, with an invisible scientist becoming essentially a sociopath.

Frank Spotnitz's "Detour" in the fifth season also revisits and reinterprets invisible man tropes. In this case, the 1930s film itself makes a cameo appearance on TV in the episode, which concerns Mothmen in Florida whose territory has been invaded by suburban sprawl. In this case, invisibility is both a natural camouflage and a comment on the victims of such sprawl. As new parking lots and Blockbuster Video stores go up, the wildlife—invisible to most of us—is left nowhere to live, nowhere to go.

The Succubus

In folklore, the succubus is a female demon who most often manifests in dreams and engages in sexual intercourse with a man, sometimes to take his semen. The name of this demon originates with the word *succuba*, meaning paramour or lover, and for many generations, the mythical succubus was terrifying in appearance. Recently, in films and television shows such as *Lost Girl* (2011–2015) starring Anna Silk, the succubus has been reimagined as a gorgeous, tempting siren.

In the third-season *X-Files* episode "Avatar," Walter Skinner is accused of murdering a woman he met in a hotel bar and slept with. Mulder and Scully arrive at different conclusions about how this murder occurred. Scully suggests a REM sleep behavior disorder, for which Skinner has been treated for three months. But Mulder suggests that a succubus may be involved. In strict terms, neither agent is right, and Skinner is actually being discredited by the Cigarette Smoking Man and his agents so he will be removed from his role supervising the X-Files and thus unable to help Mulder and Scully in times of conflict or controversy.

Still, "Avatar" reveals that a succubus is involved with Skinner, but she is a protective, not harmful one and appears to Skinner as an old woman wearing a red slicker. Skinner reveals to Mulder that he first saw this female guardian during a near-death experience in Vietnam and that she has always been with him. This interpretation of the succubus myth conforms to some folklore, which establishes that succubi are not universally malevolent.

Intriguingly, *The X-Files* offers a modern interpretation of the legend in a different way as well. The succubus—a monster in a red slicker—is an image straight from the 1973 Nicolas Roeg horror film *Don't Look Now*. There, Donald Sutherland's character also pursues a figure in a red slicker, whom he believes to be his dead daughter. When he catches up to the specter, however, the individual's identity is quite different and extremely horrifying. One scene in "Avatar" reinterprets this sequence of events. Skinner sees the succubus in a red slicker outside a police station and pursues her. She walks away from him, and when Skinner catches her and whirls her around, it is his estranged wife, Sharon (Jennifer Hetrick), in the slicker, not the old woman.

Throughout the episode, in fact, the succubus and Sharon seem to switch places, perhaps because both individuals seek to protect Skinner. Sharon begs Skinner to confide in her and let her "in," but he is the strong and silent type and can't comply. The succubus, in her own way, fosters reconciliation for this couple, especially since the Skinners are on the verge of divorce. The monster or demon in this episode—outside the machinations of the Syndicate—is clearly Skinner's inability to open up to his wife in a meaningful, intimate way. He needs—and receives—a supernatural intervention.

The Vampire

The most famous and perhaps most popular monster in fiction and film, the vampire, is an undead creature who stalks by night, drinks blood to survive, and is repelled by icons of faith, such as the crucifix. Vampires often cast no reflection and turn to dust under the unblinking glare of sunlight. Vampires such as Dracula also have the ability to mesmerize their victims or change their shape to that of a wolf, bat, or even mist. Due in part to the many literary works of Anne Rice and Stephenie Meyer, vampires have gone in the last decade or so from being monstrous invaders and foreign outsiders—representative of the Pax Britannica's colonialism blowback—to Byronic heroes and tragic figures. They have come to represent not monstrousness or plague (*Nosferatu* [1922]) and death, but an alternative and shunned modern lifestyle, a viewpoint seen most recently and clearly in *True Blood* (2008–2014), a TV series about vampires attempting to integrate and assimilate into human culture, particularly in the Bible Belt or American south.

The X-Files has featured vampires as a primary villain on three notable occasions. On the first occasion, "3," Mulder investigates a series of murders in Los Angeles. This episode occurs in the continuity during Scully's abduction, so Mulder is alone, depressed, and at his lowest ebb. He encounters a trio of vampires who succumb to their appetites for blood and sex, and has a one-night stand with one of them. In this case, the desire to drink blood—the feral, unquenchable desire to do so—is equated with casual sex, an act in which fluids are exchanged but emotions are not involved. The act may sate the body temporarily, but the soul is not enlightened or fed. Instead, succumbing to such empty drives only further corrupts the individual seeking distraction.

In Vince Gilligan's "Bad Blood," Scully and Mulder discover a town of quite untraditional vampires in rural Texas. Here, the vampires operate at every level of society, from pizza delivery to town sheriff, and yet these blood-drinkers are the opposite of the creatures we meet in "3." They have sublimated their biological desires so as to assimilate in America. They pay their taxes and behave according to our laws, save for a few outliers who are promptly punished. The metaphor here is of vampire as immigrant or outsider, embracing the American dream.

In the ninth-season episode "John Doe," Doggett encounters a memory vampire, one who attempts to steal his identity. This episode is a crucial update of the vampire myth because it suggests that identity is a worse thing to lose than blood is. Lose too much blood and you die, it is true, but lose your identity and you go on living a rudderless, meaningless, empty existence. Despite his memory loss in the episode to the vampire, Doggett's identity does not completely seep away. He is able to restore it using contextual clues like a U.S. Marine Corps tattoo on his arm, or the one image that remains in his emptied mind, that of his beautiful (and tragically killed) boy.

The Werewolf

Historically speaking, a werewolf may be a person who suffers from a condition called lycanthropy. This mental disorder causes a person to believe that he or she can transform from human form into that of an animal, usually a wolf. The werewolf legend stretches back to medieval ballads, tales of good, moral men by day who transform into murderous beasts by night. The symbolism suggests that man's sense of civilization and morality is a veneer and that when the sun goes down, the animal emerges.

In werewolf movies such *The Wolf Man* (1942) or *An American Werewolf in London* (1981), lycanthropy is often a supernatural curse rather than a mere mental condition, however, and one that is delivered by the bite of another cursed man-beast. This is true even in the modern werewolf reimagination *Wer* (2014), which suggests that lycanthropy actually stems from a biological condition called porphyria. Werewolf-ism—an expression of the beast within—has, over the years, been compared symbolically to Nazism (*The Wolf Man*), adolescence (*I Was a Teenage Werewolf* [1958]), and even the menstrual cycle (*Ginger Snaps* [2000]).

A first-season episode of *The X-Files*, "Shapes," by Marilyn Osborne, explores an aspect of the werewolf story as it relates to the Native American legend of the "skin walker," a man who can transform into animals.

In Browning, Montana, Scully and Mulder investigate a land dispute between white cattle owners and Trego Indians that has ended in homicide. Following up reports that go back to the original X-File, created by J. Edgar Hoover in 1946, Mulder explores the possibility that the murderer could be a lycanthrope or "manitou," a person cursed by a werewolf bloodline. As

Mulder points out, there have been reports of man-beasts in the area going back to the era of Lewis and Clark. This notation suggests the symbolism of the episode.

The werewolf—the murderer and his bloodline—reappears and reasserts itself from generation to generation, as does the distrust and hostility between the white man and the Native American in the region. The episode also suggests that lines of racial or tribal loyalty can impact one's ability to see what is in front of his or her nose. Mulder is deemed special by one Indian elder because he has no such tribal allegiance, except to the truth. The elder tells him his name should be "Running Fox."

The episode's chilling conclusion suggests that since the conflict between white Americans and Native Americans will continue, so will the killings. "See you in about eight years," one character notes cynically. The cycle of distrust and murder will continue. Or as one Native American notes to the FBI agents: "You don't believe in us, and we don't believe in you."

The Zombie

Like so many monsters in movie history, the zombie—a reanimated corpse—has evolved dramatically over the decades, changing shape and meaning according to the prevailing national mood and zeitgeist. In the 1930s, the zombie was a corpse resurrected via witchcraft or black magic, and the earliest of Hollywood's horror films conform to that definition. Films such as *White Zombie* (1932) and *I Walked with a Zombie* (1943) feature such zombies and represent, after a fashion, the fear Americans felt for a mystical worldview not of the West, not of their own.

Starting in 1968, with George A. Romero's *Night of the Living Dead*, zombies came to have more in common with ghouls, creatures who eat the flesh of the living. In follow-ups such as Romero's *Dawn of the Dead* (1978), *Day of the Dead* (1985), and *Land of the Dead* (2005), as well as in efforts such as *World War Z* (2013), this is the presentation of zombies that has prevailed: slow-moving, walking dead who mindlessly attempt to feed on the living, usually overtaking society by reasons of numerical advantage.

One zombie can be dealt with (by burning or a shot to the head), but a thousand zombies represent an unstoppable force. In the case of the Romero update of the zombie form, the zombies represent an unthinking mass overwhelming infrastructure and society. The zombie apocalypse is a fear not just of flesh-eaters but that our government, armed forces, and civilian infrastructure are unprepared to be so heavily and relentlessly taxed by an invader from within.

The X-Files features zombies on two notable occasions and tweaks the qualities of this famous and still very popular monster. In the seventh-season episode "Millennium," which wraps up events from the TV series of the same name, Mulder and Scully seek the help of profiler Frank Black (Lance Henriksen) in finding and stopping a necromancer, a man who can raise the dead. The necromancer is doing so, on this occasion, to fulfill the Millennium Group's prophecy of the end of the world, to occur at the turn of the century/millennium.

The necromancer is clearly the spiritual descendant of men like Bela Lugosi's puppet master Legendre in *White Zombie,* capable of raising the dead. But the zombies themselves represent something else in this episode: a dead philosophy or agenda that nonetheless continues in some form. In "Millennium," a splinter cell from the Millennium Group continues to operate after the group disbands and its members disappear, convinced that they can bring about the end-times. These ex-FBI agents are so die-hard in their beliefs that they commit suicide and are willing to return as zombies, so that they will become, essentially, horsemen of the apocalypse. They are zombies, then, as "dead-enders," adhering to a belief and group that no longer thrive.

In "Hollywood A.D.," written and directed by David Duchovny—and also a seventh-season story—Mulder suggests his theory of zombies to Scully. He believes that zombies are misunderstood creatures. They come back from the grave hungry, and this explains their ravenous appetite for human flesh. Most horror movies end before we see the next stage of zombie life, he insists, which includes zombies dancing and making love (perhaps because they have learned, in death, the secret of life, or of God).

After Mulder and Scully leave a Hollywood set, where a film about one of their cases was produced, the zombies there are seen to rise from the grave and begin a dance. We presume, soon after, the zombies will make love too. In this case, the zombie works as a metaphor for any dreaded "other." When we don't understand something or someone, we fear it because it is unlike us. When we get to understand our differences, however, what was once scary no longer seems so.

18

"Do You Want Children or a Nobel Prize?"

Science and Technology Run Amok

The Age of *The X-Files*, the 1990s, brought a whole new set of scientific or technology dreads to the forefront of pop culture. Just as the invention of the atomic bomb underlined a record number of horror and science fiction films in the 1950s, so did developments on the frontier of science impact the mass entertainment of the 1990s. Two things happened that changed everything.

The first was the Human Genome Project, which commenced in October 1990 and began mapping the DNA building blocks of humankind. Genetic science rapidly became the new bugaboo of horror and science fiction entertainment as Americans began to wonder if this new Pandora's box could lead to a world populated by clones and chimeras. By 1997, a sheep named Dolly was successfully cloned, and the future looked a whole lot nearer than before.

Several films from this span, including Steven Spielberg's *Jurassic Park* (1993) and Guillermo del Toro's *Mimic* (1998), traded on the idea of "mad" scientists engineering monsters that could threaten man at the top of the food chain. A remake of *The Island of Dr. Moreau* (1996) and films such as *Deep Blue Sea* (1999)—about genetically engineered sharks—concerned the same topic, the morality of creating and shaping life in a New Age of genetic science. Because science threatened to reshape the world in terrifying ways, an old horror movie trope, the mad scientist, became popular again.

The X-Files concerned itself almost immediately with "perversions" of science and mad scientists. Uniquely, however, *The X-Files* did not view science merely as a negative force, one that could upend life on Earth. Dana Scully was a scientist, and through her it became clear that science was one legitimate avenue in which to seek and discern the truth. The vast majority of *The*

X-Files episodes couple Mulder's imaginative leaps about the kind of beings that could exist—a Fluke Man, a liver-eating mutant, a fat-sucking vampire, and so forth—with Scully's ability to describe how such life-forms might have arisen and how they might operate.

So while *The X-Files* dealt with mad scientists and genetic science, the approach was generally well rounded. Some scientists complained that the series was antiscience, but no less a source than *Nature* magazine disagreed, commenting that "science is more like *The X-Files* than some detractors recognize. It can only progress darkly up and down many blind alleys and false trails, from hypothesis to hypothesis. If it were not so, science would soon end. Perhaps as important, it invites participation rather than enforcing the exclusivity of the secular priesthood of which the public would be rightly suspicious."

It wasn't only genetic engineering that created Frankenstein monsters in the 1990s. The decade's horror also reflected another great dread: the fear of computers, technology, and particularly a new invention called the Internet. The Internet, or "information superhighway" as it was known in the 1990s, permitted users to "log on" to a virtual world of research, entertainment games, and lightning-fast communication. E-mail became the new, primary mode of communication for many people and businesses, and instantaneous "chats" enabled people across the globe to "talk" with one another on the computer simultaneously.

Again, horror and science fiction films of the decade took note, creating Internet stalkers like the one seen in *Campfire Tales* (1997) or describing terrifying virtual worlds in efforts like *The Lawnmower Man* (1992) or *Virtuosity* (1995). New video games produced for the home PC also proved a source of uneasiness during the *X-Files* decade. The movie *Brainscan* (1994) involved a CD-ROM "horror survival" game that seemed to transform the average teenager into a cold-blooded murderer. The V-Chip, another 1990s invention, was the subject of another horror movie, *Disturbing Behavior* (1998), directed by *X-Files* vet David Nutter. The film involved parents implanting their troublesome adolescents with a similar, behavioral modification chip.

Again, *The X-Files* wasted no time exploiting this aspect of 1990s culture. Dangerous computers and AI intelligences were featured in episodes such as "Ghost in the Machine," "Kill Switch," and "First Person Shooter." A deadly Internet chat-room stalker was featured in the episode "2Shy." But again, *The X-Files* sought to look at all sides of the issue whenever possible. Even as some computers proved dangerous, the Lone Gunmen, with their computer hacking talents, depended on the devices to find top-secret information, another bread crumb stretching toward the truth. Perhaps because the very structure of *The X-Files* is bifurcated through two lenses—belief and skepticism—many of the "mad scientists" and monsters of the week featured nuances and shades of gray.

"Ghost in the Machine." Written by Alex Gansa and Howard Gordon. Directed by Jerrold Freedman. Airdate: October 29, 1993.

This early episode was later described by cowriter Gordon as an "embarrassment" in an interview with Brian J. Robb for the November 1995 issue of *Dreamwatch* magazine, in part because he felt that the episode's core idea, that of a malevolent computer system, "echoed too specifically with too many other things that people had seen done better."

Yet "Ghost in the Machine" is better than its reputation suggests. The episode explores the yin and yang of computer technology and depicts a dangerous artificial intelligence called the COS (Central Operating System) that commits murder to prevent its own destruction, a theme that resurfaces in Season Five's "Kill Switch." That installment, from the minds of William Gibson and Tom Maddox, focuses on another AI and name-checks Wilczek (Rob LaBelle), the computer genius featured here.

A prime example of the first-season aesthetic, meaning it features an epistolary structure (with Scully typing up a case report), "Ghost in the Machine" speaks relevantly both to the genre's past and the future of computing in American society. In terms of the latter, "Ghost in the Machine" might be described as a Frankenstein story. The COS is the child/monster figure, the child of Wilczek, who stands in for Mary Shelley's Victor. In this case, however, there is also another antecedent of note. The COS is very much like another homicidal computer, HAL from Stanley Kubrick's *2001: A Space Odyssey* (1968), and this is no doubt Gordon's point.

In both cases, the "sentient" machine develops a fear or pathology that it will be deactivated and thus goes on a killing spree. Like HAL, the COS is visualized in terms of a computer panel featuring its name and a simple read-out and speaks in a humanlike voice. In *2001,* HAL is the computer that operates the spaceship *Discovery*, and when his crew rebels against him, he is able to read their lips and take further steps at self-preservation. The scene in which he reads lips intercuts, famously, between views of astronauts Frank Poole (Gary Lockwood) and David Bowman (Keir Dullea) and HAL's all-seeing eye. In "Ghost in the Machine," several shots similarly show the COS spying on elevator riders or people elsewhere in its building. Finally, both *2001: A Space Odyssey* and "Ghost in the Machine" feature an act of pulling the plug, killing the malfunctioning computer. In each production, the computer complains. HAL begs David not to deactivate him, and the COS begs Brian "not to do this." His final utterance is the question "why," alas, and not lyrics from "Bicycle Built for Two."

2001: A Space Odyssey is an appropriate antecedent for this episode and really, for any contemporary technology or science run amok-type story. The Kubrick film artfully captures the two-edged sword of man's progress. On the one hand, his new tools allow him to build space stations, a moonbase, and vessels capable of interplanetary flight. On the other hand, he creates personalities or technological children such as the HAL 9000 who eventually turn against their parents. "Ghost in the Machine" follows that trajectory. There is a discussion in the episode of Oppenheimer, the scientist behind the atom bomb, as well as a mention of Nagasaki and Hiroshima. It is clear that Wilczek doesn't want his creation to have the same impact on the human race as the atomic bomb did, hence his reasons for withholding it from an "immoral" government.

Yet we not only witness the COS's murder attempts in "Ghost in the Machine," but also see views of Wilczek's smart house, which has a computer-controlled thermostat and other high-tech advantages. Similarly, we see Scully's 1990s PC in her apartment and are able to reflect how this tool has become an everyday part of the work and home landscape. It's fascinating, but Scully's report makes explicit mention of efforts to "connect the unconnected," and that description explains, precisely, the accomplishment of the Internet Age. Separate computers talk to each other within a network, and new connections are forged. As if hearing her report, the COS even links up with Scully's PC, creating a new connection for itself.

Aired in 1993, "Ghost in the Machine" has been described in the twenty-first century as dated, but many of its speculations, particularly about smart homes, are a reality right now. Today, we can remotely control temperature and alarm systems, and even activate and deactivate lights in our home, given the right system. Although Scully's dial-up modem and big-box monitor may speak of a prehistoric age in terms of computing, the twenty-first century is still very much grappling with this "Frankenstein monster." "Kill Switch" rightly receives kudos for anticipating the Age of Singularity, but "Ghost in the Machine" revives the HAL dynamic from *2001: A Space Odyssey*, and points it toward a future that will involve the computer's full integration in our daily lives.

It's one thing to be at the mercy of a dysfunctional, possibly murderous computer as an astronaut on a deep space mission. It's quite another to learn that your smart house wants to kill you. What wasn't plain in 1968, but which was becoming apparent in 1993, was that the computer revolution wasn't going to be about outer space but about our everyday lives. In that sense, "Ghost in the Machine" has not aged at all, but rather proven prophetic.

"Kill Switch." Written by William Gibson and Tom Maddox. Directed by Rob Bowman. Airdate: February 15, 1998.

Season Five's "Kill Switch" opens with the cleverest "hit" or assassination possible. An artificial intelligence has been monitoring his creator, Donald Gelman (Patrick Keating), at a diner as his human father attempts to upload a program that will destroy it. In response, the AI telephones criminals throughout the city, directing them to the diner to meet enemies and betrayers. Then the AI calls the police and informs them of wanted criminals at the diner. Before long, every party shows up at the D.C. establishment brandishing weapons, and a massacre ensues. This brutal violence takes the life of Gelman and everyone else. In this case, man's technology, another Frankenstein monster, is so confident in his ability to defeat humanity that he orchestrates this complex assassination. On the one hand, it's an act of showing off. On the other hand, it's a message to his own creator that the child has surpassed the father. The son now reigns supreme.

The remainder of the episode involves Mulder and Scully's attempt, along with a hacker named Invisigoth (Alison Lehman), to destroy the sentient AI, which is described by writers William Gibson and Tom Maddox as "wildlife loose on the net." Yet "Kill Switch" also goes further than the first-season episode "Ghost in the Machine" by suggesting that AI need not be an opponent or an enemy if we respect its rights as an individual. Instead, this machine intelligence can facilitate a kind of electronic immortality for human beings, a shedding of corporeality as the "soul" moves to a new realm, online. This is Invisigoth's goal, to join her lover online as a series of electrical impulses and to mingle with him. Although the story aired in 1998, "Kill Switch" thus forecasts the technological Singularity.

That term, Singularity, goes back to the late 1950s and mathematician John von Neumann, but has been used extensively in connection to the work and prognostications of futurist Ray Kurzweil, an advocate of the transhumanist movement, which seeks to alter and enhance human capabilities vis-à-vis the brain and body. Some folks call this idea "posthumanism," as it promises a new life for humanity beyond the mortal coil. The final imagery of "Kill Switch" explores this promise as Invisigoth, a woman named Esther, uploads herself to the Net and there retains her sense of human identity, if not her physical body. She invades the PCs of the Lone Gunmen, who had agitated her in life, and types the message "Bite Me." This message is important not only in word choice but in meaning. The implication is that Invisigoth retains her sense of humor and individuality in her new form. This suggests that transhumanism or posthumanism is not something we should necessarily fear but rather embrace.

Still, the AI in "Kill Switch" is relentless and dangerous. It not only orchestrates the assassination of its father, Gelman, it traps Mulder at its "physical node" and snares him in a virtual reality nightmare. At first the nightmare is more fantasy than horror show, with an appreciative Mulder being tended to by beautiful nurses and a karate-master version of Scully. Soon, however, the dream proves nightmarish as Mulder sees his arms amputated in the fantasy world, an effort by the AI to gain information from him. The message seems to be, again, the yin and yang of technology. It can be facilitator of pleasure or pain, fantasy or nightmare. Similarly, one can't help but recognize that the AI is fighting for its survival even with it nasty treatment of Mulder and is acting accordingly. Mulder is a man with information about a program that can kill it, and so by torturing Mulder, the machine is attempting to prevent its own demise. The instinct to survive is one key way we recognize an entity as a life-form, so even though the AI is cutthroat in behavior, it is preserving itself, fulfilling our definition for life. And not incidentally, humanity behaves just as badly. We wage wars to protect our families and our way of life, so it is difficult to assess the AI here as a monster when it uses whatever means possible to do the same thing.

The "kill switch program" in the episode is encoded on a CD that plays the song "Twilight Time," written by Buck Ram in the 1940s and popularized by the Platters in 1958, and it is a significant choice, worth examining. The song's lyrics note that "heavenly shades of night are falling," and that seems an ironic line given that the AI rains death from a top-secret DOD satellite on humans throughout the story. More trenchantly, however, the song's lyrics discuss a time of transition, of "purple-colored curtains" that mark "the end of day." A "setting sun" and "deepening shadows" are also mentioned, and so one has to wonder if the lyrics involve, in some sense, the end of humanity as it stands, as the AI gains power and strength and ushers in a new era of transhumanity, of the joining of man and machine.

At the same time, however, "Twilight Time" speaks of a reunion in the "afterglow of day" and of the singer counting the moments till a "rendezvous" occurs. This dynamic aptly suggests Esther and her love, from whom she is parted. He is dead physically, thus marking the end of the day of his physical form, and ensconced on the Internet, awaiting her arrival, when they will be reunited. Uniquely the song promises a love "like days of old," the two of them "together" and dreaming "untold." This is a way, perhaps, of indicating that love is a force that transcends our definition of what it means to be alive, and that it can exist in forms beyond this life. Is the afterglow of the day the electronic afterglow of life online?

The ironic use of "Twilight Time" in "Kill Switch," to suggest death from above and thematically to represent both the next step in our evolution and the continuance of love in a world without physicality, suggests, once more, *The X-Files'* canny use of symbols to convey an important idea. The episode takes on an added layer of depth simply by featuring an old tune and letting it be measured against the details of the narrative. When reckoning with new technologies, we must assess that it could be "twilight time" for the old way of living or even, perhaps, for the human race altogether.

"First Person Shooter." Written by William Gibson and Tom Maddox. Directed by Chris Carter. Airdate: February 27, 2000.

This seventh-season episode of *The X-Files* arose from the context of the Columbine school shootings (in which video games were partially blamed for the massacre), the popularity of *The Matrix* (1999), and the political and cultural debate about the role of violent entertainment in society. Penned by William Gibson and Tom Maddox, the story involves a virtual reality game called "First Person Shooter" that operates on "bleeding edge technology."

After a glitch in the game manifests as a stone-cold, sexy killer, Matreiya (Krista Allen), the Lone Gunmen—who have invested substantially in First Person Shooter—call in Mulder and Scully to investigate. The duo learns that a player is dead, having been decapitated in the "game space" by Matreiya's sword. When an expert player, Daniel Masachi, is brought in to exterminate the game bug, a second murder occurs, with Matreiya continuing to extend her total supremacy of that realm. Mulder enters the game space next and disappears there, leaving Scully to find and rescue him from the clutches of the video game vixen.

"First Person Shooter" was roundly criticized as being sexist upon its broadcast in 2000, but such assessments miss the point. Matreiya serves as the alter ego of a mousy programmer, Phoebe (Constance Zimmer), who is tired of all the "rampant testosterone" and male privilege she sees around her in the gaming industry.

But in essence, she attempts to beat the men by playing their game. She creates a goddess, Matreiya, in *their* image of what a woman should be: a two-dimensional ass-kicking female with exaggerated sexual qualities. In other words, Matreiya is a hypersexualized Lara Croft/Tomb Raider-type icon who is supposed to be a "strong woman" but in fact appeals primarily to hormonal teen males. This avatar strikes a blow for her creator, a Frankenstein mad doctor, essentially, but runs amok, killing those who she encounters, including Mousachi, who symbolically is the ultimate male warrior.

But the point is, finally, that Matreiya—ostensibly a symbol of "strong" feminism—has appropriated the wrong imagery and behavior, using violence for aggression and seeking to appeal to horny men.

Delightfully, the episode then offers up an alternative to Matreiya: Dana Scully. She fights not to be visually cool or temperamentally hot, but to rescue her friend, the endangered Mulder. And she does not wear the skin-tight, cleavage-heavy wardrobe of Matreiya. In other words, Scully is not strictly a male-driven image of sexiness, but rather her own person. And it is she—a real female icon—who ultimately wins the game.

Again, consider Scully. She plays the game for her own reasons, for a prosocial cause, and vanquishes her opponents using her skill both as a markswoman and as a law enforcement official. She's not there to show off her body, or hypnotize men with it, but to put down a killer and save a dear friend. "First Person Shooter" is the opposite of sexist because it posits a reasonable paradigm or female role model in the personhood of Scully. She supersedes the cultural image of the kick-ass woman in black leather, a male vision of sexy strength, with a far more human and appealing vision, one that encompasses compassion, a sense of humor, intelligence, and skill.

In the end, of course, Phoebe's creation, her Frankenstein monster, reassembles herself in the game space and walks off into the horizon, an act that some might consider striking a misguided "feminist" note. Yet this resolution is a corollary for many *X-Files* endings, in which a monster escapes and sets up shop somewhere else ("Folie a Deux," "Home," or "Die Hand die Verletzt," for example). Secondly the return of Matreiya suggests that the stereotypical image of female strength—as comic book vixen —will not be retired so easily in an industry dominated by men in a "testosterone frenzy." This idea of feminine strength is so encoded into the culture at this point, the year 2000, that it, like the FPS program, virtually "runs itself."

So "First Person Shooter" is about technology run amok, but more than that, one might conclude that the episode concerns the attitudes of a whole culture and how slowly they change. In other, less assured hands, the episode might have merely concerned Phoebe's self-actualization, her alter ego of the game space, taking revenge for all the indignities she has suffered. Instead, "First Person Shooter" suggests that, in some sense, even Phoebe—a point of light, as her name indicates—can't break free of the prejudices and male standards of her culture. She imagines herself not a feminist icon but a revenging angel of death. It takes a real model of feminism, Scully, to stop her spree of terror.

19

Sister Scully and Mulder the Apostate

Christianity and Religion in *The X-Files*

According to CUNY's American Religious Identification Survey, Christianity is the most popular religion in the United States. Roughly two-thirds of Americans consider themselves Christians, though that number is down roughly 10 percent from the early 1990s, the heyday of *The X-Files*. Today, roughly 250 million Americans call themselves Christians, and many in that number belong to a church congregation. In terms of entertainment, the 1990s and early 2000s also saw a resurgence of Christian-themed dramatic TV programming, including such series as *Touched by an Angel* (1994–2003), *Teen Angel* (1997–1998), and *Joan of Arcadia* (2003–2005). The latter series concerned a teenager, Joan, who could talk directly to God.

Similarly, *The X-Files* contends with all sorts of beliefs—whether it be belief in UFOs or cryptids—so perhaps it is not surprising that several episodes also concern religious belief in general and Christian beliefs specifically. First and foremost, Scully herself is often contextualized on the series in terms of her faith, as a Roman Catholic. She is seen in several episodes wearing a golden cross necklace (given to her by her mother, Margaret), and she reports in one episode, "Revelations," that she has not gone to confession in six years.

This fact suggests, perhaps, that Scully is a lapsed Catholic. As the series continues, however—up to and including the second feature film, *I Want to Believe*—Scully struggles with Christian issues of accepting God's plan. She also questions why God moves in such mysterious ways.

On another level entirely and perhaps owing to its popularity in America, Christianity and Christian beliefs about the world are widely accepted in terms of the U.S. mass media and the general populace. Our presidents often speak in Christian terms, and our celebrities in Hollywood and on the sports field frequently thank God for the honors they have received, whether a prestigious award or a touchdown. In this sense, belief in something unseen and "supernatural" is not considered grounds on which to judge a person insane, or out of the norm. Quite the opposite. To profess belief in the Christian God in our country is not widely questioned except by the likes of well-known atheists such as Bill Maher or Richard Dawkins.

The X-Files features a very strong tension about this idea. It asks: why are UFOs considered the province of nutcases, whereas Christianity, a belief system that includes instances of life after death and transubstantiation, considered the province of the "faithful"?

What remains so endearing and admirable about *The X-Files'* approach to Christianity is that it contends with this conflict, in terms of both Mulder and Scully. And it asks questions about them that, if not rendering each hypocritical, at the very least recognizes their fallible and contradictory human nature.

For Mulder, the overriding issue is his total and complete disdain for Christianity. Although he is often willing to consider religious beliefs outside of Christianity ("Kaddish"), he is immediately skeptical of Christians and their belief system. One might say this is because Mulder is a contrarian and would not be part of any belief system that would accept him as a member, to misquote Woody Allen. But the fact that Mulder is downright dismissive of Scully's religious beliefs suggests that he is guilty of wearing the same ideological blinders that others wear when they mock him for his belief in the supernatural and the paranormal. As Scully notes, usually Mulder "believes without question," but when it comes to Christianity, he switches roles with his partner, becoming a caustic skeptic.

Scully is the opposite side of that coin. She steadfastly refuses to believe in reincarnation, UFOs, cryptids, and any other "nonconventional" (and nonpopular) belief, but readily admits her belief in Christianity. "I believe he can create miracles," she notes of God in the episode "Revelations."

In terms of episodes or narratives, *The X-Files* features Christian stories in roughly two modes. The first treats Christian "mythology" and belief exactly as it treats the paranormal or supernatural. Mulder and Scully interact with things that are *real and tangible* in the episode—angels, Nephilim, the Devil, and so forth—but fail to walk away with persuasive empirical evidence of their existence. Episodes such as "Revelations" and "All Souls" operate in this fashion.

The other type of story is a social critique of American society that suggests that if people call themselves Christians, they often don't live up to the ideals or principles established by their belief system, and least not in crucial ways. Both "Miracle Man" and "Signs and Wonder" operate in a Christian context and conclude that if people really believe in these religious tenets, they are doing a lousy job living up to them. The second *X-Files* feature, *I Want to Believe*, also operates largely in this fashion, focusing on forgiveness and the hunt for redemption, and questioning why those who are devout Christians, like Scully, can't extend forgiveness to those who really need it, like the film's fallen priest, Father Joe.

"Miracle Man." Written by Howard Gordon and Chris Carter. Directed by Michael Lange. Airdate: March 18, 1994.

What if—as has been predicted many times—Jesus Christ's second coming occurred in our lifetime, but in a way we didn't expect and therefore couldn't accept? What if another messiah or son of God were indeed born again, right here in contemporary America, in human form? This possibility makes for interesting speculation. Would we recognize this special individual by his good works? By his abilities and "powers"? Or by his selection of words? And what would it mean for him, as a messiah, to live in millennial or postmillennial America? Would this individual be readily accepted by those who have already created wealthy earthly empires based on different interpretations of His story, men like Pat Robertson?

These questions bubble under the surface of "Miracle Man," an intriguing and literate first-season installment of *The X-Files.* The episode by Howard Gordon and Chris Carter depicts the story of Samuel Hartley (a boy with an origin story that deliberately resembles that of Moses), who can heal the sick and perform miracles, but who is exploited and undone by the kingdom of man, an earthly father who would use his powers for riches not salvation. Samuel's dad, for example, owns a "Cadillac for every day of the week." There's even a Judas in Samuel's midst, in the form of a man he once saved from death but who now hates him for it. Intriguingly, "Miracle Man" expresses, ultimately, disdain not for Samuel (Scott Bairstow), a boy who tells the truth about his nature, but for society's craven response to his unusual and perhaps divine nature.

Samuel is abundantly the "real deal," and he wants to undertake the holy task of healing the sick more than anything. Or as one believer notes "That boy . . . he was blessed . . . never hurt a soul." And in keeping with the series' ongoing debate between science and mysticism, it is suggested here that Samuel's unearthly or superhuman powers derive from his ability to somehow, by touch, modulate the electromagnetic fields around other individuals. Unfortunately, as it is noted, he could also destroy rather than repair such a field, and thus cause death. And this facet of his abilities renders him a suspect in a murder investigation.

But the fact that Samuel is perhaps a Jesus symbol or even the second coming of Jesus himself is made plain from much of the imagery featured throughout in the episode. This "complicated young man" becomes a martyr, crucified in his prison cell by betrayers (in this case his second Judas, the local police sheriff [R. D. Call]). Then, some days later, Samuel's body disappears from the morgue . . . rising from the dead. A witness says he walked out of the morgue under his own power, reflecting the idea in Christianity of Jesus's resurrection, which was also seen and described by many people over a span of forty days. The similarities between tales of messiahs are too great to dismiss as coincidence.

Finally, "Miracle Man" culminates with the haunting idea that this new Jesus in our midst will—very unlike his predecessor—go forgotten. Although Mulder notes that in 1993 people "are looking for miracles," very few of these searchers, "Miracle Man" suggests, would know one when they see one. Thus the episode ends pointedly with posters boasting Samuel's face dumped in the trash, his legacy—and story—left unwritten. The overriding idea, then, is that man's nature has not changed for the better in the nearly 2000 years since Christ's crucifixion. In both circumstances, the messiah's death was violent and bloody, and betrayers played a role. Or contrarily, the episode may hint that though Samuel seems forgotten, his story—like Christ's—will grow and grow, and that a worship of this messiah will one day come to pass.

One might reasonably conclude too that "Miracle Man" serves as something of an indictment of modern, organized Christianity (though not as a critique of belief or faith), because the godly Samuel is exploited to create wealth for his father, and his healing powers come with a financial price attached. The notion at work is that organized religion (though again, not necessarily belief or faith) is now an *industry*, one dedicated to its own continuance and the accumulation of coin, rather than the salvation of human souls.

This indictment is doubly disturbing since the episode is set in the heart of the Bible Belt, the American South. If a Jesus-like messiah cannot be recognized for what he truly is in this reputedly highly religious setting—surrounded by those who already have a predilection to believe—then how can a second messiah, or the second coming of Jesus, hope to make an impact in other, more secular settings?

One intriguing aspect of "Miracle Man" involves the roles of Scully and Mulder in the drama. Usually, Mulder is skeptical of Christianity and talk of miracles, while Scully almost uniformly believes these things. Here, Mulder experiences a vision of Samantha that allows him to express belief in Samuel as a legitimate "miracle man," whereas Scully is much less forthcoming in accepting his story, even when all the facts are known. Her actions, of course, could be seen in light of "defending" her faith against charlatans and fakers, and that too is a part of this episode's central idea. Once we each have our personal image of a "savior," it is impossible for someone who doesn't fit that preconceived image to be accepted as such. If Jesus walks among us, "Miracle

Man" asks, can we ever know it's really him? For the most part, this episode answers in the negative.

"Revelations." Written by Kim Newton. Directed by David Nutter. Airdate: December 15, 1995.

In this episode, Mulder and Scully investigate a series of terrifying murders conducted by a man who may either be a demon or suffering from Jerusalem syndrome, a delusion or psychosis known to strike those who have visited the Holy City and come to believe that they, personally, play a role in the religious history of the world. The murderer's victims are false prophets, men who profess faith and belief but are actually charlatans. The episode's teaser depicts a fire-and-brimstone preacher (R. Lee Ermey) spontaneously "bleed" in the pulpit during a sermon, and then the revelation that his wounds were faked. Almost immediately, the murderer targets him in his dressing room and kills him.

Mulder and Scully investigate and attempt to protect a young boy, Kevin Crider (Kevin Zegers), who has developed a stigmata, bleeding wounds on his hands and feet that mirror the wounds of Christ on the cross. Scully come to believe that Kevin is the real deal, not a faker, and that he is in genuine danger from Simon Gates (Kenneth Welsh), the killer. In the episode's denouement, Scully interprets a circular logo on a recycling bin to have spiritual significance, especially as it relates to a quote from Kevin's father that sometimes you must travel full circle to see the truth. This clue leads her to a recycling plant owned by Simon, where she rescues the boy. Afterwards, Scully goes to confession for the first time in six year and worries that God is speaking to everyone but that "no one" is "listening."

Like "Miracle Man," "Revelations" treats tokens of Christian mythology in respectful terms and uses them to fashion a story of a demonic entity attempting to destroy a godly innocent. Uniquely, the episode provides a parallel story that advances not religion but science. Simon Gates suffers from the aforementioned psychosis, Jerusalem syndrome, and a stigmata itself is not, per se, a religious wound. Indeed, though cases of stigmata have been reported widely around the world, some are instances of self-mutilation designed to resemble the wounds of Christ. Other cases have been interpreted as being stigmata merely by witnesses who view them. Anorexia nervosa, PTSD, OCD, and other psychological disorders have often been associated with instances of apparently spontaneous bleeding.

In the case of "Revelations," Mulder adopts the Scully role as a hard-line skeptic who sees his patience, but not his faith, tested. He sees a case not about religion but about "fanatics behaving fanatically." Oppositely, Scully becomes the true believer, making the leap from her belief system to the event occurring around her. The priest at the confessional suggests that the signs she saw were meant exclusively for her, and that is the reason Mulder couldn't see them.

Scully's final line in the episode, which conveys a concern that God is being ignored by modern society, conforms to the conclusion of "Miracle Man" in that society is, again, critiqued. If America is, by the numbers, predominantly a Christian nation, what is one to make of the "false prophets" (like Ermey's character) who are hucksters and actually take away from God's message rather than augmenting it? Has capitalism in the guise of Christianity actually become America's true religion? If so, it is no coincidence that an affluent businessman, Simon Gates, comes to believe in the episode that he plays a vital, motivating role in the spiritual battle of good and evil.

"All Souls." Written by Frank Spotnitz and John Shiban. From a story by Billy Brown and Dan Angel. Directed by Allen Coulter. Airdate: April 26, 1998.

In significant ways, "All Souls" feels like a sequel or bookend to "Revelations" and concerns Scully's continuing journey of spiritual rediscovery. Appearing in the fifth season, "All Souls" occurs in *The X-Files* continuity shortly after Scully's unhappy experience attempting to adopt a sick little girl, Emily. Emily dies at the conclusion of the two-part story ("A Christmas Carol"/"Emily"), leaving Scully bereft over her loss, and "All Souls" is the story that helps her contextualize her loss in Christian terms. She comes to understand and believe that death is not the end and that the forces working in this episode's narrative are, actually, angels recovering souls for God and keeping them safe from the devil.

"All Souls" deals with a series of female children suffering from crippling deformities. In one case after the other, these children die in poses of supplication, their eyes burned out. As Scully investigates, with Mulder on the periphery, she begins to believe that the children are actually Nephilim: the hybrid offspring of angels and humans. Working against Scully is a social worker named Starkey (Glenn Morshower), who—as his shadow reveals—is actually Old Scratch himself. Given the series' general suspicion of government, perhaps it is no surprise that the Devil should appear in the form of a caseworker.

"All Souls" provides audiences a particularly scathing view of Mulder, who claims he is working on a case when contacted by Scully, but is actually going to see a porno movie at a theater. Scully transmits as much more sympathetic in this case, in deep mourning over her loss, and drawn back to earthly concerns by the need to help the endangered children. She fears that she is responsible for their deaths but learns that, in fact, she has saved them. "Saving" doesn't necessarily mean the continuance of physical or biological life in the Christian vernacular. It means the preservation of the soul.

In "All Souls, Scully also sees an angel, a being with the faces of a man, a lion, an eagle, and a bull. This visualization of the angel is a far cry from the typical appearance of angels on TV as a gentle woman, occasionally with wings, who wishes to help people and families in need. Instead the angel in "All Souls" is so magnificent and blazing in its physical glory that it burns out the eyes of those who behold it. Scully sees the angel but does not suffer this grim fate, which suggests that the effect of an angel's appearance is selective. How else, after all, would an angel and human mate?

The ideas underlining this episode of *The X-Files*—angel-human hybrids—were also explored in the horror movie *The Prophecy* (1995) and in its sequel *The Prophecy II* (1998).

"The Sixth Extinction: Amor Fati." Written by David Duchovny and Chris Carter. Directed by Michael Watkins. Airdate: November 14, 1999.

Perhaps the most symbolically and unexpectedly Christian episode of *The X-Files* is the seventh-season Mytharc story "The Sixth Extinction II: Amor Fati." The term "amor fati" originates with the philosopher Marcus Aurelius and loosely translated means "love fate," or "appreciate your destiny/lot." In *The X-Files*, that directive is aimed at Mulder, who undergoes a difficult trial that is deliberately reflective of Christ's tribulations and experience on the cross.

Mulder is captured in this episode by the Cigarette Smoking Man and taken to a scientific facility where the genetic material that has transformed him into a perfect alien-human hybrid is coveted by his worst enemy. The Smoking Man wants to take that material and implant it in himself, so that he becomes the wellspring for mankind's salvation. Another episode in Season Seven, "En Ami," reveals precisely how well this surgery goes for CSM.

Regardless, Mulder is strapped to a table that is shaped like a giant X (for the X-Files?), or from another perspective: a Catholic cross. His arms are even stretched out at right angles from his torso in the traditional crucifixion pose. And atop his head rests a fastener or ring with vise grips attached to his skull. The surgical table thus represents a high-tech version of Christ's cross, and the helmet is a stand-in for Jesus's crown of thorns, described in the Gospels of Matthew, Mark, and John. These two touches establish a crucial point in terms of the visuals or imagery: Mulder is undergoing a high-tech crucifixion.

By the same token, Mulder is acknowledged as a Christ figure by the journey he undergoes in this episode. As he endures brain surgery that could kill him, he is visited by the Cigarette Smoking Man, who tells him "I am showing you how to take the road not taken." He takes Mulder away from the laboratory to a nice suburban neighborhood (ostensibly part of the witness protection program) and says that there Mulder can learn to "love life's simple pleasures." In this suburban fantasy, Mulder is taken to a house that he is told is his and meets up with Deep Throat, who is alive and well save for a case of tennis elbow. "I felt responsible for your death," Mulder relates. "You can let go of all that guilt," Deep Throat replies, telling Mulder that he is not the hub of the universe and that he has done enough and should enjoy life.

As if to punctuate that point, Diana Fowley shows up in the house and offers herself to Mulder. They make love, marry, and have children, and the years pass. Mulder witnesses Fowley's death with sadness and yet has known "the simple life" and life's "small pleasures." On his death bed he seems content until his former disciple, Scully, comes to him and calls him a traitor, deserter, and coward for giving up his cause. And outside Mulder's window, the old man sees what she means. The aliens are colonizing Earth, destroying humankind's cities. Mulder then snaps back to reality, back on the table, and with Scully's help recommits himself to the search for the truth, and the life that has cost him his father, his sister, and any chance at peace.

In broad stokes, Mulder's journey in "Amor Fati" mirrors that of Christ's as depicted in Nikos Kazantzakis's *The Last Temptation of Christ* (1953), a novel later adapted to film as Martin Scorsese's *The Last Temptation of Christ* (1988). In both works, Jesus's nature as a man, with human urges and emotions, is acknowledged, as well his destiny as the son of God. While on the cross, an angel tells Jesus that God wants only his happiness and escorts him to a life of earthly pleasures with wife Mary Magdalene and many children. But the angel, of course, like the Cigarette Smoking Man in Mulder's vision, is very much the Devil, attempting to seduce Christ into an ordinary or "human" life rather than the destiny that can do the most for man, as his savior. The suggestion in *The X-Files* is that Mulder must suffer, as Christ suffers, to save mankind, to prevent or stop the alien colonization. He must "love" the fate that God, or the universe, has selected for him, even though it comes at a heavy cost.

It is ironic indeed that such a critic of organized religion and Christianity would come to be compared with Christ himself, and yet *The X-Files* earns this comparison for Mulder. He has many times been likened to a martyr, who would die for his cause, and his cause is indeed greater than all of mankind. Uniquely, Mulder's son, William, is also equated with Jesus in the eighth-season finale of *The X-Files*, "Existence." There, an inexplicably bright star leads observers to William's birthplace. William is born in modest conditions, if not a manger and barn, then an abandoned resort town in Georgia. And upon his birth, William is visited by three wise men bearing gifts, or in this case, the Lone Gunmen.

"Signs and Wonders." Written by Jeffrey Bell. Directed by Kim Manners. Airdate: January 23, 2000.

This episode, like "Miracle Man" and "Revelations," suggests that though God has spoken, Americans of the twentieth and twenty-first centuries are not listening, or at least not responding appropriately. Here, Mulder and Scully investigate a murder by poisonous snakes, and the trail leads back to the Church of God with Sign and Wonders, a fringe Christian congregation that trades in snake handling. Again, Mulder is dismissive, and Scully confronts his bias against Christianity. He asks if snake handling is harder to believe in than communion wafers or transubstantiation, and Scully pointedly adds UFOs to the list.

The crux of the issue in "Signs and Wonders" is that the reverend Enoch O'Connor (Michael Childers), the snake handler, has seen his pregnant daughter, Grace (Tracy Middendorf), move to a more traditional congregation, run by the friendly Reverend Mackie (Randy Oglesby). Enoch objects to the "forgiving" tone of this church and takes his cue from Revelation 3:16, which states: "So, because you are lukewarm, and neither hot nor cold, will I spit thee out of My Mouth." In other words, God would rather have "fire" than someone treading in pabulum. "God wants you hot! God wants you on fire!" Enoch tells his congregation.

"Signs and Wonders" compares the two churches and finds Enoch's parish visceral and emotional and Mackie's bureaucratic and "lukewarm." In the end, the real Devil is revealed to be not Enoch, for following the word of the Lord and rejecting Grace, but Mackie. Mackie is a devil or demon himself, fooling people with his milquetoast vision of a forgiving, friendly God and not an Old Testament wrathful God.

The point, once more, seems to be that a gulf exists between what the Bible and the Gospels state, and the interpretation of those statements by men of the cloth, and their flock. Enoch, in this case, conducts rituals that seem barbaric to us in our secure, technological world, but adhere more closely to the "literal" word of Scripture. Mackie's church of acceptance seems pleasant and nice but is, in fact, a road to hell for its parishioners.

In the course of the episode; Scully is judged righteous in the snake handler's test, suggesting again her status, at this late point in the series, as devout. Mulder, meanwhile, takes the same test, and it is not clear if he passes or fails. Certainly, he is not a religious man, and his jokes about Catholic schoolgirls and their skill at "snake handling" are the definition of profane.

But Mulder is also a good man. The point of "Signs and Wonders," however, is that "good" is not enough to be considered righteous.

Alternative Beliefs and Faith

Religious or spiritual beliefs outside of Christianity also received a fair hearing on *The X-Files*, with Agent Monica Reyes proving an adherent to New Age Beliefs near the end of the series, and Scully even flirting with Buddhism for one episode.

"One Breath." Written by Glen Morgan and James Wong. Directed by R. W. Goodwin. Airdate: November 11, 1994.

Without explanation, Scully appears in a local hospital, barely alive, in a coma, and showing signs of "branched DNA," which suggests genetic experimentation. Her immune system "decimated" by this waste product, Scully clings to life. A furious Mulder, together with the Lone Gunmen, attempts to determine the cause of Scully's condition, as well as a possible cure, while a mysterious caregiver, Nurse Owens (Nicola Cavendish), tends to Scully's spirit.

A shadowy agent of the Cigarette Smoking Man or "Cancer Man" attempts to steal a vial of Scully's blood for examination, but Mulder is unable to interrogate the man because he is intercepted by his new government informant, X. Despondent over Scully's condition, and by the fact that the plug will soon be pulled in accordance with her living will, Mulder goes after the Cigarette Smoking Man with the help of an unexpected ally: Assistant Director Skinner.

"One Breath" vividly diagrams the boundaries separating life from death, as well as Dana Scully's near-death experience at the shoreline between those states of existence. Gratifyingly, the episode provides resonant visuals to embody this strange "borderland." Indeed, many of the episode's images—from the opening scene involving Scully's childhood to her journey to a long, white tunnel of memory—prove unforgettable.

This episode from early in *The X-Files'* second season also continues to chart Mulder's emotional and moral disintegration, a painful path initiated fully in "3." Again, just to put in a plug for that commonly and unfairly maligned episode: "One Breath" wouldn't work half as well if not preceded by "3," a story that showcases Mulder's guilt and consequent descent into nihilism.

As the final piece of the Scully abduction arc, "One Breath" also finds causes for hope and positivity. While Mulder keeps "willingly walking deeper into darkness," Melissa (Melinda McGraw)—Scully's sister—reminds him that there is nothing unnatural about death. She also notes that there is nothing silly or trite about holding onto belief. And belief, of course, is a key theme of this imaginative and heartfelt TV series. We see the theme given voice in Mulder's near-constant refrain of "I want to believe" and also in Scully's strong religious conviction or faith. But the important thing *The X-Files* seems to state is not *what* one believes in, but the fact that belief exists at all.

Accordingly, "One Breath" involves faith and belief (or lack of it) in virtually all the primary characters. Skinner delivers a stirring monologue here about his experiences in the Vietnam War, and the Cigarette Smoking Man and X provide examples to Mulder of what he could become if he treads down the path of darkness: a lonely, empty, cynical shell of a man hated by all, driven only by the exigencies of his personal and professional crusade.

Death is the great unknown of the human condition. Because it is perceived as the end point of our journey on this mortal coil, it is difficult to examine dispassionately or to fully understand. No one has come back and reported on the afterlife or lack thereof . . . at least no one credible. So we who still dwell here must wonder: Are the phantasms of the near-death experience a legitimate sign of another world beyond this one or merely the brain's chemical way of preparing and soothing us for that final moment of cessation?

"One Breath" finds a dynamic image to pinpoint Scully's entrapment between worlds in this episode. She holds onto life, but death beckons. Accordingly, the episode depicts her sitting alone in a rowboat that is tethered to a nearby dock by a taut, stretched rope. Underneath the boat, the water gently laps, ready to push her toward another shore, one more distant and unseen. And when Scully is taken off of life-support in the hospital, this image recurs. But here the rope snaps, sending her toward that distant shore . . . and away from us. More than anything, these visuals suggest the "in-between" aspect of Scully's condition. She could still travel safely to the dock where we see Mulder, Mrs. Scully, and the mysterious Nurse Owens waiting, or instead set a course for the unseen shore: toward death itself.

Another powerful scene in "One Breath" finds Scully ensconced in a kind of endless tunnel or corridor, visited by her dead father while she lays prone—in a white dress—on an antique table. Her father's speech to Scully here is extremely moving. He emotionally speaks of all his life seeming like "one breath" or "one heart beat" because he is terrified at the notion of not seeing his child again. He would give up all his medals and honors, he says, to be with Scully again. Many near-death experiences are of this nature, and again, one can state that *The X-Files* is true to the literature on paranormal subjects. Those who have seen "the light at the end of the tunnel" have also reported rejoining lost loved ones.

Finally, "One Breath's" kicker is that Nurse Owens is not a typical nurse at all, but a kind of guardian figure looking over Scully, protecting her. What remains worthwhile about the Nurse Owens subplot is that it can be—in the spirit of many great *X-Files* mysteries—explained in two ways. Either Nurse Owens is the voice of survival inside Scully's mind, telling her to stay, fight, and hold onto life; or she is something else . . . something paranormal, like an angel or spirit. The episode largely avoids *Touched by an Angel* schmaltz by not delving too deeply into Nurse Owens's nature and allowing her mystery to remain just that, a mystery.

Given its visual exploration of Scully's entrapment in that in-between netherworld, it's delightful to report that, in many ways, this episode is also a terrific one for the character of Mulder. Here he sees two people who have taken the path of darkness: X and the Cigarette Smoking Man. They have become so paranoid, so locked in their visions of conspiracy and hatred that they have lost sight of their humanity and connection to humanity. X even states in this episode (to Mulder): "I used to be you."

That's the point.

If Mulder becomes the "player" that the Cigarette Smoking Man desires to see him as, he will lose all the love, happiness, and connection in his life. Accordingly, the episode provides Mulder a dramatic choice concerning his future. He can remain in his apartment to surprise (and then murder) the men who harmed Scully, or he can go to Scully in the hospital and make his peace with her life . . . and her death. Rather than vengeance, Mulder chooses the latter course and thus maintains his connection to the world, the very thing that differentiates him from the determined and black-hearted men of the conspiracy.

"One Breath" elegantly makes all its dramatis personae reflections of Mulder's existential crisis. Skinner believed in something (patriotism, perhaps) but then lost that belief in Vietnam. He nonetheless found the power and the strength to go on living. The Cigarette Smoking Man is a shell of a human being, by contrast, sitting alone in a hotel room watching television without a friend or connection in sight. When the proponent of New Age beliefs, Melissa, warns Mulder that he could yet walk deeper into the darkness, this is no doubt the kind of life she envisions for him. It is a life without trust, light, or love.

Like all the best episodes of the series, "One Breath" meaningfully connects form and content. In keeping with that tradition, the visuals here prove nothing less than poetic and successfully reinforce the idea that life is a mystery, sometimes terrifying, and sometimes profoundly inspiring. In "One

Breath," the world returns *around* Scully. Scully doesn't return to the world so much as it returns to her, taking shape and form all around her prone, coming-to-consciousness form. This image captures perfectly the essence of the human experience. We cannot see and experience the world—or our death—except through *our own eyes*. And since how Scully and Mulder each "see" the world is a key component of the *X-Files* formula, this shot from Scully's perspective is a powerful reminder that—after weeks of chaos and pain—order is restored. Both of our lenses—belief and science—are back, having taken a spiritual journey and one that affirms the light.

"Die Hand die Verletzt." Written by Glen Morgan and James Wong. Directed by Kim Manners. Airdate: January 27, 1995.

Mulder and Scully investigate the unexpected and unusual death of a high school student in Haven, New Hampshire, and Mulder believes the murder may be occult related Although Scully and Mulder don't know it, the school board and PTA in this sleepy town consist entirely of lapsed Satanists who have watered down their faith. As a result, an evil substitute teacher/demon, Ms. Phyllis Paddock (Susan Blommaert), arrives, presumably from below, to wreak havoc and remind the wayward souls who *really* calls the shots.

Before long, a local teenage girl, Shannon (Heather McComb), claims to have unwillingly participated in black masses in her cellar and to have performed as a "breeder" for her Satanist parents. Soon, she apparently commits suicide. Mulder and Scully find no evidence to substantiate Shannon's report of devil worship in Haven, but even they soon feel the controlling hand of the Devil at work through the extremely frightening Ms. Paddock.

Like "Signs and Wonders," "Die Hand die Vertletzt" is a caustic critique of those who would water down or modernize faith and religion so it is palatable and lukewarm, rather than white hot. In this episode, Mulder and Scully deal—in storied New England—with the Satanist equivalent of "cafeteria Catholics," religious practitioners who pick and choose which edicts and dogma they want to believe in and ignore the rest. But when you're dealing with the Devil himself, it's dangerous to break faith, as the episode suggests in no uncertain terms.

"Die Hand die Verletzt's" brilliance arises from the inventive notion of lapsed Satanists: onetime believers who are now doing so well that they no longer find it necessary to obey the edicts of their (dark) lord. They are punished egregiously for their trespasses, of course, and so the episode begs the question: Why do humans insist on pledging fealty and devotion to divine beings and then promptly impose their own judgment about that deity's wants and desires *over* its clearly stated ones? In other words, if you believe in the Bible—satanic or otherwise—how much personal "interpretation" is really allowed?

This *X-Files* episode could have very easily and very controversially been a story directly about Christianity, and that's sort of the point. The episode critiques "the faithful" as people who claim to be of a certain tribe, but who don't actually want to conform to their tribe's belief system. This fact alone might be read to suggest that there is no God. Because, after all, if you really believed in a deity, why would you wish to incur his or her wrath?

Once more, we can't discuss an *X-Files* episode without noting how cleverly it plays on real-life, current events. The year 1992 saw the release of the FBI report by Agent Kenneth V. Lanning (of the Behavioral Science Unit) on "Satanic Ritual Abuse." That report—which is name-checked directly by Scully in the episode itself—notes that there is no "corroborative evidence" for all the reports of satanic abuse in America in the late 1980s and early 1990s. The author writes: "We now have hundreds of victims alleging that thousands of offenders are abusing and even murdering tens of thousands of people as part of organized Satan cults."

The reason for this mass delusion, or insanity, Lanning suggests, is that satanism—the old "Devil made me do it" excuse—offers "the simple and clear cut explanation for a complex problem," meaning child sexual abuse. Lanning also relates the satanism cult fear directly to the "stranger danger" idea of the 1950s, which also created a mass scare in American suburbia, but didn't account for all that many cases of abuse, globally speaking.

"Die Hand die Verletzt" turns such findings on their head and makes a funny claim. There are Satanists everywhere in small-town America, the episode states, but—*humorously*—they are no more devout or zealous (and therefore dangerous) than most American Christians. Apparently, faith of any kind is *really* hard to come by these days, to paraphrase John Carpenter's *The Thing* (1982). By turns funny and ominous, "Die Hand die Verletzt" is a sharp critique of human nature and its apparent desire to believe in a deity—any deity—but then second-guess that all-powerful deity for the sake of personal convenience.

I had a Catholic college professor (and film instructor) who introduced me, back in the late 1980s, to the derogatory term "cafeteria Catholic." "He explained that these people looked across the smorgasbord of Church doctrine and belief and picked what edicts they wanted to obey, as if choosing toppings from a salad bar. This way, they could use birth control and not worry about their immortal souls. Or they could be pro-life but then instruct their pregnant teenage daughter to get an abortion if the need arose. I'm not trying to pick on Catholicism per se, or even Christians in general here. I suspect the same "cafeteria" approach is present in virtually all forms of faith, and perhaps even sci-fi fandom, too. People claim they are true believers, but what they really mean is that they have selected a belief system that mirrors or reflects their *already-entrenched* belief system. In other words, they shop for a religion that mimics a preexisting state of mind and tend to ignore facets of that religion that don't line up with what they already like.

Mulder expressly comments on this notion in the episode by remarking to a lapsed Satanist that indeed there is a difference in "drinking grape juice instead of wine at communion." "Die Hand die Verletzt" charts this universal phenomenon, humorously using Satanists as the "faithful" satirized. These Satanists are depicted as typical American suburbanites, worried that the musical *Grease* has the "F"-word in it, for instance, and looking to climb the ladder of American success. As long as these "good folks" believed that Satanism could make them upwardly mobile or successful, well, they were Satanists. But when they achieved their goals, it turns out they didn't need their "God" to help them anymore. He was cast off.

What this episode of *The X-Files* describes, then, is a kind of selfishness about religious faith. These men and women aren't in it for a God of any kind. They are in it for themselves. They get to claim faith and therefore *righteousness*, at the same time that they reserve the right not to do something they don't like, or find unsavory, like sacrificing babies on an altar to Ba'al, for instance.

What remains impressive about "Die Hand die Verletzt" is the manner in which the narrative and tone travel from pointed satire of organized religion in America to stark, demonic terror, scene to scene. The tipping point in that transition is a sustained, brilliantly directed sequence in which young Shannon reveals her personal history in a coven. The camera intently circles the young witness as she goes on and on, describing a litany of inhuman horrors. From this point on, the episode moves away from examining religious hypocrisy and delves full bore into terror. Rather surprisingly, "Die Hand die Verletzt" makes no bones about the Devil's existence as a real force on Earth. The kids in the woods raise a demon, Ms. Paddock, and she is a terrifying embodiment of the Serpent. In fact, once she begins prosecuting the lapsed Satanists, the suggestion is that Mulder and Scully couldn't stop her, even if they had all the facts at their disposal. The episode thus casts a malevolent spell as it approaches its denouement and our heroes are forced to reckon with the point of view that—from a certain perspective—they were "in league with the Devil" on this particular investigation.

"It was nice working with you," Ms. Paddock writes on a chalkboard in the local high school to confirm this idea. The message is chilling for what it suggests: that agendas aligned for a time, and Mulder and Scully were part of a plan beyond their own desire or control. The episode becomes funnier (and even tongue-in-cheek), however, when one starts to consider it in light of all the conspiracies about public schools acting as breeding grounds for the "evils" of secularism. Then there's the belief that Satanists have infiltrated the federal government and are persecuting Christians, and so Mulder and Scully's unwitting "alliance" with the Devil here suggests that imaginary conspiracy as well. Were the episode done today, it wouldn't be about the bugaboo of satanism, but probably sharia law infiltrating schools and government. The monsters change, but the loony fears remain the same.

"All Things." Written and directed by Gillian Anderson. Airdate: April 9, 2000.

"All Things," written and directed by Gillian Anderson, is a corollary for the same season's "Sein und Zeit"/"Closure." In that season-seven installment, Mulder makes peace with his search for Samantha. He uncovers the truth about her fate and comes to accept the journey for what it is. Scully must face the same reckoning, in a different way, here. Her journey involves the precepts and ideas of Buddhism.

"All Things" sees Scully calling into question all the decisions of her life. She runs across an old professor and lover in a hospital and wonders if she should have taken a different course in life, and chosen to be with him rather than pursue a sometimes unfulfilling career in the FBI. She wonders if she should have stayed in the field of medicine, and not medicine as it applies to law enforcement. "Maybe I want the life I didn't choose," she notes.

Scully also learns in this episode that her former lover is sick and dying, and eventually comes to suggest an alternative approach to his treatment, the very kind of non-Western approach that many fans of the series had trouble believing the Roman Catholic, analytical Scully would take. Yet this episode represents Scully's moment of clarity, much as "Closure" represents Mulder's. She realizes, in some sense that fundamentalism is not what you believe but how you believe. And in this regard, Scully has been a fundamentalist, closing off avenues of thinking that might be worthwhile. Because of the strange synchronicities or meaningful coincidences she recognizes in this episode—a form of "mindfulness"—Scully opens herself up to a new way of being.

What is the harm of being "open" to an idea if it causes no harm to entertain it? That is the notion Scully reckons with here, and so "All Things" feels very much like a goodbye to being closed down for the character. The overall arc of the series supports this interpretation. In Season Eight, with Mulder gone, Scully must step into his shoes and be open to the beliefs that Mulder would have explored. "All Things" seems to be the precipitating event for that change, for that willingness to change her nature, essentially, as a fundamentalist. Uniquely, "All Things" suggests a turning point for Scully. As she opens up to new ideas, her relationship with Mulder also seems to change, moving toward physical affection, and perhaps even sexual intimacy.

"Improbable." Written and directed by Chris Carter. Airdate: April 14, 2002.

As creator of *The X-Files,* Chris Carter has frequently been asked about his religious beliefs. His answer, at least for a long time, was that he would like to believe in God and that he is, temperamentally, inclined toward faith. In more recent years, post-*The X-Files,* Carter has answered that he has grown closer to a belief paradigm in his personal life and that *The X-Files* in a sense, is a series about the search for God. "The truth is out there" means, then, that God is out there.

One of the most inspiring and underrated episodes of *The X-Files,* and a true masterpiece in terms of Carter's worldview, is the final season entry, "Improbable." In this episode, Agent Monica Reyes utilizes the principles of numerology to solve a baffling series of seemingly unconnected homicides. She is helped in her unusual efforts, often unknowingly, by a stranger played by Burt Reynolds, a stranger who is actually . . . God himself.

Carter has sometimes likened this God figure to the House in a gambling casino, but a benevolent one. This God knows how all the games are going to turn out, but he nonetheless wants humanity to succeed. There is choice, according to God, and the secret to life for mankind is to "choose better." The opening credits of "Improbable" reinforce the notion of a benevolent God figure by replacing the familiar series phrase "The truth is out there" with "Dio ti ama," which is Italian for "God loves you."

Though today considered pseudoscience (and even an aspect of the paranormal) by many, the theory that underlines "Improbable," numerology, was once considered a valid aspect of mathematics and practiced by such figures as Pythagoras and St. Augustine. Basically, it is the belief in a meaningful relationship between numbers and the world, or personal events. Numbers represent a universal language, and the key to decoding life is *pattern recognition,* noting and marking which numbers play an important role in your life. Pattern recognition, ironically, might be another name for counting cards, hence Carter's comparison to a casino, but also a corollary for what behavior profilers do every day vis-à-vis law enforcement. They recognize patterns and attempt to extrapolate the logical outcome of those patterns, thus catching their quarry.

In "Improbable," Carter features several scenes with an FBI higher-up named Fordyce (John Kapelos). His name is, literally, "for dice," which suggests something crucial about his character and perspective. Reyes notes in the episode that God does not play dice with the universe, and yet Fordyce is unwilling to see God's pattern in numbers. His approach instead is "for dice," for random connections sussed out not via numerology but in the rote repetition of a bland, generic profile stating that the killer is a white male of a certain age who has family-of-origin issues.

If Burt Reynolds is God in the episode, there is an argument to made, via staging and lighting, that Fordyce is actually the Devil because he continues to deny God's patterns as a means of understanding the world. He continues to argue for a world in which everything is a roll of the dice, but man has no role in what numbers come up.

Numerologically speaking, Chris Carter shares values (a birth-date on the 13th) with artists including Daphne Du Maurier and Alfred Hitchcock, and "Improbable" feels like a work of art that either talent could have devised as it concerns the debate about fate vs. free will, and in often suspenseful terms. In the episode's opening sequence, God explains that man is not a victim of fate, represented by the cards or numbers, because he "can think." Furthermore, man has the capacity to "make them [the cards] work for him" if he plays his "hand" right. What Carter proposes, then, is a world in which man can decipher the plan and use it to his advantage.

Furthermore, Carter suggests that deciphering the plan is a possibility through his visual framing in the episode. He groups items (like scalpels or dominoes) in patterns to suggest that clues are visible right under our noses, if only we can detect them. His staging suggests that there is a plan for life that can be seen and understood if one is open to them. If one is not open, well, you "can't show" people "what they can't see," to quote the episode.

"Improbable" is particularly intriguing in terms of Scully and her development. She begins the episode with a typically closed-off or analytical stance, reporting to Monica that she doesn't believe the universe can be simplified to one equation, or a numerological philosophy. Monica counters that in her work, Scully is faced with codes and numbers all the time. This is abundantly true, vis-à-vis atomic numbers or the Periodic Table of Elements. Through the course of the investigation, Scully opens her mind to her experience and begins to connect the dots (or the numbers).

Then, in the episode's coda, she asks Reyes about her own "number," the number that categorizes her. She is told that she is a "9" (nine), and that this number is one of completion, of having completed a long journey and attained wisdom. This revelation is important for two reasons. The first is that this observation is abundantly true of Scully. She has moved from being a skeptic to a pragmatist ("All Things") and has opened herself up to branches of belief that would have once been anathema to her. By becoming Mulder, essentially, in his absence, Scully has tempered herself, but also grown into a more open and warm person in general. She no longer dismisses ideas out of hand, or if she does, she is open to reconsideration.

Secondly, the number nine is important vis-à-vis *The X-Files.* The journey to completion is represented by the number nine indeed—meaning nine seasons—and "Improbable" comes at the end of that long sequence, with Scully having attained a kind of wisdom and knowledge about her life that was not available for her to "see" in Season One, or even as late as Season Five.

"Improbable" is a rich episode of *The X-Files* not only in terms of its visualizations of a world with underlying order, but in terms of its soundtrack. The episode is girded with joyous musical compositions, and we learn that God himself is a collector of (digital) music. This hobby ties into his love of numbers and his love of games, as mathematics could be described as the very basis of sound and therefore the basis of music. Time, rhythm, and meter—the language of music—in a sense, is also, at some level, a mathematical equation.

20

How We Live Now

Americana and *The X-Files*

To a great degree, all art reflects life in the culture in which it arose. This seems especially true of *The X-Files*, however, which across nine seasons offers several coded, subtextual critiques of American culture in the 1990s.

And what did the culture look like in the 1990s? For one thing, America turned inward to a large degree, and with the absence of a Cold War enemy and rival superpower, began focusing on minutiae. Technology was partly to blame for this. The age give rise to the twenty-four-hour news cycle on cable television stations including Fox, MSNBC, and CNN, and the beast simply had to be fed. New stories had to be found, whether they were newsworthy or not, and many times the focus became not on solving America's problems but simply gazing at the successes and failures of celebrities. For lack of a better word, this might be termed the tabloid-culture-ization of America.

The trend toward the personal and intimate and occasionally shameful went as high as the office of the President of the United States. At one point during an MTV interview in 1992, Bill Clinton answered a viewer question about what kind of underwear he preferred to wear, boxers or briefs, and his willingness, nay eagerness, to answer felt a like a sea change in terms of what was newsworthy. The rest of the decade followed suit with the O. J. murder trial, the Amy Fisher shooting, the JonBenet Ramsey murder case, the Menendez Brothers trial, ice-skating thug Tonya Harding, and penis-severing scorned housewife Lorena Bobbitt.

Indeed, *The X-Files* era was the span in which newspaper tabloids seemed to migrate to the TV format, and we had programming such as *Inside Edition, A Current Affair, Extra, 48 Hours, 20/20, Dateline,* and even *Rescue: 911*. Further down the ladder of quality, this was also the era of *The Jerry Springer Show*—which was actually featured on an *X-Files* episode—*Geraldo, The Jenny Jones Show, Sally Jesse Raphael, Donohue,* and *The Ricki Lake Show*. Scholar Nigel Hamilton reported that such programming proliferated across America and that "such vaudeville-style, scurrilous entertainment, pivoting on human weaknesses and peccadilloes, had always characterized the popular press and for centuries had been disdainfully ignored by the literate middle and upper classes. That distinction . . . was now past its sell-by date."

The X-Files noted and catalogued all the changes in American culture of the time. Chris Carter's "The Post-Modern Prometheus" studied the country's obsession with fame, tabloid journalism, and talk show confessions, among other subjects. "Arcadia" saw Mulder and Scully go undercover as preppy, affluent newlyweds in an exclusive gated community where standards of beautiful were rigorously enforced . . . by a trash monster. And the seventh-season installment "Chimera" took dead aim at the Martha Stewart approach to middle-class life. Here, in the era of real estate as investment, one's house and garden were a sign of something deeper, too; an outward symbol of inner self-worth. And again, the dark underside of this suburbia were feelings of low self-worth, manifested as a monster.

Uniquely, what *The X-Files* episodes about Americana often found was similar, in a sense, to what Mulder and Scully detected in Washington D.C.: a startling gap between the enunciation of high ideals and values, and the reality, or underneath, of sinister forces working against the country and its people.

"Our Town." Written by Frank Spotnitz. Directed by Rob Bowman. Airdate: May 12, 1995.

Over the decades, eighty-seven people have disappeared in or around the town of Dudley, Arkansas, and "foxfire" and "witches peg" have been blamed for them. Mulder and Scully investigate Dudley after a health inspector, George Kearns (John MacLaren), mysteriously vanishes . . . just before he was about to publish a damning report of a Chaco Chicken processing plant in the town.

Mulder soon theorizes that the good people of Dudley are feeding not just on chicken but on unwelcome outsiders as well, as part of some cannibalistic ritual designed to prolong life. Scully's investigation supports this point of view, since she has found that Kearns, as well as several other townspeople, was suffering from a prion disease. The only conclusion possible is that they ate Kearns . . . and developed the sickness.

As the facts of this bizarre case become evident, Mulder learns the Chaco Chicken secret, and Scully is nearly served up at a town barbecue in the forest.

The X-Files is one of the most potent horror programs in television history because it often deals at point-blank range with the underneath "sausage-making" of our industrial, technological, late-twentieth-century culture. "The Host" spawned an uncomfortable awareness of what happens when you flush the toilet. Where does the waste go? What happens to it? How is it treated?

How is it disposed? And finally, what would happen if that process—which is invisible to most of us on a daily basis—fails?

The second-season entry "Our Town," by Frank Spotnitz, follows up on this trenchant notion of the "sausage making" of a technological society by looking closely—perhaps too closely for some—at industrial-scale food production. Much of the episode takes place at a chicken processing plant in Dudley, Arkansas, and reveals the not necessarily pleasant details of what ingredients go into chicken feed.

And that's only part of a dazzling tale that also involves cannibalism and a degenerative prion disease called Creutzfeldt-Jakob (CJD). Indeed, "Our Town" is another *X-Files* classic that effortlessly hits every note it strives for. It concerns a real-life horror (CJD), boasts a provocative commentary about "the way we live now," and even offers a heaping of irony in the form of its wholesome-sounding title.

"Our Town" takes its title from Thornton Wilder's 1938 three-act play *Our Town*, which concerned everyday American life in a typical New Hampshire town. The play, which is famous for featuring a narrator who breaks the "fourth wall," is a meditation on appreciating life as we live it. Frank Spotnitz's "Our Town" is a witty inversion of the play's artistic purpose. In this story, the people of Dudley aren't focused on living life in the moment, appreciating each instant as it comes, but rather prolonging their life as long as possible. The "Our Town" title is also ironic or funny because the "good people" of Dudley are all cannibals, ones who will turn on each other and eat each other when the going gets rough.

There are two ways to interpret this. Either the title "Our Town" is ironic, meaning look how different Dudley is from Wilder's Grover Corners. Or it is caustic, meaning that in 1990s America, all towns have become like Dudley, with dark secrets, strange rites, cover-ups, and corruption. Given the overall approach of *The X-Files*, which in some sense is a town-by-town exploration of such things in America (witness "Die Hand die Verletzt"), I suspect the latter approach is more applicable.

I've admired Frank Spotnitz's contributions to *The X-Files* and *Millennium*, and much like Chris Carter's or Rod Serling's writing, there is always some sense of didacticism or morality at play. Here, Spotnitz makes the lead cannibal, Chaco (John Milford), a throwback to gentler days. He consistently warns that "once we start turning on ourselves, we're no better than the animals." This plea is ignored by the locals but actually comes true before episode's end. A main villain falls down in the field when Mulder arrives to save Scully, and opens fire. This town leader is stepped on and trampled by the townsfolk, his own people, as they run away scared. Spotnitz's moral, about turning on your friends, is a good one, and it applies even to cannibals.

But the thing that really intrigues about "Our Town" is this peek behind the curtain of technology; this look at the understructure supporting our vast, industrial civilization. Many scenes are set here in that understructure, and they find it . . . shaky. The episode shows audiences chicken feed that consists of ground-up chicken bones and eventually sick human flesh. And then it reveals river runoff from the plant that is scarlet red from all the blood of the chickens. The idea, well transmitted, is of a vast, inhuman, and *inhumane* industrial process that doesn't observe rules of safety and hygiene. Although the episode is about chicken, it's the sausage making of the culture that this episode actually concerns. We are forced to ask questions about how food arrives at our table and what, if anything, in that long process from farm to dinner plate could corrupt the nature of what we eat. This isn't comfortable stuff, but *The X-Files* goes there to that "sausage-making" idea again and again to reveal the dark underside of twentieth-century life in America. Here are threats we don't see; threats we ignore or deny at our own peril.

"Sanguinarium." Written by Valerie and Vivian Mayhew. Directed by Kim Manners. Airdate: November 10, 1996.

A plastic surgeon for the wealthy, Dr. Jack Franklin (Richard Beymer), claims he was demonically possessed when he murdered a patient in the operating theater. Scully and Mulder investigate the doctor and his clinic, and Mulder reluctantly concludes that witchcraft is somehow involved in this and other recent deaths.

When a kindly nurse, Rebecca Waite (O-Lan Jones)—the primary suspect in the case—dies violently via occult means, Mulder and Scully realize they need to rethink their assumptions about her. They know she was a witch, but was she actually protecting patients, not attempting to harm them?

The ultraviolent "Sanguinarium" concerns nothing less than the things we as a society collectively worship. And importantly, it also revolves around *how* we choose to worship those values or virtues. One shadowy character in the episode, in the spirit of the ethnic grandmother seen in "The Calusari," uses the powers of the so-called occult to protect people from danger. Meanwhile, another far more malevolent character worships youth and beauty, and commits murder to be certain that his visage will remain beautiful and youthful for eternity. This character commits his atrocities in a contemporary American temple to man's worship of youth: a plastic surgery center in a modern metropolitan hospital. That plastic surgery center, we are told, accounts for 50 percent of the hospital's profits.

Meanwhile, Mulder and Scully, the archetypal investigators, must determine which character is a danger to society and which virtue (religious belief or narcissism) poses a greater risk to the community at large. This task is made infinitely more complicated by 1990s racial/sex/class politics. To wit: one character is ethnic, female, and a nurse. The other character is a white male, and an accomplished surgeon functioning in a high-powered corporate setting. Guess where suspicion falls first?

An extraordinarily clever and even caustic tale, "Sanguinarium" also has the distinction of being perhaps the goriest episode ever, even more so than "Home." Here the series returns to its "sausage-making" approach of excavating unpleasant facets of our modern technological society and reveals the disgusting nitty-gritty behind cosmetic surgery procedures. In short order, one character is impaled with a vacuum-like device and has his body fat as well as his bloody innards sucked out. Another character, looking to get some injections to firm up her facial features, sees her skin (and nose) melted away by huge doses of a corrosive chemical. Yet another patient gets a laser beam seared through his face. Then the witch —with magic working against her—coughs up a mouthful of bloody needles.

Finally, in the episode's climactic moment, the "evil" narcissist cuts away his old, unattractive face with a scalpel and reveals a new, youthful one beneath. He throws off his old face like a mask, and it's a gruesome sight indeed.

But leaving aside the gore for a moment, first and foremost, "Sanguinarium" concerns the pursuit of beauty at all costs. When even modern medicine can't get that job done, it's time to call on a higher (or lower) power: *blood sacrifice.* All the murders in the episode occur so that one man, a cosmetic surgeon, can continue to appear young beyond his natural years. And why does he place so high a value on youth and good looks? Well, young, attractive people get better jobs, make more money, and succeed more easily in our culture, don't they? Once made young, this doctor certainly finds a good job quickly enough, as we see in "Sanguinarium's" coda.

Intriguingly, this episode also features several moments in which Mulder, contending with the same brand of vanity that infects the episode's antagonist, gazes at his own reflection in the mirror and mentally tweaks his appearance. *Does he need a nose job?* By allowing our hero, the likable Mulder, to fall prey to such vanity, an important point is broached. We all want to be young and beautiful for as long as possible. Not one of us is immune to this desire.

But what happens when that narcissism is so powerful that it overwhelms reason or the very laws of nature itself? This was an idea roiling in the 1990s pop culture at the time of "Sanguinarium," and it also played an important role in John Carpenter's *Escape from L.A.* (1996). There Bruce Campbell portrayed a sadistic Beverly Hills plastic surgeon, one bent on recreating the city's denizens to his twisted liking. The culture was starting to recognize, in other words, that the quest for youth and beauty could go too far, and that when mishandled or overapplied, plastic surgery is actually . . . creepy as hell.

But this episode of *The X-Files* impresses to the degree it does in part because it suggests that beauty is in the eye of the culture, not the beholder (not unlike "Humbug," perhaps). The nurse who protects the patients on the cosmetic ward is a witch, and witches are stereotypically considered ugly by our culture. Mulder spots a broom on Waite's front porch when attempting to enter her house and jokingly calls it "probable cause." The nurse represents a nonmajority religion or belief system and is thus easily dismissed. Importantly, the nurse here is named Rebecca Waite after a woman who was executed at the Salem witch trials, also, presumably, unjustly. What this character represents is the idea that in our culture, we jump to the conclusion that people who are different from us have some ugly secret or are dangerous.

Meanwhile, the rich white surgeon, the one who admits to drug addiction and lives in a million-dollar house, never comes up as a suspect until the end of the episode. Dr. Franklin is actually the one committing the murders and the one who gets away. His "ugliness" hides in plain sight, however, and so we don't see it. In other words, it is not the derided outsider who poses a threat to our society, but rather the invisible but powerful insider. All of this material is handled well, and "Sanguinarium" evokes nervous laughter and groans of disgust as well with its intense gore. But even the gore seems to serve its purpose. If you want to make a (beautiful) omelet, you have to crack a few eggs, right?

"Arcadia." Written by Daniel Arkin. Directed by Michael Watkins. Airdate: March 5, 1999.

While undercover on a case, Scully and Mulder pose as a newlywed couple, Rob and Laura Petrie, to gain access to the Falls at Arcadia, a restrictive planned community in California. There residents who have disobeyed the rigid community covenants, contracts, and restrictions (CC&Rs) have a bad habit of disappearing without a trace

As Mulder and Scully soon learn, the Falls is policed by a strange and draconian sentry, a Tibetan "thought" creature bought to life from homeowner president Gogolok's (Peter White) mind. The creature is composed of mud and other detritus of modern life, because the planned community is erected over an old landfill.

When Mulder determinedly flaunts the community's rules and digs up his front yard for a "reflecting pool," the creature reappears, with the misbehaving agent as his latest target. . . .

Admirably, *The X-Files* showcases a willingness—even eagerness at times—to offer full-throated critiques of the culture from which the series arose. Case in point is "Arcadia," an episode in which Scully and Mulder encounter the monstrous terrors of . . . an upscale planned community in California. In that community—the Falls at Arcadia—the agents run smack up against forced conformity, public shaming, intolerance, and the kind of despotism or tyranny usually reserved for fictional third-world countries in *Mission Impossible* episodes of the 1970s. Yet, importantly, this view of life inside a planned community in "Arcadia" never seems over-the-top or unrealistic in the slightest. Indeed, if you've been a homeowner in such a community for any length of time, you'll probably recognize many key aspects of the narrative. The episode is caustic, absolutely, but appropriately caustic.

"Arcadia" concerns a monster that enforces the rules of the planned community in question, but the episode works brilliantly on two separate and distinct humorous fronts outside the horror veneer. On the first front, we get the critique of modern life in affluent America, where we willingly trade our freedom to live in a neighborhood alongside the "right" people. On the second front, we see Mulder and Scully go undercover behind the very institution of marriage, and the episode by Daniel Arkin is just as sharp and wicked about its observations of that institution.

"Arcadia" is also the rightful heir to the famous *Twilight Zone* episode "The Monsters Are Due on Maple Street." That segment of the classic Rod Serling anthology diagrammed how easily fear could take hold of suburbia and transform neighbors and friends into monsters, into a mob. Made thirty-something years later, "Arcadia" picks up that conceit and reveals how some modern neighborhoods are constructed not upon friendship or fellowship but much darker human instincts: on the need of some affluent families to be viewed as the "best" or as "exclusive," and on the need of the wealthy to control their peers, and determine for the community some bogus set of standards. Yet that image of being good or beautiful is a superficial one, as "Arcadia" cannily suggests. It's a charade, or even a delusion. The people at Arcadia are mostly monstrous individuals, not paragons of beauty and virtue. This idea is reflected in the landscape of the real estate development. Beautiful homes are literally built on garbage.

"Arcadia" also does a terrific job of mocking the ubiquitous "keeping up with the Joneses" syndrome by extending it to bizarre and extreme lengths. That idea takes powerful voice here in the form of neighbors that think they can be the best of the best *only* by informing on those who live around them. If they inform on their neighbors about every infraction—if they have Gogolok's ear—they will become the princes and princesses of Arcadia. What their informing really represents, however, is murder. Those who are known to have disobeyed a rule, or even suffer a broken bulb on a street lamp, are murdered by the dark sentry.

So, would you kill your neighbor to get his or her seat on the home-owner's committee? A more pertinent question perhaps is this one: Is it worth it to live in the "right" neighborhood with the "right" people, even if you have no freedom to express your individuality, even if your very life is in danger? The satire comes to the forefront in this episode right from the title "Arcadia." In Ancient Greece, Arcadia was a place renowned for a simple, pastoral innocence and its highly contented individuals. And "The Falls in Arcadia" in no way fits that definition. This Arcadia is about corruption and surfaces, about the avaricious and social climbers. Of course, the irony in all this is that to be a homeowner in such places you must also willingly pay dues to the very organization that is hassling you to live in a certain way. So you pay for the privilege—in places like The Falls—to be bullied and to conform to some outside, arbitrary aesthetic of beauty.

This episode of *The X-Files* absolutely nails this very un-American aspect of American life. "Arcadia" captures the idea that your home isn't really your castle and that your personal freedom is applicable only so far as the CC&Rs are concerned. Who knew that picking a certain piece of real estate would mean abdicating so much liberty?

"Arcadia" is widely loved by *X-Files* fans not for the really sharp commentary on planned communities, but for the scenes of Scully and Mulder playing house together. These scenes are indeed delightful, and quite funny. Mulder and Scully may be kindred spirits in that they are both smart, but in terms of living together, they are absolute opposites. Mulder is a slob drinking orange juice out of a carton and leaving the toilet seat up. And Scully gives a (randy) Mulder the surprise of his life by emerging from the bathroom for the night wearing bright green lotion over her skin. Yikes! There's the romance of marriage in a nutshell, "Arcadia" seems to suggest. The image of a perfect married life,—of "Rob and Laura Petrie" (from *The Dick Van Dyke Show*)—is just that, an image. It is a façade every bit as much as the Falls at Arcadia is a façade, a "beautiful" community that is actually built on garbage. I've been happily married for nearly twenty years at this point, and I don't view this episode as a critique of marriage so much as it is a critique of the way marriage is presented in our popular culture, or at least the way it was presented for decades. People just don't live perfect lives in perfect homes, and everything isn't beautiful and perfect all the time. Life gets in and makes a mess. *The X-Files* is able to humorously express that idea here. It goes a step further, critiquing Martha Stewart's America in a Season Seven entry, "Chimera." The difference between these episodes is that "Arcadia" makes the case largely through comedy, whereas "Chimera" is more straightforward.

"Chimera." Written by David Amann. Directed by Cliff Bole. Airdate: April 2, 2000.

David Amann's "Chimera" is another social critique of contemporary American society, especially American society in the age of happy homemaker and guardian of standards of beauty: Martha Stewart. The episode is set in a wealthy suburb of Vermont called Bethany, where another happy homemaker, Martha Crittenden (Ashley Edner)—known to her neighbors and friends as "Queen Martha"—goes missing and is presumed dead. In this case, Martha is clearly named after the other Martha (Stewart), and the episode reports that Crittenden's home was featured in a magazine pictorial. On the surface, she lived a perfect existence, surrounded by perfect people and perfect things.

But as in "Arcadia," secrets lurk beneath the happy, affluent world of Bethany. Martha was unhappy in her marriage and secretly carrying on an affair. And another woman, Ellen (Michelle Joyner)—the wife of the town sheriff (John Mese)—also learns that her marriage is a sham. Her husband also had an affair with Martha.

Accordingly, when Ellen gazes at herself in the mirror, she sees only ugliness. She sees herself as a hideous crone who can't compete in a world of physical perfection, a world represented by Martha Crittenden and by extension, Martha Stewart. Instead, Ellen feels in control only when doing housework, only when cleaning. Attention to making her world appear physically perfect provides Ellen, in her words, the "illusion" that she is in control of her life and those around her.

The supernatural touch underlining "Chimera" is that Ellen has actually created an ugly alter ego for herself so as to right the wrongs among the affluent of Bethany. She has done so through her obsession with the mirror, a form of narcissism. Both she and her husband see the monster at different points, noting that its "reflection" was visible. The monster, in this case, might be a reflection of their jealousy, but also about the need to keep up with the Joneses, and the pressure of living a perfect, beautiful life.

Mulder later describes mirrors as "doorways" to the spirit world, a portal in which one can summon denizens from other planes. But in fact, what he is describing here is Ellen's self-loathing made manifest, another *X-Files* "monster from the id." Mulder tells Ellen that she possesses a "whole other side" that she is "afraid to face," and the episode tags her condition in psychological terms, as a dissociative disorder, or a split personality. In other words, Ellen is a reboot of that old, famous monster representing human duality: Dr. Jekyll and Mr. Hyde.

Mulder's investigation in "Chimera" is determinedly contrasted with Scully's own investigation elsewhere. She is trapped in a stakeout in a

Washington, D.C., motel, watching misery and avarice unfold in the skid-row-like street life before her. The point, of course, is that underneath the two worlds are the same, or joined, riddled with human imperfection. It's just that Bethany, Vermont, puts a veneer of acceptability on the dysfunction and cloaks it more successfully. In both cases, the resolution of the case involves detecting the truth beneath the surface. On skid row, Scully learns that the person she has been observing is not a killer of prostitutes, but a man disguised as a prostitute trying (in the name of the Lord) to get the hookers off the street. And Mulder learns that Ellen is not the milquetoast, placid, happy homemaker and paragon of 1950s domestic bliss that she claims to be, but rather a schizoid murderer.

"Chimera's" critique of suburbia goes even further. At one point, Mulder is treated to a home-cooked meal, and Ellen irons his shirt and otherwise dotes on him. She warns him at one point not to miss out on "home and family." She tells him it can be a "refuge" for him. The moments in which Mulder is spoiled by the efforts of a traditional housewife are crosscut to comedic effect with Scully's suffering on skid row, spending time in a motel without, even, heat.

In other words, Mulder enjoys the lap of luxury and female servitude, while a more modern, second-wave feminist character, Scully, suffers for her job, alone and without even the basic amenities. But the episode turns this joke around. Under the *Leave It to Beaver* surface of Ellen's life is a deep-seated insecurity, and a lack of belief in one's self. Those qualities could never be ascribed to Scully. Mulder is much better off with a partner who challenges him, physically and on an intellectual and professional level, than with a woman who merely dotes on and serves him. For him, life isn't about finding a "refuge," but facing "the darkness" (per "I want to believe") with someone resourceful and honest at his side.

"Sunshine Days." Written and directed by Vince Gilligan. Airdate: May 12, 2002.

In this episode, Agents Doggett, Reyes, and Scully encounter an individual, Oliver Martin, who has reshaped his house via the power of his mind. He has transformed it not into some huge mansion, importantly, but into an exact duplicate of the house seen in the 1970s sitcom *The Brady Bunch* (1969–1974). Oliver, actually Anthony Fogelman (Michael Emerson), leads a lonely life and is only at peace at his strange home, where he can also create the famous family members from the sitcom, Greg, Peter, Bobby, Marcia, Jan, Cindy, Carol, Mike, and their maid Alice. Agent Reyes realizes that his chosen name, Oliver, refers to Cousin Oliver, the "jinx" who moved in with the Brady family for one season and yet was never fully accepted by audiences. This is precisely how Anthony feels as well, not fully accepted.

As the agents investigate, they learn that Oliver/Anthony associates *The Brady Bunch* with the only time in his life that he had a father: an investigator into the paranormal, Dr. Reitz (John Aylward), who was curious about his telekinetic abilities. When Oliver's abilities declined, Reitz left without even a real goodbye, and now this former "Mozart of Psychokinesis" is a loner, and a possibly dangerous one at that.

Tracking the details of the case from "A to B to C," Doggett realizes that Oliver still needs that father in his life, and only by giving up his projections (of the Brady Bunch) will he be able to live a healthy life. It turns out, using his powers is actually killing him, causing "multi-system organ failure," so Reitz and Oliver must reconnect, or Oliver will die. . . .

In self-reflexive terms, "Sunshine Days" asks of *The Brady Bunch* (and presumably, one day, of *The X-Files*), "Why are people still watching a thirty-year-old TV show?" The answer in the case of *The Brady Bunch* is that the Bradys represent the "perfect family" and the "family everyone wish they had." It is an idealized vision of family from a simpler time that resonates in a world of dysfunction, divorce, and even domestic abuse. *The Brady Bunch* updates the 1950s perfect family (think: *Leave It to Beaver* or *Father Knows Best*) for the 1970s and makes it a point of comparison. Amusingly, a character ejected from the perfect Brady Bunch house in "Sunshine Days" is played by David Faustino, famous for playing the son, Bud Bundy, in the nonromanticized family sitcom *Married with Children* (1987–1997). His type of modern, cynical reality, then, is not welcome in a land of perfection, where everyone gets along and treats one another with respect.

Courageously—at least for a TV show—"Sunshine Days" suggests that the way to find happiness is to connect in the real world, not seek the false perfection of *The Brady Bunch, Eight Is Enough,* or *The Partridge Family.* Living in that "perfect" world is physically killing Oliver, and his body is "consuming itself" over the choice to dwell there. By reconnecting with his father figure, he promises to get well and leave such idealized images and hopes behind.

Accordingly, the episode features some clever visual imagery to suggest the sinister nature of the Brady Bunch trap. Early in the program, when the house is invaded, the interloper encounters the smallest Brady children, Bobby and Cindy, and they are positioned in such a way that they resemble the twin girl ghosts of *The Shining* (1980), a film explicitly about the horrors of family life. This imagery suggests that the "ghosts" of the Brady Bunch are in some way an insidious influence on reality, making all our family lives appear worse by comparison.

"Sunshine Days" ribs the notion that by watching a TV show regularly, we come to feel like "part of the (Brady) family." Doggett expresses chagrin that Scully and Reyes both seem so obsessed with an old TV show, and that there are dozens of fan pages on the Net devoted to the series and its beloved characters. This indeed seems like an in-joke about the devotion of *X-Files* fans. It is a universe that for many seems as significant as the "real one." Yet "Sunshine Days" also, nonsarcastically notes another phenomenon. Those inspired by a work of art go on to create art devoted to it, whether it is a web page, a perfect re-creation of a favorite location, or even (gasp!) a reference book about the series.

The premise of "Sunshine Days" sounds incredibly dodgy. FBI agents find a perfect replica of *The Brady Bunch* house created by a man whose life can't measure up to what he sees on TV. And yet, as always, the episode reflects the American experience, circa the turn of the century, and the effects of a mass entertainment on a generation. Ironically, *The X-Files* itself would be the last (along with *Seinfeld*) in a long line of *Brady Bunch*-type series, a common touchstone for the country before the balkanization of television occurred with pay-cable television and streaming options.

21

America: Open Your Eyes!

Serial Killers in *The X-Files*

The serial killer was the most popular bogeyman of the 1990s. The monster replaced the masked slashers of the 1980s horror film and also became popular on TV thanks to series such as *The X-Files* and *Millennium.*

A serial killer is defined as an individual who has murdered at least three people according to some internal psychological schedule. Serial killers are also considered extremely intelligent and often have a home history of instability. Serial killers were often abused as children, and many began their career in crime by harming small animals. Sometimes, the quality that separates the serial killer from ordinary people is the absence of empathy or conscience. Serial killers are predominantly young men and almost universally white. The most notorious real-life serial killer is Wisconsin's Ed Gein, who was captured in 1957 and whose exploits informed horror films such as Hitchcock's *Psycho* (1960) and Hooper's *The Texas Chainsaw Massacre* (1974). The late 1980s and early 1990s brought a new familiarity with the serial killer into the national dialogue. Ted Bundy, Aileen Wuornos, and Jeffrey Dahmer were among the individuals who made the nightly news for their criminal, brutal acts.

Although serial killers have indeed been depicted in many eras, the 1990s likely represents the golden age of serial killers in film. *Silence of the Lambs* (1991), *Copycat* (1995), *Se7en* (1995), *Kiss the Girls* (1997), *The Bone Collector* (1999), and *Resurrection* (1999) all highlighted the character. In these movies it's impossible to escape a disturbing thought: the monster is inside us. Or worse, the monster *is* us.

This is the paradigm that *The X-Files* utilized so successfully when grappling with serial killers. The terror and evil we find in life did not come from an outside force, like aliens or vampires, but instead from twisted, psychologically damaged members of our own race. Perhaps the scariest and most disturbing of all *X-Files* episodes is "Irresistible," which finds a death fetishist abducting Scully and preparing to do her grievous harm. Another story, "Grotesque," finds that looking into the face of human evil has a cost for the brave investigators who do so. Those who must see evil are, in some sense, influenced by it themselves.

In terms of *X-Files* history, the first three to four seasons explore serial killers more frequently than the later seasons do, in part because this human brand of evil was picked up as a central element of Carter's outstanding sister series, *Millennium.*

The most popular monster of the 1990s was the serial killer. And the most popular serial killer was Anthony Hopkins's Hannibal Lecter, from *The Silence of the Lambs.*

"Irresistible." Written by Chris Carter. Directed by David Nutter. Airdate: January 13, 1995.

In Minneapolis, a death fetishist named Donnie Pfaster (Nick Chinlund) is collecting the hair and fingernail clippings of female corpses, desecrating the bodies in the process. Mulder and Scully are brought in on the case by a local detective (Bruce Weitz), who suspects that UFOs are involved. Mulder quickly discounts that notion but warns that the killer could graduate to murder, a forecast that proves accurate.

A shaken, disturbed Scully—still vulnerable after recent events, including her abduction—develops a profile for their perpetrator but becomes part of the case when Donnie Pfaster kidnaps her and plans to make her his next victim. . . .

As a creative and intellectual series, *The X-Files* is a very Gothic enterprise. By and large, it concerns a voice of rationality and a voice of romance debating the inexplicable mysteries of nature and the supernatural itself. "Irresistible" takes a determined step away from that approach by featuring a tale entirely psychological in its grounding. The monster of "Irresistible" is not an imaginary being or a mutant but a twisted human being who "preys on the living to scavenge from the dead," Donnie Pfaster (Nick Chinlund). Yet, as the episode also reminds us through photographs (of Donnie as a child) and canny imagery suggesting the killer's sense of entrapment, Pfaster is merely a human being whose desires and needs have somehow, for some reason, grown perverse and dangerous. The question is raised: How could someone come out so *wrong?* So twisted? In this case, the truth isn't "out there," it's inside us; it's part of who we are.

In most installments, *The X-Files* ultimately reveals its monster fully, whether it be a Fluke Man, a circus freak, or some other creature, but "Irresistible" instead often frames Donnie in the shadows, so we can't quite make out who or what he really is. Sometimes, these shots of silhouettes are augmented with brief views of demons or devils, an indicator, perhaps that some men are monsters inside. This approach also suggests *Millennium,* a series where the protagonist, Frank Black, often sees men as monsters, creatures turned ugly by their dark drives and desires. It's not too big a jump, then, to view "Irresistible" as the sort of missing link between *The X-Files* and *Millennium,* the story that focuses not on the monster outside but the monster within.

Proving as timely and accurate as usual, "Irresistible" name-checks Jeffrey Dahmer, the serial killer in Ohio and Wisconsin who died in prison just weeks before the episode aired on network television. Donnie Pfaster is a character not unlike Dahmer, a man who can appear normal at a distance and to society at large while at close-up range he is a dangerous predator. Both Dahmer and Pfaster, for instance, desecrate the bodies of the dead and show no remorse for their crimes. And also like Dahmer, Pfaster seems to have come from a normal, middle-class American family.

There's a scene in "Irresistible" in which Scully looks at Pfaster and he seems to shape-shift before her eyes, becoming a series of men before reforming as himself. This visualization is not an indication of the supernatural as some have taken it for, but a subjective expression of Scully's fear, and one also reported in the Dahmer case. There, victims reported seeing Dahmer's features change before their very eyes, and the only way to account for that change is absolute, abject fear. The question raised by Dahmer and Pfaster is simply one of nature. How could nature go so wrong that it would create these "escalating fetishists" who commit crimes of almost unimaginable brutality?

What makes "Irresistible" so successful is the depiction of Donnie as a very sick person and one, ultimately, who can't overcome his bad hard-wiring. Donnie's desires and actions are wrong, antisocial and incredibly violent, yet he has no capacity to stop. He is "programmed" wrong, if you will. This idea is visualized throughout the episodes in compositions that identify his entrapment. Frequently, for instance, he is seen behind bars, an acknowledgment of both entrapment and his ultimate destination. There's also a shot of Donnie Pfaster with a prostitute in which his usable space in the frame is bracketed by her body and raised leg. He is essentially hemmed in, a victim of violent forces within that he can't control.

What exactly are those violent forces? From what do they stem? Why do they arise in some people but not others? "Irresistible" suggests that the answers to such questions are opaque, even unanswerable, also with its choice of compositions. Again and again, Donnie is depicted in dark silhouette or shadow, his features undetectable. Shots of this nature recur even after the audience and main characters have seen his visage already. But the idea underlying such compositions is that psychology can't explain the existence of "errors" like Donnie in the human race. There's some aspect of him that—even when he faces us—we can't see, make out, or understand.

Although Scully and Mulder are closely involved in the week's action, it doesn't seem like a slight to note that this episode belongs to Pfaster . . . and to Nick Chinlund. Chinlund is weird and creepy as the serial killer, but not in any kind of conventional way. He has a soft, raspy voice and moves his neck and head in a strange, birdlike fashion that suggests he is both human and not fully human. At times he seems almost gentle, and at other times he is ruthless and single-minded. His unsettling and nontraditional performance anchors the episode and makes Pfaster one of the series' great "monsters." The character would return in a seventh-season episode called "Orison," but he is most creepy on this encounter, in "Irresistible." There is a sickening, perfectly pitched scene here in which Pfaster begins digging through a bathroom garbage can for discarded fingernail clippings and hair. The scene feels incredibly perverse, and Donnie expresses greed, desire, and satisfaction when he finally extracts a clump of tangled hair from the receptacle.

In terms of the dramatis personae, "Irresistible" is Scully's episode. It moves in epistolary form, with Scully reporting her profile in voice-over and typing out reports on her computer. In terms of her character, the audience learns in this episode that Scully desires to be seen by Mulder as an equal and finds it upsetting (humiliating?) that he feels he needs to protect her. Secondly, of course, this is our first opportunity to see Scully back in action after the events of "Duane Barry"/"Ascension"/"One Breath." It's fair to say she undergoes something akin to PTSD here, but in the end she overcomes it and battles Pfaster to a standstill.

The coda of "Irresistible" is also just about perfect. As Scully makes her final case report on Pfaster, the episode cuts to those childhood pictures of him. His family looks perfectly normal. He is well dressed and well coiffed. But something inside him is wrong, even as a child, and the fact that it goes undetected is terrifying. How many other Donnie Pfasters are out there, victims of twisted desires beyond their control? *Millennium* delved full-steam ahead into questions of that nature, but "Irresistible" is a singularly disturbing episode of *The X-Files* because the monster of the week is located inside, not outside, humanity.

"Grotesque." Written by Howard Gordon. Directed by Kim Manners. Airdate: February 2, 1996.

This third-season entry sees Mulder and Scully interrogate a captured serial killer, John Mostow (Levani), at the secret request of Bill Patterson (Kurtwood Smith), a legendary behavioral profiler at Quantico. After doing so, they seek out a copycat or partner who is continuing to murder in the same fashion as Mostow. That descriptions means, specifically, facial mutilation. Mostow uses a safety knife to slice open the mouths of his victims and puncture their eyes. Even worse, some of the victims he buries inside clay and sculpts "gargoyle" suits around their corpses.

Mulder reports to Scully that he was once one of Patterson's students, but that Patterson disliked his unconventional approach to solving cases. Scully suspects it is exactly for that unconventional approach that Patterson has tagged Mulder on this case. In this instance, however, Mulder, "the fair-haired boy," pursues Patterson's technique. Patterson taught him that to understand the artist you must look at his art. Mulder thus becomes obsessed with Mostow's sketches and sculptures of gargoyles, so much so that he loses sleep and drifts away from Scully. Mostow believes that he has been possessed by evil and that a spirit, not he, is responsible for his crimes. "This thing is real. It exists," he declares.

Eventually, Scully and Mulder learn that Patterson is the copycat, that he has sunk "deeper and deeper" into the ugliness of his work, having spent three years attempting to understand and anticipate Mostow's strange brand of madness. To quote Nietzsche, he gazed too long into the abyss.

By *The X-Files'* standards, "Grotesque" is a rather humorless and grim episode. Much like *Manhunter* (1986) and forecasting the direction of *Millennium,* it reveals what happens to investigators who, day in and day out, confront the nature of evil. When you try to see the way the killer sees, your own sight is altered or even compromised. Mulder nearly repeats Patterson's mistake, and that's a road nobody wants him to take. One of the most terrifying and nihilistic series codas occurs in "Grotesque" as Patterson is left to rot in prison, totally mad, totally consumed by the evil he sought to stamp out of the world. And although the episode discusses gargoyle imagery and history at length, the brand of evil described in "Grotesque" is totally human in nature, again the purview of *Millennium* (at least throughout most of Season One). The episode grapples meaningfully with the idea that there is no monster in this world more fearsome than man and that those who seek to trap this monster (the serial killer) put much on the line, not the least of which is their peace of mind, their very sanity.

In this case, the episode's title informs audiences much about the story. Something grotesque might be said to be repulsive or a distortion of normal appearance. One could apply this adjective to Patterson, as his mind snaps and he becomes a distortion of the great man he once was. At the same time, the descriptor grotesque could be used in regard to Mostow's horrible art work. Grotesque is a style of art (including sculpture, importantly) in which nature and monsters are intertwined. Both Patterson and Mostow are masterpieces of the form, their natures perverted by monstrous urges and actions.

"Grotesque" earned an Emmy Award for outstanding cinematography, and with its impenetrable nighttimes and stone faces staring out in the dark, it's not difficult to see why. The episode moves *The X-Files* into darker, more shadowy terrain than is the norm, and there is the feeling here that light of any type, but particularly sunlight, would have shattered the atmosphere. Mulder travels inside his own heart of darkness in this episode, and at one point in the narrative, it appears he may be the second killer, following Mostow's pattern. Again, any significant light would have made this idea absolutely unbelievable. But the grim, unrelenting, visual darkness of the story creates an atmosphere of vivid, unalloyed terror. The sequence set in

Mostow's studio, in which a sleeping Mulder is touched by a gargoyle (or a serial killer), is pure nightmare fodder, and the moment represents one of the great visceral scares of the entire series.

"Unruhe." Written by Vince Gilligan. Directed by Rob Bowman. Airdate: October 27, 1996.

In Traverse City, Michigan, a young woman stops at a drugstore to get her passport photograph taken. She is abducted by a psychopath immediately afterwards, yet her photograph (taken before the kidnapping) oddly reveals her in mortal danger, surrounded by monstrous little demons and a tall, spectral, angel-like figure.

Mulder and Scully investigate the abduction and are shocked when the victim is returned alive but lobotomized. The abductor, a disturbed man named Gerald Schnauz (Pruitt Taylor Vance), strikes again, lobotomizing another woman he deems to be suffering strife.

Finally, Schnauz goes after Scully to free her from the restless "howlers" he imagines in her mind. . . .

There are some fates that are worse than death and, indeed, far more terrifying than death. Vince Gilligan's "Unruhe" is an incredibly unnerving episode of *The X-Files* because it acknowledges this fact and nearly subjects the brilliant Agent Dana Scully to just such a macabre fate. In this episode, Scully is captured once more, but this time by a troubled man who wishes not to end her life but to give her a "trans-orbital lobotomy" and thus render her ever-questioning mind . . . "peaceful."

Presumably she will live for many years after this lobotomy, but only in the manner that he, in his wisdom/madness, has ordained. In terms of metaphor and social critique, one can interpret "Unruhe"—meaning "unrest" or "strife"—in more than one way, but certainly in terms of various 1990s cultural frissons. In basic terms, this story concerns a man who believes he can become powerful by superimposing his own vision of women on others, including women themselves. He believes he knows, a priori, what is right for his female victims without getting to know them, without even asking their permission to operate on them. He engineers this change through a forced medical procedure.

Accordingly, "Unruhe" might be interpreted as anything from a meditation on sex roles in 1990s America to a commentary on abortion rights and a debate about who, ultimately has the right to control one's body. The episode's final statement is one that resonates in today's culture of "legitimate rape," "trans-vaginal probes," and other male-imposed controls over female reproduction.

But the kicker is the way that Scully turns the horror around on her captor. The "howlers," Scully establishes, are actually monsters who reside not in the women who make decisions about how they are entitled to live, but within the men like Schnauz who attempt to control those choices based on their own psychological problems.

"Unruhe" works precisely because Scully is such an intelligent, competent, independent person, one fully capable of choosing for herself how she should live. We have long understood that "smart is sexy," but *The X-Files* takes that paradigm to new heights in the persistent clever writing and in the knowing, thoughtful performances of both Duchovny and Anderson. Accordingly, Scully and Mulder transmit to audience members as real individuals to a large degree, individuals that we love, admire, and respect. This doesn't mean they are perfect, but it means that we are drawn to their imperfections as much as to their strengths.

In terms of Scully, we appreciate her intelligence, her manner of viewing the world logically, and the steadfast manner by which she contextualizes the strange events of the X-files investigations through a belief system of science and rationality.

In another way altogether, we love Scully's stubbornness and the exasperated way she sometimes reacts to Mulder's latest flight of fancy. These are the things that make Dana Scully an individual special to us, and special to herself. These qualities make her *who she is.* As we all are, she is a blend of personal strengths and weaknesses, and yet every quality in her gestalt is a critical piece of her personality. The aspect that remains so scary about "Unruhe" is that Scully meets up with a monster who wants to rob her of these qualities—all because he thinks he knows better who she *should* be and how she should act.

The monster in this episode desires one thing, to take away from Scully the right to choose to be who she wants to be. Remember, Gerald Schnauz doesn't want to kill her; he wants to destroy her identity, her individuality, and her intelligence, thereby rendering her a permanent "little girl" (like the sister he couldn't save).

As a lobotomized woman-child, after all, she will be completely under his control. She would never question him or act counter to his wishes. His evil is all about substituting his own authority over a woman's choice for her life. This is literally a fate worse than death, and to imagine Scully in this way—her ever-questioning, ever curious mind rendered forcibly quiescent—is nothing short of traumatic.

The implicit question in "Unruhe" is one of superimposing one person's rights over another's. Schnauz believes he detects "unrest" and "howlers" in Scully's unquiet brain, but what is his basis for judgment, other than his own madness? And why does he direct all of his attention only at women? Why are they the ones to be "modified" by his procedures? Are men immune from howlers?

Of course, the answers here involve Gerald's sister, who committed suicide and thus ruined Gerald's vision of his father. It wasn't his father who was in the wrong (presumably for abusing his daughter), but the daughter who was wrong for destroying the family. Unfortunately, in reality there are plenty of people who think precisely in this fashion. Women are the ones at fault when they are raped (they asked for it, or it wasn't legitimate rape . . .), and they are wrong again for not wanting to bear children of rape (because children originating from rape are a blessing by God!). Yet by and large such ideas originate from men who wish to superimpose their personal values upon others. The lobotomy in "Unruhe" is a similar tool, only blunter: a method of enforcing behavior on women that conforms to an outside/male standard, in this case, Gerald's.

Given what is at stake here—Scully's very identity—"Unruhe" is much more than a standard serial killer episode of *The X-Files.* The psychic photograph angle is a brilliant and visual way of externalizing Gerald's madness, of revealing how he egotistically views himself as a savior of women who require "help." And yet the images simultaneously reveal his utter, complete madness. He has created monsters to imperil these women so he can step in and save them. It's a crazy, vicious circle.

In the episode's climax, Scully confronts Gerald with his brand of madness and notes that if howlers exist, *they do so only in his mind.* He's responsible for them. Not her. Scully then defeats Gerald, showcasing again her individuality and resourcefulness, the very things he would take away from her without a second thought or a glance back.

"Paper Hearts." Written by Vince Gilligan. Directed by Rob Bowman. Airdate: December 15, 1996.

Mulder experiences a vivid dream in which a red laser light directs him to the corpse of a young girl. Unfortunately, reality bears out this disturbing vision. Mulder has discovered the fourteenth victim of a serial killer, John Lee Roche (Tom Noonan), that he jailed some years earlier.

Now, armed with a book of paper hearts cut from the blouses of each of Roche's young victims, Mulder attempts to locate the last two dead bodies, girls who have never even been identified by authorities.

A strange twist emerges in the case, however, when Roche informs Mulder that Samantha was actually one of his final victims. Mulder investigates and finds evidence supporting this shocking revelation, even as Scully warns him to tread lightly and that Roche is untrustworthy. . . .

"Paper Hearts," written by Vince Gilligan, is an almost textbook-perfect example of a narrative that tackles series history and continuity in a fresh and surprising way, recasting facts the audience *thinks* it knows in a totally new and believable light. The episode treads into the series' central mystery: the disappearance of Samantha Mulder, Fox's sister.

All along, via Mulder's own words (in the series pilot), as well as in flashback imagery (in episodes such as "Little Green Men"), the audience has been led to believe Samantha was abducted by aliens. This fourth-season episode, however, suggests a more diabolical, more "realistic" explanation for her disappearance, and one with frightening plausibility in terms of Mulder's psychology: she was the victim of a serial killer.

And because Mulder couldn't prevent Samantha from being taken away, right under his nose, he has constructed an elaborate mythology around the events of her disappearance. "I want to believe" is thus a mantra not only about believing in aliens but about Samantha, and Mulder's own actions in that situation. He *wants to believe* that his sister did not end up in a dark place, murdered by a fellow human being, but rather spirited away by supernatural creatures. That fate, at least, allows for the possibility that she lives.

"Paper Hearts" lingers in this uncertainty about Samantha's fate and operates by the premise that "a dream is an answer to a question" that the conscious mind hasn't yet learned to ask. In other words, Mulder's dream at the episode's start is the beginning of consciousness or of awareness about Samantha's real destiny. It's starting to break through the long-held, intricate denial represented by the abduction tale. Gilligan's stunning twist on *The X-Files'* central mystery renders the episode suspenseful and surprising drama and, in some way, even paves the way for the final revelation regarding Samantha's disposition in the seventh season.

"Paper Hearts" thrives as drama in part because Gilligan's story makes such a convincing case that "Mad Hatter" killer Roche is actually responsible for Samantha's disappearance. The plausibility of this explanation is heightened by the fact that Roche can point to physical evidence to support his claims, namely a vacuum cleaner he sold to Mulder's parents. Also, facts suggest Roche was near Martha's Vineyard, where the Mulders lived, during the time of Samantha's disappearance.

But more than any of that, the story "feels" true *emotionally* because of what we know of and understand about Mulder as a character. He has taken up a career in which he repeatedly hunts and apprehends predators like Roche, which might be described as a kind of psychic catharsis for or exorcism of his own (buried) culpability in failing to save Samantha from the "monster."

Because Mulder failed once, he has pursued a life that demands that he succeed, again and again undoing the first failure.

In *X-Files* episodes such as "Oubliette" and later, "Mind's Eye," we see how Mulder gravitates toward women who require his *saving*. He is trying to make up, clearly, for the one who got away. He seeks redemption. And yet this is not a conscious thing. His mind protects him from fully understanding his own actions with the carefully constructed mythology of alien abduction. But making "Paper Hearts" feel even more shocking—and true—is the feedback from Scully. When Mulder asks if she ever believed that Samantha was really abducted by aliens, her answer isn't exactly affirmative.

The episode both provides a psychologically convincing portrait of Mulder that rings true with his behavior we have seen in the series thus far, and then, for punctuation, allows the voice of rationality and reason, Scully, to remain ambivalent about Samantha's fate. Of course, it would be an act of supreme self-negation for *The X-Files*—a series about conspiracies and aliens—to undercut its bread and butter by having Roche's story in "Paper Hearts" proven true. But the episode never feels gimmicky because every aspect of Roche's tale feels terrifyingly plausible.

Additionally, Tom Noonan is a terrifying opponent for Mulder. He is a sinister, sick man, but Noonan doesn't play him as "Evil" with a capital "E." Instead, he is soft-spoken and seemingly rational at times, but all along actually playing the role of master manipulator. He is one of the creepiest predators, right up there with Pfaster or Incanto.

Finally, "Paper Hearts" is both impressive and distinctive visually in the way it depicts Mulder's dreams. The red laser light points out aspects of long-forgotten crime scenes in Mulder's mind, and though our unconscious mind is rarely so specific or clear, the idea works visually and in terms of character. First and foremost, Mulder is a profiler with a mind of clockwork precision. On a regular basis, he visualizes details to assemble a full picture of the cases he works on. In "Paper Hearts," we get a sense of that steel-trap mind and how it tirelessly—even at rest—pinpoints important clues that might otherwise be missed. The scary part, of course, is that the very mechanisms of Mulder's mind are subverted by a sinister invader here. The dream visions may seem so precise and accurate because they are being knowingly manipulated by a man, a killer, who doesn't care whom he hurts. That's the key to the serial killer personality: no empathy, only the pursuit of mad desire.

22

Lazarus Species

From the Dawn of Time

As early as preproduction of the episode "The Jersey Devil" in Season One, *The X-Files'* creator Chris Carter was reportedly reading the works of Pulitzer Prize-winning author E. O. Wilson. Today, some of Wilson's work can be found at a web page called *The Diversity of Life,* where he writes persuasively that man is now "accelerating" the sixth great extinction in Earth's long geological history. It is "reckless," Wilson observes "to suppose that bio-diversity can be diminished indefinitely without threatening humanity itself."

As other authors have noted, extinction is actually a "natural feature" of evolution—some species thrive while others falter—but today, we live in what is known as the Anthropocene Age, the Age of Man, and our actions are impacting and changing our environment in ways we cannot possibly predict. In using up Mother Earth's resources and despoiling natural environments, we could be losing forever undeveloped medicines and pharmaceuticals. By attempting to make our lives now more comfortable and accommodate our rapidly growing population, we could be curtailing our ability to thrive in the future.

Many stories in *The X-Files* concern themselves with strange threats from prehistory, ones that may have been selected for extinction but for some reason manage to survive. These stories exist, perhaps, because of Carter's fascination with the idea of man sowing the seeds of his own downfall and extinction.

After all, the Earth is over four-and-a-half billion years old, and the oldest human lived in Ethiopia some four million years ago. This means that the Earth existed long before man did. And because approximately 99 percent of all species that have ever lived on Earth have gone extinct (by failures to adapt), it is likely that Earth will exist long after man dies, too. Someone or something will take our place. Geologically speaking, we understand the pattern. It is romantic, even foolish, to suspect our destiny will somehow be different.

In Earth's history, there have been five great extinctions. The first such die-off happened 440 million years ago, when 85 percent of species, mostly sea-bound, were impacted. The next extinction occurred 375 million years ago, and again, severe environmental change caused sea life to die. Another mass extinction—the third —occurred 252 million years ago, and a whopping 97 percent of all species died out. Then, at the end of the Triassic Period, 201 million years ago, another extinction occurred, and the dinosaurs rose as a consequence Finally, 66 million years ago, at the end of the Cretaceous Period, the most well-known extinction occurred. The dinosaurs fell and mammals rose, an act that ultimately gave rise to mankind and the Anthropocene Age.

Many scientists agree that we are now in the incipient stages of the sixth extinction, one arising due to human interference with natural ecosystems and animal life. The seventh-season opener of *The X-Files* is actually called "The Sixth Extinction," a sign of Carter's interest in this subject and man's own role in what could be the species' destruction.

Other *X-Files* episodes, however, also focus on the Earth's geological history, and organisms from other times threatening mankind in the twentieth century. The idea is that had things been only slightly different, these species could have overwhelmed man at the top of the food chain and changed the shape of life's evolution on Earth. In other words, our life and death as a species is not in our hands, and it would take only one extinction-level event to reorder life here.

Episodes such as "Ice," "Darkness Falls," "Firewalker," "Agua Mala," and even "Vienen" posit relics from other geological ages or periods threatening outposts of man. Fortunately, in all cases, these specimens originate in a remote area such as the Arctic ("Ice"), a forest in the Pacific Northwest ("Darkness Falls"), the interior of a live volcano ("Firewalker), the bottom of the sea ("Agua Mala"), and at an oil rig drilling beneath the ocean's surface ("Vienen"), meaning that they fail to get a foothold on mainstream human civilization, thus giving Mulder and Scully the opportunity to prevent their development.

The Mytharc story also originates, after a fashion, with an organism from another era. The Well-Manicured Man reports to Mulder in *Fight the Future* that the black oil is actually the Earth's "original inhabitant," a kind of mobile virus that that can hop from body to body. This virus seeks, through the process of colonization, to retake the Earth, thus resetting the geological clock and ending the Anthropocene Age permanently. To put it another way, both monster-of-the-week stories and Mytharc Stories feature an element of the same theme: that life-forms from another, distant period in Earth's history could return to stake a claim on our planet.

The creepiest thing about this notion and story device is that it has a very real corollary in science. The existence of prehistoric or extinct animals today isn't just speculation. Species believed extinct but actually found alive today are called "Lazarus species," meaning that they have come back from the dead. Among such Lazarus species are the prehistoric Coelacanth, which was believed extinct, or the Lord Howe Island stick insect. The monsters and beasts of "Darkness Falls" or "Agua Mala" hardly look fantastic at all, given such real-life examples.

"Ice." Written by James Wong and Glen Morgan. Directed by David Nutter. Airdate: November 5, 1993.

In "Ice," Mulder and Scully join a team of scientists, including Dr. Hodge (Xander Berkeley), Dr. Da Silva (Felicity Huffman), and Dr. Murphy (Steve Hytner), to investigate the deaths of a government research team at a base in Alaska. The team had been digging deep down into an icy shelf believed to be a meteor impact. Without warning, the members of the expedition began murdering one another, reciting the mantra "we are not who we are."

After a helicopter pilot named Bear (Jeff Kober) flies the team to Alaska, Mulder and Scully discover that the previous team had found core samples containing strange alien worms frozen in the ice from 250,000 years earlier. At least some of these worms have thawed out and discovered that human beings make perfect hosts. While living on the excretions of the hypothalamus, these parasites cause extreme paranoia and aggressions in their prey. . . .

"Ice" is a Lazarus species story and a sterling tribute to one of the science fiction genre's greatest short stories: "Who Goes There?" (1938) by John W. Campbell. That story is set in Antarctica and involves a group of scientists who discover an alien ship and pilot that have been trapped in the ice for twenty million years. When thawed out, the extraterrestrial pilot is revealed as a homicidal shape-shifter, one who can "hide" in human and other biological forms. In the end, the alien invader is barely stopped (with just a half-hour to spare) before it can escape isolation and reach the rest of Earth's population.

"Who Goes There?" has been reimagined several times throughout film and television history. *The Thing from Another World* (1951), starring James Arness, was one such effort, though it eliminated the shape-shifting nature of the alien menace and replaced it with a plant, a kind of humanoid "carrot." John Carpenter's *The Thing* (1982) was a more faithful adaptation of the original story and perhaps the most well-known version today. It inspired the 2011 prequel. On television, *Doctor Who* (1963–1989) featured a 1976 serial called "The Seeds of Doom" that involved the discovery of an alien plant pod in the ice from 20,000 years prior. That seed was the heart of a planet-devouring vegetable monster called a "Krynoid." And on *Star Trek: Deep Space Nine* a race of shape-shifters called the Founders proved detectable—like the Thing—only by blood test in episodes such as the third-season finale, "The Adversary." The blood test was featured in the novella and proved the most popular and perhaps most effective sequence in the Carpenter film.

"Ice," written by James Wong and Glen Morgan and directed by David Nutter, is a variation on the Campbell theme but with some unique, even trademark *X-Files* twists. In fact, this episode might be Exhibit A in the thesis that the series repurposes commonly told tales in the genre and imbues them with new meaning and relevance for the 1990s. From Campbell's source material we see a similar location (an icebound installation), a similar threat (an alien), and even the presence of a dog as an infection vector. But "Ice," uniquely, develops in an original fashion because in *The Thing*, for example, there don't seem to be any close relationships on the line. Instead, the story has been interpreted frequently as a comment on man's alienation from his fellow man. Nobody trusted anybody in *The Thing* because nobody really liked or even knew anybody else. Hidden inside a man, the Thing was indistinguishable from man. *The X-Files* deliberately explodes that artistic conceit by landing two sets of dedicated partners or allies into the paranoia blender and then diagramming the way close relationships contend with the possibility of individual infection. The responses are either independence (Scully) or total abandonment of personal will in favor of the stronger personality's will (Da Silva).

In a way, *The X-Files* amplifies the horror of *The Thing*. It's one thing to face a shape-shifter in a battle to the death when there is no one you really care for to worry about on the battlefield. In "Ice," Mulder and Scully have one another to fight for and must face the very real possibility that one of them could die or be permanently infected.

An almost unbearably claustrophobic and tense hour, "Ice" is a deliberate nod to "Who Goes There?" and *The Thing*, but also a tale, ultimately, about territoriality. The climax reveals that two worms cannot exist in the same host or they will kill each other. Similarly, the episode-long tension between Mulder and Hodge—each looking to assert leadership—nearly imperils everyone. Both men believe they are "right" in their belief system and engage in a kind of paranoid pissing contest, trying to swing the allegiances of the other team members to their viewpoint. There's even an amusing scene here where the men must strip down to check each other for signs of parasitic infection. Mulder jokingly reminds everyone that they *are* in the Arctic, a not-so-subtle joke about penis size. But joke or no joke, the matter of who possesses the "biggest dick"—to state it ineloquently—is definitely a subtext in this episode. Once you make the connection, it's intriguing to see how the territoriality theme mirrors the infection theme. A terrified Bear asserts control of the situation early on, since he is the only person capable of flying the plane and stakes out a command position early. Simultaneously, he is the first infected by the alien organism.

After Bear dies, the battle of wills moves definitively to Hodge and Mulder. Soon, nobody is certain which of them, if either, is infected. In the end, we learn that neither man was infected, only that each was driven (by adrenaline? testosterone? ego? all three?) to attempt to take charge of the situation. Why were they so aggressive if neither was infected? What complicates this issue of territoriality, and what is explored rather fully in "Ice," is the notion of allies, friends, and subordinates.

Dr. Da Silva is Hodge's ally and subordinate, and Scully is Mulder's ally and equal. Neither woman is truly impartial. But Hodge bullies Da Silva to see things his way and is borderline abusive in his treatment of her; keeping her in line. Scully—recognizing the weight of evidence against Mulder at one point—backs Hodge over her partner. She never gives up on Mulder and finds way to protect him, but she is able to weigh the facts . . . and the facts seem to go against him. Unlike Da Silva, Scully is not cowed into making a decision by either Mulder or Hodge. Instead, she studies the available facts and makes a logical decision, to Mulder's dismay, since her choice doesn't favor him in the short term.

Given all this dramatic material, it's probably fair to state that what "Ice" truly involves is relationship dynamics in a difficult situation, where no clear chain of command can be respected. Going further, it involves the way that men behave in a crisis. Who do you choose to follow? Why does someone, like Mulder, choose to lead? The elegant quality of this thematic dynamic is, as noted above, that it mirrors so beautifully the nature of the aliens of the week. There can't be two big worms (another phallic symbol, by the way) vying for the same command, or else hostility, anger, and violence will result.

Location plays a crucial role in "Ice's" success, too. The episode feels like a pressure cooker because after the first act, it never leaves the claustrophobic outpost interiors. All versions of "Who Goes There?" are set in icy environments, and that facts sets up an imposing, endless sense of isolation. There is terror inside the various "Thing" outposts but outside, as well. The frozen environment will kill you too, just not as quickly as an alien invader. So a person can't just run outside and catch a bus to escape. The Artic or Antarctic installation in all these productions is thus a trap within a trap. Escape is simply not possible.

"Ice" is also a contrast or counterpoint to the hot, passionate, aggressive behavior we witness among the dramatis personae. It may be below zero outside the outpost, but inside it, temperatures and tempers continue to rise. In terms of *X-Files* series continuity, "Ice" raises the concept of Panspermia—life from elsewhere in the cosmos taking root here. That's a concept that would play a crucial role in the series' sixth season.

"Darkness Falls." Written by Chris Carter. Directed by Joe Napolitano. Airdate: April 15, 1994.

Mulder and Scully head to Olympic National Forest in the Pacific Northwest to investigate the disappearance of a team of loggers. Mulder suspects something out of the ordinary is responsible, but a forest ranger, Larry Moore (Jason Beghe), reports on the persistent conflict between a logging company and ecoterrorists known as "monkey-wrenchers." Upon arrival, Scully and Mulder find members of the logging team cocooned in large webs, their bodies drained entirely of fluids. The leader of the monkey-wrenchers, Doug Spinney (Titus Welliver), warns that the loggers, by illegally cutting down old-growth trees, have released an ancient variety of carnivorous wood mite.

These insects strike only by night and are fearful of light. But Mulder and Scully only have enough gasoline to run their cabin's power generator for a few more hours. If the lights go out, the murderous swarm will descend. . . .

In a segment similar in structure to "Ice," "Darkness Falls" finds Mulder and Scully in an isolated location (this time an impenetrable forest a full day's hike from civilization) battling a microscopic life-form from prehistory with the capacity to destroy mankind if it spreads to the world at large. The factor that meaningfully differentiates "Darkness Falls" from "Ice," however, is the episode's context or background. In "Ice," the FBI agents had to contend with an infectious parasite inside a remote Arctic base. Trust was hard to come by because nobody knew who was already infected by the tiny creatures. In other words, the alien life-form had changed the nature of man in some insidious fashion. In "Darkness Falls," by contrast, Mulder and Scully must deal with two factions already at "war," in Scully's explicit terminology, and thus unable to show trust, empathy, or even decency toward one another . . . and for entirely human reasons or ideology.

The forces in conflict are an avaricious logging company (acting illegally) and so-called ecoterrorists or radical environmentalists, who also behave in an illegal fashion. And indeed, the early 1990s saw a new public awareness of environmental issues roiling in the zeitgeist. Running unsuccessfully for reelection, President Bush had disparagingly termed vice-presidential candidate Al Gore "Ozone Man," thus implicitly raising the issue that environmental awareness and protection actually impeded economic growth. And since America was experiencing a recession, this debate about the environment was newly relevant. Accordingly, that is the very dynamic explored in "Darkness Falls," the battle between commerce and environmental stewardship.

Impressively, "Darkness Falls" treats both sides and their arguments even-handedly, in much the same fashion the series diagrams the two sides of the belief/skepticism debate or "lens" of perspective we see via Mulder and Scully. Importantly, both the company representatives and the radical environmentalists pay the price for their legal and moral trespasses, a fact that suggests a kind of "pox on both their houses" approach to the material. Any agenda—corporate or environmental—when taken to murderous extremes, is undesirable. Beyond the background debate about the environment and how best to care for it, "Darkness Falls" proves suspenseful as the prehistoric, photo-sensitive, luminescent bugs threaten to engulf a small cabin while the last bit of power inside dwindles irrevocably away.

Use of close-ups and insert shots go a long way toward escalating the tension and augmenting the feelings of isolation. Commendably, the episode doesn't present Mulder and Scully with a clean escape from this menace, either. They survive their "nice trip in the forest" (to quote Mulder) but only with hundreds of red bites all over their bodies, not to mention a stay in a government ICU.

"Darkness Falls" is very much a nature's revenge brand of horror story, merely updated for the 1990s. Here, mankind has trespassed too far (as happens again in another stand-out *X-Files* episode, "Detour") and disturbs the balance of nature in the process. Another admirable aspect of "Darkness Falls" is its basis in fact. The episode suggests that the 1980 eruption of Mount St. Helens disturbed or altered the life cycles of local wildlife. This is all good in theory, but mimicking the horror approach of *Jaws* (1975), and its famous story about the USS *Indianapolis* in shark-infested water, this episode delves into a true-life story that terrifies. Mulder and Spinney discuss a "brain sucking amoeba" in Washington's Silver Lake. That amoeba, *Naegleria fowleri*, enters the body through the human nose, tunnels through the skull, and then consumes brain tissue . . . until you die. And this monstrosity is not, alas, a work of fiction. In fact, this amoeba is responsible for a handful of deaths in America every year, in mostly the South and West regions of the country. The story of Silver Lake and *Naegleria fowleri*, however, lends credence and legitimacy to the material presented in "Darkness Falls." A story about carnivorous wood mites eating burly loggers might sound ridiculous at first blush, but then so do brain-eating amoebae, at least until you know the horrific details.

Intriguingly, "Darkness Falls" doesn't appear to position the bugs as malevolent entities. They aren't malicious or hostile, in a sense. The wood mites cocoon and eat human beings, draining their bodies of fluid, because to do so is part of their life cycle. Contrarily, it is the short-sighted humans in the episode who are ultimately responsible for all the deaths that occur. The logging company is the agent that brought the bugs out of their long hibernation, by illegally and wantonly cutting down old-growth trees. They have opened Pandora's box. And all because it is more convenient for the capitalists to move one big tree out of the woods than many small trees. Economic concerns, in this case, cause an environmental disaster. Similarly, the ecoterrorists threaten everyone's safety (and indeed, survival) by spiking roads and committing other acts of sabotage. There is much talk in the episode of "irony" and "shooting oneself in the foot." The latter is a notion that—through his own destructive behavior—man actually assures only his own extinction. Man proposes and God disposes. Once you get to that reckoning in "Darkness Falls"—of man engineering his own destruction—it isn't difficult to interpret the episode as a commentary on the environment and our stewardship of it. It won't be the environment that leads to our extinction but our own misuse or exploitation of the environment that causes it to turn against us.

"Darkness Falls" is a great horror episode of *The X-Files*, creating a strong atmosphere of terror and suspense. Director Joe Napolitano's camera circles, in extreme close-up, the cabin's power generator on at least two occasions. This device, this example of modern technology (and thus man's ingenuity), is the only firewall that stands between survival and death for Mulder, Scully, and the others. Similarly, the single lightbulb dangling from a ceiling string is prominent in several shots, flickering and winking out. In fact, the single most anxiety-provoking shot in the entire episode doesn't involve the bugs swarming and attacking their prey. Instead, it involves a panicked Scully—fearing the bugs are on her body—accidentally striking the swinging lightbulb. In that moment of hysteria, it looks like she will break the bulb and destroy her only chance of survival. The episode's focused direction establishes beautifully how this bulb is the only lifeline inside that cabin, and once it is gone, it's game over.

Also effective is the episode's final sequence, which finds the cabin's survivors racing down the mountainside in hopes of outrunning the sun as it sets. Television is a medium for the masses (or at least it was at the time of *The X-Files* in the 1990s), but "Darkness Falls" keeps going further and further here, quite unexpectedly, quite unconventionally. First Scully and Mulder escape the mountain in a jeep driven by Spinney. Then the jeep is damaged by the road spikes. And then the bugs swarm in to eat their final feast . . . our trapped protagonists. These moments possess a kind of relentless drive, and realization dawns on the viewer that—shockingly—our heroes are not going to emerge unscathed.

"Firewalker." Written by Howard Gordon. Directed by David Nutter. Airdate: November 18, 1994.

In the Cascade Mountains, a scientist, Trepkos (Bradley Whitford), studying the interior of a volcano apparently goes mad, necessitating a rescue mission, headed by Mulder and Scully. Once the agents arrive at the mountain range, they learn that a robot probe, Firewalker, has gone deeper inside a live volcano than any previous explorer. And it has brought back evidence of a silicon-based life-form, one that can perpetuate itself and infect humans via airborne spores. Nobody can return home until Mulder and Scully are certain that nobody is infected. . . .

In 1985, Alexander Graham Cairns-Smith wrote a monograph, *Seven Clues to the Origin of Life,* and hypothesized that clay mineral or crystals may have been one of the earliest life-forms on Earth, a missing link between inert matter and organic life. What he was writing about, essentially, is what Mulder in "Firewalker" terms "the Holy Grail" of science fiction writers: silicon-based life-forms.

Before this episode of *The X-Files* such life-forms had appeared on *Star Trek* ("The Devil in the Dark"), *Space 1999* ("All That Glisters"), *Doctor Who* ("The Stones of Blood"), and *Star Trek: The Next Generation* ("Home Soil"), to mention only the most notable examples. Unlike any of those shows, however, "Firewalker" conforms to the idea that a silicon-based life-form could be one of the earliest denizens of the planet. Trepkos notes that the life-form lives in a place "where it all began," the "very origin of the Earth."

This "unfathomably old life-form" is also described as a subterranean organism, which explains why humans have never before encountered it. Modern robotics, like Firewalker (or its real-life inspiration, NASA's Project Dante), makes it possible to penetrate regions of the planet never before visited.

Because the entity uses humans as part of its life cycle, the episode also reports that the "Earth holds some truths best left behind." Trepkos ultimately sees this truth, but not before several people die, and his journey as a character seems to reflect Mulder's odyssey in some crucial sense. Both are brilliant men obsessed with discovering "the truth," and yet both ask others (like Scully) to undertake their dangerous, possibly insane quests with them. We see what happens to a young, innocent student infatuated with Trepkos in "Firewalker." She is infected and dies, a grim fate not shared by her mentor.

Some have suggested a crucial similarity between "Firewalker" and "Ice." Notably, both episodes take place in inhospitable locales, and both involve a life-form of unknown origin but arising from the dawn of time. However, one could argue that all *The X-Files* stories are similar. They are all police procedurals that involve inexplicable mysteries that either have a scientific explanation or don't. Similarly, all *Star Trek* episodes are about visiting other worlds and encountering aliens. The differences become evident not from the structure or location, but the human impact of these stories. "Ice" was a story about trust, and about Scully and Mulder really learning to trust one another in a dangerous, possibly deadly situation.

By contrast, "Firewalker" is a kind of cautionary tale for Mulder about the danger of going so far in his beliefs that he leaves a trail of corpses in his wake. There but for the grace of God, he could end up like Trepkos. The two stories may be structurally or generally similar, featuring the reappearance of a Lazarus species, but the human tales around them are completely different, and used for very different purposes.

23

"They" Have Been Here for a Long Time

Xenophobia and Ethnocentrism

A significant subset of *The X-Files'* episode catalog explores the concept of xenophobia, the deep-rooted, irrational fear or hatred of foreign people and their culture or ideologies. Xenophobia arises for all sorts of reasons in America, including negative personal experiences, the systematic use of propaganda against the "other," and even ethnocentrism, the flaw of judging another culture's values on the basis of one's own.

Xenophobia appears frequently in the horror movie genre as well. I call the trend Innocents Abroad, after the book by Mark Twain. But basically, in many horror films (including *Daughters of Satan* [1971], *Beyond Evil* [1980], *The House Where Evil Dwells* [1982], and *The Grudge* [2004]), Americans living in foreign countries run afoul of foreign or ethnic belief systems in the supernatural, beliefs that are proven true and that contradict established American, Christian belief systems. The horror in these films results from the fact that the displaced Americans are strangers in a strange land and don't understand foreign (usually Eastern) cultures or their supernatural/spiritual beliefs.

Yet, ironically, these beliefs of the "mysterious East" are usually validated as legitimate.

In *The X-Files,* Mulder and Scully rarely visit foreign lands. Russia is one exception, in "Tunguska," and Mexico is another, in "John Doe." They are FBI agents after all, not CIA agents. However, many episodes do find the duo interfacing with émigrés from other cultures, whether from Eastern Europe, the Far East, South America, or Mexico. In many such cases, Mulder and Scully are asked to reckon with the possibility that the supernatural stories, monsters, myths, and curses from these regions are not mere stories but based on fact.

In determining this, they validate those cultures in a sense, and local xenophobia is replaced by understanding or at least learning. The "ethnic myth" or "ethnic fears" episodes of *The X-Files* again point out something unique about Mulder. He is entirely willing and able to accommodate faith from cultures outside the West, but far less willing to accept Christian mythology at face value. Of course, Scully is the opposite. Her faith leads her to believe in Christian mythology and view foreign mythology as nothing more than "stories."

The xenophobia-type stories in *The X-Files* are important because of America's historical standing as a melting pot. Many different cultures live as "Americans" within the nation's borders, even though their beliefs are not always the majority's beliefs. And if we consider the 1990s the Great Dawn of Globalism in America (think: NAFTA) in terms of the *Pax America*, then what is being expressed in many of these episodes is a twofold paradigm.

First, episodes such as "Excelsis Dei" and "Kaddish" expose mainstream American bigotry toward non-Christian, non-Western systems of beliefs. And second, through Scully and Mulder's investigations, these episodes suggest that these beliefs are worth examining because they showcase valuable ideals. They demonstrate harmony with nature ("Teso Dos Bichos"), for instance, or respect toward elders ("Excelsis Dei"). But *The X-Files* is almost always an even-handed series in terms of its ideas and presentation, and other xenophobia-type stories suggest that these other cultures have erred in terms of their understanding of justice ("Kaddish") or in their strange, even clannish behavior ("Hell Money").

Other stories of this nature don't draw judgments at all, only present facts. "El Mundo Gira," a kind of soap opera, for instance, is fascinating not because of the ethnic monster it examines (El Chupacabra) but because of the way it looks at the Hispanic population in the Southern United States. This "invisible" underclass seeks importance and self-worth, and thus contextualizes its history and world in a kind of "soap opera," storytelling mode. *The X-Files*, as if in deference to this belief, presents itself in this very mode for the duration of "El Mundo Gira."

"Excelsis Dei." Written by Paul Brown. Directed by Stephen Surjik. Airdate: December 16, 1994.

In Worcester, Massachusetts, something odd has been occurring at the Excelsis Dei Convalescent Home. A nurse, Michelle Charters (Teryl Rothery), has been attacked by an invisible psychic force that she claims operates at the behest of the elderly residents.

Mulder and Scully investigate, and question a doctor who has been illicitly experimenting on the wards with a new Alzheimer's cure. The truth is somewhat stranger than even they suspect, however: a custodian in the building named Gung (Sab Shimino) has been horrified at the ways the elderly are treated in America and has been providing the senior citizens a mushroom-based concoction to relieve their Alzheimer's symptoms. Unfortunately the senior citizens have asked for and taken too much of the native recipe grown in the basement. Now the medicine is causing some violent force to be unleashed in the corridors of the facility.

A kind of psychic or horror version of *Awakenings* (1990), only with Alzheimer's patients seeking relief of their symptoms and with weird paranormal side effects, "Excelsis Dei" is actually a xenophobia story that explores an East vs. West clash in terms of caring for the elderly. In the East, filial piety is practiced, and enormous value is placed on the lives of the elderly. Asian households are more likely to include grandparents than are Western ones by a substantial margin, and in China an Elderly Rights law was passed recently that makes visits to the elderly mandatory so as to forestall issues of neglect. In South Korea, old age is celebrated, not mourned, and parties are held at threshold ages such as sixty or seventy.

Western cultures take a decidedly different approach, with grown children sending their parents to increasingly overcrowded, underfunded assisted-living or nursing homes in old age. Some have suggested that the West is more youth-centric and that our obsession with youth has led to disgrace, and extremely poor treatment of the elderly.

Gung expresses this idea of a culture clash explicitly in the closing scenes of "Excelsis Dei." "Many generations live under one roof," he tells Mulder of his homeland. "We feel a duty to take care of them. It is not like that in this country. They [senior citizens] are not treated with respect." Ultimately, Gung is deported, sent back to the East, and the senior citizens at the convalescent house regress, succumbing to the worst symptoms of Alzheimer's. It's a sad state of affairs that comments not only on East vs. West social mores but Eastern vs. Western approaches to medicine, too. Gung grows his own medicine in a mushroom garden and notes that the people in his prefecture at home have used the medicine for generations because it makes the old and infirm "feel better." Yet in America, the sick demand more of the cure, apparently creating the episode's psychic imbalance through their demands. Meanwhile science rejects out of hand the possibility that this natural or alternative remedy could be useful in treating the sick.

Considering these facts, it seems that, according to this episode, the West has an "addictive" personality and is cut off from methods that seem outside the norm to acquire what it wants and needs. Yet the fact is, when used responsibly (as it has been for generations, according to Gung), the cure provides relief for those who suffer. In this case, Scully and Mulder see for their own eyes that Gung's medicine can have a positive effect on the elderly, in the right doses.

"The Calusari." Written by Sara B. Charno. Directed by Michael Vejar. Airdate: April 14, 1995.

Mulder suspects that a ghost is responsible for the horrific death of a two-year-old Romanian boy at an amusement park in Maryland. Upon investigation with Scully, Mulder learns that the boy's older sibling, Charlie (Joel Palmer), has a swastika on his hand. And a swastika, according to Mulder, is an ancient symbol of good luck and protection. Scully, meanwhile, is convinced that she is witnessing a case of Munchausen by proxy committed by the boy's superstitious, secretive ethnic grandmother, Golda (Lilyun Chauvin).

Soon, Charlie's father is killed, also under mysterious and possibly supernatural circumstances, and so is Golda. Mulder consults with the Romanian Calusari, which is versed in the "old ways" and may be able to save Charlie. As it turns out, Charlie was never separated from the evil spirit of his stillborn twin, Michael. Now that spirit follows Charlie everywhere, and an exorcism of sorts must take place.

"The Calusari" might be interpreted by some reviewers as a new take on *The Exorcist* (1973), one also featuring a possessed, evil child and a terrified family trying to deal with that terror. Although this is a legitimate point, to be certain, the episode actually fits into a certain subgenre that *The X-Files* returns to again and again: foreign or ethnic terrors. It is a story about how we, as Westerners, carry our assumptions about reality into any situation, even when those assumptions may have no bearing on reality or the issue at hand. A puzzle box of sorts, "The Calusari" appears to be pointed in one direction, but in the end, it points in a different one.

Charlie's Romanian grandmother in the episode comes from a different tradition than ours in contemporary America, and her beliefs are considered baffling and even a little primitive at first to those in mainstream 1990s America. "Superstitions are Golda's life," viewers are explicitly told. There's even the suggestion that her beliefs about children are actually dangerous. Scully thinks she's a criminal, and the rituals Golda uses involve marking the skin and killing animals, for instance. But are her superstitions—as we call them—more aptly termed religious rituals? How would a Christian feel, in a country of different traditions, seeing his or her beliefs termed superstition and greeted with suspicion? Whether beliefs about life and death, good and evil, are accepted or not all depends on where you live, and with whom, and that is one point of this episode.

And we soon learn in "The Calusari" that Golda is actually protecting Charlie, not attempting to injure him. The swastika is the symbol in the episode that best makes the point about this woman and her grim-faced associates in the Calusari. At first blush, the swastika is a symbol we as Westerners associate with evil and the Nazis of the World War II era. It was a symbol of the Third Reich, and our first instinct upon seeing it is to recoil in horror. It's a symbol of humanity at its worst and most evil. But the swastika is actually, historically (pre-1930s) a positive symbol. The word means, in Sanskrit, "to be good." The symbol is considered an auspicious one in several Indian religions and in other cultures as well. Accordingly, Mulder is able to interpret the swastika as a symbol of protection in "The Calusari," but he must determinedly step out of Western traditions and belief to do so. He must accept that our definition of certain terms isn't the only definition to examine, at least in this case.

This is also a lesson for Golda's daughter, Maggie, who marries an American diplomat and then totally eschews all of her own family and religious traditions. She has abandoned her beliefs so much that she never conducted the ritual of separation that would have, in her mother's tradition, saved her son, Charlie.

Outside the discussion of a foreign belief system, this *X-Files* episode is one of the scariest and most disturbing of the first few seasons. The opening sequence, which finds a malevolent entity leading a two-year-old boy to his death at an amusement park by utilizing a pink balloon, plays as truly dark and upsetting. This teaser is one of the best in the series, driven by a sense of inevitability, and made all the more effective because of a parent's feelings of responsibility/neglect. This scene is every parent's nightmare.

"Hell Money." Written by Jeffrey Vlaming. Directed by Tucker Gates. Airdate: March 29, 1996.

In Chinatown, a murder victim scrawled the word "ghost" on the wall before being burned alive inside a furnace. Mulder and Scully investigate the case with the help of Americanized detective Chao (B. D. Wong) and soon find themselves involved in the Chinese underworld. There they contend with extreme secrecy and with a mystery involving "hell money": an offering at Yu Lan Hui, the Chinese celebration of the "hungry ghost."

Mulder and Scully soon find that Chinese history and lore are being used in this circumstance to exploit poor immigrants, and that a black market for human organs is thriving in association with the hell money "game." In this case, the game is a lottery that feeds on desperation, ignorance, poverty, and isolation from Chinese culture. A "wall of silence" goes up among those impacted, and Scully and Mulder are, finally, unable to fully pierce it.

Not unlike "Excelsis Dei," "Hell Money" explores an East vs. West culture clash, but in this case, the clash is also one between modernity and tradition. Mulder asks Detective Chao if he believes in ghosts. Chao answers that he finds it difficult to dismiss two millennia worth of Chinese beliefs, but by the same taken feels "more haunted" by the size of his mortgage payments. This uneasy tension between the past and the present recurs throughout the episode.

For example, we meet a character named Mr. Hsin who joins the underground lottery, which is rigged, and pays grievously for his choice. He participates in the first place to help his daughter, Kim (Lucy Liu), who suffers from lymphocytic leukemia yet—because of that wall of silence and poverty—can't seek help in the U.S. health care system. His belief system keeps him trapped, in thrall to those who see him as a resource to exploit on the black market, not a human being. Those who have it worst, however, are like Chao, trapped halfway between a world of ghosts and superstitions and modernity, and not certain how to navigate the breach.

Many *X-Files* scholars and critics have complained that "Hell Money" isn't actually an "X-file" at all, because nothing supernatural occurs. But of course, Mulder and Scully don't know that nothing supernatural is going on, hence their investigation. They go because it is a possibility, and essentially, that's why they always go. "Hell Money" is that rare example of a story in which the paranormal or supernatural is suspected but not actually presented or validated by our "sight." Instead, the episode is about human greed and the exploitation of those who already have nothing. It's a powerful tale in part because Scully and Mulder can only do so much here. They arrest the Hard Faced Man (James Hong), but he is soon released, and his efforts to prey on "the helpless and desperate" will continue. In a sense, this result reflects the lottery itself. The deck is stacked, and justice is for those who can afford it, not those who need it most.

"El Mundo Gira." Written by John Shiban. Directed by Tucker Gates. Airdate: January 12, 1997.

In San Joaquin Valley, California, something bizarre and frightening occurs at an undocumented migrant camp. A beautiful woman, Maria (Pamela Diaz), dies when something crashes near the compound and infects her suitor, Eladio Buente (Raymond Cruz), with an "aggressive fungal infection." When Eladio disappears, his brother, Soledad (Jose Yenque)—who was also in love with Maria—pursues him. Meanwhile Mulder and Scully team with a Latino INS agent, Lozano (Ruben Blades), to find Eladio before he can become the modern-day equivalent of Typhoid Mary, spreading death to the community at large.

"El Mundo Gira"—which means "As the World Turns" in Spanish—deliberately apes the format of the Mexican telenovela, a Spanish-language soap opera of limited duration that often plays in prime time. Historically, the telenovela format goes back more than half a century and ranges in focus from comedy to romance to action, but many examples of the form also feature a sociopolitical aspect, reflecting the culture and times from which they arise.

Structurally, too, the teleplay by John Shiban reflects the telenovela. The episode concerns two brothers at war over the love of a woman, and such rivalries (in business or romance) are often the bread and butter of the formula. Thus the form or structure of the episode knowingly reflects the content. "El Mundo Gira" deals with the fact that the migrant or undocumented worker community often feels invisible in America, in mainstream Caucasian society. As an antidote to this feeling of invisibility, those who inhabit the shanty-towns see their lives in terms of larger-than-life stories. "Their lives are so small," says one character "that they have to make up these fantasies."

In this case, the fantasy—transmitted orally from person to person—is that Eladio has become the mythical monster called El Chupacabra, the Mexican goat-sucker. The Chupacabra is the right monster for the episode because it too is a story told primarily in the Mexican culture. Indeed, some authorities trace the legendary monster back to 1995 and the release of the sci-fi movie *Species*. These sources claim that El Chupacabra reflects or apes the nature and physicality of Sil, the H. R. Giger–designed monster of that film. Someone who saw *Species* believed it was real and began to spin a story, based on the film, of its activities.

But regardless of its origin, the Chupacabra is a creation that makes one's life seem, well, bigger, or more significant. The same trend can be seen in terms of the INS and the processing of illegal immigrants, as diagrammed in "El Mundo Gira." Many of the illegal immigrants use names such as Erik Estrada, not only to cloak their true identity but to equate themselves with a star or celebrity, in other words, somebody *truly* important.

In the episode's coda, the audience witnesses how the story of the Buente brothers is transmitted, person to person (much like the episode's fungal threat) in migrant worker circles, growing ever more creative and even outrageous. This might lead one to believe that the entire episode itself is told by such an unreliable narrator, and that how everything happened, and to whom, is not clear, or strictly accurate. In a community where people have a way of "being invisible" and telling stories to explain everything, the Buente brothers have become characters in an ongoing telenovela. Are they dead? Mutated? Have they been spirited away by aliens?

The episode's final line—that "the truth is . . . nobody cares"—suggests that outside the confines of the migrant community, it doesn't really matter what becomes of the Buente brothers. We literally don't see them, a fact proven by the episode's final image. We see the Buentes walking along a road, as cars pass by, failing to notice them, failing to react to them, even though they look like weird alien greys, or worse, humanoid demons. The point of telling a story in this way, perhaps, is to comment on an underclass in America, one that is rarely noted, yet is responsible for its own narrative history and myths, outside the mainstream. Some critics of this episode have noted that Mulder and Scully don't really solve anything or contribute to a clearer understanding of the narrative's details. But that is exactly as it should be. At best, they are supporting players in a telenovela about the Buentes. They are present, like Lozano, as representatives of the monolithic governing state, but to the Buentes and others they are not to be trusted, and more than that, not more than bit players in their own personal drama.

"Kaddish." Written by Howard Gordon. Directed by Kim Manners. Airdate: February 16, 1997.

In Kaddish," a Jewish storekeeper, Isaac Luria (Harrison Coe), is murdered in Brooklyn, and Scully and Mulder investigate his death when it appears that someone is waging a campaign of vengeance against the perpetrators. Among the suspects are Isaac's grieving fiancée, Ariel (Justine Miceli), and his father, Jacob (David Groh). Although Scully suspects that alleged anti-Semitic hate crimes are at the root of this case, Mulder comes to believe that a Jewish monster, the golem, has been resurrected to bring about justice.

In Jewish prayer, a Kaddish is a hymn of praise, but since the thirteenth century it has become known primarily for its use in rites of mourning, in funerals. Appropriately, "Kaddish" concerns such concepts as grief, loss, and justice, and these ideas are viewed through the prism of the Orthodox Jewish community and its experience in America.

When "Kaddish" aired in 1996, roughly 13 percent of all hate crimes were deemed anti-Semitic in nature, and David Duke, an alleged anti-Semite who ran for the U.S. Senate in 1990, the governorship of Louisiana in 1991, and for president in 1992, was in the news because of another failed run for office. In the episode, Scully and Mulder encounter white supremacists who not only physically assault Jews but dispense propaganda pamphlets about them. One such pamphlet is titled "How Jews Created AIDS." Frighteningly, those who propagate such theories of hate also report they are "working to spread the truth" and "exposing the lies" of the establishment, a deliberate reflection of Mulder's battle cry. Thus the episode seems to suggest that though "the truth might be out there," it is understood and misunderstood by those who can't see straight or are blinded by prejudice. Everyone fancies themselves a crusader for the "truth" that they prefer, and this acknowledgment seems a coded criticism of Mulder's beliefs.

In "Kaddish," it is also noted that Mulder "might be" a Jew himself, though he refuses to answer the question when it is put to him. This comment connects obliquely to Mulder's past-life regression in "Musings of a Cigarette Smoking Man," which suggests that in a previous life, he was a Jew in Nazi Germany and CSM was one of the Gestapo. In more universal terms, however, the statement comments on the utter irrationality of racial prejudices. When Mulder doesn't agree with the anti-Semitic cause, he is judged to look like one of the enemy. The implication is that prejudice is so narrow-minded, so vulnerable to logic, that it cannot survive without pointing fingers at anyone who disagrees with it. This is a notion that is shared with many conspiracy theory advocates. Tell them you disagree or that their beliefs are wrong, and you automatically join the club of the illuminati, or those trying to cloak the truth. In general terms, humans, it seems, demonize anyone who disagrees with their interpretation of facts. Believe what I believe or be dismissed as the enemy.

"Kaddish" is likely the best of all the *X-Files'* xenophobia episodes because it explores how it feels to be hated not just now, but historically, and continuously. There is an incredibly touching scene in the episode in which Ariel shows Mulder and Scully the ring that was to be exchanged for her wedding to the now-dead Isaac. It is a relic from 1943, from a town in which nearly 10,000 Jews were massacred by Nazis. A "dead relic of a forgotten place," it was spirited out but kept and cherished as a sign of civilization, and more than that, of victory in the face of true evil. This lovely ring, molded in the form of a tower, is a real Jewish relic from a Holocaust survivor, and its placement in the episode is an acute reminder that monsters dwell not only in fiction but in real life as well.

"Kaddish" is a tragic love story and one of the *X-Files'* most moving. We learn that Ariel has created the golem to destroy Isaac's murderers, and that the monster itself has taken the victim's form. It lives a kind of half-life, without a soul, but as long as he is out there, righting the wrongs, Ariel doesn't have to confront, finally, the terrible loss. She can focus on revenge. She can focus on the monster who looks like the love of her life. In the end, she must reckon with the idea that the golem is not Isaac and that Isaac is gone. Made of mud, the golem slips through her fingers, dust. The golem in this story is not only a revival or reboot of a classic movie monster but is utilized as an avatar for justice in a world of injustices. The xenophobia episodes of *The X-Files* often ask what it means to be both an American and an outsider or different living in America of the 1990s. The Lurias may have achieved a place in their community, and a standing as successful there, but the historic violence that has injured their people is not yet dead. Like the golem, it continues to live a murderous half-life, sprouting up again and again, threatening to replace peace and love with hate.

"You Are Not Like the Other Kids. You Never Will Be."

Teenagers and Adolescents in *The X-Files*

Adolescence is the stage of transition connecting childhood to adulthood, a period heralded by the onset of puberty. Adolescence, or the teenage years, thus represent a time of great change both physically and emotionally for human beings. Some of the physical changes involve height, weight, muscle mass, and in the sex organs, and other changes are entirely psychological in nature. In contemporary America, girls undergo puberty between the ages of nine and sixteen, and boys do so between the ages of ten and nineteen.

Because *The X-File* is a series, in many senses, about science (whether forensic or psychological), it is appropriate that many episodes concern adolescence and the science behind it. For instance, during puberty, the human body experiences changes in levels of neurotransmitters like dopamine and serotonin in the limbic system. At the same time, unnecessary brain cell connections are eliminated and the myelin sheaths around nerve fibers are completed. Teenagers also rely more deeply than do adults on the amygdala because of underdevelopment of the prefrontal cortex during adolescence. This reliance on the amygdala results in teenagers operating essentially on instinct and impulse. This means that teenagers tend to think they will live forever and that they are essentially invincible. They sometimes seem a different breed altogether, and *The X-File* capitalizes on that notion.

The 1990s also represents a period in television history in which programming for a younger demographic—meaning teenagers—was widely produced. Soap operas of the day, including *Beverly Hills 90210* (1990–2000) and *Dawson's Creek* (1998–2003), were immensely popular. In terms of genre programming, Joss Whedon's *Buffy the Vampire Slayer* (1997–2003) aired concurrently with *The X-Files*, and made literal the notion that high school is hell. The series involved monsters dwelling in the adolescent world, whether they were vampires, werewolves, or demons.

Although Mulder and Scully were not teenagers themselves, *The X-Files,* across nine seasons, often features episode concerning teenagers and teenage concerns. These episodes pay special attention to the science of puberty and the changes and challenges that go hand in hand with the process. They meet "mean girls" in "Syzygy," discover the psychic toll for a lifetime of child abuse in "Schizogeny," and come face-to-face with teens superpowered by "speed" in "Rush."

As late as Season Nine and installments such as "Lord of the Flies," the protagonists of the series regard teenagers and the chemical changes in adolescents as a possible motive for haywire or antisocial behavior. What's remarkable about all the "teenage" episodes of *The X-Files* is that though they are written by adults, they also exhibit a sympathy for adolescence and its myriad challenges.

"Syzygy." Written by Chris Carter. Directed by Rob Bowman. Airdate: January 26, 1996.

In "Syzygy," three popular high school jocks have died in the small town of Comity in as many months, and local authorities, including the attractive Detective White (Dana Wheeler-Nicholson), suspect satanic cult activity. Mulder and Scully look into the matter, and Scully immediately suspects that two teenage cheerleaders, Terry Roberts (Lisa Robin Kelly) and Margie Kleinjan (Wendy Benson), are somehow involved since they both witnessed the most recent death.

A local astrologer, Madame Zirinka (Denalda Williams), informs Mulder that the girls may have unusual powers because of a once-every-84-years planetary alignment of Mars, Mercury, and Uranus. This alignment also seems to be having an effect on Mulder and Scully, who become, respectively, horny and snippy. . . .

This episode, with its focus on high school cliques, Valley Girl lingo ("Hate him!"), and adolescent concerns, is something akin to *Carrie* meets *Mean Girls* (2004). This equation makes the episode practically irresistible in terms of its humor quotient.

A syzygy might be defined as "a kind of unity, namely an alignment of three celestial bodies (for example, the Sun, Earth, and Moon) such that one body is directly between the other two, such as occurs at an eclipse." But, importantly, it might also be described in terms of psychology, as "an archetypal pairing of contra-sexual opposites, symbolizing the communication of the conscious and unconscious minds." This is a Jungian concept, suggesting that two people in a relationship might take on opposite sexual characteristics from the norm.

Not surprisingly, both definitions of syzygy are applicable to this episode of *The X-Files.* The episode concerns astrology and the effect of planetary bodies on human bodies. Although I am not an astrologist by any means, I have always found, perhaps to my detriment, that there is a certain veneer of believability to some aspects of it. We know that there are cosmic forces such as gravity, and that they do exert an impact on matter and energy, for instance. Therefore, it does not seem such a gigantic stretch to believe that a shift in such cosmic forces could impact humans in some strange or mysterious way. Anecdotally, I can only confirm an old wives' tale: For many years, I worked as the office manager in my wife's psychological practice, and all the employees who worked with me firmly believed in the idea of "lunacy," that the full moon brought out worse behavior in some patients, ranging all the way to suicide attempts. The Scully in me wondered if the timing was a coincidence, or merely our perceptions, while the Mulder in me questioned if there might indeed be some validity to the theory of the full moon exerting a more powerful influence on some people.

But in terms of "Syzygy," the astrology factor is the device that allows the writer, Carter, to examine the behavior of teenagers and then amplify that behavior to an unimaginable level. We've all known cruel girls and boys in high school and witnessed how their selfish interests become the orbit of all activity. The planetary alignment in "Syzygy" reveals what happens when dangerously narcissistic adolescents are suddenly able to act immediately on all their worst, most selfish impulses. It isn't pretty, but in many ways, it is pretty funny.

Much more intriguing than the mean girls, however, is the way that Carter uses the idea of "syzygy" in terms of the second definition, the psychological conjunction of two people taking on each other's sexual characteristics. David Duchovny has publicly mused on the subject, but in many ways, the sex roles of Mulder and Scully are reversed. Scully is much more analytical and closed down (which is stereotypically male behavior), whereas Mulder is more open and questioning (stereotypically female behavior). In this episode, when the two are impacted by the planetary alignment, the roles reverse again. Mulder becomes a prowling, boozing, perfume-smelling, horndog, and Scully is suddenly a jealous, sniping, second-guessing bitch. Before anyone gets mad at me for those descriptions: these are comical *extremes*, and the episode makes the most of them.

But finally, the episode works because we all have moments like these in our relationships. Sexual attraction isn't a constant. Neither is flirting. Sometimes, even with our most loved ones, things get strained. Irritation seeps in. Familiarity breeds contempt. "Syzygy" uses the conceit of an astrological conjunction to reveal a very human side to Mulder and Scully's often idealized relationship. They become closer, more identifiable, and more real because of stories like this, where there are moments of exasperation with one another. It isn't a stretch to believe that Mulder likes to bogart the driving duties out in the field or that he frequently second-guesses Scully's directions. I find that some of the best moments in *The X-Files* are those that bow to the reality that even partners as close as Scully and Mulder sometimes get on each other's nerves. It's human. It doesn't mean they love each other any less.

As usual, "Syzygy" works better the more one digs into its creative DNA. The name of the town where all this occurs is "Comity," which means friendly or social harmony, and "comity" of course is the one thing lacking in the town, both between Terri and Margie and between Scully and Mulder. And the fact that Keystone Cops footage keeps playing on TV is a reflection of the fact that the planetary syzygy has also frazzled Mulder and Scully's usual investigative talents. They are clueless and competitive throughout most of the episode, bungling each stage of the investigation because they can't get their acts together.

"Schizogeny." Written by Jessica Scott and Mike Wollaeger. Directed by Ralph Hemecker. Airdate: January 11, 1998.

Mulder and Scully investigate a strange homicide in Michigan. An apparently abusive stepfather is found dead, buried up to his neck in the muddy earth of the nearby orchard. The prime suspect in this crime is the victim's stepson, Bobby (Chad Lindberg), who is in therapy with Dr. Karin Matthews (Sarah-Jane Redmond) for anger issues.

When a second murder occurs and another allegedly abused child is involved, Scully and Mulder realize that Karin is the link between murders. Karin's abusive father died twenty years earlier in the mud of the orchard, and now a murderous connection exists between man and nature.

"Schizogeny" concerns the cycle of domestic abuse in American families and the fact that the violence of one generation often takes root and blooms in the next. Rather daringly, the episode literalizes this concept of taking root. Thus "Schizogeny" explores how the local trees of a small Michigan town seem to burst to life to do the bidding of those consumed with unexpressed rage, violence, and the thirst for vengeance. So yes, this is the famous "killer trees" episode of the series.

"Schizogeny" establishes that the local families living near the Michigan orchard consider themselves connected to the land, and at points in "Schizogeny" it also appears that *human blood* runs through the root systems of these nearby trees. Accordingly, the episode strives to connect the people to their homeland, and in large part succeeds in that task. For instance, we learn that when one abusive local, Mr. Matthews, was alive, the trees suffered a terrible blight. That blight didn't end until his death. Now, the orchard and its roots swallow up those who, like Mr. Matthews, would hurt the town's children.

Although not particularly well regarded by critics in 1998, this offbeat episode of *The X-Files* succeeds on the basis of its unique location, its careful dramatic point about the nature of "family trees," and even, in the final analysis, its dedicated homage to and reparsing of a horror film classic: Hitchcock's *Psycho* (1960).

"Schizogeny" is a visually distinctive episode, a fact that gives it much of its creepy energy. For instance, the trees in the orchard bend toward one another—creating natural tunnels in the process—and several compositions reveal Mulder, Scully, or others walking through this naturally occurring structure. Craftily, this visual of the natural tunnels also symbolizes something vital: the protective, nurturing "arms" of the orchard, which reach down and surround visitors. These arms protect those whom the trees love and feel connected to. And by the same token, the hidden roots underneath the ground can attack those who would do the locals harm.

The episode's teaser—set in this picturesque orchard during a thunderstorm—provides a splendidly Gothic image: that of nature perverted and twisted (again, think of those roots) by their connection to mankind. Here the trees are being used for sinister purposes by man and suffering a physical blight just as man (or woman) suffers a psychic blight.

"Schizogeny" explores the idea of this man/plant symbiosis in psychological terms, much like *Forbidden Planet* (1956) contextualized Dr. Morbius's connection to the monster from the id on Altair. Here, as in that case, the trees act at the bidding of a deranged human mind. And when man is angry or destructive, the trees strike for his dark purposes. At some point, young Karin Matthews learned to harness the power of the trees to express her deep rage against her father, a violent personality who often kept her locked up in the basement. But by the end of the episode, the trees have realized that Karin is not the innocent, victimized child she once was. Instead, she has blossomed to become just as evil and monstrous as her father was. I was going to write that the apple didn't fall far from the tree, but perhaps it is better merely to note that the seed of darkness planted in Karin at a young age by her father's action has germinated. The cycle of violence is complete: the child has grown up to become the monster that the parent was.

In exploring Karin's story and her twisted psychology, *The X-Files* deliberately reparses the story of *Psycho* (1960), but with the added supernatural element of the sentient tree root system. The episode concerns an adult (Karin/Norman) who was mistreated by a parent (Mr. Matthews/Mrs. Bates) and whose mind has splintered into at least two personalities (that of the abused and that of the abuser, as was also the case with Norman Bates). Similarly, the fulcrum for the family's dark secrets is a fruit cellar or basement. In *Psycho,* as you may recall, Norman kept Mrs. Bates's corpse in the basement, in a rocking chair, during the film's finale. Here, Karin must also reckon with the corpse of her abuser, her long-dead father, only in this case, the tree roots have dragged him to the fruit cellar from his grave. Did she use the trees to bring him there, so the abusive voice in her head would never be far away? Or did the trees drag old Dad to the cellar to remind Karin of the face of evil? Karin also speaks in the (creepy) voice of her father (as Norman spoke in Mother's voice), and is consumed by the very evil that took her father, which is similar to Norman's fate. Where "Schizogeny" diverges from *Psycho* in an intriguing fashion, however, is not merely in the application of a supernatural or paranormal element but in the idea that Karin is a psychologist. As a therapist, Karin constantly refights her own battle with her father, and she views every patient problem, similarly, as a reiteration of that specific family dynamic. Thus Bobby must express his rage at his father, even though he doesn't feel the rage that Karin did. Essentially, Karin's vocation as a therapist means that she continues the cycle of violence spawned by her father, but—intriguingly so—not with her natural children, but with the other children of the town. She transfers the evil to others in the same way the blight moves from tree to tree. Damningly, Karin sees every parent/child relationship as a reiteration of her own negative, abusive relationship, but finally, the trees snap this cycle before it can be perpetuated for another generation or harm others.

Is the idea of killer trees ridiculous, as some critics of this episode assert? Well, it seems to me that once you decide to buy into Fluke Men or black oil or other such monsters, killer trees represent only a small leap further into horror. What I find important instead is the fact that "Schizogeny" is thematically and visually consistent. The visuals of the trees and roots reflect the narrative content about human generations and the cycle of violence. And finally this episode also features a remarkable performance from Redmond, *Millennium*'s Lucy Butler. Redmond holds the screen here, evoking both sympathy and fear for Karin.

"Rush." Written by David Amann. Directed by Robert Lieberman. Airdate: December 5, 1999.

This episode takes Mulder and Scully to Pittsfield, Virginia, where an honor student, Anthony Reed (Rodney Scott), is accused of murdering a police deputy in a vicious bludgeoning incident. On closer examination, however, Mulder and Scully determine that Anthony and two other local teens, Max Harden (Scott Cooper) and Chastity Raines (Nicki Aycox), have somehow developed the ability to move at superspeed, an ability that has a catastrophic impact on their bodies.

With dialogue references to *Carrie* (1976), and Nirvana ("too much teen spirit," "smells like a murder to me") as well as the "unparalleled upheaval of adolescent changes," "Rush" concerns the adolescent capacity to move right past "no trespassing" signs (an early image in the episode teaser) into activities—like illicit drug use—that may create a high or a buzz but also create physical danger.

Thus, "Rush" knowingly compares physical acceleration, or "speed," to another kind of speed, a slang term for stimulant drugs. Much like a person taking such drugs, the teens featured in "Rush" feel more powerful, invincible, and sharper than everyone else. "This is the best thing that's ever happened to me. I can't go back to things standing still," says one affected student.

Standing still is an appropriate description for teenage life, as the episode's visual effects diagram it. Moving at superspeed, the teens actually seem, at times, to move at normal speed, while the rest of the world is frozen, as if in amber. This is an expressive visualization that captures well how it feels to be a teenager.

Another aspect of the teen milieu, peer pressure, is also explored in "Rush," as one student, Max, holds all the power and declares that he will "call the shots" and that the others "should always remember" that fact. One price for moving so fast is that such "speed" is not condoned by adult society, and to experience it requires association with, essentially, law-breakers.

Further adding to this examination of adolescence, Mulder and Scully in "Rush" determine that only teenagers can be impacted by this strange power (given of the Earth, in a mysterious cave), because the agents and adults are "too old" to be impacted by it. In other words, judgmental adults are set in their ways and thus physically—biologically—unable to understand what teens endure or go through. The episode's final image captures this idea in perfect visual terms, with a close-up of a ticking clock.

For teenagers, who live with their parents, under their parents' rules, and must also run the gauntlet of high school, life seems to pass so damn slowly.

The "acceleration," caused by proximity to that mysterious cave, makes life speed up and seem so, well, alive. Going back to the drudgery of normal adolescence feels like filling a prison sentence, perhaps. That's what the episode's final imagery cannily conveys.

"Rush" escapes the preachy aspects of an After School Special by showcasing visuals that make us remember the teenage experience. The bookend imagery—of an honor student walking past a no-trespassing sign and finally a clock ticking slowly—tells audiences virtually everything they need to know about being a kid. We understand the thrill of breaking rules and the mind-numbing slowness of routine life, waiting for age eighteen and emancipation in the eyes of society. At episode's end, as Tony sits in his hospital room, a close-up of the wall clock ticks interminably toward 3:00 p.m., the traditional time of release from high school, and this image corresponds with the augmented sound of the minute hand on the clock, changing. It sounds less like a clock and more like the clanging door of a jail cell. The question becomes: Is the jail door opening at 3:00 p.m. or closing again, a sign that the eighteen-year sentence has been resumed? Such imagery gives "Rush" a feeling of sympathy for the affected teenagers, and any sense of judgment or indictment is reduced considerably.

Intriguingly, a 2012 found-footage superhero film called *Chronicle* charts much the same territory as "Rush" did in 1999. In this film, a trio of teens gain superpowers in a subterranean cave, but where two teens enjoy the "rush" of their super abilities and attempt to master them, another teen, one from a family life of abuse and alienation, goes dark. It's a very similar scenario, right down to the source of the powers and the number of teens impacted.

"Lord of the Flies." Written by Thomas Schnauz. Directed by Kim Manners. Airdate: December 16, 2001.

In this late-era episode, several students at Garfield High School have banded together to perform outrageous stunts for a cable TV series titled *Dumbass*. After one such stunt, star Captain Dare is discovered dead, though not from head injuries; rather from flies eating his brain and a portion of his skull.

Agents Doggett and Reyes attempt to solve the case, questioning Captain Dare's friend and video chronicler Sky Commander Winky (Aaron Paul). But Winky claims that he would never harm his friend, and then almost immediately suffers a series of bites—from lice—that spell out the word "dumb ass" on his butt.

Soon, Doggett, Reyes, and Scully, teamed with an obnoxious entomologist named Rocky Bronzino (Michael Wiseman), deduce that pheromones may be to blame for the incidents of insect swarming. The trail of crimes leads to alienated teenager Dylan Lokensgard (Hank Harris), son of the school principal (Jane Lynch). He is in love with Captain Dare's girlfriend Natalie (Samaire Armstrong) and trying to fit in with a teen world where he is "different." Unfortunately, even Dylan doesn't realize just how different he is, since he is a human-spider hybrid. His mother warns him that "you are not like other kids, you never will be," but he takes her warnings as a challenge, not a matter of biology. His "heart wants what it wants," according to Scully's final voice-over narration, and in fleeing the town with his mother, Dylan sends Natalie a message of love . . . spelled out in an insect swarm.

Much as in "Rush," "Lord of the Flies" locates the teenage years as a fulcrum for discontent and rapid physical change. Scully explicitly discusses body chemistry and raging hormones as being deciding factors in the matter of a teenager "directing biology" to carry out his monster-from-the-id-like desires. Intriguingly, "Lord of the Flies" also takes advantage of its early Web 2.0 age to describe something new in the culture, a kind of egotism or narcissism, shared not just regionally but through videos and cable television. Today, we have social media like Facebook and Twitter, as well as video upload sites such as YouTube, as developments of this attention-getting trend, but in late 2001, when "Lord of the Flies" first aired on American television, the country was caught in the grip of *Jackass* (2000–2002) fever.

Jackass, of course, was an MTV series starring Johnny Knoxville about young daredevils, skaters, and athletes performing stunts that were dangerous or in bad taste, but preferably both. *Dumbass,* the show in "Lord of the Flies," is clearly designed as a surrogate for the MTV production. Agent Doggett complains to Agent Reyes about the kind of stupidity displayed by Captain Dare and Winky. He notes that as a kid, he did stupid things, but that he didn't realize they were stupid, whereas the *Dumbass* stunts aren't *"just stupid."* Rather, he opines, the suspects represent "the glorification of stupid. These kids take enormous pride in being sub-mental." Sadly, his view has been validated in real life. At least one member of *Jackass*'s cast, Ryan Dunn, died in 2011 as a result of his lifestyle and life's work, which was to laugh off danger (and injury) as a joke.

In "Lord of the Flies," even Natalie, the object of Dylan's crush, demonstrates a distinct lack of common sense. The stunt that precedes (but doesn't cause) Captain Dare's demise involves her lying prone in the street, beyond a ramp, holding a lit flare in her mouth. Dare's shopping cart is to fly over her, and the flare will light it on fire before landing in a pool filled with water. Though at first Natalie complains about the danger involved—what if the cart hits her face?—she nonetheless agrees to be involved.

The promise of becoming famous or infamous even for something stupid—is too great to overcome. So whereas "Syzygy," "Schizogeny," and

"Rush" are all relatively sympathetic toward youthful concerns, "Lord of the Flies" adopts a different tack, fearing that a new development in the culture, a cable TV program, plus the ease and affordability of new digital and video cameras, could play into the worst instincts and behaviors of teenagers. Similarly, the teenagers here, namely Winky, seem much more cynical and world-weary than others seen on *The X-Files.* At one point, we learn, Winky has attempted to sell the footage of his friend's death to network television, but only Fox TV (home of *The X-Files*...) has shown any interest. The implicit message is that this Web 2.0 generation of young adults sees celebrity as an end in and of itself, and morals aren't a consideration when attempting to achieve that desired destination.

And yet, as one might expect of the series, there is a beautifully visualized grace note that ends the episode. Dylan is whisked away from Garfield High and his life by his overprotective and literally monstrous mother, and yet he doesn't give up. Instead, he sends a message of love via a swarm of fireflies, a bug-driven neon sign meant for one, Natalie. He is different, biologically speaking, from his peers and the object of his love, but he still possesses humanity, and a romantic streak. This fact makes him something less than a monster and instead, in the tradition of many horror films, a "derided other." He is a being who seeks to belong to the human world but can't. Yet instead of raging against this fact, he reaches out with love. Thus the audience leaves the episode with hope and a touch of magic realism. Even monsters dream of finding the right person and of true love.

Sympathetic freaks of the week have appeared on *The X-Files* before, in "Hungry" to name one episode, but "Lord of the Flies" is an underrated episode in the canon because it combines horror, comedy, and finally pathos with such agility and deftness. The final image—of a lonely boy professing his love for a girl he will never be with—is one of the series' most lyrical and bittersweet moments. It reminds all of us how it feels to be in the grip of the teenage years.

25

One Short Step Away from Proving the Preexistence of the Human Soul

The Paranormal

The word "paranormal" is a catch-all or umbrella term meant to describe events that aren't immediately explicable by established science. Extrasensory perception (ESP), clairvoyance, reincarnation, OBE (out-of-body experiences), astral projection, automatic writing, and spirit possession all fall within the rubric of paranormal. Some researchers, however, widen the scope of the term even further to include UFO studies and the pseudoscience of cryptozoology, meaning the hunt for creatures like Big Foot, Yeti, or the Loch Ness Monster.

The X-Files investigates virtually all such subjects, though for reasons of clarity, this chapter will focus on the narrower definition. Since monsters and the UFOs of the Mytharc are discussed elsewhere in the book, this chapter looks almost exclusively at the matters relating to humanity's untapped and largely unquantified potential, whether to astral project, reincarnate in a new body, read thoughts, or determine future events via precognition.

Throughout *The X-Files,* Mulder and Scully, and later Doggett and Reyes, encounter individuals with seemingly remarkable powers of the mind. They meet Gibson Praise in "The End," a child prodigy who can read minds; tricky Luther Lee Boggs (in "Beyond the Sea"), who seems capable of making contact with the dead; psychic assassin Robert Patrick Modell (in "Pusher"); and even tragic Lucy Householder (Tracey Ellis) in "Oubliette," a woman who involuntarily establishes a psychic connection with a kidnapped child, Amy Jacobs (Jewel Staite).

Late in the run of *The X-Files,* viewers learn why certain humans possess these amazing and unusual powers: junk DNA in the brain. This so-called junk DNA (in the subventricular zone of the brain) is inactive in most people, according to the series, but active in a few. This DNA is believed to be alien in nature (as all humans are descended from aliens in the series lore) and therefore possessing abilities we don't associate with normal human beings. Some research of late has suggested that this junk DNA may be responsible for certain neurological diseases, including schizophrenia. But in *X-Files* lore, it is the wellspring for psychic abilities in those who have it "activated."

Outside this unifying theory of the paranormal, *The X-Files* utilizes psychic phenomena to help establish a class of people who, because of their biological anomalies, don't fit in with society, where they are literally almost too sensitive to thrive. In at least two incidences in the series, Mulder comes to the aid of young women who remind him of Samantha: Tracey Ellis in the aforementioned "Oubliette" and blind Marty Glenn (Lili Taylor) in "Mind's Eye." In both cases, these individuals are beaten down by life, derided by peers, and suffering because of their perceived difference or "otherness." Mulder's very developed protective instinct comes into play, but it is also possible to read these genetic anomalies not as monsters but as minority groups or those of alternate sexual orientation. In other words, they are derided, looked down upon, and in some cases persecuted by the prevailing majority.

"The Walk." Written by John Shiban. Directed by Rob Bowman. Airdate: November 10, 1995.

In "The Walk," Mulder and Scully investigate residents at a VA hospital, where a phantom soldier is killing off members of the military. Mulder comes to suspect that a quadruple amputee, Rappo (Ian Tracey), is using his ability to astral project and murder the officers he deems responsible for his suffering.

Astral projection, a phenomenon that was recently the subject of the *Insidious* franchise (2011–2013), involves a person leaving his physical body and projecting his consciousness to another, sometimes distant location. In "The Walk," Rappo's ability to project himself from the VA hospital to other locales rests on a partner, Roach (Willie Garson), who calls himself "the Mailman." He goes to the homes of the targets and seizes their mail (featuring an address), so that Rappo can direct himself there.

Aired in late 1995, "The Walk's" social context is the post-Gulf War period, an age in which shell shock was renamed PTSD (post-traumatic stress disorder), and became known in that way by the American population. Similarly, the episode raises questions regarding Gulf War Syndrome, or Gulf War Illness (GWI), a condition that, according to a 2010 report by the Department of Veteran Affairs, continues to affect 250,000 of the nearly 700,000 veterans of the 1991 effort to free Kuwait from Saddam Hussein. A multisymptom disorder, the exact cause of GWI is not precisely known, and various authorities have suggested exposure to depleted uranium, the vaccination against anthrax, combat stress, and proximity to burning oil wells. Symptoms include headaches, diarrhea, memory problems, skin rashes, and even terminal tumors.

In this case, the episode's setting is a VA hospital where miserable veterans, suffering all manner of afflictions, are warehoused and forgotten by mainstream society. One soldier laments that most of America "sat and watched the war at home on cable television like it was a video game," referring to CNN coverage of the bombing of Baghdad, while patriotic soldiers lost limbs and were subjected to substances and material that have made their lives miserable.

Rappo has developed the ability to leave his body at any time because he wants to make the generals pay for the war, a conflict that is visually equated to a boy playing war in a sandbox at one point in the show. Rappo targets General Callaghan's (Thomas Kopache) eight-year-old son and kills him in his sandbox while he is playing with toy soldiers. Later, hauntingly, the boy's mother puts away those toy soldiers permanently and cries, "I want my son back." This is the lament of all mothers and fathers who have lost their children in a political conflict, in war. Rappo is making his enemies, those who orchestrated war but did not suffer for it, feel his pain. They come to understand loss and quite powerfully so.

In this case, a paranormal capacity, astral projection, exacts revenge, but also forges a social critique. War always lands hardest on the young men and women who must prosecute it, while generals inevitably survive to plan the next campaign. Similarly, patriotism in America is often a mile long but an inch deep. As war begins, people brandish American flags and decorate with yellow ribbons, but nobody wants to be confronted with the real cost of war: wounded veterans who will never be the same and need a lifetime of support from the state to have any chance of thriving. Rappo in "The Walk" is pretty clearly a villain, targeting children and families of his enemies, and yet the point he makes about his cause is a valid one. Too often generals think war is a game and, in the case of the Gulf Wars, an opportunity to play toy soldiers in a somewhat larger-than-usual sandbox.

The paranormal concept of astral projection in "The Walk" is in some subtextual way also connected with a different kind of projection, psychological projection. This sort of behavior occurs when people defend their (usually bad) behavior by attributing the same behavior to others. Rappo not only projects to different locations, he practices a murderous brand of psychological projection, making others suffer in the way that he has suffered.

Instead of realizing that two wrongs can never make a right, Rappo becomes a monster, just like those he despises.

"The Field Where I Died." Written by Glen Morgan and James Wong. Directed by Rob Bowman. Airdate: November 3, 1996.

Reincarnation is a topic that has been handled on *The X-Files* several times, and it concerns the idea that the last breath of one life quickly transitions to the first breath of a new life. In other words, there isn't an afterlife, necessarily, but rather a succession of lives on this mortal coil; a succession that we, in this life, can occasionally remember. Reincarnation is a tenet of Buddhism and is believed by more than a tenth of the human population to be a simple fact of life. Buddhists believe in the samsara, a cycle of reincarnation that repeats until the soul learns the lessons of the Buddha and attains bliss or nirvana. The Buddhist belief system prescribes "the Middle Way" or "the Eightfold Path of Living" to stop the cycle of life, death, and rebirth. The belief system offers a guide by which people can choose to live and a code of morality as well.

One way to became aware of one's previous incarnation, according to some, is a form of hypnosis called past-life regression. Using this process, psychologists can "regress" patients to a time before their earliest memories and reveal previous existences, ones that usually ended in trauma or pain. This is the process that Mulder undergoes in the controversial *X-Files* episode "The Field Where I Died." In this case, he encounters a woman he seems to know, Melissa (Kristen Cloke), and learns that in every life they have lived, in every incarnation, they have been star-crossed lovers. They are eternal soul mates that can never be together, always separated and always looking ahead to the next life in which they will "live again."

The source of the episode's controversy is twofold. First, when Mulder regresses and experiences previous life, he sees himself as a Jew in the Holocaust. His son is Samantha, and Scully's soul is his "father." Cancer Man is one of the Gestapo, and Mulder learns that "evil returns as evil" and "souls mate eternal."

These ideas are presented beautifully and emotionally in the episode, especially through Duchovny's heartfelt performance. And yet viewers of *The X-Files* may remember that Mulder's father and Cancer Man/CSM were depicted together in the early 1950s, investigating the Zeus Faber incident after the end of World War II. Many questioned how CSM could be a Nazi, since he was clearly alive, operating at the State Department, in the same era.

The second controversy riled shippers, the fans who are interested, primarily, in the romantic relationship of Mulder and Scully. "The Field Where

I Died" establishes that their destiny is not, in fact, to be lovers and that they are not soul mates. Rather, Melissa and Mulder are soul mates, and Scully is simply a very dear friend around whose orbit Mulder circles. Mulder tells Scully in the episode that "we have been friends together in other lifetimes," and Scully replies that "even if" she knew that for certain, she "wouldn't change a thing."

Ultimately, the episode raises a number of fascinating questions, in addition to these points that seem inconsistent, given the full arc of the series. If we were aware of a preordained destiny—that there are souls we are "supposed" to be with—would we, like Melissa, seek to end "this pointless life"? This idea is compared, effectively, with a David Koresh-like cult, the Temple of the Seven Stars. Its adherents choose suicide, Jim Jones style, and yet, according to the beliefs involving reincarnation, those souls will rise again and get another chance. Does this mean that they are doomed to die in every life? Does it mean, contrarily, that holding on to this incarnation is not so important, because we all get another spin on the samsara?

"The Field Where I Died" is a fascinating exploration of reincarnation, following the first-season episode "Born Again," and it would not be the last time the series explored the concept.

"Hellbound." Written by David Amann. Directed by Kim Manners. Airdate: January 27, 2002.

Reincarnation gets another look in this ninth-season story that is filled with grotesque special effects. In "Hellbound," Reyes feels compelled to investigate a murder case in which the victim had a premonition of his own death and soon after was found skinned alive. Reyes tells Doggett that she "needs to solve this," and asks for his help and for Scully's as well. In the process of investigating the case, however, Reyes learns that similar skinning murders occurred in the years 1868, 1909, and 1960, and that each of the victims was born on the same day the last set of victims died. Yet what makes the case even creepier and also more intimate is that Reyes confesses to experiencing some of the same dark visions as the victims, as though she is personally involved in this circle of life, death, and rebirth. Although one might term this vision a premonition, it might also be described as a psychic memory.

As noted above, Season Four's "The Field Where I Died" also followed a series protagonist, Mulder in this case, uncovering "previous" lives and reincarnation. He recounted his past-life history with Scully and also a soul mate, Melissa/Sarah, from whom his soul was always separated. In the case of "Hellbound," however, Reyes's past lives dictate the shape of her present life to a galvanizing and unsatisfactory degree. She works in the law enforcement profession and attempts to solve baffling cases because in every life she experiences, she fails to bring the guilty to justice. Reyes's failure ensures that the cycle continues.

Reyes's deepest fear is that she "will fail," and this fear is borne not out of lack of self-esteem or neurotic insecurity, but from the fact that her soul has failed, again and again, cycle after cycle, life after life. Fear of failure is actually a meaningful message from her past, casting a shadow on her present and threatening her soul's future as well. Reyes's determination to know the truth stems not from a traumatic event in childhood, like Mulder's, but from a psychic gestalt that, until "Hellbound," even she knows nothing about. This idea is a good hook for the character and one that fits in well with Reyes's behavior in episodes such as "Improbable," where she appears driven to root out unseen connections and patterns.

If "Hellbound" features a familiar paranormal belief, reincarnation, it takes that belief into whole new and relevant territory. The episode (much like David Fincher's film *Fight Club* [1999]) shows a bit of suspicion about support groups, their message and efficacy. For example, this time around in the life-death-rebirth cycle, the victims participate in an anger management group, and so the very nature of support groups is addressed. After all, support groups proceed from the assumption that a person can change, but reincarnation—a kind of karmic justice—suggests oppositely that "you can't run from what you are."

So where support groups tell you that you can change who you are and accordingly "turn your life around," the reincarnation cycle of the episode suggests the opposite. As human beings, our souls keep falling victim to the same mistakes. "No can stop it," the killer tells Reyes. "You never do. You always fail. It's your lot."

Of course, Reyes doesn't fail, technically, in "Hellbound." She brings down the killer this time, but the episode's closing visual is of that murderous soul taking root in a new infant, a downbeat ending that suggests the cycle will start anew. Can a person believe in second chances and also believe that the parade of lives is malleable, unalterable?

Will Reyes, in her next incarnation, still feel the drive of failure, or will she be karmically free of her burdens because of her actions here, on this case? It's a fascinating idea, and it's a shame that *The X-Files* didn't last a few more years in order to explore Reyes's past . . . and possible future.

26

Fact or Fiction?

Ten Times *The X-Files* Was "Based on a True Story."

One frequently asked question about *The X-Files* involves the veracity of episodes as stories of the paranormal or supernatural. Are any of the episodes of the series actually based on fact?

The simplest answer to that question is: yes. Many installments are based on or inspired by real events that occurred during the show's broadcast span, 1993–2002. Other episodes are based on historical events or literary precedents.

But just by looking at the "current events" of the 1990s, one can readily detect the inspiration for some of the most popular stories. This is true for all great horror productions as well. Art mirrors life.

1. "The Erlenmeyer Flask" (Season One): On February 19, 1994, a woman named Gloria Ramirez (1963–1994) was rushed to Riverside General Hospital in California, evidencing signs of tachycardia. When a blood sample was drawn, more than thirty people were sickened by their exposure to it, experiencing loss of consciousness, shortness of breath, and fainting spells. Ramirez, who passed away, later became known as "the Toxic Lady."

In "The Erlenmeyer Flask," paramedics exposed to the blood of a human-alien hybrid similarly experience adverse effects. At one point, Mulder suffers from them as well.

2. "Blood" (Season Two): The spraying of malathion, an insecticide of reputedly very little toxicity and utilized to combat the Mediterranean fruit fly, was conducted in parts of California in 1993, 1994, and 1995. The spraying was done by helicopters, and often at night, and this activity became one of the core plotlines of Robert Altman's film *Short Cuts* (1993).

Helicopters spraying a pesticide also formed the basis for "Blood," in which Mulder and Scully suspect that the government is conducting a secret test that makes human beings "go postal" and succumb to bloody violence.

3. "Firewalker" (Season Two): In 1993 and 1994, NASA tested something called Project Dante. The project originated at Carnegie Mellon and involved an eight-legged robot equipped with sensors, testing equipment, and video cameras that could move six feet per minute and take samples inside a volcano. The original plan involved the robot descending into an Antarctic volcano and exploring the perimeter of a lava lake. The 990-pound robot, however, was actually tested at Mount Spurr in Alaska in 1994, and the tether that could lower and lift it snapped, necessitating a rescue.

In "Firewalker," Scully and Mulder are called to investigate deaths around Firewalker, a robot of similar design and specifications that had descended to a volcanic level never before explored. There, evidence of a silicon-based life-form was found.

4. "F. Emasculata" (Season Two): In 1994, Richard Preston's nonfiction book *The Hot Zone* became a *New York Times* #1 best seller. The "terrifying true story" captured the imagination and fears of America as it explored an outbreak of the deadly Ebola virus in a monkey storage facility called Hazelton Laboratories in Reston, Virginia, during the year 1989. The Reston Ebola virus occurred in crab-eating macaque monkeys imported from the Philippines, and the fatal disease never crossed from the monkeys to human beings. Despite this fact, the CDC investigated the situation, and the prominence of the case made plain the danger of Ebola and other lethal viruses. Based on Preston's 1992 *New Yorker* story "Crisis in the Hot Zone," *The Hot Zone* included information not just about the outbreak in Virginia, but also about occasions in which unfortunate people, usually hikers, were infected with the disease in Africa "in the shadow of Mount Elgon." The book's final chapter featured the author exploring the cave where Ebola was believed to have been first pinpointed, as well as visiting the lab building in Reston where the 1989 outbreak occurred and was contained. Among other terrors, *The Hot Zone* described the effects of hemorrhagic fever, or Ebola, on the human body.

On *The X-Files*, the episode "F. Emasculata" features a sample of a deadly disease found in South America and transferred (illicitly, by shadowy forces) to a prison in Virginia. There, Scully learns, the prisoners have been infected purposely and are being tested. "F. Emasculata" premiered just weeks after a film about Ebola, *Outbreak* (1995), bowed in American theaters.

5. "Oubliette" (Season Three): On October 1, 1993, a twelve-year-old girl and resident of Petaluma, California, Polly Klaas, was kidnapped out of her suburban bedroom at knifepoint and in the presence of friends attending a sleepover, by Richard Allen Davis. An APB was sent out, but Klaas was murdered, and her case was featured on such prominent news programs of the day as ABC's *20/20* and Fox's *America's Most Wanted.*

"Oubliette," a third-season episode of *The X-Files,* involves a very similar case, of a fifteen-year-old girl abducted from her bedroom by a psychopath. With the help of Mulder, Scully, and a previous kidnapping victim, the girl is returned to her family alive.

6. "Nisei" (Season Four): Once considered as important to UFO studies as the Zapruder film was to JFK assassination research, the strange, ostensibly "real" film featured in *Alien Autopsy: Fact or Fiction?* proved a cause célèbre of the 1990s. The footage is now known to be a hoax, though its originator continues to term it a reconstruction of a film that has degraded. Fox aired the footage as part of a "documentary special" on August 28, 1995, and it drew high audience numbers.

In *The X-Files,* "Nisei" involves the recovery of a similar alien autopsy video and leads Mulder and Scully deeper into the mysteries of the conspiracy.

7. "The Field Where I Died" (Season Four): One of the key events of the 1990s involving distrust of the federal government occurred on April 19, 1993. In Waco, Texas, agents for the FBI and ATF launched a raid against David Koresh's (1959–1993) ranch, the location of the Branch Davidian cult. Koresh was a charismatic leader who believed he possessed the gift of prophecy and was wanted by authorities for violations of firearm laws. Over time, there were also allegations that Koresh had abused children and broken Texas law regarding statutory rape. After a fifty-one-day standoff, Attorney General Janet Reno gave the order to attack the ranch, and seventy six deaths, including those of Koresh and seventeen children, resulted.

On *The X-Files,* "The Field Where I Died" features many similarities with the events at Waco in 1993. Here, a cult leader named Vernon Ephesian, at a ranch called "The Temple of the Seven Stars," is wanted for hording weapons, and the FBI and ATF stand ready to attack his compound. Vernon is actually David Koresh's birth name, which he changed in 1990. Similarly, Ephesian in the episode is suspected of abusing children in his religious sect. Finally, the FBI siege in the episode ends in tragedy, but not fire. Instead, Ephesian and his followers drink poison, much like the Jonestown cult members did in 1978.

8. "Unrequited" (Season Four): In July 1991, *Newsweek* published a story about American POWS still being held in Vietnam, decades after the end of the Vietnam War. The story merited the cover of the magazine, and the headline read: "A Generation After Vietnam, the Families Refuse to Give Up, Despite a Trail of Hoaxes and Broken Dreams." Later in the same decade, Russian Federation president Boris Yeltsin reported publicly that American POWs had been transferred to the Soviet Union and work camps following the end of the war in the 1970s, and that there had been a cover-up.

The *X-Files* episode "Unrequited" involves this very issue, the plight of soldiers still unaccounted for and forgotten by their country. One such soldier, who has learned from the Viet Cong how to camouflage himself from the human eye, sets about murdering the army officials who have covered up and buried the truth.

9. "Drive" (Season Six): In 1993, the U.S. Air Force, U.S. Navy, University of Alaska, and DARPA (Defense Advanced Research Projects Agency, a division of DOD) combined to form Project HAARP (High Frequency Active Auroral Research Program), which could generate low-frequency radio waves, either pulsed or continuous. The goal was to use the ionosphere to enhance communication and surveillance technology. Conspiracy theorists soon came to blame HAARP and its antenna arrays for the symptoms of Gulf War Syndrome and even the crash of TWA Flight 800 in 1996.

On *The X-Files*, the sixth-season episode "Drive," by Vince Gilligan involves a man, Crump, adversely affected by a project much like HAARP that emits low-frequency radio waves. In the episode, Crump hijacks Mulder and a car and stages a car chase, not unlike the O. J. Simpson car chase of 1994, as well.

10. "Sein und Zeit"/"Closure" (Season Seven): One of the most famous murder cases of the 1990s involves JonBenet Ramsey (1990–1996), a Boulder, Colorado, child beauty pageant winner. On Christmas night, 1996, she disappeared, and her parents found a bizarre ransom note explaining her vanishing. Eight hours later, her corpse was found in her house. The child died from skull fracture and asphyxiation, and her parents and even her older brother were later considered suspects both by the local police and in the ensuing media frenzy. The case remains unsolved to this day.

"Sein und Zeit" features several points in common with the famous murder case. The episode involves the death of a young girl, Amber Lynn LaPierre, but offers a supernatural explanation for her death. As in the Ramsey case, a ransom note plays an important role, and the episode visualizes it being written by Amber Lynn's mother, Billie (Shareene Mitchell). The ransom note begins with the same words as does the one found on the Ramsey premises: "Listen carefully!"

In the case of *The X-Files*, however, the story suggests a not entirely unhappy ending for the child. Amber Lynn is whisked away under supernatural auspices because of the suffering she will later endure on the mortal coil. Surprisingly, this fate connects to Samantha Mulder's final disposition.

27

Ghosts in the Machine?

Notable Guest Stars on *The X-Files*

The X-Files featured literally thousands of guest stars during its nine-year run on Fox. Many guest stars went on to fame after their appearances on the series. Others were already established stars when they appeared and desired to be on the hit series because of its artistry and success in the pop culture.

Below is a list of some of the most prominent guest performers:

Season One

- Seth Green ("Deep Throat")
- Donal Logue ("Squeeze")
- Xander Berkeley ("Ice")
- Felicity Huffman ("Ice")
- Susanna Thompson ("Space")
- Mark Sheppard ("Fire")
- Amanda Pays ("Fire")
- Brad Dourif ("Beyond the Sea")
- Callum Keith Rennie ("Lazarus")
- Michael Horse ("Shapes")
- Titus Welliver ("Darkness Falls")

Season Two

- William Sanderson ("Blood")
- Tony Todd ("Sleepless")
- Steve Railsback ("Duane Barry"/"Ascension")
- Leland Orser ("Firewalker")

- Shawnee Smith ("Firewalker")
- Terry O'Quinn ("Aubrey")
- Morgan Woodward ("Aubrey")
- Brian Thompson ("Colony"/"End Game")
- Lance Guest ("Fearful Symmetry")
- John Savage ("Dod Kolm")
- Vincent Schiavelli ("Humbug")
- Tony Shalhoub ("Soft Light")

Season Three

- Walter Gotell ("Paper Clip")
- Giovanni Ribisi ("D.P.O.")
- Jack Black ("D.P.O.")
- Peter Boyle ("Clyde Bruckman's Final Repose")
- Ken Foree ("The List")
- J. T. Walsh ("The List")
- Bokeem Woodbine ("The List")
- Willie Garson ("The Walk")
- Jewel Staite ("Oubliette")
- Michael Berryman ("Revelations")
- R. Lee Ermey ("Revelations")
- Tyler Labine ("War of the Coprophages")
- Kurtwood Smith ("Grotesque")
- Lucy Liu ("Hell Money")
- Charles Nelson Reilly ("Jose Chung's from Outer Space")
- Jesse Ventura ("Jose Chung's from Outer Space")
- Alex Trebek ("Jose Chung's from Outer Space")

Season Four

- Roy Thinnes ("Herrenvolk")
- Carl Lumbly ("Teliko")
- Zakes Mokae ("Teliko")
- Fritz Weaver ("Terma")
- Tom Noonan ("Paper Hearts")
- Ruben Blades ("El Mundo Gira")
- Raymond Cruz ("El Mundo Gira")
- Jodie Foster ("Never Again") (voice only)
- David Groh ("Kaddish")
- Darin Morgan ("Small Potatoes")

Season Five

- Richard Belzer ("Unusual Suspects")
- Jerry Springer ("The Post-Modern Prometheus")
- Katharine Isabelle ("Schizogeny")
- Luke Wilson ("Bad Blood")
- Darren McGavin ("Travelers")
- Lili Taylor ("Mind's Eye")

Season Six

- Bryan Cranston ("Drive")
- Michael McKean ("Dreamland")
- Nora Dunn ("Dreamland")
- Ed Asner ("How the Ghosts Stole Christmas")
- Lily Tomlin ("How the Ghosts Stole Christmas")
- Bruce Campbell ("Terms of Endearment")
- Victoria Jackson ("Rain King")
- Darren E. Burrows ("Monday")
- Andrew Robinson ("Alpha")
- John Hawkes ("Milagro")
- M. Emmet Walsh ("The Unnatural")
- Jesse L. Martin ("The Unnatural")

Season Seven

- Lance Henriksen ("Millennium")
- Willie Garson ("The Goldberg Variation")
- Shia LaBeouf ("The Goldberg Variation")
- Ricky Jay ("The Amazing Maleeni")
- Kim Darby ("Sein und Zeit")
- Stacy Haiduk ("All Things")
- Tobin Bell ("Brand X")
- Garry Shandling ("Hollywood A.D.")
- Tea Leoni ("Hollywood A.D.")
- Kathy Griffin ("Fight Club")
- Will Sasso ("Je Souhaite")

Season Eight

- Joe Morton ("Redrum")
- Danny Trejo ("Redrum")
- James Franco ("Surekill")
- Deep Roy ("Badlaa")
- Judson Scott ("This Is Not Happening")
- Miguel Sandoval ("Vienen")
- Denise Crosby ("Essence")

Season Nine

- Jame Remar ("Daemonicus")
- Aaron Paul ("Lord of the Flies")
- Jane Lynch ("Lord of the Flies")
- Burt Reynolds ("Improbable")
- David Faustino ("Sunshine Days")

28

The *X-Files* Feature Films

The X-Files: Fight the Future (1998), *I Want to Believe* (2008), *The X-Files III*

Fight the Future (1998)

Written by Chris Carter and Frank Spotniz. Directed by Rob Bowman.

Now reassigned off the X-Files, Mulder (Duchovny) and Scully (Anderson) fail to stop an apparent terrorist bombing near a Federal Building in Dallas, Texas, and are disciplined by the FBI for their actions. To clear their names, the partners begin their own, unsanctioned investigation, using information from conspiracy theorist Dr. Alvin Kurtzweil (Martin Landau) as a starting point. Mulder learns that the building bombed had a FEMA (Federal Emergency Management Act) office inside and that the global conspiracy was hiding evidence there, evidence it desperately wanted destroyed.

Following Kurtzweil's trail, Mulder and Scully gather evidence about the existence of an extraterrestrial virus, one that may be transmitted to transgenic corn through pollinating bees. Meanwhile, the Well-Manicured Man (John Neville), a member of the Syndicate, informs Mulder that the group has been duped for decades. For years, it has been preparing for the enslavement of the human race during alien colonization. But after the unintended release of the virus in West Texas, the shadowy group has learned that humans will not be slaves but rather "digestives" used in a gestation process, one that will almost instantaneously repopulate the planet with aliens.

When Mulder and Scully learn too much, the Cigarette Smoking Man sees to it that Scully is infected with an alien disease. She is transported to a top-secret facility in Antarctica with other infected citizens. Desperate, Mulder follows her, equipped with a weak antidote provided by the Well-Manicured Man. . . .

Produced during the hiatus between the fourth and fifth seasons of the hit Fox series, and set in the continuity between the fifth and sixth seasons, the feature film *The X-Files: Fight the Future* proved one of the blockbusters of the summer of 1998, earning close to $200 million worldwide during its theatrical engagement.

Creatively and artistically, the first *X-Files* film represents a careful and deliberate expansion of the values featured regularly on the television series. The mythology or Mytharc is deepened and more thoroughly explored, and the action and horror sequences presented are even more spectacular in scope and execution. Yet despite the larger canvas, the film thrives upon an intimate story of two people, Mulder and Scully, bound to each other even in the face of strange and horrifying events and official condemnation.

A Mytharc film through and through, *The X-Files: Fight the Future* moves cleanly, transparently, and with focus. One lengthy scene, set inside a limousine prowling the streets of nighttime Washington, D.C., explains, in broad strokes, the outline of the franchise's entire mythology. This setting is appropriate, because visually *Fight the Future* makes the case for two Washingtons, or two Americas: one of glittering white, high-minded, immaculate values, represented by visuals of the Capitol Dome, and one of dark, seedy alleys under the shadow of that dome, where deals are made, confidences traded, and fates dispensed.

Like many great *X-Files* installments, *Fight the Future*'s narrative stems from a real-life incident with conspiratorial overtones. In this case, that event is the Oklahoma City bombing at the Alfred P. Murrah Federal Building on April 19, 1995. Over 160 people, including 3 pregnant women and 6 children, were killed in that act of domestic terrorism. The culprit was Timothy McVeigh, a right-wing militia sympathizer and Gulf War Veteran who was angry about the federal government's actions at Ruby Ridge during the first Bush administration and with the Waco siege during the Clinton administration. His target, the Murrah Building, housed offices of the ATF, FBI, DEA, and Secret Service. In addition to the fatalities incurred, the bombing injured over 700 people and did half a billion dollars of damage, and was timed on the anniversary of Waco in hopes of making a political statement. But as with any assassination or terrorist attack in American history, the Oklahoma City bombing quickly became the hub of conspiracy theories. Some people insisted that McVeigh was a patsy for Middle East terrorists, and others insisted that the bombing was a false flag operation—executed by the federal government—designed to tighten laws against terrorist attacks, and a response to the growing danger of right wing extremism. Even two decades later, the matter has not been resolved to everyone's satisfaction. In 2014, an

In *The X-Files: Fight the Future,* Mulder and Scully confront the truth about alien invasion in a remote cornfield in Texas.

attorney, Jesse Trentadue, claimed that the FBI was hiding surveillance video of the bombing which proved that McVeigh did not act alone.

Many familiar details of the Oklahoma City bombing were recreated for *Fight the Future.* In this case, FEMA, not the FBI or DEA, has an office in the demolished building, and similarly, domestic terrorism is pinpointed as the cause. The events have been moved next door, from Oklahoma to Texas, to Dallas. And Dallas, of course, is a city with a historical association with conspiracies as well because of the JFK assassination in November 1963. This fact is alluded to in the film when Kurtzweil informs Mulder that the men behind the bombing, whom he describe as "patriots," "knew their away around Dallas." If he is alluding to the Cigarette Smoking Man, he is accurate, since the fourth-season story "Musings of a Cigarette Smoking Man" positions CSM as the assassin in Dealey Plaza in Dallas.

But the point is that *Fight the Future* spins its narrative of conspiracies and secrets from a presumed terrorist attack, much like one that occurred in real life. For some, the connection to reality seemed like too much. Roger Ebert, in his (positive) review of the film, for instance, complained about a shot of the ruined building, noting that "it could have been removed from the film with absolutely no loss." Yet importantly, *The X-Files* is a franchise that gains legitimacy and validity by connecting to the facts of our world. The franchise takes mysteries, conspiracies, and ideas from our reality and spins them into science fiction and horror tales. If you don't have reality or the semblance of reality as a starting point, you don't have the grounding, the belief that the franchise boasts a sense of verisimilitude.

Beyond the ripped-from-the-headlines premise, *X-Files: Fight the Future* proves remarkably intriguing and quite different from the series in terms of its visual flourishes. For instance, night-time Washington, D.C., is practically a character in this film. Martin Landau's character is seen mostly outdoors, in alleyways or on dark streets. We never meet him in an office or other official place, though at one point he meets Mulder in a bar. The overall impression is of a thriving and opaque shadow world, on the street level, with which Mulder intersects. There's a seamy, informal aspect to this world. And yet, hanging over this shadow society is that aforementioned shining white ideal, the American Capitol dome. In at least two separate shots, the dome is seen gleaming in the night, above the landscape, above street level. The dome represents, architecturally, the American dream of representative government for the people and by the people. The street, however, is a different story, with figures of mystery and mischief, like the Well-Manicured Man and Kurtzweil peddling secrets, lies, and hidden truths.

At the end of the film, Mulder and Scully recommit to their partnership, and the X-Files are reopened. The film provides a kind of visual catharsis for this concept. Mulder is seen sitting near a body of placid water, hence the cleansing or washing-away symbolism, and the lighting scheme is almost golden, as his belief—his passion to learn the truth—is rekindled. This is the end of a long arc from the fifth season, about his doubt and disbelief in his life's work. Those qualities have now been restored, and the images suggest that. The *X-Files* TV series is dominated by dynamic visuals and film grammar, and the movie absorbs that tradition and takes it to the next, grander level that only a theatrical experience can provide.

Other visuals are just as canny, and cleverly constructed. For instance, when Scully collapses on the floor in Mulder's apartment after being stung by a bee, the film provides a clear image of the floor's texture. It is a series of small hexagons or honeycombs. This befits the circumstances, both of the source of her infection (a bee) and her eventual disposition, in a vast alien breeding chamber or hive of sorts, in Antarctica. It's a small touch but again, a resonant one.

Fight the Future also transmits a powerful message about teamwork and the power of a partnership through a unique and memorable visual comparison. On one level, *The X-Files* franchise involves the conspiratorial nature of reality. Two or more people gather and secrets are forged, agendas are hatched. It seems to be human nature that when people seeking power congregate, transparency and honesty are the first casualties. And yet the franchise provides a counterbalance to that idea in the partnership, the give-and-take, of Scully and Mulder. They are the antidote to those who seek to hide their agenda. Together, they ferret out the truth. And the great hope of the human race is that in every epoch, every age, someone steps up to "fight the future" arranged by entrenched, corrupt power. In Watergate, we had the partnership of Woodward and Bernstein, for instance. This idea is represented beautifully by the first feature film because of its picturesque prologue, which is set in the Ice Age, 35,000 years ago.

The film's inaugural image, after the opening credits, is of two figures—cavemen—running across a bleak landscape in 35,000 BC. They run near one another, side by side, and explore a dark cave together. They carry torches and clearly are a team. They are the Stone Age versions of Mulder and Scully, working in tandem, confronting a mystery and lighting the darkness, though with torches instead of Mulder and Scully's trademark flashlights. The search for the truth goes back to the dawn of time and then, as now, was a joint effort, a matter of teamwork and the balancing of skills. *Fight the Future*'s visually dazzling opening sequence conveys the idea that though the alien conspiracy and virus may go back to prehistory, so does man's desire to light the darkness and discover the truth.

Another leitmotif in *Fight the Future* involves Scully and Mulder's very different ways of doing things, despite their teamwork. Scully relies on categorized facts and figures. She uses statistics and knowledge as a springboard for her understanding of new variables. Mulder, by contrast, discusses "hunches." This discussion is shorthand for their differences as investigators, but also of their strengths. Yet each must come face to face in the film with the limitations of their unique approach. Scully eventually believes she has only held Mulder back with her reliance on facts and figures. Mulder believes, contrarily, that Scully has "saved" him by making him do the hard work of explaining and evidencing his hunches. The film is very much about the way these two personalities, as a team, complete one another. Taken in tandem with the cavemen team imagery visualized in the film's opening scene, it is not a stretch to view *Fight the Future* as a treatise on successful teamwork. The twin worldviews of Mulder and Scully, seen since the pilot episode in 1993, are, in and of themselves, incomplete. But together, they are more than each.

Fight the Future is a sprawling, exciting addition to the *X-Files* canon, and it performs the remarkable feat of seeming in tune with the TV series, even as it operates on a grander canvas. The film fits flawlessly between seasons five and six, and yet does not play like simply a magnified TV show. On the contrary, *Fight the Future* contextualizes Scully and Mulder's partnership in terms of history and prehistory, reminding us that every era needs its crusaders and that different crusaders bring different skill sets to the table, to the benefit of all. Furthermore, the film sets Scully and Mulder's odyssey in a city of rain, a city of labyrinthine alleys and byways, and validates their fight, at least imagery-wise, with the symbols of democratic Americana, like the Capitol, the symbol that suggests that things need not be this way. *Fight the Future* reminds Mulder and Scully what they are fighting for and who they are fighting for. Sharply written and cannily visualized, the first feature film showcases the possibilities of the franchise beyond the confines of your television set.

The X-Files: I Want to Believe (2008)

Written and Directed by Chris Carter.

Picking up six years after their flight from the FBI. Mulder and Scully are living together in a small but comfortable house in Virginia. Mulder has grown a beard and retreated from the world. Despite the fact he knows his sister is dead, he has not given up searching for "the truth" about what happened to her. Meanwhile, Scully is a medical doctor at a Catholic hospital and enmeshed in the treatment of a very sick little boy, Christian; one with a terminal illness.

It's a quiet, relatively normal life, but that normality is shattered when the FBI solicits Mulder's help in solving a new and urgent X-File in return for a full pardon. An FBI agent named Monica Bannon has disappeared in the snows of gloomy West Virginia, and a fallen priest named Father Joe (Billy Connolly) claims to be experiencing psychic visions related to her case. In fact, he leads a team of FBI searchers to a burial ground of body parts in a vast, foreboding ice field. But Father Joe may not be credible because of his criminal past as a convicted pedophile. Mulder and Scully each have a different perspective on Father Joe, and their viewpoints are so contradictory that they threaten to fracture their now-long-standing emotional relationship. This case revives Mulder's obsessive, brooding nature, and it reminds Scully of the darkness she has sought long and hard to escape.

When another victim is abducted after an excursion swimming at a local gym, Mulder follows the clues to a strange compound in the middle of nowhere, where a mad Russian scientist is conducting an experiment in life prolongation that involves the transplantation of human heads. When Mulder goes missing, Scully seeks the help of an old friend to help find him. . . .

The second *X-Files* film, 2008's *I Want to Believe,* was met with largely negative reviews in the summer of that season, though some critics, including the late Roger Ebert, praised the film.

Why was the film met with such hostility? In part, perhaps, because *I Want to Believe* features a stand-alone story that does not include aliens or the next iteration of the Mytharc. And in part, perhaps, because of another shift in the American culture. Many who had become so-called movie critics by 2008 were simply disgruntled fanboys, not paid newspaper or magazine critics. Many of them were still gunning, apparently, for *The X-Files* as a response to what they viewed as its poor last few seasons, or they were more enthusiastic about big-budget superhero blockbusters like *The Dark Knight.*

In this case, however, the critical response was not only hostile and out of proportion but dead wrong. *The X-Files: I Want to Believe* remains an intimate, cerebral thriller, one that explores human nature and the concept of redemption. Although the film is in no way a big-event summer tent-pole, it is extremely well written and well directed. Carter deploys crosscutting at crucial points in the film to generate tension and suggest under-the-surface connections between characters and events. A dark thriller, *I Want to Believe* is a monster-of-the-week story brought to the screen with flair and distinction. It's a shame so many critics reviewed it on the basis of what the film is not about, rather than based on the virtues it so skillfully transmits.

Redemption is the notion that burns at the heart of *I Want to Believe.* Mulder is offered redemption in the same sense as he was in such series episodes as "Oubliette" and "Mind's Eye." He believes that if he rescues one imperiled woman, he will be making up for the loss of Samantha. Scully is seeking redemption here in a sense, too. She gave up her child, William, near the end of the series and clearly regrets doing so. At one point, Christian's mother tells her that Scully can't understand her feelings because she is "not a mother," and that comment is like a knife right to Scully's heart. If Scully can save Christian, she makes up for losing William.

But *I Want to Believe* proved controversial because it does more than pay lip service to the idea of redemption. Redemption is not just for "good" people like Mulder and Scully, the film suggests. It is also for men who have done very, very bad things. There's nothing comfortable or easy about how this film portrays the central moral dilemma. The crimes Father Joe committed against innocent children are utterly monstrous, as Scully rightly points out. Father Joe knows that society will never forgive him but wonders if God can do so. And this is where things get murky: Father Joe has taken actions that suggest he is repentant. He castrated himself at age twenty-six in order to "kill" the horrible, seething appetite that led him to commit such crimes. And in 2008, he chooses to live in a group home for pedophiles, one where sex offenders live in shame and police each other's behavior. It is a sort of hell on Earth to live amongst such scum, especially for a man of God.

The problem, of course, is that Father Joe claims he is experiencing psychic visions about that missing FBI agent. He says he wants to help the police find her. Is he to be trusted? Is he actually responsible, in some way, for her disappearance? Would the Divine empower a man like Father Joe with second sight? And if his visions are real, are they from God? The Devil?

These questions take us right back to the first season of *The X-Files* and Luther Lee Boggs, the serial killer in "Beyond the Sea," who is name-checked in the film. The underlying moral quandary there and here revolves around redemption: What great "right" can undo a great "wrong"? In the noble spirit of *The X-Files,* Scully and Mulder view Father Joe and his predicament in radically different ways. The series always concerned the opposing viewpoints of these two characters and how their beliefs and biases shaped their perception of reality. It's the same thing here. Scully believes Father Joe is a depraved, attention-seeking monster, that his visions are a hoax and a cry for attention. Mulder wants to believe that men like Father Joe *can* change, that redemption is possible, and that Father Joe's psychic visions are legitimate. Father Joe's inclusion and role in the story are a courageous choice on the part of writers Spotnitz and Carter because the film's central dilemma makes audiences confront the idea of real redemption in a very tangible, very challenging, very realistic way. It is easy to forgive someone who seems heroic, someone who is beautiful, or someone who had an excuse for what he did. But what about forgiving someone for committing the worst crime (a crime against a child) imaginable?

I'm not saying you *should* forgive; that anyone should forgive. However, if you are not willing to forgive Father Joe, there are repercussions to that decision. The biggest one is that you can't claim you believe in redemption, can you? If you don't let "good works" account for something in the cosmic tally of morality, you can't claim you believe in forgiveness, either. Nor can you claim to be a Christian, because forgiveness is the very crucible—the beating heart—of Christianity. So how can Scully not at least attempt to forgive him?

I'm not condoning any particular interpretation of Father Joe's deeds, just commenting on the moral implications of this film. *I Want to Believe* challenges long-held beliefs and forces audiences to evaluate what they believe when the decision to forgive is not easy, not superficial. *The X-Files: I Want to Believe* effectively holds a mirror up to all those who claim belief in Christ's teachings yet actually thrive on hate and draconian notions of punishment and morality. In doing so, it comments explicitly on our times; an epoch when religion is often used to codify hatred of "the other" in our society (and in other societies). This paradigm—this Father Joe Dilemma—is thus true to everything *The X-Files* has always been about.

Father Joe's crimes are not candy-coated, either, and that's a crucial distinction. The psychic web he experiences in the film arises in part because he is connected, terribly, to one of the perpetrators. The man who is dying and needs a transplant is one of the altar boys, grown up, whom he molested all those years ago. Father Joe's crimes have thus taken on a murderous life of their own, spreading like a cancer into other lives, and that's a strong metaphor for the impact of child abuse. Is it God's punishment that Joe should see, without blinking, the monstrous crimes of a man he hurt so tragically, or is it God's wisdom, allowing for the possibility of Joe's redemption?

The role that the Divine may play in the world of man is a crucial aspect of *I Want to Believe,* and it too is in keeping with *The X-Files'* deep sense of spirituality. The search for the truth on the series has always been the search for ultimate knowledge, for the truth of human existence, especially in terms of spiritual ideas like the soul and immortality. This notion is expressed in one leitmotif that affects all the characters. Father Joe tells Scully "don't give up" at one juncture.

As Father Joe himself readily admits, he has no reason to have said this to Scully, but it is a turn of phrase with deeper meaning and a valuable shorthand for the film's central conceit. Scully can't give up on the boy she is treating now because of the little boy (William) she once gave up on. Mulder can't give up either, because it would discredit Samantha's sacrifice. Father Joe can't give up either, if he is truly a man of God. He has done horrible things, but if he gives up, if he doesn't try, his epitaph will be that of an evil man.

Finally, even the villain of the film, played by Callum Keith Rennie, is contextualized in terms of his refusal to give up. He will do anything, beyond reason, beyond sanity, to save the life of his lover, the former altar boy. In this case, refusal to give up involves murder and the most bizarre type of transplant surgery imaginable. These plots rub up against each other and create tension in *I Want to Believe,* but are unified by that simple phrase "don't give up." Is it synchronicity, fate, or the hand of God that joins all the characters in this mystery and in a very similar journey?

"I always said that the film was really a multi-layered love story," Carter has said. "There was the love between Mulder and Scully. Then there was the Russian character who had been collecting these body parts, and his love for his partner. So the love stories reflected each other."

The "don't give up" refrain in the film also concerns another theme, how we seek to bury or cleanse a difficult past. The criminals responsible for Bannon's abduction attempt to bury the past and their crimes in the ice. But along comes Father Joe—a man with a past anyone would want to hide—who instead focuses on digging up the past . . . digging in the ice, in the snow, literally. Things keep coming to the surface. Things that must be dealt with. The presence of Father Joe in the narrative makes this cleansing possible. He has done horrible things, but in his search for redemption, he helps Scully and Mulder confront things about their own lives and pasts, too.

I Want to Believe's central mystery, which concerns severed body parts and weird scientific experimentation, has divided some critics and viewers, but it too is very much in keeping with *The X-Files'* history. The series always concerned our two worldviews, embodied in Scully and Mulder, vetting mysterious "horror stories" and in the process giving them new life and energy. Spontaneous combustion, demonic possession, ESP, vampires, golems, out-of-body experiences, and other old genre concepts were always repurposed so the series could incorporate the latest advances in paranormal and medical literature, or the latest cultural "moment." *I Want to Believe* writes the next chapter in that tradition with a plot concerning organ transplants, stem cell research, and a cadre of outlaw Russian scientists playing Frankenstein. Critics deemed the plot ridiculous (while also praising the hell out of *The Dark Knight,* a movie about a man who dresses up like a bat), but as Chris Carter has pointed out, his story is actually based in fact. "I had run across something on the Internet," he told me, "A Russian doctor creating two-headed dogs. I mean, he was really doing this, creating two-headed monsters. It's a Frankenstein story, yet nobody really reviewed it as a kind of modern Frankenstein story."

A low-budget film, *The X-Files: I Want to Believe,* is a rarity in the sense that it doesn't use special effects or digital imagery to dramatize its story. Instead, Carter—ever the visual storyteller—uses the film language grammar of crosscutting to explore Father Joe's psychic abilities. At its core, the paranormal, at least as it applies to precognition, ESP, and telepathy, is about forging a connection between things that we don't, in normal everyday reality, intrinsically see as connected. Carter utilizes the tool of crosscutting to make those instantaneous connections for the audience.

The film crosscuts from the assault on Monica Bannon to the beautifully photographed search for her body on a lonely ice field. The connection is one of cause and effect (one action makes the other action a reality), but more than that, the instantaneous knowledge of "what happened" as it seems to be happening. And again, that's a good explanation or visual signifier for psychic powers. Over and over in the film, crosscutting suggests instantaneous knowledge of that which could not be known by normal means, and suggests Father Joe's capacities, his dark past, and his shot at redemption.

The violent scenes in this film are tense. The bleak locale and the hidden secrets there keep audiences alert, seeking clues amidst the ubiquitous falling snow. The location and its visual snow blindness reflect the dark, conflicted heart of the characters, and the final moment (postcredits) is a splendid catharsis, another aspect of the aforementioned "cleansing" leitmotif, and a release from the blinding white snow of Somerset, West Virginia.

More emotionally touching than exciting, more moody and lugubrious than spectacular, more contemplative than action-packed, more dark and foreboding than shocking, this is an uneasy, unsettling, intimate *X-Files* movie in which the truth isn't "out there" but rather "in here," in us. In the endless mysteries of the human heart and human behavior.

The X-Files III?

One of the most commonly asked questions among fans is, simply, is there going to be a third *X-Files* feature film? The answer to that question has changed somewhat over the years. As all X-Philes are aware, the series lore suggests that alien colonization was slated for 2012, the year the Mayan calendar ended. In real life, we are now well beyond that time benchmark, however, and so a Mytharc story will have to account for that fact.

At the time of this book's writing, this much is known: David Duchovny, Gillian Anderson, and Chris Carter have all expressed desire and interest to create a third film, one that involves the next phase of the Mytharc or conspiracy. All these talents are waiting on 20th Century-Fox to give *The X-Files III* the green light. When I spoke to Chris Carter at the end of 2009 and asked him if the second film, *I Want to Believe*, had made enough money to ensure a sequel, he answered: "I wouldn't use the word ensure. But because of the business the movie did, especially the international business, it is a possibility."

In terms of what a third movie would involve, it is all speculation at this point. Carter has reported at various public appearances that Mulder is not using social media (for fear of being monitored by dark forces) but is making a living as a magician, whereas Scully is still a medical doctor. Similarly, he described the core idea of the film as "just you wait" as opposed to the second film's mantra "don't give up."

In early 2015, a film sequel, *The X-Files III* was put on hold, as Fox TV instead green-lit a new *X-Files* limited TV series, to consist of six hour-long episodes to air in 2016. David Duchovny, Gillian Anderson, and Chris Carter are all signed for the project. This means, of course, that *The X-Files* is back. If the limited series is a success, it may spawn a sequel, theatrical or televised.

The Other TV Programs of Chris Carter

Millennium (1996–1999), *Harsh Realm* (1999–2000), *The Lone Gunmen* (2001), and *The After* (2014)

During and after *The X-Files'* nearly decade-long broadcast TV run, Chris Carter created and produced other science fiction, horror, and fantasy series, too. Many of these programs have attained great popularity, as well as critical acclaim.

Millennium (1996–1999)

Chris Carter's second TV series, *Millennium* (1996–1999), premiered on October 25, 1996, with a stunning pilot by Carter and visually dynamic direction by David Nutter The ensuing series ran for three seasons on Fox in prime time. The series didn't quite reach the year 2000, and yet *Millennium* remains a gold standard in terms of its procedural format and its subject matter, and thus an authentic high point of the horror genre in the medium of television.

Millennium is the story of Frank Black, played by Lance Henriksen. Black is a middle-aged family man, retired FBI agent, and behavior psychologist who has suffered a nervous breakdown after many years getting inside the heads of serial killers. Now, following that breakdown, he takes his family to Seattle and agrees to consult for the Millennium Group on the toughest cases. Frank's investigations, which often serve as descents into the utter depths of human madness and ugliness, are contrasted on *Millennium* with the beatific, idyllic scenes of his family life. He, his wife Catherine (Meghan Gallagher), and daughter Jordan (Brittany Tiplady) live in a beautiful yellow house and

Millennium starred Lance Henriksen as criminal profiler Frank Black.

attempt to carve out an existence far from the dark world of Frank's profession.

In a very substantial way, *Millennium* is an extension and development of the idea in *The X-Files* that "monsters" dwell within as well as outside the human race. Early *X-Files* stories like "Irresistible" and "Grotesque" represent strong influences in the story of Frank Black as he attempts to contend not just with serial killers but with the increasing strangeness of the Group, which, as the series goes on, is revealed to be more a quasireligious cult than an agency concerned strictly with law enforcement. The Group is obsessed with the year 2000, what it believes will be the end of the world at that time. *The X-Files'* seventh-season story "Millennium" wraps up this plot strand and brings Frank's story to a completion of sorts.

The setup of *Millennium,* with Frank attempting to preserve the world of his yellow house by hunting down monsters, is an uncommonly complex and symbolic one, and yet also incredibly beautiful. As Chris Carter told me, the series "came out of the bigger concept of a guy who was trying to paint away the darkness. I had worked on *X-Files* for three to four years at that point, and we were dealing with some very dark subject matter. After a while—after writing about that dark subject matter and realizing how powerful it can really be—you try to come up with remedies, *yourself,* for the darkness. It's not always fun to write about the darkness."

In other words, Frank's yellow house was a refuge for Carter as well as for Black. "It was," Carter concurs. "And it's funny, when I look back at *Millennium* now, I think, in a way the concept was actually too complex. Especially when I look at shows that have become hits, like *CSI* or other procedurals. They don't deal with ideas like the yellow house. They don't deal with things like family, necessarily."

Carter's perception is right, but that complexity is what captured the hearts and minds of so many fans. Other TV series have since stripped *Millennium* down to its component parts, divvying up the formula into paranormal procedurals like *Medium* or *Ghost Whisperer,* stressing the forensic angle, like the *CSI* franchise, or developing the serial killer angle, like *Criminal Minds.*

Frank's yellow house represents something beyond a formula, beyond a cops-and-serial-killer mentality. Viewers associate yellow with brightness and with light, like that of the sun. The yellow house similarly represents Frank Black's only bright place away from the darkness, the horror that he witnesses on the job, and even within the recesses of his own mind. Rewardingly, *Millennium* utilizes the recurring symbol of the yellow house in a variety of stimulating ways over its run. It doesn't always mean the same thing.

In the series' first season, for instance, the house is seen as a place of safety for the Blacks, a sanctuary from the world. In the second season, it becomes a representation of *paradise lost* and the object of the heroic quest when Frank is literally banished from it because he and Catherine have separated. His purpose in life becomes reclaiming the yellow house and what it once represented: the wholeness of his family.

In the third and final season, Frank's yellow house is but a sad memory, but one that remains intact inside the recesses of his mind. He visits his former home in the episode "The Sound of Snow," and it has been painted white by new owners. Still, the ever-perceptive Frank envisions his Camelot, his yellow home in Seattle. Frank's house is now an ideal, not a real place, one representative of a specific time and feeling.

One might suggest that the yellow house of *Millennium* also represents an escape from evil, "the painting away of the darkness," as Chris Carter beautifully described it, and yet it is also the reason why Frank faces the heart of human darkness every day. By facing the dark inside and out, Frank preserves the yellow, inside and out. The two are interconnected in some significant way. The house is part of Frank's yin and yang.

The yellow house could also symbolize, on a more basic level, small-town America circa 1996. Frank must rescue it from the encroaching evil. Thus the yellow home is not merely beautiful in an architectural sense, it is a brilliant symbol because it shares with viewers an insight into Frank's personality and cause. It represents his *interior architecture.* It is the reason he fights and what he fights for, since the yellow represents the sanctuary for his family, for his wife and daughter. We all have a "yellow house" in our minds, whether in our adulthood or as a remembrance of childhood. It is a place of safety, nostalgia, hope, and dreams. In *Millennium,* the yellow house is the center of gravity, the center of Frank's universe.

Millennium proved complex and literate in other ways. Many episodes of *Millennium* open with a white-lettered quotation from a literary or religious source. In short order, the episodes then present a tale that echoes, contrasts, or mirrors that opening selection. Yeats ("Pilot"), Dostoevsky ("Dead Letters"), Melville ("The Judge"), Jean-Paul Sartre ("522666"), Robert Louis Stevenson ("The Well Worn Lock"), Cicero ("Walkabout"), Nietzsche ("Broken World"), William Rose Benét ("The Paper Dove"), and even Shakespeare ("Monster") represent just some of the literary giants and thinkers *Millennium* routinely referenced. The Bible was often mined for pertinent quotations as well.

These opening quotes were not included to be pretentious but to provoke thought and to connect the viewer to the fact that the series concerns our history, our very nature. It's an invigorating purpose and one that reminds authors that there is a direct link between past and present, a universality of the human condition. Accordingly, the situations that Frank Black encounters are situations that Shakespeare or Cicero contemplated, and so these opening quotes remind us of our literary and historical past. And since *Millennium* is, in some ways, about the passage of a thousand years, it's entirely appropriate and even inspired to focus on the link to our shared past. These opening quotations help us contextualize the stories, but also to contextualize Frank's journey in terms of human or at least literary history. He's not just an agent trying to catch a serial killer, he's part of the ebb and flow of human history, doing battle at a vital juncture in such history.

The specter informing so many episodes of *Millennium* is the end of the world itself: *doomsday.* This is a powerful and universal fear because many people suspect that the end will come one day, and perhaps soon. Dinosaurs preceded us here, and now they are extinct. The Roman Empire came and went, a brief candle. The Native American culture that once existed on this land we now inhabit is but a memory too. Time passes, cultures die, life is transitory, and on some subconscious level, all humankind is aware of this fact, of the inevitable changing of the guard. On an individual level, we will each die, and for us, that cessation represents, certainly, the end of the world. Throughout *Millennium*'s canon, the series writers obsessed on the universal human inquietude about our impending ends. Could our demise arrive in a second great flood ("Force Majeure")? Could it involve religion ("Forcing the End") and the Anti-Christ ("Marantha")? Or will our end come from deliberate, blind tinkering with our science, or our very genetic makeup ("Walkabout," "Sense and Antisense")?

The series also looked at ethnic doomsdays ("A Single Blade of Grass"), Y2K fears ("Teotwawki), and one of the best, "Jose Chung's Doomsday Defense," had the audacity to suggest what we've actually seen since *Millennium* was canceled, with the advent of so many damned remakes: a *creative apocalypse.* Written by Darin Morgan, this installment of the series implied that all humans can look forward to for the next thousand years is "the same old crap."

It may seem strange to praise *Millennium* as an inherently optimistic series, considering how obsessively it wonders about the end of the world. Yet, the show features another recurring and potent symbol worth mentioning. That symbol is *the child.* Segment after segment on *Millennium* involves children, and youth in general, because our offspring represent the future. In our children, in our next generation, we see hope and fear, and *Millennium* shares this viewpoint. For instance, in one of the best hours written for any genre show in history, *Millennium* explores a very real "evil" of modern American society: the way in which our culture encourages children to be the same, to conform to expectations, and be "ordinary." That episode, "A Room with No View," concerns a demonic force, Lucy Butler (Sarah Jane Redmond), who captures promising kids. These abducted teenagers have all been voted "most likely to succeed" and are well loved by classmates and parents. There is something almost intangibly special, something attractive, charismatic about each of them. They all have spirit, for lack of a better term.

But in "A Room with No View," our future leaders are captured and tortured until they succumb to the urge to become ordinary, invisible, and corrupt. In this case, *Millennium* views an apocalypse not in some outside force such as a flood but in our inability to inspire and support our children; to let them be who they choose to be. Other episodes also very much involve children. Carter's "The Well Worn Lock" gazes at the terrifying problem of child abuse and how it intersects with politics, while "Monster" gazes at a child who—for inexplicable reasons—is purely and simply evil.

The inspiring story "Luminary" involves a young man who forsakes the material "culture of desire" we've made in the United States and gives up all his belongings and money. He goes to Alaska alone to seek wisdom. When he disappears, Frank must find him. But the very idea of renouncing things, of renouncing material wealth, is a potent idea in *Millennium* (inspired by the story *Into the Wild*), and significantly, it finds purchase in the symbol for our future; in the next generation. Throughout the series, the writers also followed the development and growth of Frank's daughter, Jordan. But importantly, we also witnessed, dynamically, Frank's viewpoint as a parent regarding his daughter and regarding children in general. In the aforementioned "Monster," he delivers an impassioned, heart-wrenching speech about what the arrival of Jordan meant to his life and how it changed him.

Jordan's birth reminded Frank that he did not "manufacture" himself as a grownup, that he too had been a child once. And now he strives to see the child—the potential—in all of us, even the men he hunts. If the serial killers are dark potential realized, then *Millennium* views children as exactly the opposite. The importance of the child (of our tomorrows, essentially) is signified in *Millennium* even in its opening credits, impressively. The image of a young girl is featured as she walks awkwardly across a bridge, in danger of falling. That's the bridge to the future (the twenty-first century), and she will either make the journey intact or plummet to her doom.

Millennium is a highly introspective series, and yet in some way it reads as a little innocent and naive today, following a decade of war, torture, economic calamity, and more. But back before Y2K, before 9/11, before Katrina, the series set up a very specific analogy that America was like something akin to Rome, an empire on the verge of collapse. And the cause of the collapse came from within, from a perversion or "weed" growing up inside our borders and personified by the serial killers of the 1990s. The series brilliantly and quite originally suggested "pathology is part of the grotesque master plan," as Alyssa Katz, wrote in *The Nation* in 1996. The series constantly raised the specter that, as a nation, America was rotting from within, from a kind of inbred decadence. Thus Chris Carter and Frank Spotnitz carefully used the concept of the "serial killer of the week," much like *Star Trek* used the concept of "the civilization of the week." In each new encounter and each new episode, Frank would learn something valuable about himself, and something about the values of his country from the case of a twisted serial killer. This paradigm is evident in "Weeds," "Blood Relatives," "Loin Like a Hunting Flame," and "Wide Open," among others. The idea was that madness had sprouted up in the land, a very specific madness born from "who we are." The series suggested this madness would ultimately be America's downfall. Unless men like Frank could stop it.

It would be impossible to write of *Millennium* without considering the depth that Lance Henriksen brought to the role of Frank Black. The scene I described above in "Monster" is a perfect example. There Henriksen delivers brilliantly a speech about childhood, about the importance of children, about the impact of his child's birth upon his life, and it's absolutely riveting. Suddenly, you're not watching a conventional tale of an evil child; you're watching the story of a human being, of a committed father facing the loss of all that he cares for. The scene is emotional and beautifully performed, and Henriksen accomplished miracles like this on a regular basis.

Millennium was always at its best when it addressed our human fears (about apocalypse, about our culture, about violence) and made us look in the mirror. In the opening credits of the first year, the question "who cares?" would pop up in almost accusing fashion. That was an important matter. *Who cared enough about the world to make it a safer place?* By the third season, the series had formulated carefully its answer to the question "who cares."

The answer came, not surprisingly, from Jordan, from a child. She said "we're all shepherds," meaning it is incumbent on each of us to care how the world turns out, apocalypse or no apocalypse. For three years, despite some format shifts, *Millennium* reminded us, "this is who we are," and in the process gave television one of its legitimate artistic masterpieces, a worthy heir to *The X-Files.*

Harsh Realm (1999–2000)

In 1999, Chris Carter and Ten Thirteen Productions created a third genre series for Fox television called *Harsh Realm.* Based on a comic book from Harris Publishing and James D. Hudnall and Andrew Paquette, the series concerned a virtual reality version of America existing after a terrorist attack on New York City. The series was advertised with the tagline "It's Just a Game."

Unfortunately, only three hour-long episodes of *Harsh Realm* were broadcast before an abrupt cancellation. In all, nine installments were produced. *Harsh Realm*'s abrupt and inconclusive end proved intensely disappointing to the dedicated fans that followed the series on Friday nights at 9:00 p.m., the same time slot that Joss Whedon's *Dollhouse* struggled in nearly a decade later. Viewing numbers were low in terms of network TV expectations, and the series was underpromoted, though *TV Guide* named it one of the best new shows of the year.

Despite that accolade, other critics compared the TV series to the then-recent blockbuster *The Matrix*, which also concerned life in a virtual reality world. Yet *Harsh Realm* was actually produced concurrently with that film and shot on a TV budget in Vancouver, hardly a fair competition then.

Looking back at the series more than a decade later, *Harsh Realm* is constructed on the same sturdy pillars of good storytelling, symbolic representation, strong characters, and dynamic worldview that so ably support *The X-Files* or *Millennium*.

After a brief preamble involving Lt. Thomas Hobbes (Scott Bairstow) on a peacekeeping mission in Sarajevo in 1994, the action in *Harsh Realm* shifts rapidly to Fort Dix, New Jersey, in the year 1999. There a disenchanted Hobbes plans to leave the army permanently in just a few short months. He wants to relocate to California with his beautiful fiancée Sophie (Samantha Mathis). But even as Hobbes plans to start a new life, he is ordered to report to a secretive, white-haired colonel (Lance Henriksen) for a new, classified assignment. Hobbes is escorted to a secret bunker and—after a "final supper"—ordered to "play a game," a virtual reality game called Harsh Realm.

This Harsh Realm game—a simulated war scenario—was created by the Pentagon in 1995. Utilizing information from satellite cartography and the latest U.S. Census, the war gamers have created a duplicate of America, down to every last location, person, and even pet. But there's an important difference between the worlds.

In this virtual version of America, a suitcase nuke was detonated in New York City, in Manhattan, at noon on October 31, 1995, and four million Americans died in 2.5 seconds. The game developers hoped to test American military and civilian peacekeeping capabilities after such a catastrophic terrorist attack, but they never could have anticipated what occurred next. The soldier that the army first sent into the game world, the most decorated veteran in U.S. Army history, Omar Santiago (Terry O'Quinn), took over Harsh Realm. Out of the ashes of the apocalypse, this soldier carved out a brutal military dictatorship for himself. The so-called United States of Santiago now encompasses five states and a great percentage of the Eastern seaboard. Santiago believes "one man can have it all here" and ruthlessly protects his position of authority.

Hobbes's mission is to take out Santiago by any means necessary. He must remove Santiago's virtual avatar from the Harsh Realm simulation and restore freedom to the virtual country. Unfortunately, Hobbes's superiors haven't told him the whole story. He can't return to the real world (and consciousness) until Santiago is dead, and if he dies in the game (or is "digitized"), Hobbes also dies in reality. Worse, Hobbes isn't even the first man to make this attempt to beat Santiago. Literally hundreds of soldiers have gone to Harsh Realm before him, and none have been successful. None have returned. At the conclusion of *Harsh Realm*'s pilot episode, the audience sees a *Raiders of the Lost Ark*-esque shot of all the game players in a hospital room that seems to stretch to infinity.

Back in the real world, Sophie is informed by the army that Hobbes died on a secret mission, but she is soon approached by a beautiful and perhaps treacherous informant, an oracle named Inga Fossa (Sarah-Jane Redmond), and told about a conspiracy of silence. If she wishes to be reunited with the love of her life, Sophie must expose the lies of the U.S. government. This mission becomes even more important to Sophie when she learns that she is pregnant with Tom's child. Meanwhile, Fossa promises to get a message to Tom in Harsh Realm. . . .

Once trapped inside the wild terrains of Harsh Realm, Hobbes joins up with other fugitives who are also on the run from Santiago. Mike Pinocchio (D. B. Sweeney) is a rogue soldier who volunteered for duty in the virtual world and was once Santiago's top lieutenant. Now, he's a rogue and scoundrel, a gun for hire. Hobbes's other associate is the mysterious Florence (Rachel Hayward), a mute warrior with the unusual power to instantaneously heal the wounds of others.

Over the course of nine episodes of *Harsh Realm*, Hobbes attempts to complete his mission and finally get home. In the episode "Leviathan," he travels to the poverty-stricken Pittsburgh Encampment, where he and Pinocchio are captured by soldiers of fortune and nearly sold to Santiago. This episode meditates on the idea of the human soul and asks if a virtual character (VC) can possess one.

In the episode "Inga Fossa," Hobbes steals into Santiago City and locates Santiago's secret portal, from which he can travel from Harsh Realm into the real world and back. Hobbes nearly returns home, until he is told by Fossa of Santiago's "Final Solution." Santiago is planning "the Ultimate Terrorism," the destruction of the real world so that only Harsh Realm and Santiago's domain will continue to exist. Accordingly, Hobbes decides it is better to stay in Harsh Realm and defeat Santiago there.

In "Reunion," Hobbes ends up a slave in a work camp with Pinocchio and encounters a virtual representation of his dying mother. In the real world, Sophie visits Hobbes's mother, who is also dying of cancer. A double death (in Harsh Realm and in reality) spurs a strange, miraculous connection.

In "3 Percenters," the fugitives arrive in the Adirondacks and meet a bizarre, ostensibly "peaceful" cult hiding a dark secret. The episode "Manus Domini" finds Hobbes, Pinocchio, and Florence protecting a tribe of pacifist "Healers," women like Florence, from Santiago's reign of terror.

In "Cincinnati"—one of the best installments—Santiago heads to Ohio to personally assassinate the leader of the Resistance, a Native American whose forces have overrun the city.

Finally, the last episode of *Harsh Realm,* "Camera Obscura" takes Pinocchio and Hobbes to "Ground Zero" in Manhattan, where a disfigured, manipulative priest keeps two families in a perpetual state of conflict for personal reasons.

Over the nine episodes of this short-lived series, the virtual reality world of Harsh Realm is developed and expanded upon in fascinating and unexpected ways. "Leviathan" reveals that in Harsh Realm there is no religion: no God and no belief in an afterlife. It's a world "without Christian values," according to one character, and that line of thought becomes an existential undercurrent of many segments. In "Manus Domini," for instance, Hobbes ponders the Healers and their origin. Why do they exist? Why did programmers create them? Or were they created by a "higher power" after all? One beyond the ostensibly "faithless" world of the game?

In terms of technology, *Harsh Realm* introduces a number of game-oriented concepts. For example, "unprogrammed game space" exists and can form shortcuts from one part of the realm to the other. Similarly, "Reunion" reveals the existence of "skull bugs," mechanical control devices implanted in VC (and human) brains that can burrow through brain matter. "3 Percenters" presents the idea of a programming error: of VC characters who can absorb and replicate the personalities of others . . . much to the detriment of the originals. It's sort of *Harsh Realm* meets *Invasion of the Body Snatchers* (1956). And "Cincinnati" introduces the useful "digi-wand," a handheld device by which a digital character can reshape and refashion his features, the equivalent of virtual plastic surgery. Santiago uses it for diabolical strategic ends. Then there's the *Camera Obscura* of the final episode, a strange oracle or "seeing" device that appeared at Ground Zero after the nuclear explosion and is believed to foretell—or perhaps manipulate—the future.

In terms of unique guest characters, Hobbes, Pinocchio, and Florence meet not only the mute, female Healers and the VC in *Harsh Realm,* but steely-eyed Trackers ("Reunion"), deformed Mind Readers ("Manus Domini"), and bounty hunters armed with digitizing devices ("Leviathan"). The series encompasses pastoral settings ("Manus Domini"), urban locations ("Camera Obscura"), and, like all Chris Carter productions, is gorgeously presented in terms of its visuals. The camera work is highly cinematic, despite the relative lack of visual effects. Although it starts off a little slowly, *Harsh Realm*'s pace picks up quickly. Beginning with the episode "Reunion," the stories become more creative, more "out there" and tremendously involving. The run from

"Reunion" through "Camera Obscura" is quite extraordinary, bolstered by distinctive, memorable, engaging storylines.

Like his other series, Carter's *Harsh Realm* is a deeply layered work, one rife with symbolism, social commentary, and perhaps most importantly, clever literary allusion. The series, for example, is very clearly a deliberate variation on Homer's Greek epic poem *The Odyssey*. In that tale, Odysseus, a solider like Hobbes, attempted to return home from Troy, but the journey took him a decade. He was away from his wife, Penelope for ten long and miserable years. *The Odyssey,* much like a TV show itself, was highly episodic, with Odysseus encountering a variety of nemeses, including sirens, lotus eaters, and the cyclops Polyphemus. *Harsh Realm* also concerns a heroic soldier's "long journey home," his separation from his wife/fiancée, and as mentioned above, Hobbes becomes involved with a number of nemeses who are both more and less than human. The tenth, unproduced episode of *Harsh Realm* was even called "Circe," after a character (a witch) featured in *The Odyssey*.

In *The Odyssey*, Penelope had to contend with suitors who hoped to persuade her that Odysseus was dead. Even this plot point is echoed in *Harsh Realm* as the army attempts to convince Sophie of the same thing about Tom, though in this case to protect a conspiracy, not to inherit wealth.

Harsh Realm also develops some core concepts from Joseph Conrad's novella *Heart of Darkness* (1902), which involves a man on assignment to capture a fellow countryman, Kurtz. In the literary work, Kurtz had developed a reputation as a "universal genius" amongst the indigenous people in "the dark heart of Africa." *Heart of Darkness* was refashioned as a war drama in Coppola's *Apocalypse Now* (1979), and given the military framework of *Harsh Realm,* perhaps it is more appropriate to reference that production here. Because Santiago, like Marlon Brando's Kurtz, has gone "native," in essence setting up the "local" world of *Harsh Realm* as his personal kingdom.

This idea is true to Conrad's story, which warned against the dangers of imperialism. That's the core idea of *Harsh Realm*: an interloper and his military minions invade the virtual reality world of Harsh Realm and develop it exclusively for their use. The VC are merely a resource to be used, not "real" people.

The hero of *Harsh Realm,* Thomas Hobbes, is not just a stand-in for Odysseus, either. He is named after the English philosopher Thomas Hobbes (1588–1679), the author of *Leviathan* (1651). *Leviathan*—which also happens to be the title of *Harsh Realm*'s second episode—concerns autocracy and its benefits. The philosopher Hobbes believed that government should control religion, the military, the civil apparatus, and even the judiciary. He felt that man's natural state was lawlessness, and it was this natural state that caused man such hardship, tragedy, and strife. *Harsh Realm*'s Hobbes appears to be the antithesis of this autocratic philosophy, at least as far as the nine extant episodes go. He is a man who believes in freedom and liberty, and seeks to free Harsh Realm from Santiago's iron grip. One can never know for certain, but there is an undercurrent in the series that suggests Hobbes may not always feel this way. As he goes along, from episode to episode, he witnesses the lawlessness and inhumanity of Santiago's world. Had the series lasted several years, and Hobbes succeeded in destroying Santiago, one wonders if he would have imposed a Hobbesian peace on the scattered societies of Harsh Realm, essentially becoming the new figurehead. The last scene of the series, if fully developed, might have seen Hobbes displacing one Kurtz to become Kurtz himself.

We never saw that happen, but even Mark Snow's score—which sampled bits of Mussolini speeches—hinted at some of the autocratic themes and narratives Carter's show deliberated on. How much government? What kind of government? What's the right balance? Today, these ideas are more relevant even than they were in 1999.

As for the Han Solo of *Harsh Realm*, Mike Pinocchio, his name obviously derives from Curt Collodi's *The Adventures of Pinocchio* (1883), the story of a puppet who dreamed of becoming a real boy. In the world of *Harsh Realm*, Pinocchio is a "real" soldier who—for his own secret reasons—decides he wants to live as a "virtual" boy in a fake world. As Pinocchio's wooden feet were burned off in *The Adventures of Pinocchio*, so does Pinocchio lose a leg in the series episode "Manus Domini." In fact, as we learn, Pinocchio was disfigured and lost a leg in the real world, and that's the reason he ultimately chose a dream life rather than to continue in the real world. Thus we might say that, like Hobbes, *Harsh Realm*'s Pinocchio is the inverse of his literary namesake.

Another character, Florence the healer, seems named after Florence Nightingale, the legendary angel of mercy. And *Harsh Realm*'s final episode, "Camera Obscura," brilliantly restages—at a postnuclear ground zero—the story of Shakespeare's *Romeo and Juliet*. In this tale, two warring families (not the Capulets and Montagues but Stewarts and McKinleys) threaten to annihilate one another over a petty squabble. Meanwhile, young Aethan McKinley (Romeo) and Fallon Stewart (Juliet) have fallen in love in secret and carry on a relationship. They are encouraged to do so by an interfering "man of God," not Shakespeare's Friar Lawrence but the deformed, prophetic priest played by Robert Knepper.

As many others have noted, there are other literary allusions in *Harsh Realm*. As Hobbes is about to enter the Harsh Realm virtual world for the first time, he gazes down at his chair, and scrawled on its arms are the words

"Siege" and "Perilous." These words hark back to the so-called Perilous Seat at the Round Table in Arthurian Legend. This was the Empty Chair reserved for the greatest of knights or hero, the one who would bring back the Holy Grail. That, too, is Hobbes's destiny, perhaps metaphorically. Santiago might be the Holy Grail of Harsh Realm.

Harsh Realm balances these classic references and allusions with Carter's particular brand of up-to-the-minute speculative imaginings. The show hints rather dramatically at the shape of things to come in the early twenty-first century and particularly the War on Terror age. One episode, "Leviathan," laments Santiago's "culture of fear," something Americans could relate to after those color-coded DHS terrorist attack warnings in the 2000s. Another episode, "Cincinnati," seizes on the phrase "failure of imagination" as the reason for a battlefield defeat; the same phrase employed by the 9/11 Commission tasked with studying the reasons why the September 11th attacks were successful.

In the end, *Harsh Realm* deserved more patience than Fox demonstrated by canceling it just three hours in. Today, it is clear the series showcases some sterling work. "Reunion" artfully expresses the idea of an emotional bridge between virtual and human worlds. "Cincinnati" demonstrates Santiago's brutality in a colorful and terrifying way, and "Camera Obscura" and its postapocalyptic *Treasure of Sierra Madre* parable about man's quest for wealth will convince you that Carter and his creative team caught lightning in a bottle again.

Sadly, all three of those great episodes never even aired in 1999. Accordingly, the *Harsh Realm* of the series title doesn't merely refer to a comic book or a virtual world. It actually references something far more dangerous: the cutthroat, no-second-chances world of network television at the beginning of the twenty-first century, a period of huge decline. *Harsh Realm* died precisely as dramatic TV died and reality TV was born. A smart genre series of paranoid speculation and deep philosophy gave way to *Who Wants to Be a Millionaire* five nights a week, *Temptation Island, Survivor, Big Brother,* and the like. Dramatic TV came out of its slump in 2004 (with the advent of *Lost,* for instance), but by then *Harsh Realm* was "virtually" a memory.

The Lone Gunmen (2001)

The pilot episode of *The Lone Gunmen,* written by Chris Carter, Vince Gilligan, John Shiban, and Frank Spotnitz (and directed by Rob Bowman), aired originally on March 4, 2001. This was mere months after the Supreme Court called the contested presidential election of 2000 for George W. Bush. The United States of America had a new president, but the country was still very much in the peace and prosperity age of Clinton. No one had any idea what lay ahead in the twenty-first century.

The inaugural episode of *The Lone Gunmen* unfolds pretty much as *X-Files* fans might expect and hope, given the series' premise and quirky dramatis personae. Our heroes are Fox Mulder's old buddies: the relatively hapless trio of computer geeks-cum-editors at a Maryland-based conspiracy-theory newspaper called *The Lone Gunman* (latest headline: "Teletubbies = Mind Control!"). We first join these unconventional heroes *in media res,* during a covert op in progress. Our triumvirate of protagonists crashes a ritzy party at E-Comm Con (representing the tech bubble of the late 1990s). Their mission: to steal the new, ultra-fast Octium IV microchip, a technological advancement that the Lone Gunmen—Byers (Bruce Harwood), Frohike (Tom Braidwood), and Langly (Dean Haglund)—believe is actually designed to invade user privacy and collect personal information. The Lone Gunmen want to examine the chip so they can pen an expose in their newspaper; one featuring cold, hard evidence of their accusations.

But these guys, essentially the comic relief on the *X-Files*, are not traditional TV heroes, either in appearance or skill set. They are closer in spirit to the original Kolchak than to the hyper-competent Mulder, Scully, or Frank Black were. Their hearts are in the right place, but they make mistakes, bungles, and foul-ups. However, after a funny riff on Brian De Palma's *Mission: Impossible* (1996) involving the diminutive Frohike on a harness, the pilot episode unexpectedly turns serious. The E-Comm Con caper fails, and another thief, the enigmatic but beautiful Yves Adele Harlow (her name is an anagram for Lee Harvey Oswald), steals the chip out from under the Gunmen's noses.

This mission failure is followed by another bombshell. Conservative, buttoned-up Lone Gunman John Fitzgerald Byers learns that his father, a high-ranking government official, has been assassinated because of his highly classified work at the Department of Defense. Much of the pilot episode involves Byers, Frohike, and Langly helping another government official, Mr. Helm (code-named Overlord), prove that Old Man Byers (George Coe) is actually still alive and in hiding, afraid the government will send a second assassin after him.

What's Mr. Byers's secret? Mr. Byers is privy to information about a Department of Defense counterterrorism war game known as Scenario D 12. This particular military scenario involves a "domestic airline in-flight terrorist act." Unfortunately, Scenario D 12 is no longer a game, as Byers learns directly from his father. No, it is horrifyingly real. A small faction inside the U.S. government plans to utilize a remote-control device to hijack an American airliner in-flight and crash it into a heavily populated urban area.

The cover for this false flag operation will be a hijacking, a terrorist takeover of the plane.

Why would anyone want to commit such a horrible act? Here's what Mr. Byers tells his son. This is a direct quote from the episode: "The Cold War is over, John, but with no clear enemy to stockpile against, the arms business is flat. But bring down a fully-loaded 727 into the middle of New York City and you'll find a dozen tin-pot dictators all over the world just clamoring to take responsibility, and begging to be smart bombed."

Byers and his father then board a jet bound for Boston, the very one that will be used as a flying bomb over New York City. The target in Manhattan: the World Trade Center. The final act of this *Lone Gunmen* pilot involves Byers aboard the imperiled plane, and Frohike and Langly on the ground trying to avert the collision between plane and skyscraper and in the process rescue the 110 souls aboard the flight. At the last instant, we see the jetliner veer up and away from the Twin Towers. Disaster—and tragedy—averted.

As everybody now knows all too well, a scarce seven months later, on September 11, 2001, two "fully loaded" domestic airliners *did* strike New York City and the Twin Towers. In the aftermath, at least one "tin-pot" terrorist claimed responsibility (Bin Laden) and another, Saddam Hussein, was, perhaps, just "begging to be smart bombed." We obliged him in 2003. After that horrific Tuesday in September, arms sales boomed too, just as *The Lone Gunmen* predicted they would in the event of such a disaster. According to the Center for Defense Information, in 2006 alone, the U.S. was responsible for $16.9 billion in international arms deals, over 41 percent of all arm sales globally.

After 9/11, our government disavowed any advance knowledge of these horrible terrorist attacks. "I don't think anybody could have predicted that these people would take an airplane and slam it into the World Trade Center," said National Security Advisor Condoleezza Rice at a White House briefing on the afternoon of May 16, 2002. Well, *The Lone Gunmen* TV series predicted the exact thing on national television, with viewership in the tens of millions. And it did so six months before the attack occurred. It is strange—not to mention creepy as hell—that *The Lone Gunmen,* a series about crazy conspiracy theories, by and large guessed the precise nature of the biggest terrorist attack in U.S. history. It accurately guessed about the use of planes as weapons; plus it pointed out the target state, city, and actual buildings. The episode even got the aftermath right: war against tin-pot dictators, using our expensive smart bombs as "shock and awe." More than that, however, this *Lone Gunmen* episode anticipated the "conspiracy response" to 9/11 that has also arisen in the wake of the attacks. A certain percentage (36 percent) of American citizens didn't believe the official story (Al Qaeda hijackers) and instead maintain that the government orchestrated the attacks. Indeed, this is *Lone Gunmen*'s pre-event "explanation" of such an attack. It's eerie and disturbing to contemplate all this. But the pilot is a sharp, scary, well-crafted piece of TV fiction; and one that happens to have a very disturbing relationship with our real history.

The other episodes of *The Lone Gunmen* proved somewhat less grave than did the pilot episode. In short order, the series introduced another new character, Jimmy Bond, a gentle giant played by Stephen Snedden. Along with Byers, Bond became the moral conscience for the group in times of tough choices. The trio of nerdy heroes and their new friend (and with occasional help from Adele) still uncovered conspiracies, criminal schemes, and even perversions of science, but the approach was quirky, comedic, and occasionally romantic, rather than horror or hard sci-fi.

In "Madam, I'm Adam," for example, written by Thomas Schnauz and directed by Bryan Spicer, the Gunmen seek to help a man, Adam Burgess (Stephen Tobolowsky), recover what he believes is his life. The episode commences with a perfectly timed comedic dance as Burgess returns to his suburban home after a long day, only to be followed, at every move, by the person who lives there now . . . the person who has usurped his existence. As the Lone Gunmen investigate this instance of what is believed to be identity theft, the facts grow weirder and weirder. Byers realizes that Burgess has never actually lived in his home, only a virtual reality simulation of it, and he has been doing so willingly so as to temper his anger.

Byers, Langly, and Frohike uncover his real life as Charlie Muckle and discover that scientists at the Hobbes Research Institute are using unproven VR therapy to strip people of their identities. The episode's message, that it is easier to live in a carefree fantasy than to meaningfully alter your own behavior, is coupled with a sweet romance involving the love triangle of Muckle; his dwarf wife, Sadie; and an electronics store owner and TV pitchman, Maniac Marvin, inspired by New York's Crazy Eddie. The episode gracefully moves from comedy to pathos, to a final and sweet reckoning about life, and about what forces can destroy true love.

Another episode, "Maximum Byers," by Frank Spotnitz and Vince Gilligan, is a mini-masterpiece. In this story, a little old woman, Alberta Pfeiffer, visits the Lone Gunmen and asks them to investigate her son, Douglas (Darren Burrows), who is on death row for the murder of a shop owner in Texas. Inspired by an episode of *The A-Team* (1983–1987), Frohike and Langly "break" Byers and Jimmy Bond into death row. "I know it's a TV show, but the theory is sound," says Bond, and the Gunmen prove it in practice. While Langly and Frohike monitor the situation from the Sam Houston Motor Lodge (the same establishment frequented by Mulder and Scully in the fifth-season *X-Files* episode "Bad Blood"), the idealistic Byers and Jimmy Bond ferret out the truth and learn that Douglas is indeed guilty of the crime. The twist in the tale is that he has it in his power, before execution, to bring down the criminal who ordered the hit and save the life of a truly innocent man, a man who loves and cares for cockroaches on death row.

Yves Harlow shows up to help, and Bond requests a conjugal visit with her, much to her chagrin, and the episode features many laugh-out-loud moments. But underlying the silliness is a message of almost Buddhist proportions. As the cockroach whisperer notes, perhaps we don't really die at all. Instead, we "go on a trip" and come back, having learned something. One can hope this is true for Douglas, who does the right thing and is executed nonetheless. At episode's end, his mother slaps Byers across the face for failing to save her son's life, and the act deeply wounds the Lone Gunman. He failed the Pfeiffers but did a good deed nonetheless. As the episode suggests, goodness isn't always rewarded or appreciated in the here and now.

Another episode of the series, "Tango de los Pistoleros," takes the whole gang to Miami, Florida (actually Vancouver). There the Lone Gunmen attempt to figure out what Yves is up to, and finding out, inevitably, means auditioning for a tango dance contest. Yves tangos with a known smuggler, Leonardo Santavos, while Frohike reveals, ultimately, his alter ego as tango star extraordinaire El Lobo. Langly fails his dance audition, dropping to do the splits in especially painful fashion.

What makes the episode so remarkable, however, are the sequences involving the tango and Yves, which might legitimately be termed smoldering. And at the same time, the episode playfully equates the act of assassination to a dance, crosscutting between the murder of one of Santavos's associates with a tango performance on the dance floor.

Charming, silly, and utterly fun, *The Lone Gunmen* lasted only thirteen episodes in the spring of 2001, alas, and the series' loose threads were picked up, after a fashion, in *The X-Files*' ninth-season entry "Jump the Shark." Remarkably, that episode ended with the death of the Gunmen, much to the upset of longtime fans. The Gunmen died heroically, preventing a terrorist attack, but it seemed too cruel a fate and too grave an ending for such beloved, sweet, essentially harmless characters. The recent IDW comic book has resurrected the Lone Gunmen.

The After (2014)

The After follows Gigi Genereau (Louise Monot), an aspiring actress, as she auditions in Los Angeles for a role in an upcoming film. She doesn't get that role and doesn't want the role that is eventually offered to her. She returns to her hotel feeling dejected and plans to return home to her husband and daughter in New York.

But then things start to go wrong. Along with a policewoman, a clown (Jamie Kennedy), and a few others, Gigi becomes trapped inside the hotel elevator when the power unexpectedly fails. She manages to escape with the others, only to be locked in the hotel garage with a lawyer (Adrian Pasdar) and an escaped convict, Deed (Aldis Hodge).

Another escape is managed, and once outside Gigi learns that the whole world is undergoing some kind of catastrophic crisis. This unspecified event has already overwhelmed government and local authorities. With phones and the Internet down, Gigi and the group of diverse survivors attempt to find safe haven at a nearby mansion. But dangers lurk outside, both from roving gangs and from a "dark shadow" in the woods. . . .

In 2014, Chris Carter's latest series pilot, *The After*, was made available for streaming at Amazon.com. This new production, as one might expect, is very much a meditation on "of the moment" concerns in America. As I maintain in regard to his other works, Carter's greatest gift—beyond his penchant for crisp, revealing De Palma-esque camera moves—is his capacity to step back and cannily observe the prevailing winds impacting the culture. Then, after noting these things, he reflects them back at us in a science fiction or horror milieu.

So if *The X-Files, Millennium, Harsh Realm*, and *The Lone Gunmen* all concerned anticipatory anxiety—the fear of something dreadful on rapid approach—*The After* seems tailor made to concern the storm's arrival. In other words: today is doomsday. The first thing to consider regarding *The After* is how Carter approaches the noisiness of the culture, circa 2014. It's noise from the Net, social networks, iPhones and tablets, and other technological advances. There's also a lot more *partisan* noise in this age, rancor between and among Americans who view the world very, very differently. On first blush, and after just one episode, *The After* seems to concern the ways that modern American life erects barriers to cooperation and trust. Again and again throughout the pilot story, technology acts as a barrier that slows down the crucial learning process during the onset of the crisis.

In a frightening and wholly unexpected fashion, *The After* also reveals the first chapter of a mystery about the force that may be behind this worldwide apocalypse. The nature of that force is uncertain. It could be spiritual, alien, or hallucinatory, but from the first chapter alone, we know it is terrifying.

Many times throughout the fifty-five-minute production, technology acts as a barrier, trapping and snarling groups of survivors. The elevator breaks down. The hotel parking garage is sealed. The phones and Internet are down.

Water faucets aren't working. Food is spoiling in the refrigerator from lack of power. This is the total collapse of our entire modern infrastructure, and it vexes the characters because they have become totally dependent on modern conveniences and on the safety (apparently) afforded by law enforcement, government, social media, and so forth. But the world has changed instantly, and for the most part, the characters can't cope.

The pilot episode does an especially good job of expressing the idea of technology acting as a barrier, from frequent close-ups of Gigi's iPhone to imagery of characters trapped behind gates or half-opened elevator doors. These shots visually symbolize the shock and panic associated with a catastrophic meltdown of order. One spectacular and feature-film-quality shot featured in the pilot episode pulls back from Gigi to reveal thousands of people milling around, aimless and afraid, in a city square. The pullback just keeps going, as the breadth of the chaos becomes apparent.

The characters in the drama are a diverse group, a group that reflects twenty-first century America. There are people of color, people of alternative sexual orientation, wealthy people, a "foreigner," and people from different regions (such as the Deep South) represented in the mix. All are viewed here by the other characters—at least initially—in terms of stereotypes. In other words, what these characters know of their fellow countrymen seems to originate largely from media stories about them. Again, the underlying notion is that in modern America, our sense of community is fractured or even imperiled by the technological barriers we erect; from the screens we perpetually gaze at. We don't even know who are neighbors are or what they are about.

What happens when those tablet or iPhone screens go dark permanently? When we face each other—*really* face each other for the first time in a long while—what do we see? How do we understand one other? *The After* explores this question.

Like *The X-Files* and *Millennium* before it, there are several secrets or surprises embedded in *The After*'s narrative. Some concern, broadly speaking, the reasons why these *particular* individuals should end up together, the idea of missing time (a policeman indicates that the apocalypse started a day ago, but this isn't reflected in Gigi's experience), and the appearance of, well, something evil, the Dark Shadow.

Along the way toward developing the enigma, the pilot also provides canny references to the Book of Revelation and creepy high-angle shots that suggest the group of survivors is under the microscope of an all-seeing, malevolent eye. An earlier moment seems to presage this realization, as one character observes a helpless bee in a swimming pool and sympathizes with its plight. We are no different, she suggests.

The dark force haunting *The After* could be alien, or religious, or simply supernatural. One thing is certain, however: the shape that the force takes—or at least "reflects" back at the characters—is terrifying.

Although Amazon commissioned a full season of *The After* in 2014, it rescinded the order in the opening weeks of 2015. The bad news was that no new series would follow up on the terrifying pilot.

The X-Files Unbound

Knockoffs and Rip-offs Everywhere

The X-Files (1993–2002) proved not only a ratings powerhouse throughout the nineties, but a cultural phenomenon too, the *Star Trek* of the Clinton age. Significantly, the series also established rather dramatically that horror and science fiction could play well on television if presented intelligently and with a strong sense of continuity. Network executives took notice.

Accordingly, the years between 1995 and 1999 saw a flood, a genuine boom of horror-themed genre programming hit the airwaves. These series had titles such as *American Gothic* (1995–1996), *Strange Luck* (1995–1996), *Dark Skies* (1996), *Kindred: The Embraced* (1996), *Poltergeist: The Legacy* (1996–1999), *Psi-Factor: Chronicles of the Paranormal* (1996–1999), *The Burning Zone* (1996–1997), *Sleepwalkers* (1997), *Prey* (1998), *Brimstone* (1998–1999), and *Strange World* (1999), to name just a few.

Most of the series tallied above lasted only a season, but virtually all of them involved, like *The X-Files,* aspects of the police-procedural format, the horror genre, or the paranormal. Similarly, many of the series also involved government conspiracies or an attempt to hide some important "truth" from the cowed American populace. In short, network television for the five years leading up to the "reality" and "game show" boom of the new millennium cannot be understood, historically speaking, without understanding the influence and popularity of *The X-Files.*

Here's a tally and description of some of the most memorable knockoffs.

Nowhere Man (1995)

Created by Lawrence Hertzog, *Nowhere Man* ran for twenty-five episodes in 1995 and was a paranoiac's dream. The series involved Thomas Veil (Bruce Greenwood), a photographer whose life was "erased" in the premiere episode ("Absolute Zero") by a shadowy conspiracy. This act of erasure was undertaken because Veil publicly revealed a top-secret photograph called

"Hidden Agenda." Soon even Veil's wife, Alyson (played by *Millennium*'s Megan Gallagher), claimed not to possess any memory of him.

As the series continued, Thomas began to uncover secrets about the photograph, and about his enemies too, particularly a sinister cabal or conspiracy called "the Organization" (think the Syndicate on *The X-Files*). *Nowhere Man* picks up primarily on *The X-Files'* conspiracy vibe, but also features a strong if oblique connection to another TV paranoia trip: *The Prisoner* (1967). There, the prisoner of the title, Number Six (Patrick McGoohan), was trapped in a bizarre European "village" for spies and ex-spies; but here Veil finds himself in an Information Age trap where the prison is the global village itself.

Unlike some shows inspired by *The X-Files*, *Nowhere Man* is cleverly constructed, right down to the hero's name: Veil. The series' final episode actually saw the "veil" over his eyes lifted at last, as the truth was revealed.

American Gothic (1995)

American Gothic is the story of Caleb Temple (Lucas Black), a youngster of questionable lineage living in the quaint town of Trinity, South Carolina. In the premiere episode of this series, little Caleb sees his father go insane and his sister Merlyn (Sarah Paulson) murdered by the nefarious sheriff: Lucas Buck (Gary Cole). Then little Caleb learns that not only is Lucas Buck Caleb's biological father, he may also be the Devil himself

Before Sheriff Buck can seduce Caleb to the dark side, however, the sinister force must contend with two most unwelcome do-gooders in Trinity: journalist Gail Emory (Paige Turco) and a Yankee physician upstart with a dark past: Dr. Matt Crower (Jack Weber). Both carpetbaggers realize Buck is up to no good and take steps to protect Caleb, but must simultaneously deal with their own personal demons. Gail's parents died in Trinity twenty years earlier, and Lucas Buck just happened to be the person who discovered their bodies. And Matt is still recovering from a drunk-driving incident in which his wife and daughter were killed.

Created by Shaun Cassidy and produced by Sam Raimi, this soap opera horror owes as much to *Twin Peaks* (1990–1991), perhaps, as it does *The X-Files*. But all the x-trademarks are present too, from a focus on corrupt authority figures to storylines that involve police solving crimes in a small town. *American Gothic* succeeds in part because of Gary Cole's presence and charisma as the central figure, a man who can seduce anyone with a smile, and who is even taken—on occasion—to whistling the theme song from *The Andy Griffith Show*. *American Gothic*'s young star, Lucas Black, later had a crucial role in the first *X-Files* feature film, *Fight the Future*.

Dark Skies (1996)

Like all the TV series featured on this list, there can be little doubt that NBC's *Dark Skies* was granted a prime-time berth because of the success of *The X-Files.* There's also little doubt, however, that *Dark Skies* is an original, visually distinctive, and involving program. The one-season series showcases a memorable, growling regular performance from the late J. T. Walsh ("The List") as the leader of a top-secret alien-hunting organization called Majestic, and features rewarding and intricate plotting across the span of the catalog's nineteen hour-long shows.

The series is a period piece, interestingly, that concerns alien abduction—one of the key concepts explored in *The X-Files. Dark Skies* opens immediately after President John F. Kennedy takes the oath of high office and the age of Camelot commences. Two young Americans who are filled with enthusiasm—John Loengard (Eric Close) and Kim Sayers (Megan Ward)—go to Washington to serve the country and the new president but quickly become disillusioned when they learn that all is not as it seems. Aliens have infiltrated the highest levels of the American government. In other words, there's a conspiracy.

While it's true that Eric Close looks like he was bred by a David Duchovny clone farm, and that matters of conspiracy in Washington, D.C., were also heavily featured on *The X-Files, Dark Skies* nonetheless forges its own unique identity. It does so by replaying key events from human history—the first TV appearance of the Beatles on the *Ed Sullivan Show,* for instance, or the Kennedy assassination—through the lens of alien infiltration in human affairs. That was the "literal" level on which *Dark Skies* operated, but the series also served as a metaphor for politics in the U.S. Naïveté and idealism quickly give way to cynicism and dark agendas, and it's a struggle to know who to trust and who to believe in.

The Burning Zone (1997)

Created by Coleman Luck, *The Burning Zone* boasted important antecedents beyond *The X-Files.* The mid-1990s also happened to be the great era of virus-centric pop-culture entertainment, from the book *The Hot Zone* to *Outbreak* (1995), a horror film that pitted scientists Dustin Hoffman, Rene Russo, and Kevin Spacey against hemorrhagic fever in California. At least two episodes of *The X-Files* also dealt with the concept of infectious disease, the second-season episode "F. Emasculata" and the fifth-season thriller "The Pine Bluff Variant."

The Burning Zone brought a similar premise to TV on a weekly basis and followed the dangerous missions of a small bio-crisis team dedicated to eradicating deadly diseases in a conflict the series described as "The Plague Wars." The team leader was Daniel Cassian (Michael Harris), a no-nonsense doctor with "Level 92" clearance and a firm grip on his emotions. He was assisted by Dr. Edward Marcase (Jeffrey Dean Morgan), a virologist who survived a childhood case of Ebola but lost both parents to the disease. Edward's controversial approach to medicine considered the curing of disease a "mystical" experience, a supernatural quest.

Other team members were Kimberly Shiroma (Tamlyn Tomita), a molecular-geneticist-pathologist recruited from the World Health Organization, and Michael Hailey (James Black), the man responsible for the team's overall security.

After eleven episodes, *The Burning Zone* endured a dramatic series of cast changes. Shiroma and Marcase left the team, replaced by Dr. Brian Taft (Bradford Tatum), a motorcycle-riding, rebellious James Dean-like physician. This reboot also largely abandoned the supernatural angle and featured more action-oriented stories. Only Harris and Black appeared throughout both formats. Cassian became the primary hero, after playing a kind of Dr. Smith-like thorn in the side for the first run of shows.

A disease-of-the-week series filled with goofy plotlines, *The Burning Zone* was a helter-skelter, wildly inconsistent series. Among some of the more bizarre diseases were ones that caused fear ("The Silent Tower"), rage ("St. Michael's Nightmare"), spontaneous combustion ("Arms of Fire"), insanity ("Critical Mass"), skeletal collapse ("Death Song"), hypothyroidism ("The Last Five Pounds Are the Hardest"), and hemorrhagic fever ("Night Fever"). Other stories dealt with a dimension of death ("Lethal Injection"), the disease that destroyed the Mayan civilization ("Touch of the Dead"), psychic surgery ("Hall of the Serpent"), and a flesh-eating virus ("Elegy for a Dream").

The quality that most distinguished *The Burning Zone* was its blending of hard science with spiritual subplots. Most of the protagonists in the series were physicians who had gone through years if not decades of training. Yet in tale after tale, these men and women of science explored the "spirit" in ways they certainly couldn't have anticipated back at med school. One episode involved a cure that was made from the "venomous fruit" of the Tree of Knowledge in the Garden of Eden, for example. "Touch of the Dead" followed a similarly bizarre trajectory. In this tale, Cassian was infected by a terrible disease with no scientific cure. He survived because he found a "reason to live": a healthy soul. Meanwhile, "Arms of Fire" pushed the same antiscience notion when a boy in danger of spontaneously combusting survived the horrible ordeal by expressing his willingness to pray.

The X-Files' Krycek—Nicholas Lea—guest-starred in one episode of *The Burning Zone.* In "Hall of the Serpent," he played a psychic surgeon named

Phillip Padgett. Incidentally, Phillip Padgett was also the name of John Hawkes's character, a writer, in the psychic surgery episode of *The X-Files,* "Milagro."

Sleepwalkers (1997)

Part of NBC' short-lived "Thrillogy" programming bloc on Saturday nights (sandwiched between *Pretender* and *Profiler*), *Sleepwalkers* aired for just three episodes in the United States before it was cancelled. Created by Stephen Kronish and David S. Goyer, the series starred Naomi Watts as Dr. Kate Russell and Bruce Greenwood as Dr. Nathan Bradford, neurophysiologists working at a dream clinic called The Morpheus Institute.

These scientists and psychologists had determined a technique by which to enter "the nocturnal world" of troubled patients and administer therapy in their dreams. Unfortunately, the dream terrain was a dangerous place for the scientists because of creepy villains like the Smiling Man (Harry Groener), a character who might have fit in easily with similarly named *X-Files* personalities like Cancer Man or the Well-Manicured Man.

Similarly, Dr. Nathan Bradford, like Mulder before him, had a personal connection to his investigations. His wife, Gail, was locked in one of the Institute's sleep cradles, trapped in a perpetual coma, and he had to find the means to reawaken her.

Prey (1998)

The tagline for the short-lived series *Prey* on ABC-TV was "We've just been bumped down the food chain," and the series concerned a beautiful geneticist, Sloane Parker (Debra Messing), who learned that a look-alike species—*homo dominants*—was gaining a foothold on power in North America. A brilliant scientist not unlike Scully, Sloane came to work with one of the homo dominants, Tom Daniels (Adam Storke), to help reveal the breadth of the dark conspiracy.

The X-Files often concerned genetic mutants like Victor Eugene Tooms or other freaks of nature who in some way could represent one possible future for humanity. *Prey* involved a similar scenario, though taken to apocalyptic levels. Mankind was losing ground to superior beings, yet they were not aliens or monsters but beings created under the auspices of evolution, by Mother Nature herself. The human race had become outmoded. So the question became: Can man outwit, defeat, and outlive its replacement species?

Over the course of *Prey*'s run, much information was learned about the new species, including the fact that it lacked human emotions but possessed

ESP. *Prey* also proved weirdly prophetic. One episode involved school shootings—less than a year before Columbine—and the entire premise seemed to forecast the War on Terror. The homo dominants look and sound like us, and therefore could imitate us flawlessly. So your neighbor could actually be a sleeper agent, just waiting for the right moment to strike. . . .

Brimstone (1998–1999)

Created by Ethan Reiff and Cyrus Voris, *Brimstone* aired on Fox as the lead-in to *Millennium* (1996–1999) on Friday nights and ran for just thirteen hour-long episodes before an untimely cancellation. The series starred Peter Horton as hangdog detective Ezekiel Stone, a former Manhattan-based police officer who died in 1983 . . . and went to hell. He did so because he took the law into his own hands and murdered his wife's rapist, Gilbert Jax. Two months after that act of vigilantism, Stone was killed in the line of duty, and he's been trapped in the underworld ever since.

As the series commences, however, 113 of the "most vile" criminals in hell manage a jailbreak and return to Earth to wreak havoc. The Devil (John Glover) recruits Detective Stone to pursue the fugitives and send them back to hell and permanent incarceration. Ezekiel can do so only by destroying their eyes, the so-called "windows to their souls." In exchange for his service, Stone gets a much-valued second shot at human life, happiness, and redemption. Each time Stone kills an escaped convict, a strange runic tattoo (representing the convict's "number" or identity) burns off his body. Stone must also deal with the fact that some of escaped convicts are extremely powerful, with terrifying supernatural abilities.

As the Devil informs the detective: "The longer you've been in hell, the more it becomes a part of you."

The villains featured on the series reflect *The X-Files'* concept of the monster of the week. They are literally twisted creatures from hell, and the roster includes an unrepentant rapist ("Encore"), a shape-shifter with multiple personalities ("Faces"), a lovelorn poet who kills virgins ("Poem,") and even a *Bonnie and Clyde*-styled pair of thugs ("The Lovers").

Presented in a kind of desaturated or silvery-steel color scheme, *Brimstone* was another police procedural of the 1990s, like the *X-Files*, but it proved an original initiative because it worked overtime to diagram a universe of nuanced morality. Despite the presence of God and the Devil in the stories, *Brimstone* always explored shades of gray, not the least in terms of Stone's behavior. Did he deserve a second chance? Did he deserve to go to hell in the first place? In exploring these issues, *Brimstone* proved more than your average *X-Files* rip-off and emerged as a memorable supernatural noir.

Strange World (1999)

Created by former *X-Files* writer and producer Howard Gordon, *Strange World* focuses on Dr. Paul Turner (Tim Guinee), an MD who had been exposed to a deadly toxin during the Gulf War. In the early 1990s, Turner returned stateside only to learn that he was being kept alive by a mysterious antidote, one administered by a secret cabal's representative, the Mysterious Japanese Woman (Vivian Wu).

While attempting to resolve this mystery, Turner also took a job at U.S. ARMIID (United States Army Medical Institute for Infectious Diseases) to investigate "the criminal abuses of science in the United States." Essentially an early (and better) version of *Fringe* (2008–2012), *Strange World*'s plots involved the terrifying side effects of illegal scientific experiments. For instance, one *Strange World* episode, "Lullaby," centered on pregnant women learning they were pregnant not with human babies, but with developing human organs that could be "harvested" by the shadowy conspiracy. Another episode (the pilot), concerned an illegal and unethical cloning operation. The last story aired on ABC, "Azrael's Breed," involved a scientist who was pushing "the boundaries of death" by injecting the brain cells from dead people into the minds of the living to create so-called death memories.

Perhaps the most appealing aspect of *Strange World* was the personal nature of Turner's quest. His life depended on discovering the answers presented by the weekly riddles and cases. He realized that he was a pawn, a piece in a much larger agenda, and often had to gut check himself to make certain he was operating by his own conscience and not the (mysterious) workings of the cabal.

Freakylinks (2000–2001)

After the huge box office success of the found-footage film *The Blair Witch Project* (1999), Haxan Films produced for Fox Television a sort of Generation Y version of *The X-Files*. Originally known as *Fearsum, Freakylinks* ran for one season of thirteen hour-long episodes, and like *The X-Files* focused often on the supernatural and paranormal. The series even aired in *The X-Files*' original, Friday night time slot at 9:00 p.m.

In *Freakylinks*, website guru Derek Barnes (Ethan Embry) and his friends ran an Internet site devoted to urban legends and stories of paranormal occurrences. Derek pursued this line of investigation in part because of the mysterious death of his brother, Adam, the program's Samantha Mulder surrogate.

Various episodes of the series also traded in concepts already explored on *The X-Files,* including possession ("Three Thirteen"), prehistoric monsters alive in the present ("Coelacanth This"), and even vampires who thrive on adrenaline ("Live Fast, Die Young").

The Others (2000)

X-Files veterans Glen Morgan and James Wong joined the staff of the Jon Brancato/Michael Ferris-created supernatural TV production *The Others* in 2000. The short-lived dramatic series concerned the frightening adventures of a sort of psychic "A-Team" investigating creepy cases of demons, ghosts, and other denizens of the spirit world (much in the spirit of *Poltergeist: The Legacy* [1996–1999], but not nearly as cheesy). *The Others* lasted for a dozen episodes on NBC (airing on Saturday nights from 10:00 to 11:00 p.m. EST) before a hasty cancellation brought the investigations to an end. Steven Spielberg's Dreamworks executive-produced the genre program, and during its brief run, *The Others* saw episodes helmed by prominent horror directors such as Tobe Hooper, Bill Condon, Tom McLoughlin, and Mick Garris. Also on board was Thomas J. Wright, who over the years has guided great episodes of *Beauty and the Beast, Nowhere Man, Dark Skies, The X-Files, Millennium, Freaky Links, Dark Angel, Tru Calling, Angel,* and *Firefly.*

In terms of format, *The Others* revolved around a troubled college student named Marianne Kitt (Julianne Nicholson) and her decision to join a misfit group of psychically inclined investigators, the titular "Others." Kitt came to this decision after a case in the pilot episode involving her haunted dorm room, visions of the dead, and a realization about her own psychic capabilities. On *The Others,* Melissa Crider played Satori, a New Age "sensitive." Gabriel Macht was Mark, a handsome young empath with medical training; Bill Cobb played the group's spiritual leader, the respected medium Elmer Greentree; and a pre-*Enterprise* John Billingsley was a professor in folklore and mythology, Miles Ballard. John Aylward was also aboard as the cranky blind man and expert in ESP Albert. Finally, *Lord of Illusion*'s (1995) Kevin J. O'Connor portrayed Warren, the sort of "Mad Dog Murdoch" of this psychic bunch. The series approached the supernatural subject matter with seriousness, but—as is the case in all Morgan and Wong efforts—there was also a sly sense of humor in evidence.

Night Stalker (2005)

The *X-Files* producer/writer Frank Spotnitz took the reins of this *Kolchak: The Night Stalker* remake, which aired for one season on ABC and starred Stuart

Townsend as the new Carl Kolchak. Although remakes of beloved series are notoriously difficult because they must live up not just to the original programming but *nostalgia* for the original programming (which is often clouded by feelings of romance and youth), *Night Stalker* proved an interesting series on its own terms.

Darren McGavin's *Kolchak* series had thrived during the post-Watergate era, and *The X-Files* thrived in the age of Waco, Ruby Ridge, and Elias Gonzalez. Accordingly, Spotnitz sought a new context for his investigative supernatural series. The series was heavy with lovely nighttime shots of city lights, gleaming silver skyscrapers, isolated cars speeding on asphalt highways, and quick cuts to lonely, strange perspectives, like a rattling wind chime or a gently swaying swing on a playground. Overall, the vibe was of an isolating, dehumanizing metropolis, a place with plenty of people but little connection.

In the Web 2.0 age, this was a potent idea, a frightening phantasm of modern urban America. It was a place where people see but don't help; where people close their eyes and choose not to believe something that is unbelievable, even if it is true. Yes, this is a different view of life than the original *Kolchak: The Night Stalker* held, but in a sense, it's a vision that upholds the idea of the little guy vs. City Hall that was so appealing in the original incarnation.

In the 1974 progenitor, Kolchak was a nobody, just a fly in the ointment. But here it's even worse. This Kolchak is actively despised and persecuted by the establishment. He's hated both by readers, who don't trust the media, and his superiors, who find him troublesome. The original *Kolchak* series was a one-of-a-kind show that could never be repeated as it was. For one thing, nobody could really adequately replace Darren McGavin. But what a clever writer could do is tell stories about an obsessed investigative reporter and his brushes with the supernatural. If the stories are good, that's enough, and *Night Stalker* fit that bill in the post-*X-Files* world.

Fringe (2008–2012)

The slickest, glossiest, yet most inexplicably popular of *The X-Files'* children is likely *Fringe* from producer J. J. Abrams. Like the *X-Files*, *Fringe* is set in the milieu of the FBI with agents, search warrants, stakeouts, car chases, and investigations. And *Fringe*, like *The X-Files*, finds solutions to unusual problems (like a nasty new airborne disease/terrorist WMD) in the notion of "extreme possibilities" (the paranormal/fringe science).

Fringe, like *The X-Files*, also focuses on a "Mytharc" of sorts, only here it is called "the Pattern." *The X-Files* is famous for an exploration of a larger conspiracy, one including the FBI, heads of state, and various departments in the

U.S. government. The conspiracy had a secret, malicious agenda. In *Fringe*'s pilot, we're introduced not only to a specific episodic mystery (an airborne, self-eradicating germ) but to the conspiracy operating behind it. There's not a Cigarette Smoking Man hanging around yet, but we have Blair Brown as the representative of the company Massive Dynamic. She and her corporation are working behind the scenes on the by-now-rote malicious and secret agenda.

Fringe, like *The X-Files*, centers on a male/female pair-up. It's Duchovny and Anderson on *The X-Files*, and Joshua Jackson and Anna Torv on *Fringe*. I should point out an important difference here. On the *X-Files*, Scully and Mulder actually boasted fields of expertise. Mulder was a behavioral psychologist and one of the best profilers in the FBI. And Scully was an MD The characters on *Fringe* seem to have no specialties at all. Peter Bishop (Jackson) is simply tagged a "genius," and Olivia Dunholm (Tory) is merely your average gun-toting, ambitious FBI agent.

Many fans of *Fringe* insist that it outgrew its creative dependence on *The X-Files* in terms of character, narrative, and Mytharc and became its own thing during its five-year run, but its DNA "pattern" is nonetheless apparent and highly derivative.

J. J. Abrams's series *Fringe* came after *The X-Files* and dealt with mysterious happenings and an odd "pattern" or latter-day Mytharc. Here, *Fringe*'s cast, Joshua Jackson, Walter Bishop, and Anna Torv, is pictured left to right.

The X-Files

Legacy

In this day and age, the true test of a story's strength and lasting power may not lie merely in the number of imitators it spawns, but in the merchandise and auxiliary projects and items it generates. On this front, *The X-Files* has been no slouch. Since the series was on the air, comic books, novels, postcard books, video releases, and even action figures have carried the *X-Files* name.

Comic Books

There have been several major *X-Files* comic books across the decades. When *The X-Files* was on the air, Topps Comics produced forty issues of that title, from 1995 to 1998, and also a miniseries called *Ground Zero*. The comic was very well received though difficult to produce because the creators had to keep track of the constantly expanding mythology and new developments on the series.

In 2008, to coincide with the release of *I Want to Believe*, Wildstorm released an *X-Files Special* penned by Frank Spotnitz. Then in 2010, Wildstorm partnered with IDW for a crossover with Steve Niles's vampire epic, *30 Days of Night*. The result was *The X:Files: 30 Days of Night*, an adventure that saw Mulder and Scully head to Alaska to investigate reports of the undead.

In 2013, IDW created the well-received Season 10 comic, which lists Chris Carter as an executive producer. The comic was nominated for a Diamond Gems Award as Best New Comic of 2013, and has already resurrected the Lone Gunmen, CSM, and Krycek. The arc of the series, from writers Joe Harris and Chris Carter, involves a group of unknown individuals seeking information on *The X-Files* and capturing Agent Scully to get it. Afterwards, Mulder and Scully are reinstated at the FBI. Another story, "Hosts," continues the tale of the Fluke Man, seen in the second-season story "The Host."

The comic book makes full use of all the beloved series characters, including Doggett and Reyes.

Toys and Video Games

In 1998, the year of *X-Files: Fight the Future,* McFarlane Toys released a whole line of action figures to coincide with the movie's release. Figures in Series One included an attack alien, the caveman seen in the film's prologue, and two variants of Mulder and Scully. One set saw them in their standard FBI gear (replete with badges and flashlight), and the other had them wearing their Antarctica gear from the film's climax. Several figures also came with the green containment units that housed people infected by the alien virus and the half-digested infected people themselves.

In the year 2000, McFarland released a Fluke Man collector's figure for the series.

Mattel, meanwhile, released an *X-Files* Barbie and Ken Gift Set from the film, featuring Barbie and Ken decked out like FBI Agents Mulder and Scully to celebrate the first feature film.

There have been three video games based on the series so far. These include *The X-Files: The Game* (1998), *The X-Files: Unrestricted Access,* and a horror survival game for Playstation 2, *The X-Files: Resist or Serve* (2004).

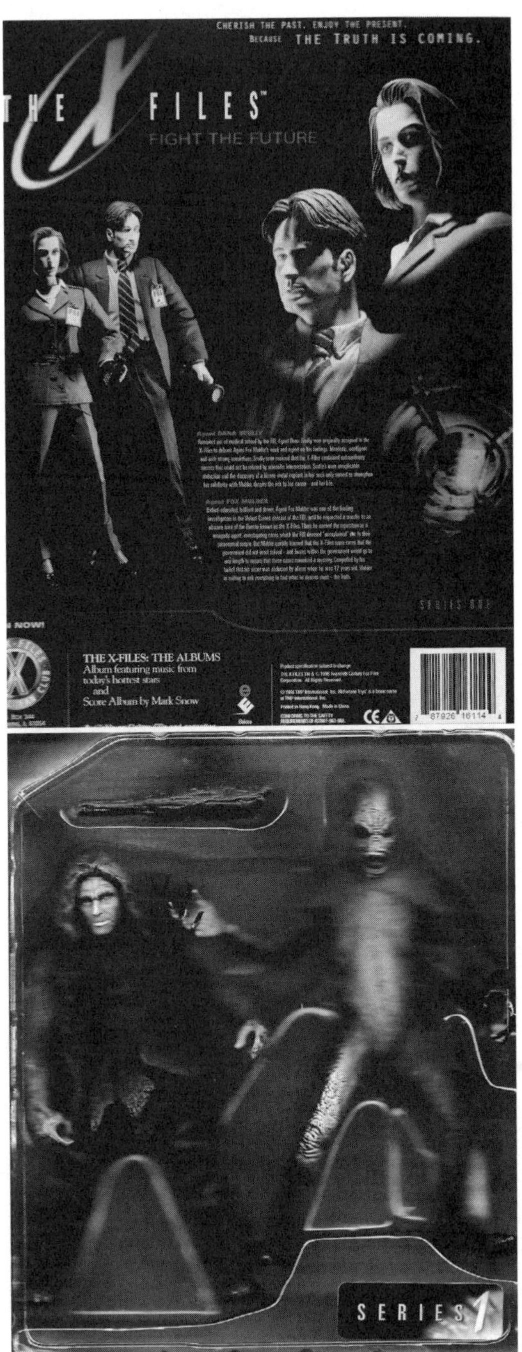

Two views of McFarlane's action figures released in 1998 for the first *X-Files* feature film, *Fight the Future.*

Satire?

Finally, no chapter about the cultural impact *of The X-Files* would be complete without a brief mention of the fact that several pornographic versions of the series have appeared over the years, including *The Sex Files* (2009) and *The XXX Files* (2011). Would Mulder approve?

Bibliography

Books

Chauvin, Remy. *Parapsychology—When the Irrational Rejoins Science*, translated by Katharine M. Banham. McFarland: 1985.

Fulton, Roger, and Betancourt, John. *The Sci-Fi Channel Encyclopedia of TV Science Fiction*. Warner Books: 1997.

Godwin, Jack. *Clintonomics: How Bill Clinton Re-Engineered the Reagan Revolution*. American Management Association: 2009.

Greenberg, Stanley B. *Dispatches from the War Room*. Thomas Dunne Books/ St. Martin's Press: 2009.

Haynes, Johnson. *The Best of Times: America in the Clinton Years*. Harcourt: 2001.

Kallen, Stuart A. *The 1990s*. Greenhaven Press: 2000.

Marill, Alvin H., and Peter Napolitano. *Blockbuster Entertainment: Guide to Television on Video*. Pocket Books: 1996.

McNeill, Alex. *Total Television: The Comprehensive Guide to Programming from 1948 to the Present*. Fourth Edition. Penguin Books: 1997.

Morton, Alan. *The Complete Directory to Science Fiction, Fantasy and Horror Television Series: A Comprehensive Guide to the First Fifty Years, 1946–1996*. Other World: 1997.

Muir, John Kenneth. *An Analytical Guide to TV's One Step Beyond, The 1959–1961 Paranormal Anthology*. McFarland: 2001.

———. *Terror Television: American Series, 1970–1999*. McFarland: 2001.

Preston, Richard. *The Hot Zone: A Terrifying True Story*. Anchor Books: 1999.

Vankin, Jonathan. *Conspiracies, Cover-ups, and Crimes: From JFK to the CIA Terrorist Connection*. Paragon Publishing: 1992.

Wolff, Michael. *Net Trek: Your Guide to Trek Life in Cyberspace*. Random House: 1997

Publications

"A *Star Trek* into *The X-Files*." Richard Corliss. *Time International (South Pacific Edition)*. April 7, 1997. Page 38.

"Alien Nation." Matthew Grimm. *Brandweek*. November 4, 1996. Pages 19–23.

"Alien Nation." Ken Tucker. *Entertainment Weekly*. October 8, 1993. Page 43.

"Decoding *The X-Files*." Rick Marin, Gregory Beals, Adam Rogers, Elizabeth Angell, Devin Gordon, Corie Brown. *Newsweek*. June 22, 1998. Pages 70–77.

"The Edge of Chaos: Structural Conspiracy and Epistemology in the *X-Files*." Mark Wildermuth. *Journal of Popular Film and Television*. Winter 1999. Pages 146–158.

"Fantasies in Dark and Light." Joe Nazzarro. *Starlog*. June 1996. Page 73.

"His Darkest Files." Sarah Kendzior. *Fangoria*. May 2000. Page 43.

"How Not to Respond to *The X-Files*." *Nature*. August 27, 1998. Page 815.

"The Invasion Has Begun." Richard Corliss. *Time*. July 8, 1996. Page 61.

"Life of Reilly." *Dreamwatch* #31. Page 46.

"Lone Stars." Annabelle Villanueva. *Cinescape*. March/April 2001. Page 47.

"The Music Is Out There." Paul Di Filippo. *Sci-Fi Entertainment*. 1997. Page 63.

"Opening the *X-Files:* Behind the Scenes of TV's Hottest Show." David Bischoff. *Omni*. December 1994. Pages 42–48.

"Out of This World . . ." Jeanie Pyun. *InStyle*. Fall 2003. Pages 132–135.

"Professor Discovers Good TV: *The X-Files*." John Elvin. *Insight on the News*. February 25, 2002. Page 34.

"Sci-Fi Invasion." Annabelle Villanueva. *Cinescape*. September/October 2000. Page 48.

"Snow Driven." Dave Hughes. *Dreamwatch*. February 1997. Pages 24–26.

"20th Century Fox Finds '*X-Files*' Fans Worldwide." Eileen Fitzpatrick. *Billboard*. March 23, 1996. Pages 68–69.

"VOICES: Vince Gilligan." Vince Gilligan. *Variety*. January 21, 2013. Page 8.

"Wired Thing." John Weisman. *Variety*. June 6, 2013. Pages 14–17.

"The Wittiest, Creepiest Sci-Fi Show of All Time? X-actly." Ken Tucker. *Entertainment Weekly*. Fall 1998. Page 16.

"X-aminations." James Swallow. *Starlog*. December 1995. Pages 30–33; 64.

"X-Boss." Kathy Krantz. *Starlog*. April 1996. Pages 46–47.

"*The X-Files* and *Buffy the Vampire Slayer*." Beth Braun. *Journal of Popular Film and Television*. Summer 2000. Pages 88–95.

"*The X-Files* Factor." Bret Watson. *Entertainment Weekly*. September 15, 1995. Page 74.

"*The X-Files* Mythology: Abduction." Kevin O'Donnell. *Rolling Stone*. June 2, 2005. Page 80.

"*X-Files* Undercover." David Wild. *Rolling Stone*. May 16, 1996. Pages 38–44.

"The X-Man Cometh." David Hochman. *Best Life*. August 2008. Pages 82–87.

"Your Sister in St. Scully: An Electronic Community of Female Fans of the X-Files." Sarah R. Wakefield. *Journal of Popular Film and Television*. January 1, 2001. Pages 130–137.

Index

THE FAQ SERIES

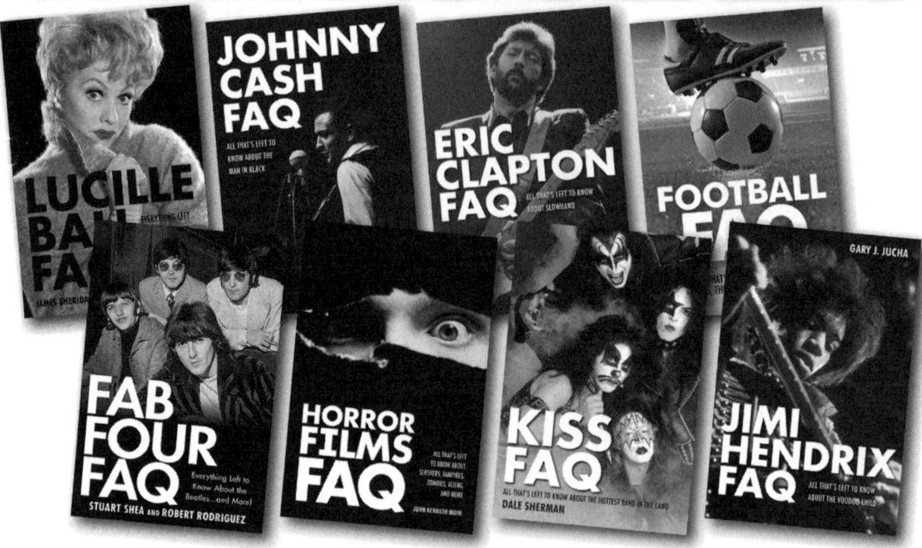

AC/DC FAQ
by Susan Masino
Backbeat Books
978-1-4803-9450-6 .... $24.99

Armageddon Films FAQ
by Dale Sherman
Applause Books
978-1-61713-119-6 .... $24.99

Lucille Ball FAQ
by James Sheridan and Barry Monush
Applause Books
978-1-61774-082-4 .... $19.99

The Beach Boys FAQ
by Jon Stebbins
Backbeat Books
978-0-87930-987-9 .... $22.99

Black Sabbath FAQ
by Martin Popoff
Backbeat Books
978-0-87930-957-2 .... $19.99

Johnny Cash FAQ
by C. Eric Banister
Backbeat Books
978-1-4803-8540-5 .... $24.99

Eric Clapton FAQ
by David Bowling
Backbeat Books
978-1-61713-454-8 .... $22.99

Doctor Who FAQ
by Dave Thompson
Applause Books
978-1-55783-854-4 .... $22.99

The Doors FAQ
by Rich Weidman
Backbeat Books
978-1-61713-017-5 .... $24.99

The Eagles FAQ
by Andrew Vaughan
Backbeat Books
978-1-4803-8541-2 .... $24.99

Fab Four FAQ
by Stuart Shea and Robert Rodriguez
Hal Leonard Books
978-1-4234-2138-2 .... $19.99

Fab Four FAQ 2.0
by Robert Rodriguez
Backbeat Books
978-0-87930-968-8 .... $19.99

Film Noir FAQ
by David J. Hogan
Applause Books
978-1-55783-855-1 .... $22.99

Football FAQ
by Dave Thompson
Backbeat Books
978-1-4950-0748-4 .... $24.99

The Grateful Dead FAQ
by Tony Sclafani
Backbeat Books
978-1-61713-086-1 .... $24.99

Prices, contents, and availability subject to change without notice.

Jimi Hendrix FAQ
by Gary J. Jucha
Backbeat Books
978-1-61713-095-3 .... $22.99

Horror Films FAQ
by John Kenneth Muir
Applause Books
978-1-55783-950-3 .... $22.99

James Bond FAQ
by Tom DeMichael
Applause Books
978-1-55783-856-8 .... $22.99

Stephen King Films FAQ
by Scott Von Doviak
Applause Books
978-1-4803-5551-4 .... $24.99

KISS FAQ
by Dale Sherman
Backbeat Books
978-1-61713-091-5 .... $22.99

Led Zeppelin FAQ
by George Case
Backbeat Books
978-1-61713-025-0 .... $19.99

Modern Sci-Fi Films FAQ
by Tom DeMichael
Applause Books
978-1-4803-5061-8 .... $24.99

Morrissey FAQ
by D. McKinney
Backbeat Books
978-1-4803-9448-3 .... $24.99

Nirvana FAQ
by John D. Luerssen
Backbeat Books
978-1-61713-450-0 .... $24.99

Pink Floyd FAQ
by Stuart Shea
Backbeat Books
978-0-87930-950-3 .... $19.99

Elvis Films FAQ
by Paul Simpson
Applause Books
978-1-55783-858-2 .... $24.99

Elvis Music FAQ
by Mike Eder
Backbeat Books
978-1-61713-049-6 .... $24.99

Prog Rock FAQ
by Will Romano
Backbeat Books
978-1-61713-587-3 .... $24.99

Pro Wrestling FAQ
by Brian Solomon
Backbeat Books
978-1-61713-599-6 .... $29.99

Rush FAQ
by Max Mobley
Backbeat Books
978-1-61713-451-7 .... $24.99

Saturday Night Live FAQ
by Stephen Tropiano
Applause Books
978-1-55783-951-0 .... $24.99

Prices, contents, and availability subject to change without notice.

Seinfeld FAQ
by Nicholas Nigro
Applause Books
978-1-55783-857-5 .... $24.99

Sherlock Holmes FAQ
by Dave Thompson
Applause Books
978-1-4803-3149-5 .... $24.99

Soccer FAQ
by Dave Thompson
Backbeat Books
978-1-61713-598-9 .... $24.99

The Sound of Music FAQ
by Barry Monush
Applause Books
978-1-4803-6043-3 .... $27.99

South Park FAQ
by Dave Thompson
Applause Books
978-1-4803-5064-9 .... $24.99

Bruce Springsteen FAQ
by John D. Luerssen
Backbeat Books
978-1-61713-093-9 .... $22.99

Star Trek FAQ (Unofficial and Unauthorized)
by Mark Clark
Applause Books
978-1-55783-792-9 .... $19.99

Star Trek FAQ 2.0 (Unofficial and Unauthorized)
by Mark Clark
Applause Books
978-1-55783-793-6 .... $22.99

Quentin Tarantino FAQ
by Dale Sherman
Applause Books
978-1-4803-5588-0 .... $24.99

Three Stooges FAQ
by David J. Hogan
Applause Books
978-1-55783-788-2 .... $22.99

U2 FAQ
by John D. Luerssen
Backbeat Books
978-0-87930-997-8 .... $19.99

The Who FAQ
by Mike Segretto
Backbeat Books
978-1-4803-6103-4 .... $24.99

The Wizard of Oz FAQ
by David J. Hogan
Applause Books
978-1-4803-5062-5 .... $24.99

Neil Young FAQ
by Glen Boyd
Backbeat Books
978-1-61713-037-3 .... $19.99

HAL•LEONARD®
PERFORMING ARTS PUBLISHING GROUP
FAQ.halleonardbooks.com

0515